Culture and
Customs of France

France. Cartography by Bookcomp, Inc.

Culture and Customs of France

W. SCOTT HAINE

Culture and Customs of Europe

GREENWOOD PRESS
Westport, Connecticut • London

Library of Congress Cataloging-in-Publication Data

Haine, W. Scott.
    Culture and customs of France / W. Scott Haine.
        p.   cm. — (Culture and customs of Europe)
    Includes bibliographical references and index.
    ISBN 0–313–32892–7
    1. France—Social life and customs.   2. France—Civilization.   I. Title.   II. Series.
    DC33.7.H26   2006
    944—dc22   2006017935

British Library Cataloguing in Publication Data is available.

Copyright © 2006 by W. Scott Haine

Library of Congress Catalog Card Number: 2006017935
ISBN: 0–313–32892–7

First published in 2006

Greenwood Press, 88 Post Road West, Westport, CT 06881
An imprint of Greenwood Publishing Group, Inc.
www.greenwood.com

Printed in the United States of America

The paper used in this book complies with the
Permanent Paper Standard issued by the National
Information Standards Organization (Z39.48–1984).

10 9 8 7 6 5 4 3 2 1

To my father, Charles Allen Haine.
Also to Charles C. McLaughlin and Mary Anderson:
your presence is missed but your inspiration still guides.

Contents

Series Foreword

THE OLD WORLD and the New World have maintained a fluid exchange of people, ideas, innovations, and styles. Even though the United States became the de facto world leader and economic superpower in the wake of a devastated Europe in World War II, Europe has remained for many the standard bearer of Western culture.

Millions of Americans can trace their ancestors to Europe. The United States as we know it was built on waves of European immigration, starting with the English who braved the seas to found the Jamestown Colony in 1607. Bosnian and Albanian immigrants are some of the latest new Americans.

In the Gilded Age of one of our great expatriates, the novelist Henry James, the Grand Tour of Europe was de rigueur for young American men of means, to prepare them for a life of refinement and taste. In a more recent democratic age, scores of American college students have Eurailed their way across Great Britain and the Continent, sampling the fabled capitals and bergs in a mad, great adventure, or have benefited from a semester abroad. For other American vacationers and culture vultures, Europe is the prime destination.

What is the New Europe post–Cold War, post Berlin Wall in a new millennium? Even with the different languages, rhythms, and rituals, Europeans have much in common: they are largely well educated, prosperous, and worldly. They also have similar goals and face common threats and form alliances. With the advent of the European Union, the open borders, and the Euro and considering globalization and the prospect of a homogenized Europe, an updated survey of the region is warranted.

Culture and Customs of Europe features individual volumes on the countries most studied and for which fresh information is in demand from students and other readers. The Series casts a wide net, inclusive of not only the expected countries, such as Spain, France, England, and Germany, but also countries such as Poland and Greece that lie outside Western Europe proper. Each volume is written by a country specialist, with intimate knowledge of the contemporary dynamics of a people and culture. Sustained narrative chapters cover the land, people, and brief history; religion; social customs; gender roles, family, and marriage; literature and media; performing arts and cinema; and art and architecture. The national character and ongoing popular traditions of each country are framed in an historical context and celebrated along with the latest trends and major cultural figures. A country map, chronology, glossary, and evocative photos enhance the text.

The historied and enlightened Europeans will continue to fascinate Americans. Our futures are strongly linked politically, economically, and culturally.

Preface

"Who, at one time or another, hasn't dreamed of leaving one's life behind and moving to Paris?"

Suzy Gershman's *C'est la Vie* (2005)[1]

WHILE ONE CAN easily cite great thinkers, writers, poets, and painters on the centrality of French culture to world history, quotes such as the one above show how deep an appreciation of French culture is found in the United States and around the world. In *Almost French: Love and a New Life in Paris* (2004), the Australian Sarah Turnbull shows what can happen when one makes the pilgrimage permanent. Indeed, this sentiment is found in many books aimed at a mass consumer market in the English-speaking world.

Just browsing on Amazon.com can provide an amazing amount of references aimed at improving everyday lives with some French flair. For example *Entre Nous*, by Debra Olliver, carries the subtitle *A Woman's Guide to Finding Her Inner French Girl* (2004), and Edith Kunz promises in her book, *Fatale*, to show us *How French Women Do It* (2000). But it is not only the exotic that draws interest. Robert Arbor and Katherine Whitside in *Joie de Vivre* explore *The Simple French Style for Everyday Living* (2003). Naturally, Gallic eating and drinking fill the Anglophone imagination; for example, William Clower's *The Fat Fallacy: The French Diet Secrets to Permanent Weight Loss* (2003) is merely one books touting what has become known as the French paradox: the ability to eat well and not gain weight at the same time. The most recent bestseller along this line is Mireille Guilian's *French Women Don't Get Fat: The Secret of Eating for Pleasure* (2004).

These specific cultural references must be placed in the larger context of the abundant references to France on the World Wide Web. Using the widely popular search engine Google, or in fact any search engine, you find that France outpaces Mexico, Great Britain, and Latin America in the number of links provided (as of November 2005).

France:	745,000,000
China:	689,000,000
Germany:	649,000,000
Mexico:	496,000,000
India:	443,000,000
England:	326,000,000

But does this mean that we are still in the era of Gene Kelly dancing on the Seine with Leslie Caron in *An American in Paris* (MGM, 1951)? The answer, sadly, must be no. The war in Iraq has merely brought to the surface tensions and shifts in the Franco-American relation that have been going on for decades. Since the 1960s, and in United States schools from grammar school through higher education, historians have traced the decline in the number of students and the number of classes in the French language.[2] By the end of the 1960s young Americans usually went to Asia rather than France to find enlightenment. In 1971 Jim Morrison, lead singer of the legendary 1960s rock band The Doors, went to Paris; certainly he wished to find new inspiration, but he wound up dying. Since the 1970s writers are more likely to go to New York or Los Angeles than Paris for the contemporary art and culture scene.

Nevertheless, France remains a formidable presence in the world. Along with Germany, it is at the center of decision making in the European Union. Overall its economy is the fifth largest in the world. It agricultural exports rank second only to those of the United States. France is spoken in over 50 countries in the world, and through its Association of Francophone nations French language and culture continue to be dominant, especially in much of Africa. Moreover France and Paris remain the number one tourist destinations in the world.

ACKNOWLEDGMENTS

First to Wendy Schnaufer and Kaitlin Ciarmiello at Greenwood: thanks for all your patience and expertise! Then to Julia Rosen and Emily Johnston at Apex Publishing: thanks for all of your hard work! For reading chapters, Marie-Pierre Ulloa, Michael D. Sibalis, Emmanuelle Chapin, Bertram M. Gordon, Jeffrey H. Jackson, and Philip Whalen were perceptive and encouraging. For reading and editing another whole manuscript, Polly Tooker showed her mastery of the English language. An especial thanks to Daniel Colagrossi for his superb and original photographs. Charles Rearick took time out from his own groundbreaking work on the history of Paris and French culture to show and inspire with deft reference. Many other colleagues, friends, scholars, and artists also were of great assistance. Thanks to Leonard A. Macaluso for some tips on Napoleonic sources; James A. Winders for his vast and pioneering knowledge of African music in France; Donna Evleth for tracking down sources and vital tips for getting around Paris; Armel Louis in Paris for always showing me new titles in his book stores; the artist Joseph Nechvatal for his great help both in Paris and via email; Sarah Sussman, curator of the French and Italian collections at Stanford's Green Library, for always being there when I needed as were innumerable staff at the Bibliotheque National de France François Mitterrand and INSEE (the National Institute of Statistics) near the Gare de Lyon; and finally the staff of the University of Maryland University College online library, for their patient and prodigious help and sources. In addition, two scholars and friends living and teaching in Paris—Jessica Tree and Mark Cramer—showed me not only sources but the spaces where French life and culture happen. Finally, and fully, my wife Gano, daughter Emily, and son Bert were always there when I needed.

NOTES

1. Suzy Gershman, *C'est La Vie: An American Woman Begins a New Life in Paris and—Voila!—Becomes Almost French* (New York: Penguin, 2005), inside front dust jacket.

2. Bertram M. Gordon, "The Decline of a Cultural Icon: France in American Perspective," *French Historical Studies* 22 (1999): 625–651.

1

The Land, People, and History

FRANCE IS AND HAS ALWAYS been in some sort of cultural ferment or crisis, such as a revolution, an invasion, a riot, a religious conflict. This history of upheaval may stretch as far back as the conflict between the Neanderthals and Homo Sapiens, but had certainly emerged by the time of warring Celtic tribes (from 700 B.C.E.); the country began an especially fruitful, if conflicted, interaction after the Roman conquest by Julius Caesar (58–51 B.C.E.) when Celtic culture retreated in the face of the powerful Roman civilization. At the end of the Roman Empire in the fifth century C.E., France became the cradle of the new Medieval civilization that spread across Europe, especially with its Gothic architectural style and monastic orders, such as those of the Clinic and Cistercian, that continued until the Italian Renaissance. The Catholic Church battled against what it saw as pagan survival from the age of the Celtic Druidic priests.

With the rising power of the French monarchy, the crown had to combat recalcitrant nobles reluctant to give of their local powers, and towns people and rural peasants fearful of higher taxes and growing royal power. The cultural fruits of absolutism would become apparent in the age of Louis XIV (1643–1715), which brought dramatic refinements to aristocratic life. During the eighteenth century the Enlightenment (1715–1789), brought a demand that commoners not just nobles be allowed to share in a society growing rich through trade and industry and more powerful with the scientific and industrial revolutions. Democratic aspirations moved to the center of French and European society. With the French Revolution and Napoleonic Eras (1789–1815), France dominated the European world not only culturally but also militarily and politically.

During the nineteenth century Britain eclipsed France with its empire and industrial revolution, and both the United States and Germany surpassed it in terms of economic dynamism. Yet France enjoyed another cultural golden age with Paris, the cultural capital of the world, for virtually the entire period 1840–1940 (especially evident at the time of the World's Fairs of 1889 and 1900 that produced the Eiffel Tower). This was also the age of writers such as Honoré Balzac, Charles Baudelaire, and Marcel Proust, and the emergence of modern art from Gustave Courbet to the Impressionists to Pablo Picasso. The interrelation between industrial development, democratic rights, and artistic integrity was at the heart of the nineteenth-century cultural dynamism. France's colonial empire that emerged at the end of the nineteenth century was second only to Britain's and ensured the penetration of its culture, especially in much of Africa, the Middle East, and the South Pacific.

World War I brought the emergence of new secular ideologies promising to transform the world, communism and fascism, and these ideologies added a new impetus for cultural ferment. After World War II, existentialist philosophy and writing, the school of Parisian artists, and cinematic innovators such as the New Wave directors continued to keep France as the forefront of world culture. After 1960, an energetic central government endowed Paris and France with a new generation of museums—such as the Pompidou Center in Paris and the renovated Louvre—to music, dance, and other cultural festivals, such as the Fete de la Musique. During these recent decades immigration from France's former colonies and other non-European nations has provided new riches and energies for French cultural flowering. These trends should ensure France's continued cultural prominence around the world across the twenty-first century.

In the following chapters will show an ever-shifting cultural dynamic at work. French culture started with paintings in the caves of southern France by tribes of hunter gatherers, then shifted to the chiefs, priests, and artisans of the Celtic tribes. These tribes then had to accommodate the penetration and transformations wrought by the Romans, who in turn had to accommodate the penetration of Germanic warriors and Christian missionaries then priests, monks, and nuns. The emergence of Feudalism brought to the fore an aristocratic culture whose patronage would extend down through the centuries, with such luminaries as Saint Louis (ruled, 1226–1270) Francis I (ruled, 1515–1547) and Louis XIV (ruled, 1661–1715). The age of the French Revolution and the romantic and modern periods that followed witnessed the emergence of the heroic artist that reached its apogee in Picasso, who by the end of his life was not merely a great artist but also a wily entrepreneur and cultural icon. The growing power of the consumer that had been glimpsed in the emergence of the World's Fairs and the development of middle class tourism, with Paris as one of its primary destinations, became much more palpable with the development of first cinema; then radio; then television across the first half of the twentieth century; and now at the turn of the twenty first century, the ascension of the internet and other digital technologies that have made music and films increasingly personal accoutrements of the individual consumer.

The result is the emergence of a mass culture increasingly based not only on the personal whim of the consumer—hence terms such as *surfing* or *zapping* that have become as current in French as in English—but also on participation, either in going to museums, attending concerts or festivals, or writing books. Ironically, while the early twenty first century witnesses a decline in the number of readers, it is also seeing a dramatic increase in the number of writers. In short, in all spheres of the history of culture, patronage, creation, and consumption, France has been at the forefront.

THE PLACE

Spanning the worlds of the North Sea, the Atlantic, the Mediterranean, the Alps, and the Rhine, few nations face in as many geographic directions and contain as many microclimates as France—a vital reason for its fame in wine production. Yet France, bounded by water and mountains, also has great geographical coherence. Since World War II, the French have adopted a favorite term to describe their nation: "the hexagon."[1] Indeed, the Atlantic seaboard, the English Channel (which the French call La Manche), the border with Belgium, the Rhine River, the Alps, the Mediterranean, and the Pyrenees do indeed compose a coherent six-sided shape to the French border, with these sides demarcated by mountains or water. With 547,030 sq km, France covers more territory than any other nation in Western Europe or the European Union. (In U.S. terms, France is about twice the size of Colorado.) Mount Blanc in the Alps, at 4,807 m, is the highest point in France, with the Rhone River delta the lowest, at 2 m below sea level.

In addition, France has extensive overseas territories. These include four overseas departments that are fully part of France—French Guiana in Latin America, Guadeloupe and Martinique in the Caribbean, and the Indian Ocean island of Reunion—and four overseas territories—the islands of Saint-Pierre and Miquelon off the coast of Canada, the island of Mayotte in the Indian Ocean, and the islands of New Caledonia, Wallis, and Futuna in the Pacific and Terre Adelie in Antarctica. These latter territories are at varying degrees of integration into or rebellion against the hexagon. Relations between France and New Caledonia, for example, have been periodically tense over the last quarter-century, but no definitive solution has yet been found; that is, neither independence nor full status as a department has been achieved.

Although no longer a world empire, France still has international reach through these territories and through the International Organization of La Francophonie (an association of all French-speaking nations). In 1986, President François Mitterrand convened a meeting at Paris of French-speaking nations and regions (such as Quebec in Canada), which created this organization. The mission of this 51-member organization is to promote the education and culture of French speakers around the world. Since 1987 this organization has met every two years and has set up an intergovernmental agency and founded Senghor University of Alexandria, Egypt (named after the great Senegalese president Leopold Senghor, who was also a major twentieth-century French poet and a founder of African cultural liberation; see the concept of *negritude* explained later in chapter 6). In 1997, the first secretary-general was installed, the former UN secretary general Boutros Boutros-Ghali of Egypt. Thus French language and culture continue to radiate (*rayonnment* being a favorite French term) out from the hexagon.

Looking at the hexagon one is struck by both the coherence and the diversity in the French landscape. In essence, mountainous terrain in the central and eastern parts of the nation provides the waters to irrigate the alluvial plains that stretch along the borders and coastlines of France. The broad central mountain range (known as the Massif Central) and the Alps to the east are the origins of most of the rivers flowing through France. These rivers stretch from the Rhine, at the border between France, Germany, and Switzerland, across the plain of Lorraine, Champagne, and Flanders—with the rivers Meuse, Somme, and Seine flowing to the English Channel—and down the coast, past the Breton Peninsula, to the Loire river, and down the Atlantic coast to the Dordogne and Garrone Rivers, flowing past Bordeaux, to the border with Spain (in the Bay of Biscay). Flowing past the Alps are the Soane and Rhone rivers, which pass by the Mediterranean port of Marseille. At the northeast juncture of this broad alluvial plain (fed by the mountainous regions) is the region known, due to its dense river network, as the Ile de France, and in which the capital, Paris, is located. An ideal center for grain production and horse-rearing, this would be the nucleus upon which the modern French nation would be built following the crowning of Hugh Capet in 987. For centuries after this date French knights, warriors, and soldiers spread out to secure what would become France. Indeed, France under kings such as Louis XIV and emperors such as Napoleon Bonaparte would pioneer in political centralization and bureaucratic organization in the modern world.

The division of the French landscape has undergone a fascinating and complex evolution. Under the Old Regime (that is, monarchal rule before the 1789 Revolution) the kings divided their kingdom into provinces. Even after the king incorporated a province into his crown, the king and his successors frequently let the province retain many of its traditional laws and customs. Until 1789, the monarchy made a distinction between Pays d'États and Pays d'Élections. Pays d'États (Land of States) provinces had control over their own administration and often had their own high court of justice (known under the Old Regime as a *parlements);* they often also had control over their own administration and had their own high court of justice (known under the Old Regime as a *parlement*) which usually had the power to block royal edicts that it felt violated the traditions and customs of the province. On the other hand, the monarch and his officials, especially the intendants, directly ruled over the Pays d'Élections (Land of Elections) and the Pays d'Impositions (in essence provinces newly acquired through conquest or diplomacy). The parlements of France, of which the Parlement of Paris was the most prominent, having not only the capital but one-third of the nation within its judicial mandate, upheld the customs and cultures of the provinces under their jurisdiction and prevented monarchical meddling and domination. In this way the particularities of aristocratic Old Regime France preserved and enshrined cultural diversity. The most important provinces had their own parlements, which met in the provincial capitals: Rouen (Normandy), Rennes (Brittany), Bordeaux (Gascony), Toulouse (Languedoc), Pau (Navarre), Aix-en-Provence (Provence), Grenoble (Dauphiné), Dijon (Burgundy), Metz (Lorraine), and Tournai (Flanders).

On the eve of the Revolution of 1789 much of the population of France did not speak French and often had customs that varied greatly from those of Paris. For example, Bretone, a Celtic language, held sway in Brittany, with a unique set of customs. To the northeast, Normandy still felt the influence of the northmen, that is, the Vikings for which it was named. On the eastern border, facing the Rhine, the German language and customs pervaded the provinces of Alsace and Lorraine. In general France has two main dialects, named after the word for "yes." South of a line stretching from Bordeaux to Grenoble were the speakers of th*e langue d'oc;* north of this boundary, including the Paris region, were the speakers of the *langue d'oil.* Gradually, over centuries, the northern Parisian dialect gained supremacy, providing a clue as to why the French are so particular about pronunciation. Other variations disappeared much more slowly. For example, only after World War II did the traditional distinction between Southern France cooking (emphasizing olive oil) and Northern French cooking (using butter) begin to dissipate as both butter and olive oil became plentiful throughout the nation. Moreover, northern French towns and villages tend to have a more enclosed and private architecture, while southern French towns and villages have more patios and terraces facing onto the street, as in many other

Mediterranean societies. In southern France, too, bullfighting has always been popular—another continuity with Spain just to its south.

At the start of the French Revolution, the Enlightenment inspired rationalists sitting in the National Assembly to abolish these ancient provinces and redraw the administrative map. A set of almost uniform governmental units, or departments, now covered France in a virtual administrative grid. As much as was feasible, these 89 units were uniform in terms of geographic area and population. The goal was to create uniform and equal French states. Provincial differences were to be effaced and erased and a national culture implemented. This vision would take more than a century to be implanted and would never be fully complete. Key moments in the consolidation of a national culture occurred with the completion of a national railroad network, the implementation of a national system of primary education, and universal male military service, all fully in place by the end of the 1880s. Over the course of the nineteenth century, Paris, as the capital of the most centralized nation on earth, became all the more powerful not only in terms of politics, administration, and economics but also in culture. Indeed, it is a virtual consensus that this city of political revolutions and world's fairs was indeed the cultural capital of the world across the late nineteenth and into the early twentieth centuries.

One can make a strong case that Paris as the world's cultural center was at its peak during the 1920s. While the city of light may have attracted the world, many French artists, writers, and administrators increasingly felt that Parisian domination was stifling French life. The famed theatre directors Jacques Copeau in the 1930s and Jean Vilar in the 1940s would leave Paris looking for new vitality in the provinces. When the leftist Popular Front government came to power in 1936 their immediate implementation of paid vacations allowed a large swath of the French working class, especially in northern cities, to explore the southern and rural parts of France. After World War II, J. F. Gravier wrote a best-selling condemnation of Parisian centralization as having created a French "desert" *(Paris et le désert française)*. Indeed, during the 30 glorious years (as the post–World War II boom years 1945–1975 are known in France), the bulk of French funds for redevelopment and renovation went to areas outside of the capital. For the first time in over a century, provincial cities grew faster than Paris.

The impetus for decentralization reached a decisive moment during the first years of the presidency of the Socialist François Mitterrand. Between 1982 and 1986, under Minister of the Interior Gaston Defferre, important powers were given and institutions created for a new set of provinces with their own set of elected counsels with extensive powers over education, transportation, culture, the environment, and health, labor, and consumer affairs. The departments have not been abolished, but France once again has a functioning set of regional entities for the first time since the Old Regime. Part of the initial logic of this move was to empower local democracy, but as the European Union has evolved and globalization become more apparent, this plan of decentralization has been part of a broader regional revival across Europe. These provinces have become an important channel for the distribution of funds for cultural development and sites of lively political debate (with opposite ends of the political spectrum—the environmental Greens and the extreme right National Front—sometimes gaining control of provincial councils).

The 22 contemporary regions roughly replicate the Old Regime's 33 regions. The provinces of France, moving clockwise from the north to the south and back up to Paris, include the Nord-Pas-de-Calais, Picardy, Champagne-Ardenne, Alsace, Lorraine, Franche Comté, Rhone-Alps, Provence, Alps Côte-d'Azur, Corsica, Languedoc-Roussillon, Midi-Pyrennes, Aquitaine, Limousin, Poitou-Charentes, Auvergen, Bourgogne (Burgundy), Centre (Loire Valley), Pays (country) de la Loire, Brittany, Normandy (currently split into two regions, lower and upper), and the Ile (literally island) de France, including the capital, Paris.

The Nord-Pas-de-Calais (population 3,985,000; capital Lille), with its flat broad plain and its windmills, canals, hearty beer, and Flemish influence, at first glance might remind one more of Holland than France. But Gothic Cathedrals, the medieval Chateaux de Bours, the World War I battlefields and cemeteries of the Somme, and the ports of Dunkerque (Dunkirk) and Calais are forever part of the history of France and the English-speaking world in the twentieth century. From the mid-nineteenth to the mid-twentieth centuries, Lille and her neighboring cities were at the heart of the French textile and coal industries. The decline of these industries after the mid-1970s has been offset recently with the emergence of the area as a transportation hub, with the Channel tunnel and the TGV-Nord bullet train.

Immediately south is Picardy (population 1,847,000; capital Amiens), which shares many of the same cultural and historical features as the Nord-Pas-de-Calais. For example, the Notre Dame Cathedral at Amiens is one of the masterpieces of the Gothic style. Its chateau dates from the seventeenth and eighteenth centuries, and it features one of the great gardens designed by Le Notre, who also did those at Versailles and at Chantilly under Louis XIV. World War I battlefields also cast a somber and reflective note on the terrain. It is traditionally more agricultural than its northern neighbor (with grain and sugar beets) but now is benefiting from its proximity to the great Paris region and becoming a producer of tires and chemicals.

If Picardy does not conjure an immediate impression, the province to its immediate east, Champagne-Ardenne (population 1,351,000; capital Châlons-en-Champagne), definitely does. Famous not only for its unique sparkling wine but also for creating the notion of *appellation controle* (from the original *L'appellation d'origine contrôlée,* or appellation of controlled origin) and *terroir* (roughly translated as soil), this region also contains Reims Cathedral, the place of the coronation of French kings and subject to devastating damage during World War I. Not surprisingly, tourism is a major industry and has helped offset the decline in metal and textile production. Each year, within the "sacred triangle of champagne"—Epernay, Reims, and Chalons-sur-Marne—tourists come for such festivals as the "Nights of Champagne" in Troyes at the start of November.

To the east of Champagne-Ardenne, the Provinces of Lorraine (population 2,295,000; capital Metz) and Alsace (population 1,649,000; capital Strasboug) can be treated as a whole due to their German heritage, especially apparent in the architecture and the cuisine, which features sauerkraut and Riesling. Seventy years of war (1870–1945) saw the two provinces move back and forth between France and Germany. The slowly elevating plain that leads to the Vosges Mountains of Alsace was a prize for Lorraine's steel industry and coal mines during the Industrial Revolution (the 1850s through 1960s), but now, with these industries largely obsolete, the area searches for a new economic base. Nestled between the Vosges Mountains and the Black Forest of Germany, Alsace has been able to take advantage of being at the crossroads of the two great Western European economies to create a broad-based economy in such fields as engineering, textiles, chemicals, and breweries. In addition, the capital Strasbourg is the seat of the European Parliament. Across these two historically contested regions the landscape is dotted with fortresses and cemeteries.

Between Burgundy and Switzerland lies the Franche Comté (population 1,107,000; capital Besançon). As one moves from the western to the eastern part of the province, one ascends from farmland to the Alps. Along with dairy farming, woodworking, and watch- and clock-making, the province is home to the Peugeot automobile company. Directly south is the second most populous and economically dynamic province of France, Rhone-Alps (population 5,495,000; capital Lyon). This diverse and dynamic region featuring Alpine vistas hosted the 1992 Olympics at Albertville and produces some of the best cuisine in France, in Lyon. It is the home base of the famous chef Paul Bocuse, among others. After Paris, Lyon is the second most important city in France and is a financial, manufacturing, and university center.

Within the Provence-Alpes-Cote-d'Azur region (population 4,375,000; capital Marseille), we reach the Mediterranean after moving through mountainous terrain. This is the third most populous French province and includes Marseille, France's largest port and the second largest in Europe, after Rotterdam. In addition, the province has Cannes, home of one of the world's most important film festivals, as well as the French Riviera. Since the turn of the twentieth century the French Riviera has become one of the great magnets of international tourism. The affluence of high-end tourism results in the region having the highest concentration of French and foreign banks outside of Paris. Gambling at the principality of Monaco or Nice is world famous. In recent years, the technological park of Sophia Antipolis boasts one of the highest concentrations of high-tech companies in Europe. Off the cost is the mountainous island of Corsica (population 253,000; capital Ajaccio). Famous as the birthplace of Napoleon and today for a thriving tourism industry, the island also has had a small but dedicated movement demanding its independence since the 1960s.

Returning to the mainland, Languedoc-Roussillon sits across from Provence (in the Gulf of Lion). Divided between a coastline of flat beaches attractive for tourists and a hilly and mountainous interior, which traditionally has produced half of France's inexpensive table wines, this province has a sizable population of 2,183,000. This expanse of the Mediterranean coast has recently seen a growth in tourism, a diversification of agriculture, the arrival of high technology around its capital, and university center at Montpellier. These recent developments have offset the decline in low-end wine due to France's increasing emphasis on appellation wines (which now compose over 55 percent of all consumption within France). To the east is the city of Nimes, in which Roman ruins and baroque architecture blend in a magnificent synthesis, especially in the Jardin de la Fontaine, one of the most beautiful parks in France. The influence of Catalan and Spanish culture is also felt here with the popularity of bullfights.

In between Mediterranean and Atlantic France is the Midi-Pyrenees (capital Toulouse). The largest of France's 22 regions within the hexagon, it has a population of 2,471,000 and boasts one of France's most dynamic cities today, Toulouse. The classic red tiles of its buildings now compete with the French aerospace center and the factories that assemble the European Union's Airbus. Not surprisingly, it has also emerged, behind Paris, as the second most important region for high technology in France. The diversity that is France is also manifest in this region. Nestled in the Pyrenees near the Spanish border is Lourdes, the most popular Christian shrine in the world, according to *National Geographic*.[2] The mountains of the region are also the best-preserved wilderness region in Western Europe, home to many rare species and to the great stone-age painting in the caves at Lascaux and Eyzies. Like much of rural France, a steady population decline over the past 30 years has created almost ghost towns among the famous Bastides, fortified towns built during the medieval period to combat heresy, which once flourished in this rocky and inaccessible terrain.

Moving to the Atlantic coast—Aquitaine—we come to one of the greatest, if not *the* greatest wine-producing region of the world. Famous for its exquisite reds, such as Chateau Petrus, and its cognacs and armagnacs, this province contains a population of 2,842,000 and has Bordeaux as its regional capital. Along with its vineyards, the province is also renowned for its extensive pine forests and its seaside resorts of Biarritz, Saint Jean-de Lux, and Arcachon. The province also has connections to Spain: It contains France's Basque population (primarily located in Spain) and has an ancient pilgrimage route to the Cathedral of Santiago de Compostela in Galicia (Spain). At present, despite its rich heritage, the province has not been as successful as other provinces at attracting new industries.

Above Aquitaine lies the province of Poitou-Charentes, which stands at the western base of the Central Massif mountains. Situated between the Gironde and Loire river valleys, this is a predominantly agricultural region. It is one of the less-populated provinces (1,617,000), and its capital of Poitiers boasts the university at which one of the great masters of French literature, François Rabelais, taught and wrote. Within the mountainous (dotted with extinct volcanoes) interior are the two provinces Limousin and Auvergne. These provinces, at the heart of France *(la France profound),* have populations roughly the same size as Poitou-Charentes and regional capitals (respectively) at Rouen and Clermont-Ferrand. These traditionally remote regions have supplied the Paris region for centuries with much of its population and work skills (Limousin stone masons and construction workers and Auvergnat water carriers and café owners). Although both provinces remain primarily agricultural, they have world-famous industries and companies. While Aubusson has been renowned for its tapestries since the fifteenth century, Limoges has been famous since the eighteenth century, when kaolin (which remains white even after being baked) was discovered for use in its white porcelain china. The Michelin family has produced their world-famous tires at Clermont-Ferrand since the 1890s. The region also contains the famous thermal spa at Vichy, which became the capital of the collaborationist government of France during Nazi occupation in World War II. Vichy was chosen in part due to the large number of hotel rooms and its location in a rural France that was deemed more pure than the corrupt Paris that had led to France's downfall.

Above the Auvergne stands the other, along with Bordeaux and Champagne, premier wine-growing region of France, Burgundy (capital Dijon). This crossroads of France and Europe contains the superb architecture of the medieval dukes of Burgundy (who once rivaled the kings of France in power). Although not highly populated, at 1,614,000, the economy is highly diverse: from wine, beef, mustard, and restaurants to metallurgy and tourism.

The Loire Valley lies west of Burgundy. It contains the provinces of the Center and the Pays de la Loire and is the home of the magnificent Renaissance chateaus, erected during the reign of Francis I (1515–1547) to serve the royal entourage as they constantly traveled to display and maintain power. Today these provinces are the biggest grain-producing (Center) and livestock-breeding (Pays de la Loire) regions of France. The Center (population 2,440,329), with its capital Orleans, the city liberated by Joan of Arc, has a lucrative tourist industry not only for the chateaus but also for the crown jewel of Gothic architecture, Chartres Cathedral. The Pays de la Loire (population 3,222,061; capital Nantes) is not as rich in historical treasures but boasts the fourth-largest port in France (Nantes Saint-Nazaire) and has a growing high-tech sector and superb beaches for tourists (it is just two hours from Paris on the high-speed French trains, TGV, the French initials for trains of great speed).

Improved transportation, including the TGV, has helped open up the Breton peninsula to the northwest. A once remote and exotic region, with prehistoric stone Celtic monuments after the fashion of Stonehenge, it spoke the Celtic language of Breton and sent thousands of its daughters and sons to Paris. Brittany now plays a vital role in agricultural production, industry, high technology, and the tourist industry. Its population stands at a robust 2,828,000, and its regional capital of Rennes is the center of automobile production. The Celtic language, clothing, and customs that once seemed an affront to a centralizing nation are now a magnet for a globalizing economy.

Above and to the east of Brittany stands Normandy. Now divided into two provinces, Basse and Haute Normandie—having 1,404,000 and 1,760,000 in population and provincial capitals at Caen and Rouen respectively—the two areas have grown increasingly differentiated. Lower Normandy has shifted from agricultural production to agricultural processing and added production of household consumer good and electronics while maintaining its oceanfront tourism and its coastal connections to England (Cherbourg and Caen). Upper Normandy, with Le Havre and Rouen, now France's second- and fifth-largest ports, has made the most of its proximity downstream from Paris. Agriculture, the oil and chemical industries, and tourism also play important roles in the economy.

Finally we come to the Paris region, the Ile de France. With the national capital and 18 percent of the population, just over 11 million, the Paris region leads in almost every area of industrial and cultural production. Moreover, it is also headquarters for two important international bodies: the cultural branch of the United Nations (UNESCO) and the Organization for

Economic Cooperation and Development (OECD). Much of the cultural history of Paris will be explored in the next section of this chapter. Suffice it to say here that having one of the world's most famous and important cities is an invaluable asset for France in a globalizing economy, because it is one of the most important poles of attraction for human and economic capital.

THE PEOPLE

France ranks second in population to Germany in Western Europe and the European Union, with 62,400,000 people as of January 2005. But an overall tally of the total population does not provide a sense of the recent growing diversity or the rich history of the French population. As France forms a geographic crossroads of Europe, so its population, through the 1940s, was composed of the main ethnic stocks of the continent: Germanic, Mediterranean, and Celtic. The Germanic influence was especially apparent when the Germanic tribe known as the Franks overran the Roman province of Gaul after the fourth century C.E. The reign, especially under the Merovingian line of Clovis, brought the change in the name of the country. During this era of the migrations and invasions of Germanic peoples, some of the displaced Celtic population of the British Isles joined their ethnic cousins on the peninsula of Brittany. Along the Pyrenees resided the Basque population, with their unique language, perhaps the oldest spoken in France. In southern France, however, the Romanized population continued to predominate and up until the French Revolution based its legal code on Roman, not Germanic law. To this day, the people of southern France often remind one more of Italians and Spanish and the people of northern France more of the people of Holland, Germany, or even Scandinavia, than of some average French "type."

From the fall of the Roman Empire (around 500 C.E.) to around 1650, France had the largest population in Europe. Even in 1814 its population of 30 million was larger than all of the various parts of a still disunited Germany. This demographic weight helps explain French military prowess from the time of Charlemagne through the Crusades, Louis XIV, and Napoleon. After Waterloo, however, French demography started to diverge from that of the rest of Europe. For example, between 1814 and 1914, the start of World War I, the population of Germany soared from about 22 million to 67 million, while the population of France barely reached 40 million.

France's lagging birthrate had become an obsession by the 1880s. In compensation, the nation's scholars helped pioneer the scientific study of population (demography), and the nation's politicians and military carved out an empire second only to that of Great Britain. Even before the guns of August 1914 began firing, French leaders planned to use the resources of its colonial population in the struggle against the larger German foe. After the merciless bloodletting of World War I (which saw the death or dismemberment of five of the eight million men mobilized), the French pioneered, albeit slowly, in creating a welfare state that would encourage large families. In lieu of a demographic upswing during and after World War I, France welcomed unprecedented numbers of immigrants from across Europe. At a time when the United States was restricting access, France became the new destination for millions of people wanting to start life anew. Italy, Poland, Russia, Spain, and Portugal supplied most of the immigrants. Once the Great Depression hit France in 1932, however, the welcome mat was rolled up.

These measures, many of which were implemented right before the outbreak of World War II, could not prevent France's disastrous defeat in the war. However, by the middle point of the Nazi occupation, the French birthrate suddenly increased and, between 1943 and 1973, would produce the biggest surge in population since the eighteenth century. The unprecedented postwar economic boom demanded more workers than France could provide, and so continued immigration from southern and Eastern Europe was encouraged. But even these nations could not provide enough, and so the colonies, or excolonies, provided increasing number of workers after 1960— the primary year of French decolonization. After the end of the postwar boom with the oil shock of 1973–74, France limited the number of new immigrant workers but did allow those already in France to bring their families.

By the 1980s it was apparent that the hexagon was evolving into a truly multicultural society. A young second generation of Africans, either from the North—Morocco, Algeria, and Tunisia—or from the sub-Sahara—especially Senegal—and Asians from Vietnam and China grew to adulthood feeling fully French (while retaining ties to the nations of their parents). After 1960 a growing number of French citizens from the Caribbean departments, the vast majority of them of Afro-Caribbean descent, also exercised their right to move to the metropole, thus adding to an ever-growing cultural mosaic. It is impossible to know exactly how many French citizens can be classified as "minorities" (in the American sense) because the government does not keep records on a person's race or religion. This is part of the French Republican ideology that subordinates cultural diversity to political equality. It is also a legacy of the battles between the Catholic Church and the Republican governments since the French Revolution (1789) over the question of the role of church and state in society. In 1905 the Third Republic officially separated the French state and the church. Since that time the Fourth and Fifth Republics have tried scrupulously to keep the two spheres separate. One result has been high-profile conflict over the wearing of "conspicuous religions symbols"[3] (a subject we shall explore in the chapter on religion).

The best estimate is that today about 10 percent of the French population is what Americans would call "nonwhite." Undoubtedly, even with one of the highest birthrates in Europe, but still below the replacement level of 2.1 births per female, France will need millions of immigrants over the coming decades to maintain a sufficient labor force for its industry and enough workers to sustain the social security system. Thus France will have to adapt not only to an increasingly global economy but also to an increasingly diverse population. As of now, France proposes an alternative model to the multiculturalism of the United States. The French Republican model postulates that legal equality buttressed by educational opportunities and a robust welfare state provides a better means of integration into a modern state than rights or privileges given to certain groups.

Some of the best indexes of a new multicultural French society can be seen in a wide variety of cultural spheres. We shall see later that some of the freshest voices in French music, literature, dance, and painting are to be found among those whose ancestors came from beyond the hexagon. The most climatic moment in recent French history came when a team that was "black, blanc, beur" (black, white, and North African) won the world championship of the most popular sport in the world: soccer. (*Beur* means Arab in a form of contemporary French youth slang that originated in the poor immigrant suburbs of Paris and other cities and is known as *verlan* which involves reversing a word's syllables.) In all aspects of French culture today we find an extraordinary *metissage* (mixing and interaction). History shows us that throughout French history diversity has been key to the extraordinary creativity of this country.

HISTORY

Since the Middle Ages, French culture has usually been at the center of European civilization. Following its apprenticeship under the Roman Empire, as Gaul became transformed into France, a creative fusion of religion and politics occurred. After succeeding his father as king of the Salic Franks in 481, Clovis went on to found the Merovingian dynasty and make Paris his capital. When he married a Catholic princess, Clotilda, he converted from the Arian Christianity common among other Germanic tribes and would thus lay the foundation for the first Catholic kingdom in the West, sworn to protect the Roman pope. This close connection between church and state became even more intimate when Pepin the Short, a descendent of Charles Martel (the general who had turned back the Muslims at Poitiers in 732, deposed the feeble last Merovingian and became king). To gain legitimacy, not only was he elected by an assembly of Frankish nobles, but he also was anointed by Pope Stephen II at Saint Denis (outside of Paris). His son, the mighty Charlemagne, would achieve even greater prestige by being crowned Holy Roman Emperor by Pope Leo III in Rome in 800.

With Charlemagne's death in 814, his son, Louis the Pious, divided the empire among his three sons and thus helped given birth to modern France. In the emerging centuries of its development, religious concerns played a central role, for example, the founding in France of the Cluniac monastic system (at Cluny in 910), which would stretch across the entire continent and provide the pope with devoted servants and local areas with agriculturalists and educators. Under the French pope Urban II in 1095 came the launching of the first Crusade against the Muslim world (the last Crusade would end under the French King Saint Louis in 1270).

As Charlemagne's temporary restoration of centralized monarchical authority faded, political authority again fell into the hands of local aristocratic warriors. As a result, the Catholic Church played a vital role in unifying the kingdom. This was true from the time of the first Capetian king, Hugh (elected in 987), through to his last continuous heir, Louis XVI (died on the scaffold, 1793). For example, advisors to Hugh Capet's son, Robert II (the Pious) promulgated the belief that the king could cure scrofula, a skin disease, by his mere touch. Suger, abbot of Saint Denis and counselor and strategist for kings Louis VI (the Fat; ruled 1108–37) and his son Louis VII (ruled 1137–80), depicted the king as God's anointed, deposited the bones of French kings in a chapel at Saint Denis, and give tangible form to the Capetian dynasty's claims of power and sanctity by encouraging a style of architecture that would become known as Gothic. The Cathedral at Reims, the site at which the French were coronated with holy water, is a particularly fine example. The style's diffusion across Europe shows the powerful reach of medieval French culture. During the eleventh and twelfth centuries, French monarchs and prelates were also at the forefront of creating the rituals and sacraments of marriage and fusing them with the rules of feudal property.

Out of southern France in the twelfth century came troubadour poetry, which would develop a new elite culture in France and other Western societies: courtly love. Inspired by the love poetry of Muslim Spain across the Pyrenees, this poetic form would have a profound influence on Dante and Petrarch and in the emergence of aristocratic courts society across Europe. But it also became implicated in the Albigensian heresy, which stemmed from a group, the Cathars, that the Catholic Church labeled heretical because they revived the Manichean belief in a strict and equal theological dualism between good and evil, God and Satan. This movement was brutally crushed after 1209 when Pope Innocent II called northern French knights to a Crusade. In the process, southern France and its culture were brought forcefully under the rule of the north, a move that still stirs passions even today in the Midi.

During the Renaissance and baroque era of Italian artistic dominance, French kings patronized Italian masters such as Leonardo da Vinci (Francis I) and Gian Lorenzo Bernini (Louis XIV). Francis I, a great patron of learning and the arts and a champion of the French language, created a college free of the restraints of the Sorbonne. At this new institution, later known as the College de France, such innovative subjects as Hebrew and Latin philology were taught. An ordinance of Villers-Cotterets in 1539 stipulated that royal business be "pronounced recorded and delivered . . . in the native France language, and not otherwise."[4] The same ordinance also required the systematic recording of births, marriages, and deaths. Finally, Francis I built a chateau that introduced the Italian Renaissance style to France. Across the following century, the French aristocracy pioneered a distinctive French architectural style found especially in the chateaus of the Loire Valley. At the start of his reign a young Louis XIV brought the reigning genius of the new Italian artistic style, the baroque, to Paris to add new additions to the Louvre. His stay was short due to his denigration of the French style. Nevertheless, the magisterial bust of the young king became the paradigm for royal portraiture for the next century.

But the sixteenth and early seventeenth centuries were not among the most lustrous periods in the history of French culture, because France experienced an age of religious warfare (1561–1598) and then extensive rural and urban revolts (1648–1653). After the death of Henry II in a jousting accident in 1559, at the moment when a vigorous new French form of Protestantism emerged in the work of a young lawyer from Noyon in Picardy—John Calvin—the monarchy fell into feeble hands. Although Calvinism failed to take root in France, this austere doctrine of predestination (that is, God has already determined who will be saved and damned even before the start of a person's life), which inspired hard work and sober living, spread throughout much of Europe from the French-speaking city of Geneva, especially into Holland and Scotland. Calvinism would provide one of the main foundations of the Protestant work ethic that has increasingly become both secular and universal around the world.

Henry IV (ruled 1598–1610) would restore order to France and begin an ambitious building program in Paris (including the Place des Vosges, the Pont Neuf, and the Grande Galerie at the Louvre). Indeed, Henry let hundreds of artists and artisans inhabit and create in the basement of the Louvre (a custom ended only under Napoleon I). The stability Henry brought to France ended tragically with his assassination by a Catholic zealot and with the outbreak of the Thirty Years War in the German states.

France's involvement, which led to crushing taxes on peasants and the urban poor, led to a series of popular revolts across France during the childhood of Louis XIV. Known as the Fronde (after the slingshots that streets urchins used to hurl mud at passing carriages in Paris), this revolt consumed much of the territory for five years.

Under Cardinal Richelieu (in essence filling the role of prime minister for Louis XIII) and Louis XIV, seventeenth-century France riveted the attention of the entire continent and much of the world with its dazzling cultural accomplishments. The monarchy created the French academy to preserve and promote the French language and a host of other academies for the arts. The Sun King's patronage helped stimulate one of the great ages of French culture. The golden age of French theatre, of Corneille, Racine, and Moliere, occurred during his reign. In painting, Nicolas Poussin became one of the founders of the new artistic style known as classicism. To facilitate the new classical school, Louis XIV created a French academy at Rome and a salon for living artists where they could exhibit their newest works. His assiduous patronage of the arts took its most dramatic turn with the construction of the largest palace (and building) in Europe at Versailles. The construction of the building called upon and honed the talent of French architects, artists, and artisans as well as glass, porcelain, and tapestry makers and set the standard for royal residences for the following centuries.

Louis XIV brought to a sublime culmination the projection of cultural power that had been at the heart of the French monarchy for centuries, and Louis helped make France the center of European culture and French the language of diplomacy. Moreover, to secure his image in the minds of the French and European population and to spread the image and word of his beneficence and bountiful rule, he lavishly spent to broadcast his image through statues, paintings, engravings, songs, and broadsheets, an early form of newspaper. During his reign France secured its reputation as the center of European if not world fashion and taste, with items ranging from cafés to clothes and umbrella and luxury stores, with opulent storefront window displays and a fashionable nightlife.

His successors would not realize the centrality of culture to power and would pay a steep price. Louis XV (ruled 1715–1774, but only from 1730 in person) paid more attention to his exploits as a hunter and lover than his role as a benefactor. As a result subsidies to writers declined at a time when ideas subversive to royal and religious authority began to circulate. In what would become known as the age of the Enlightenment (roughly 1690–1789), French writers such as Voltaire, Denis Diderot, and the expatriate French-speaking Swiss Jean-Jacques Rousseau kept European eyes riveted on France as they campaigned against the arbitrary and irrational authority that they found within French society, usually in the actions of the monarchy and the Catholic Church, and championed a culture that would be based more on a close study of human psychology and sociology than on the Christian Bible. By the late eighteenth century, an emerging notion of a "public sphere" tied to the rise of newspapers, provincial academies, salons, and cafés and the growing publication of books and the rising rate of literacy brought the ideas of these "enlightened" *philosophes* (the French word for philosopher and the word by which these writers were known across Europe) to an ever-widening audience. To try to counter unbelief and sedition, the monarchy and the Catholic Church tried to censor or ban much of the literature that questioned the divine right of kings to rule society and the primacy of Catholic Christian dogma over findings of modern science and the scientific method of free inquiry and empirical proof.

Monarchal and Church repression made these Enlightenment ideas seem all the more alluring and important even among the aristocracy (who did not seem to realize that their privileged position could be lost in a more democratic society). As France suffered humiliating defeats in Europe and in the colonial world at the hands of a seemingly "enlightened" nation Great Britain, especially during the Seven Years War (known in the United States as the French and Indian Wars [1754–1763]), many writers and a growing number of the political and economic elite called upon France to imitate its competitor across the English Channel. (Voltaire had extolled England as a land of rationalism, commerce, and prosperity in his *Letters on England*, as early as 1733.) It was extremely logical that French public opinion would view England as a more successful society. During the Seven Years War France lost all of its North American Empire, except for the islands of Saint-Pierre and Miquelon, and incurred a massive debt (unlike England it lacked a national bank that could tap the wealth of the upper classes and issue the equivalent of war bonds).

The stirrings of American independence after the French and Indian War led to a cultural and then a political alliance between the nascent North American Republic and France. Thus a long-standing Franco-American affinity was born at this time. Leading American revolutionaries such as Benjamin Franklin, John Adams, and Thomas Jefferson all went to France as diplomats for the fledging nation. These American dazzled French intellectual and high society in that they seemed to be putting into practice the ideas of the French philosophes. When French aristocratic officers, such as the Marquis de Lafayette, went to fight for American independence, they too would be proclaimed national heroes in France.

Ironically, the young French king Louis XVI, in allying with the new American Republic in order to undermine the power of the age-old British foe, helped unleash a revolution in his own domain. Monies used to aid American independence by sending over army and naval units helped drive the French court further into bankruptcy. When combined with an agricultural crisis and a population explosion at the end of a period of unprecedented prosperity (roughly 1720 to 1770) the result would be the first great modern worldwide revolution, the French Revolution (1789–1815).

The cultural ramifications of the Revolution were almost as great as the political. Philosophes such as Rousseau in France and Johann Gottfried von Herder in the German lands had already waxed lyrical about the creativity and genuineness of ordinary people, especially peasants in their villages, who were seen by these and other authors as the true creators of the language and customs of a people. Now this protoanthropological and democratic notion of culture began to surface in France. After deposing Louis XVI, the revolutionaries would turn the Louvre, previously the royal residence in Paris, into the first modern museum. Moreover, in a series of public festivals glorifying the Revolution and the French people, in part inspired by Rousseau's writings, the revolutionaries would redefine and reorient political and cultural life away from the monarch and the Church and towards the nation and the citizen. Unlike the subject of a king, the citizen of a nation, in theory, had not only duties and responsibilities but also rights and prerogatives. The people of France took advantage of this newly won liberty to engage in new forms of sociability, such as the planting of liberty trees, the development of new revolutionary songs (the "Marseillaise," or the "Ca Ira," for example), dances, communal meals, and new sartorial styles, such as the Phrygian bonnet and the tricolor uniform. In addition, a vigorous anticlerical and anti-Christian movement emerged. Under the Civil Constitution of the Clergy (July 1790), priests ceased to be primarily representatives of Christ and the Roman pope and instead became functionaries of the French state. This act proved to be one of the most divisive during the French Revolution. It helped to inspire counterrevolution in regions that supported priests who refused to swear allegiance to a secular government and to foster the de-Christianization campaign in Paris and other cities, which often resulted in churches being turned into "temples of reason."[5]

The implications of revolution and democracy for culture would be incalculable and would place France at the center of European culture long after its political predominance had withered. (The era of France as the foremost political and military power on the European continent would end with Napoleon.) In essence, the Revolution showed that culture, like politics, could change radically if organized groups desired a transformation. Just as in politics, where France would be at the forefront of emerging political notions of liberalism, socialism, conservatism, and communism over the two centuries after the Revolution, so it would be in art, with such artistic and cultural movements as romanticism, realism, symbolism, impressionism, fauvism, cubism, and surrealism.

The revolutionary generation (1789–1815) had a multifaceted effect on culture. One the one hand it continued the tradition of government patronage of the arts; on the other hand it produced an unprecedented "market" in cultural goods. Along with opening the Louvre as a public museum, the early years of the Revolution witnessed the establishment of the Ecole National des Beaux-Arts and the Institut de France. From 1797 what would become known as the Ecole would gain the right to name the winners of the Prix de Rome. Under Napoleon the bureaucratic infrastructure of these institutions developed. Across the nineteenth century, this "academy" retained the exclusive rights to train musicians, painters, sculptors, and architects. The greatest annual moment in French art was the salon that the academy would host, encompassing all art deemed most worthy. Increasingly "academic art" became the foil of new artistic movements intent on forging new styles.

The revolutionary era also opened up a new relationship between the artists and writers and the general public based upon market forces. Within two years of the Revolution's outbreak (1789) the regulated economy of guilds was abolished and freedom of commerce was proclaimed. This was an event of immense cultural as well as economic significance. Theatres, concert halls, newspapers, and book publishers, as well as restaurants and cafés, now had to compete in an open market without subsidies or privileges. As a result, a cultural public sphere emerged in which critics flourished as they told a growing public what were the best plays, books, painters, and sculptors—much less cafés and restaurants—to buy or to frequent. Although academic art might have survived, it now had to compete in a much more competitive environment in which not only royal and aristocratic patronage but also middle-class taste set the criteria (based on its ability to sell).

After the fall of Napoleon, French governments, until the Popular Front in the mid-1930s, for the most part left culture to the whims of the marketplace. Aside from the government's overseeing of the academy, censoring work deemed seditious or obscene, or later, during the 1880s, creating a national system of secular free primary education, the French government did not intervene in a continuous fashion. Periodically, from the 1790s, the French government funded and hosted international expositions, but these early forms of world's fairs also drew upon funding from French private industry and commerce.

The implications of capitalism increasingly influencing culture have been debated, as we shall see, throughout French history. In the decades following the Revolution writers and artists became increasingly frustrated at the "philistine" (a Biblical reference to a tribe lacking in culture) attitude among the general public about art. Increasingly it seemed that "good" art was measured by popularity and accessibility rather than by refinement and complexity. In short, art seemed to be reduced to just another commodity, such as a piece of soap. Increasingly, France's cultural creators asserted that artistic creation and its production had a spiritual or, if they were revolutionaries, an emancipatory value. Writers such as Honoré de Balzac chaffed at the fact that they often had to write best sellers in order to earn enough money to compose works of quality (such as his novel series *The Human Comedy*).

The first great revolt against the imperatives of the marketplace taking precedence over artistic inspiration occurred during the height of romantic rebellion in France, in the 1830s and 1840s. Romanticism came late to France, in part due to the turbulence of the Revolution and the wars of Napoleon. When it did it took a more iconoclastic and revolutionary turn than in Britain or Germany. The poet Gerard de Nerval mocked middle-class pretensions to respectability and decorum by walking a lobster in the most fashionable area (then) of Paris, the Palais Royal. In response to stares he quipped: "Why should a lobster be any more ridiculous than a dog . . . or any other animal that one chooses to take for a walk? I have a liking for lobsters. They are peaceful, serious creatures. They know the secrets of the sea, they don't bark, and they don't gnaw upon one's monadic privacy like dogs do. And Goethe had an aversion to dogs, and he wasn't mad."[6] Such behavior asserted the right of artists to live differently and to go beyond convention. On the theoretical level, the most important statement of the age came from de Nerval's friend, Théophile Gautier. Beginning as a painter and then turning to literature, Gautier pondered the relation between art and life and developed the concept of art for art's sake. This theory of artistic and cultural autonomy from the imperatives of economic and social life appeared in the preface of his novel *Mademoiselle de Maupin* (1835). Gautier argued that art's sole purpose was to embody beauty and to convey a higher consciousness than that found in ordinary life. His theory of plasticity, that the various arts can learn from one another and that a writer can use words like a painter or a painter use colors like a writer, would have a profound influence on future generations. In the short run it helped pave the way for new schools of poetry, such as the Parnassians and symbolists.

The notion of art for art's sake (*l'art pour l'art*) helped inspire the growth of an artistic bohemia and an avant-garde in late nineteenth-century Paris. The notion of an artistic avant-garde developed analogously to the military concept of those who scouted or led the attacking army. By the 1830s, the image of artists in their garrets (the inexpensive attics or sometimes basements of

Parisian apartments) and cafés was becoming commonplace. Other informal institutions of leisure and recreation such as dance halls, popular concerts, and country taverns also became the favorite haunts of this artistic world. The artistic increasingly strove to discover the new and the creative in all forms of human endeavor, which seemed impossible if they devoted their lives simply to making money and achieving social mobility based on the opinion of others rather than on their own genius.

One of the greatest and most influential writers of the generation after the romantics was Charles Baudelaire. Often grouped among the symbolist poets, Baudelaire was one of the first to define the aesthetic of artistic modernism. He called for poets and painters to be students of their own age and to record the incredible transformation going on about them with industrialization and urbanization. (Baudelaire himself would provide indelible images of Paris's urban renewal during the 1850s and 1860s.) Rather than paint or depict the gods and nymphs of classical mythology, writers and artists should reveal the nature of the modern city: its cafés and train stations, the workers, the unemployed, and those on the margin such as prostitutes. Baudelaire was good friends with Edouard Manet, one of the most innovative painters of mid- to late nineteenth-century Paris and a mentor to the impressionists.

The modern notion of the bohemian (the ancestor of the beatnik or the hippie) became codified in the novel of a Parisian writer by the name of Henry Murger. Referring initially to young students or aspiring artists on the Left Bank of Paris, lodging in attics and frequenting cafés, these seemingly aimless, rootless, and exotic figures seemed similar to the "exotic" peoples of Eastern Europe—gypsies, or in this case the natives of what is today the Czech Republic, Bohemians. Written between 1845 and 1848, Murger's novel became the basis for Giacomo Puccini's popular opera, *La Boheme* (1890), which carried the figure of the bohemian from the literary to the musical world.

The fact that Murger's novel depicted Parisian life leading up the 1848 revolution is crucial. Paris through the 1890s (when the Dreyfus Affair raged and many thought France was on the verge of yet another revolution) was as haunted by a fear of political revolutions, which erupted in 1830, 1848, and 1871, as it was inspired by artistic innovation. In some cases, such as Gustave Courbet, this link was direct. Courbet had been a pioneer in the realist school of painting in the 1840s and 1850s, depicting the plight of peasants and workers sympathetically and heroically. Then, as a member in charge of artistic affairs during the revolutionary Paris Commune of 1871, he had directed the destruction of Napoleon I's Vendome Column—made from captured canons—due to its militaristic symbolism.

But artists did not have to be explicitly political to face government repression. Stylistic innovation and the use of the theme of adultery could bring government repression. Baudelaire and the novelist Gustave Flaubert both went on trial for offending public morality under the regime of Napoleon III (president 1848–1851, then emperor after his seizure of power in December 1851).

Yet nineteenth-century French culture also showed that the young bohemian radical could turn into the old bourgeois conservative. This point can be illustrated through the history of the school of painting that gave birth to modern art, the impressionists. Growing up in the 1850s these aspiring artists were part of the first generation of painters that had to come to terms with a new technology, the photographic camera. With the traditional function of art, realistic depiction, now challenged, the impressionists would turn away from the outside world to begin an exploration of the way in which the human mind perceives the world. This is the essential turn that marks the rise of all forms of modern art. Not surprisingly, in an age of political turmoil and one in which the Ecole de Beaux arts and its annual salon still dominated the market for painting and sculpture, their art was viewed as an abomination. Indeed, the term impressionism, now used to characterize the movement, was then used pejoratively.

In order to mediate the growing conflict between academic and nonacademic art, Emperor Napoleon III intervened and allowed art rejected by the academy to be shown at a "Salon des Refusés" in 1863. Now often seen as the birth date of the artistic avant-garde, it then proved to be a disaster; as most critics ridiculed the mishmash of different styles and genres, only a few of the paintings shown were by the impressionists. Nevertheless, over the next few decades the artistic tide turned against academic art and increasing number of Parisian artists, roughly 12,000 in the late nineteenth century, turned from tradition to innovation. The French art establishment, however, did not support, much less collect, the new waves of artistic innovation that flowed from impressionism. For example, in 1895 the government rejected the bequest of the impressionist painter Gustave Caillebotte of 29 paintings, including some by Cezanne, Monet, and Manet.

Impressionist painting became popular in large part due to the growing American love of French culture and the new artistic styles of Paris. The late nineteenth century saw the rise of American industry and commerce, and many of the newly wealthy Americans saw their best chance to cement their claim to elite status in the purchase of new French art. This is an important reason that so much of the impressionist canon is in the United States (for example, at the Art Institute of Chicago). Thus the affinity between French and American culture continued to be sustained.

Impressionism strove to explore the dynamics of human perception, especially how the eye comprehends light; the movement also provided an invaluable historical record of the transformations in the popular culture of urban and rural life. Painters in the school such as Claude Monet, Pierre-Auguste Renoir, Alfred Sisley, Camille Pissarro, Edgar Degas, Edouard Manet, and Mary Cassatt recorded the ambiance of the horse race, the café concert—a venue for popular music—the opera, café life, train stations, home life—from raising children to holding dinner parties—and private musical concerts. Indeed, the period after 1830 saw a dramatic increase in the number of cafés, first in the provinces and then, from the 1860s, in Paris. Political repression after the 1848 revolution through the Paris Commune could not hold back this venue of popular entertainment and intellectual and artistic discussion and debate. Indeed, as noted above, the French version of the music hall emerged from café life. Parisian newspapers innovated across the nineteenth century by reducing the price of the newspaper and increasing the quality (adding color and photographs). By the end of the nineteenth century, Paris had some of the largest newspapers in the world. Events such as the Dreyfus Affair (1894–1904) and the assassination of the newspaper editor Gaston Calmette by Madame Caillaux, the wife of a prominent politician, riveted Paris and the provinces. In the latter case the nation was so entranced by the murder trial that the events leading up to the start of World War I were pushed to the sidelines.

By the 1880s impressionism seemed spent in the eyes of many artists. Between this decade and World War I, a wide variety of new artistic movements would appear. Usually grouped under the term postimpressionism, these works depict Parisian, provincial, or colonial life in the work of such artists as Paul Cezanne, Vincent van Gogh, Paul Gauguin, and Henri de Toulouse-Lautrec and such movements as pointillism (Seurat and Signac), nabism (Bonnard and Vuillard), and fauvism (Matisse). After 1900, with the arrival of an increasing number of artists from around the world, France gave birth to the cubism of Picasso and Braque and the early dadist works of Marcel Duchamp.

Literature flourished as well in what has become known as the fin de siècle and belle époque periods (roughly the 1890s through World War I, 1914–1918). The realism of Flaubert in the novel and symbolism of Baudelaire in poetry sparked innovations such as Emile Zola's novelist "naturalism" and Stéphane Mallarmé's concern with the self-contained nature of a poem's meaning. The playwright Alfred Jarry in the late 1890s experimented on the Paris stage with the use of absurd or pornographic dialogue, and the post-1900 poets Max Jacob and Guillaume Apollinaire with a "cubist" form of poetry. Apollinaire was one of the first great champions of Picasso's painting, thus carrying on a French tradition, dating back to Diderot but especially developed by Baudelaire, of the writer as art critic.

Paris during this time also saw the birth of modern cabaret and the cinema. A mixture of song, theatre, dance, mime, and poetry, cabaret first flourished on the Parisian Right Bank on the hill of Montmartre. Singers such as Aristide Bruant became famous not only through the posters of Toulouse-Lautrec, but also as someone who tapped into the languages and gestures of the Parisian working class and created a new synthesis of elite and popular culture. As railroad and steamship networks drew the world closer and connected Paris in particular much more easily to the Anglo-American world, modern tourism emerged, with Paris as one of its prime destinations and Bruant as a major attraction. The first public showing of film occurred in a Paris café in 1895. This presentation launched the careers of the Lumière brothers, who were soon joined by another powerful film maker, Charles Pathé. From this moment, Paris and France fell in love with the new medium and would dominate worldwide production until World War I.

Virtually all of these cultural initiatives occurred outside of government patronage. The government of the Third Republic (effectively in power from 1880) nevertheless did provide some inspired cultural patronage. We have noted earlier its most lasting legacy, the creation of a system of secular primary schools, but its boldest move was to hold two inimitable World's Fairs. The 1889 fair was a celebration of the centennial of the French Revolution and the secular scientific culture that was emerging. The Eiffel Tower was meant to show that republican France could produce worthy monuments to compare with anything the Catholic Church or the monarchy had produced. The great success of this fair, along with another one in 1900, helped restore France's position in the world after its defeat at the hands of the new German Empire in 1870–1871. Since the time of Louis XIV Paris had been famous for its illumination at night, but due to the dazzling use of electricity during these world's fairs, Paris became known as the "city of lights."

When an average French person in 1900 looked out at the cultural condition of her or his nation, however, lamentation rather than celebration was more common. The French press constantly bombarded the population with unfavorable comparisons with Germany. In particular, the low French birthrate had become an obsession; consequently, the fear that France would lack the manpower to stand up to Germany in another war became pervasive. Popular and increasingly mass culture was usually blamed for French infertility. Constant mention was made that France consumed more alcohol and had more drinking establishments than any other nation on earth and that its press was corrupting the youth. For many cultural conservatives urban culture was a disaster, and the only hope was to inspire higher fertility among the French peasants and a celebration if not a return to the peasant farmers and their culture.

Education in the schools of the Third Republic was devoted to weaning the peasants from Catholicism and the workers from socialism. Although much was written on the need for more physical education, French schools remained among the most academic in the industrialized world, and French nationalism and the benefits of a republican society were emphasized, especially in history and civics classes. Nevertheless, education in the late nineteenth and early twentieth centuries did not lead to much democratization, since few (primarily sons), of the lower classes could go even to the French equivalent of high schools, much less college. These basic schools were equivalent to American grammar schools stressing basic skills of reading, writing, and national culture, with little focus on elite culture or advanced mathematics or science.

The status of women had not improved much over the course of the century. In the minds of even female republicans the average French woman seemed too attached to the parish priest and the Catholic Mass. A stereotype of the time pictured French men at the café and their wives at church. Fear that women receiving the right to vote and full legal equality would bring a further decline in the birthrate and the election of Catholic governments led many republicans to oppose women's emancipation. Only a few women in education, in the arts, or in journalism could break out of the stereotypical dichotomy of the woman as either housewife or harlot.

Initially, the start of World War I brought an unprecedented unity among the French people. Radicals among the Socialists, the workers, and the peasants, who had sworn never to fight in an "imperialist war," now joined forces in a "sacred union" to protect republican France from Prussian militarism. As the war dragged on, however, and as millions of French soldiers and civilians were killed or wounded (most of World War I on the Western Front was fought on French soil), French culture became polarized. On the one hand, the French political Right demanded that the nation become moral, sober, and disciplined to fight the war for as long as necessary. On the other hand, in reaction to what seemed like senseless slaughter, the French Left, along with the artistic avant-garde, increasingly developed a more radical critique of Third Republic society and culture.

Victory in late 1918 only temporarily quieted a growing culture war between the French Left and Right. In general, on the one hand, the French Right came out of the war unified in demanding revenge against Germany, reparation of the nation, and renewal of the culture. For most critics on the Right, a return to Catholicism, the implementation of sport, a rise in the birthrate, and a repression of cafés and other forms of popular culture would lead to French regeneration. On the other hand, the France emerged from the war deeply divided over the new Russian Revolution. The result would be a split of the old French Socialist Party into two: a Socialist Party and a Communist Party (PCF). In general, the Left wanted a vast increase in government intervention to solve the problems of housing and unemployment and to provide France with what we now know as a welfare state. At the epoch making Congress of Tours in 1920, this split occurred as revolutionaries who wanted to follow the example of Lenin's Bolsheviks in Russia and create a Soviet France expelled members of the old Socialist Party (SFIO) who championed reform through the parliamentary system. Some artists called for a return to French classicism to defeat German barbarism, and even painters such as Picasso did return to classical motifs for a period during the 1920s, the war radicalized the artistic avant-garde. In Switzerland and in Paris young writers and artists revolted against a civilization that seemed to have gone mad. In Zurich a young Romanian, Tristan Tzara, created a type of anti-art that would become known as dada (intentionally meaning little more than the rhyme in a children's game and signaling that notions of cultural hierarchy must be overturned). In Paris a young doctor who had treated frontline soldiers suffering from shell shock, Andre Breton, was turning to Sigmund Freud and the new discipline of psychoanalysis in order to try to understand the effects of the human unconscious on life and art.

After World War I Tzara would come to Paris and link up with Breton. At the same time other disaffected artists, writers, and composers from around the world were flocking to Paris to try to make sense of the great events that had just transformed human life and culture. Indeed, Paris during the 1920s would reach the zenith of its cultural influence over the world, including African American jazz and Latin American dances such as the tango. Russian refugees from the Bolshevik Revolution, African writers, and Asian artists all descended on the city. The French call the 1920s the "crazy years" due to the mixture of desperation and celebration that ensured after the end of the shooting and shelling. Seldom had people danced more, and after an initial sober interlude during and following the war, drunk so much. Especially for American writers and artists escaping a provincial and prohibitionist United States, Paris seemed a revelation. One of the most enduring stars and symbols of this age was the African American expatriate dancer and singer Josephine Baker. She would remain a superstar in France from the 1920s until her death in the 1970s, having served in the French Resistance during World War II.

By 1920 Montparnasse had eclipsed Montmartre as the center of the artistic avant-garde. James Joyce, Ernest Hemingway, and Pablo Picasso are among the thousands of names that graced such famous cafés as Le Select, Le Dome, and La Coupoule. Andre Breton refashioned dadaism into surrealism and held court at a number of cafés across Paris. Never before or since had the intellectual and artistic life of Parisian cafés been so rich.

Over the next two decades, Breton's surrealist group would include many of the most important writers, artists, and thinkers, not merely French but of world culture, of the era. Max Ernst, Salvador Dali, Giorgio de Chirico, René Magritte, and Yves Tanguy among painters and Louis Aragon, Rene Daumal, Paul Eluard, and Jacques Prevert among writers all spent some time within this broad conversation on the nature of the human mind and its relation to culture held by Breton. In general Breton believed that Western Civilization was terminally ill, if not dead. Only new sources of creativity from outside the traditional sphere of rational elite white European male power—for example African, Asian, and Native American art and cultures, the working class, women, and the inspiration of the human unconscious—could create a more humane and just society in the future., Toward this end, in the late 1920s, with the onset of fascism and the rise of Nazism, Breton tried to link surrealism with communism. When he became disenchanted with Soviet Marxism he turned to the exiled Leon Trotsky in Mexico.

Breton was also a tireless cultural entrepreneur organizing protests and exhibitions that almost always drew intense media scrutiny. After the war he and fellow surrealists heckled some of the nation's most venerated writers, Anatole France and Maurice Barres, for their conservatism and pomposity in the case of the former and the racism and militarism in the case of the latter. The surrealists also protested the 1931 French Colonial Exhibition, stressing the political oppression and the cultural insensitivity that imperialism entailed. Breton also issued numerous manifestos on the artistic and political meaning of surrealism. During the 1920s writers who had come to maturity before the war achieved some of their greatest success. This was especially true of Marcel Proust and Andre Gide. Proust would finish his magisterial artistic ruminations on the meaning of memory and place by the time of his death in 1922. Andre Gide would be one of the first writers to grapple with homosexuality and then later, in the late 1920s and early 1930s, with the question of colonialism and political commitment, excoriating European colonialism in Africa and then praising and joining and then condemning and leaving the Communist Party following trips to the Soviet Union.

Although the war had ended French domination of international cinema, it did not disrupt its hegemony over fashion, industrial design, and architecture. As with the world's fairs of the late nineteenth century, so here the government played a vital role in promoting and hosting the 1925 International Exposition of Decorative Arts and Modern Industries. What has since become known as art deco had begun to emerge by 1910 but reached its high point around this exposition and continued to dominate much of the architectural and industrial design around the world through World War II. Although streamlined, art deco continued, though modified, the beaux arts tradition of ornamentation, and art deco buildings did not break radically from the beaux arts tradition that Baron Haussmann had used in rebuilding much of Paris in the 1850s and 1860s (and that has influenced the city beautiful movement in the United States). During the 1920s, however, a visionary architect appeared on the French scene. Charles-Edouard Jeanneret, from the French-speaking part of Switzerland, would become known in the world of architecture as Le Corbusier. With his radical new conceptualization of architecture, declaring the street dead, the car the wave of the future, and modern buildings "machines for living," Le Corbusier mapped out a radical plan to transform much of central Paris by tearing down a wide swath on the Right Bank beside the Louvre Palace. His visionary ideas found little support before World War II, but many imitators, usually without his genius, afterwards.

The 1920s did not come to as sudden a crash in France as in the United States or Germany, because the nation had not been as fully industrialized. Only at the end of 1931 did the economic downturn hit. Although the French rate of unemployment did not hit 20 percent, as in most other advanced Western nations, the less-developed industrial infrastructure took longer to recover. As a result, with a birthrate that continued to decline and Nazi Germany across the Rhine after 1933, French anxieties increased to new heights. For the Left this reached a fever pitch when in February 1934 a right-wing demonstration in front of the French parliament appeared to be the prelude to a fascist takeover in France, just a year after Hitler's rise to power. To combat the fascist specter, the French Left put aside its feuding, and Communists, Socialists, and the Radical Party (in name only) formed a Popular Front. Two years later, in 1936, the Socialist Leon Blum ran at the head of a Popular Front electoral alliance aiming to become the first Socialist prime minister in French history.

Artists, writers, and intellectuals played a central role in this mobilization against fascism. In 1932, the Communist Party created the Association of Revolutionary Artists and Writers (its initials in French being AEAR) to rally the nonfascist artistic and intellectual intelligentsia for coming battles. In 1935 the first international conference in defense of culture was held in Paris (the second would be held two years later in besieged republican Spain) and brought together most of the prominent leftist intellectuals and writers of the world. Two years later, the AEAR launched a series of houses of culture whereby intellectuals, writers, teachers, and workers could come together to mobilize against fascism. One of the members of this movement was the young writer and future culture minister, Andre Malraux. The tragedy of the time is that right-wing intellectuals were almost as numerous and well organized. However, in the short run the French Left appeared to triumph over the Right when, in the following year, Blum and the Popular Front coalition won the 1936 parliamentary elections.

After its victory the Popular Front turned immediately to cultural issues. Even when it mediated a sit-down strike that had closed most of French industry, it gained not only a higher salary and a renewal of the 40-hour workweek but also two weeks of paid vacation. The Popular Front was the first French government to establish a subsecretariat for leisure and sport, first connected to the Secretariat of Public Health and then to Education. The goal of this subsecretariat was to spread high culture among the French population. A reduced workweek and increased vacation were seen as vital means of giving the population more time for culture and leisure (seen as integrally interrelated). Public reading centers were set up and library buses (known in France as the *bibliobus*) were sent out into the remote areas of the country previously excluded from cultural activity. An attempt was also made to bring theatre to the provinces, something the famed avant-garde director Jacque Copeau had been trying to do since 1924. The director of this subdepartment, Leo Lagrange, also tried to coordinate radio and cinema production and broadcasts so that a large population would be exposed not only to high culture but also to republican values. Towards this end in 1936, on the anniversary of the fall of the Bastille (one of the heroic events at the start of the French Revolution of 1789), the Romain Rolland play *14 July* was staged at the Paris House of Culture. Finally, to provide great appreciation of France's rural cultural heritage, the Museum of Traditional Arts and Customs was founded. Never before had a French government viewed culture in such sociological and democratic terms (with leisure and education being complementary and not contradictory, as had often been thought, especially in terms of café life).

The victory of the Popular Front, however, proved to be short-lived, as Blum remained in power for only one year and the coalition dissolved by the end of the second. Although cultured and gentile, Blum provoked hysteria on the Right. A popular saying on the Right at the time held: "Better Hitler than Blum." By the 1930s the French Right had made a momentous transition: It viewed Nazi Germany as less of a threat than Soviet Russia. Thus there could be no real *union sacré* as war approached in 1939 as there had been in 1914. Indeed, for many on the Right, France's fast defeat at the hand of the Nazi blitzkrieg brought more gloating than weeping.

When Marshal Philippe Petain (hero of the Battle of Verdun in World War I) stepped forward to assume leadership of a conquered France, many on the Right felt they had finally gained a chance to transform French culture according to their own image. The "rootless cosmopolitan elitist"

Parisian culture, along with Jews, freemasons, and café owners and alcohol producers, became some of the targets of the new regime that settled in the southern spa town of Vichy. Catholicism and traditional rural life became official models for French regeneration. The Ecole des Beaux Arts, rather than the avant-garde, again became the approved model for high culture. The dream of a return to a "classical," "orderly," and "healthy" civilization was at the root of Vichy cultural policy. Plans for urban renewal stressed overcoming the density and disorder of modern cities and the creation of sporting institutions and venues to refashion a national physique that did not seem to measure up to the Germans. The trio of republican values—liberty, equality, and fraternity—enshrined since the French Revolution of 1789 were replaced by a new trio—work, family, and country.

Ironically, this collaborationist government that wished to be a partner in Hitler's "new order" merely modified many efforts begun under the Popular Front. Cabinet-level positions for youth and general-education sport emerged, and Popular Front attempts to organize the cinema were brought to fruition with the creation of the Comity of Organization for the Film Industry (initials in French: COIC). Moreover, Vichy trained an elite body of administrators to reanimate French culture at the Ecole des cadres at Uriage in the mountainous Rhone-Alps region near Grenoble, and created youth organizations such as Young France (*Jeune France*). Although lack of time and funds and changes in Vichy's leadership hindered the effectiveness of these organizations, they embodied both continuities from the Popular Front and legacies that would be developed by the Resistance government and the Fourth and Fifth Republics.

For all the deprivation and devastation of occupied France, new cultural currents did begin to flow. A more rationalized film industry produced some major classics, such as *The Children of Paradise* (Marcel Carné), and the philosophy of existentialism blossomed in occupied Paris with Jean-Paul Sartre's *Being and Nothingness* (1943) and his and Albert Camus's stage plays. Indeed, it was during the occupation that the Saint Germain des Pres neighborhood of Paris (west of the Latin Quarter and north of Montparnasse) became a cauldron of cultural creativity. Although this cultural renaissance helped usher in a new France after the war, it was also a propaganda coup for the Nazis, who could argue that their rule could be beneficial. The Resistance movements, which helped the allies and Charles de Gaulle and the French army unite to liberate Paris and France, naturally had a cultural vision for the new France. Not surprisingly it drew heavily upon the cultural democratization and decentralization advocated by the Popular Front. But in a major irony, the Resistance drew many of its ideas and leaders from Vichy cultural policy (in fact many early supporters of Vichy had switched sides by 1942).

The concern with a stronger healthier France that would have more sports stadium and fewer cafés was a theme that the Resistance shared with Vichy (despite the proud record of café owners and habitués in the Resistance). The café, a center of both urban and rural French life from the French Revolution to World War II, began a decline that has not been reversed: The number of cafés decreased from 509,000 in 1938 to 315,000 in 1945, 220,000 in 1962, and 47,000 in 2005.[7]

The liberation of Paris and of France in the summer and fall of 1945 brought a new government and a new cultural flowering. A Germany and Italy devastated by fascism and defeat and a Spain still under the boot of Franco posed little competition to a Paris that seemed to pick up where it had left off in the 1920s as far as the world capital of culture. The new philosophy and sensibility of existentialism made Jean-Paul Sartre and Albert Camus world famous and inspired the first great philosophical text of modern feminism (Simone de Beauvoir's *The Second Sex* [1949]). At the same time modernist masters such as Picasso, Matisse, and Braque were still working and attracting yet another young generation of American painters. Cultural activists from the Popular Front and Vichy periods such as Jean Vilar tried to infuse culture—in Vilar's case classical theatre—into French provincial life. More broadly, after decades of stagnation and social conflict France wished to become a fully modern nation. Towards this end the 40 percent or so of the population still in rural areas engaged in a dramatic economic and cultural mobilization via agricultural organizations to modernize the French countryside and bring all the modern technologies, from tractors to central heating, radios, and later television, into the lives of rural and working-class France. The associational and organizational transformation, with cooperatives and agricultural improvement associations, that the French peasant initiated spread to the rest of society.

Between 1945 and 1975 France would experience "thirty glorious years" of economic growth and urbanization that changed the parameters and even the definition of culture. By 1975 the French were housed, clothed, and fed better than they had ever been before. Living rooms with televisions and stereos had become the norm, and almost every family owned a car. As a result, the conditions of cultural consumption changed radically. Increasingly, cafés, music halls, theatres, and even cinemas were deserted as the French enjoyed movies, music, and the new television fare in the privacy of their homes rather than in some public venue. At the same time, as cultural and leisure activity in daily life was becoming more private, the emergence of the car and air travel also saw an unprecedented development of mass tourism. Two of the most characteristic and distinctive French traits of this new cultural expression were the emergence of the French company Club Med (Club Mediterranee) and the purchase of second homes in the countryside.

Starting out as a nonprofit association in 1950 to provide rustic retreats in exotic locations, Club Med has emerged since the 1960s as one of the great innovators and largest corporations in world tourism. At the same time as the French were traveling in unprecedented numbers to foreign countries, they also became the nation with the most second homes, per capita, of any nation in the world. In short, one of the most dramatic developments in French culture and customs over the past 60 years has been the shift of the countryside as a place of production (even though French agriculture still remains one of the most efficient and profitable in the world, only 3 percent of the population still works on the land, compared to 40 percent in 1945) to a place of consumption and leisure. (Indeed a fear in France developed in the 1990s that rural villages would largely disappear.)

Until the return of Charles de Gaulle to power in 1958, postwar French governments had not implemented an ambitious cultural policy. Despite fears of American cultural hegemony, from film—with the Blum-Byrnes accords (1946) that opened up the French film market to Hollywood—to the growing spread and popularity of Coca-Cola, no systematic governmental response emerged to promote French culture in the late 1940s through the late 1950s. This was an era in which French intellectuals, especially on the Left, developed a thoroughgoing critique of American culture as one debased by the profit imperatives of large corporations.

The Fourth Republic (1946–1958) would disintegrate over the question of French colonialism, especially in Algeria. Should this overwhelming Muslim nation still be part of France or should it gain its independence? War hero Charles de Gaulle, the leader of the Free France movement in London after 1940 and its first provisional president in 1945–46, stepped forward to create the Fifth Republic and eventually (1962) to end French involvement in Algeria. He believed that Algeria could not be assimilated into France, that its high birthrate would pose, if it remained within France, a threat to its cultural identity in the future, and that its underdevelopment would be a drag upon a rapidly modernizing society.

De Gaulle wanted to reassert French prominence in the world, and culture was a vital part of his strategy. Thus he chose one of his longtime advisors, prominent writer Andre Malraux, to be minister of culture. This was an innovative move. Although the French state for centuries had promoted the nation's culture, it was only under de Gaulle that a ministry specifically dedicated to this task was created. Indeed, de Gaulle's creation inspired many former French colonies, most of whom obtained their independence in 1960, to create their own ministries of culture.

Although under de Gaulle the ministry was not well funded, Andre Malraux's prestige and immense energy and ambition ensured that the post was highly visible and had great impact. Malraux's vision was threefold: conserving France's cultural heritage, promoting cultural creation, and bringing the cultural heritage of France to its people and the world. For his administration Malraux drew upon many of the former colonial bureaucrats in the French empire and told them "What you did with the Africans, why not do the same in France?"[8] These cultural bureaucrats then leapt into a program of "cultural action" that featured among its most innovative aspects the creation of houses of culture *(maison de la culture)* in 12 provincial cities. These multifunctional spaces could show art exhibits, movies, and plays, and host seminars and classes. Malraux hoped that they would abolish the cultural gap between Paris and the provinces and hoped to build almost 10 more, but no more were built after he left the ministry. Another high-profile measure Malraux took was to clean the monuments of Paris (a task that continues to this day). One of his most important and momentous acts was to provide funds for a young generation of filmmakers in the late 1950s who went on to become the famous new wave *(nouvelle vague)* that reenergized the industry.

Beneath the surface prosperity, French society, and the elegance of its traditional French high culture, new currents transformed mass and youth culture during the 1960s. The French baby boomers, indeed known in France as *le baby-boom,* not only became infatuated by U.S. rock 'n' roll and then later the arrival of the "British invasion," but also dedicated themselves to producing their own generation of rock stars (the *yéyés,* so named for the French translation of "yea-yea"). The first major French rock star was born Jean-Philippe Smet in Paris in 1943, but he would become known to France during the 1960s as Johnny Hallyday. This transformation indeed reflects the new cultural currents emerging in the 1950s. Soon after his birth his parents separated and he spent much of his youth on the road with relatives in the theatre. By the age of nine he was performing the Ballad of Davy Crockett on stage (the saga of this frontiersman being a staple of the Walt Disney studios during the 1950s). But the moment that changed his life came in 1957 when he saw the Elvis Presley movie *Loving You.* Determined to be a rock star, Johnny went on the television program *Paris Cocktail* at the end of 1959. He was immediately spotted as a major talent, and his first record appeared a mere three months later. By this point he had taken a new name (inspired by the boyfriend of his cousin, Lee Halliday, but naturally connoting America). This is one early indication of the insight of contemporary French sociologist George Friedman that those growing up in the 1950s and 1960s were "the first generation raised more by media than by school." One result would be that cultural forms such as rock 'n' roll would create new bonds among youths that would complicate, if not supplant, the bonds of social class.

As French youth became more exposed to television (especially images of the Vietnam War), rock 'n' roll, and the sartorial styles of an emerging counterculture they became more politically engaged and radical. While youth activism was global during the 1960s, in France it assumed a traditional French cultural form: a revolution. Thought the events of May–June 1968 did not wind up overthrowing de Gaulle's government, for many that was the intent.

While many student leaders used the language of Marxism and Third-World liberation, the proliferating posters on Paris streets, which were among the most innovative aspects of the events, put the spotlight on cultural change. The essential message critiqued a society that cared more about discipline than knowledge, more about wealth than wisdom, and more about constraint than freedom. Particularly gratifying to the student radicals was that their demonstrations and protests, first at a new university in the drab Parisian suburb of Nanterre and then in the university district of Paris (the Latin Quarter), sparked the largest strike in the history of the French working class, involving 10 million workers, a third of the labor force.

After initial fumbling and disorientation in early and mid-May, Charles de Gaulle regained his composure and was assured of the military's support. At the end of May the general made a dramatic television appearance calling for a return to order, dissolving the National Assembly, and calling for new parliamentary elections. One of the most dramatic moments came in early June with a march in support of de Gaulle down the Champs Elysées featuring Andre Malraux, among others. This march through the affluent part of Paris countered the earlier demonstrations through traditional working-class eastern Paris between the Place de la Bastille and the Place de la Republic and showed that the general retained wide public support. De Gaulle's political charisma worked one more time when in late June 1968 the French electorate gave his party a decisive advantage in the parliamentary elections.

But de Gaulle's tenure in the French white house (the Elysée Palace) was virtually at an end. Sensing that France indeed needed a more participatory and decentralized government, he proposed a constitutional amendment in the spring of 1969 that would have turned the French Senate into a body representing occupational groups and would have created regional councils. De Gaulle made clear that if his measure failed to pass he would resign; when it did not pass in late April, he proved as good as his word and resigned. Malraux followed de Gaulle into retirement as he had into service. Until the election of François Mitterrand in 1981, the culture ministry would drift, with 9 ministers in 12 years, and with total funding increasing but its percentage of the budget decreasing.

Although the goal of the revolution may have failed, a new demotic culture began to emerge based on informality, tolerance, and openness. At its most palpable, a figure such as Jean-Paul Sartre stopped wearing suits and ties; at its most profound, a whole new series of social movements emerged that dramatically altered the nature and notion of culture. This is perhaps best seen in the work of a philosopher who would become especially prominent in the 1970s and early 1980s, before his tragic death in 1984: Michel Foucault. By the mid-1970s, reflecting on the meaning of May 1968, Foucault asserted that the tolerance spawned by this open and diverse movement had helped create the climate in which gay liberation could emerge. Nevertheless, as one of the principal student-leaders in 1968, Daniel Cohn-Bendit, confessed in the 1980s, "In May '68 we didn't really worry about those problems. It was in the 1970s that there occurred the growth of what we call 'specific movements': the women's movement, the homosexual movement, taking into consideration sexuality in all its forms."[9]

Following the events of May–June 1968, a whole new set of liberation movements emerged. Looking back after 20 years one former participant in the 1968 movement saw the moment that involved "the act of a generation," which "involved the desire for a radical break with the values, norms, and institutions of the established order."[10] Women, gays, lesbians, regional minorities, and ecologists achieved unprecedented prominence, in part because each group set about creating not merely a political movement but also a cultural flowering. Neighborhoods, bookstores, musical styles, publications, demonstrations, and festivals all became associated with these once invisible or marginal causes.

French feminists, like their American counterparts, became radicalized when they saw male militants treating them as men had traditionally treated women. As one French feminist remembered: "it was a guy's movement. . . . We [women] did the cooking, made the sandwiches, looked after the guys . . . We were the revolutionaries' maids. . . . These young guys were completely misogynist."[11] Such behavior led to women ceasing to follow the traditional French leftist dictum that class oppression must be ended before gender oppression. In this context Simone de Beauvoir's *Second Sex* became a founding theoretical text for a new generation of French feminists. In 1968, some of the founding documents and organizations of the new French women's liberation emerged: for example Françoise Paturier wrote her "An Open Letter to Men" and the highly influential group Psychanalyse et Politique (usually abbreviated Psych & Po) emerged. Two years later (1970) the group Féministes révolutionnaires engaged in media events to highlight male oppression. In April 1971, the Manifesto of the 343, which asserted that "A million women have abortions in France each year. Because they are condemned to secrecy" and signed by Simone de Beauvoir and Marguerite Duras, helped put the question of legal abortions at the forefront of French politics.[12] In 1974 the National Assembly rescinded the law banning abortion and, with feminist Simone de Beauvoir at their side, formed the League of Women's Rights (Ligue du droit des femme).

Although gay militancy had been periodically part of the events of May 1968, it was only three years later that a militant gay organization emerged. Homosexual Front for Revolutionary Action (FHAR, or *Front Homosexuel d'Action Révolutionnaire*) erupted into French life not as in the Stonewall riot when in New York gay men refused to be intimated by another police raid on a gay bar, but when lesbians and some gay male friends took over a live and public radio broadcast on March 10, 1971. They deemed the theme of the show— "Homosexuality, that Painful Problem"—demeaning and degrading and made their opinions known. Soon after this media coup, the demonstrators created FHAR, and by April 1971 they had penned a manifesto. A former 1968 militant who had been discreet during the events, Guy Hocquenghem, emerged as the director who got the manifesto published in the Maoist newspaper *Tout!* As an increasing number of men joined the organization, women dropped out, feeling that they no longer had much influence. As the 1970s progressed, rituals of "coming out," as developed in France by Guy Hocquenghem, became a new ritual of liberation.

Much of the political impetus of student revolutionaries turned from trying to overthrow the state to connecting with the ordinary people and their experience of daily life in order to build a mass movement from the ground up. Inspired by the ideas of the Italian Communist theoretician and leader Antonio Gramsci and the French Marxist thinker Louis Althusser, almost three thousand radicals took jobs in the factories to try to implant (or "establish," hence the French term *etabli* used to describe them) a radical consciousness in the workers and at the same time to learn what it meant to be a member of the laboring classes. By the mid-1970s most of these militants had left the factories but found a new cause in the regional struggles for autonomy that gained force following May 1968. One of the most important struggles involved the peasants of the Larzac plateau in the Auvergne who fought, eventually successfully, the creation of a military base. The interaction between local farmers, outside intellectuals, and representatives of anticolonial struggles from around the world who were invited there by the farmers is one of the sources for the current antiglobalization movement.

While popular and alternative cultures flourished during the late 1960s and early 1970s, traditional bastions of elite culture faltered. Paris after 1968 was no longer the center of the art world, and younger generations of French painters did not wield the same influence as Yves Klein. In literature, after the high visibility of postwar existentialists, such as Sartre and Camus and the theatre of the absurd of the 1950s—with such writers as Becket—the later trends and schools, such as the new novel of the late 1950s and 1960s, were unable to win the same prestige around the world. For many critics and much of the reading public, authors such as Alain Robbe-Grillet seemed to turn from grand themes of life to explore the complexity of language and the conventions of the novel. By 1968 even the convention of an "author" was called into question by the structuralist critic Roland Barthes.

Yet the same decades were a remarkable time for philosophy and social theory. Indeed, terms such as Third World, deconstruction, gender, postmodernism, and globalization had much of their original impetus among French intellectuals. For example a French scholar of population (demography) created the term Third World in 1955, after an analogy of the Third Estate during the French Revolution (in contradistinction between the First, the developed Western world, and the Second, the communist states). The author who turned this concept into the basis of a radical critique of inequality in the modern world was Frantz Fanon. Originally from the French Caribbean island of Martinique, he served in the French army during World War II, then gained degrees in medicine and psychiatry at the University of Lyon in the early 1950s, and then practiced in Algeria. Fanon joined the Algerian liberation movement during the 1950s and early 1960s and wrote the groundbreaking *Wretched of the Earth* in 1961. Deconstruction was developed by the philosopher Jacques Derrida during the 1960s; postmodernism was developed by Jean François Lyotard in the 1970s. French feminists also helped to pioneer gender analysis during these same decades. The concept of globalization had much of its impetus in the historical work of Fernand Braudel, who studied civilization and culture in a global context (with his multivolume studies of the Mediterranean and capitalism and civilization).

Conservative to liberal presidents who followed de Gaulle took some steps to open up French culture. His immediate successor, Georges Pompidou, a great lover of modern art, initiated a revolution in French museum building. His plan for a new art museum near the impoverished old central market district of Paris (les Halles) was completed after his death in 1974 (opening in 1977). The immediate success of this new concept of museum, one that opened out onto the exterior world and was meant to encourage creation as much as exhibit it, was inspiration for Mitterrand's *grands projets* in the following decade. Along with completing Pompidou's project, his successor, the liberal Valerie Giscard d'Estaing, embarked on his own museum project, one for nineteenth-century art, in the belle époque Orsay train station on the Seine (which would become the Musée d'Orsay).

Giscard also took initiatives on some cultural matters, but had no overall vision. After winning a close election over François Mitterrand in 1974, he legalized abortion and set up a cabinet-level position in the government concerned with women's issues. He started to deregulate television, radio, and book prices. In addition, his most innovative minister of culture, Jacques Duhamel, set up cultural charters *(chartres culturelles)* and funds for cultural intervention (FIC) to encourage local and popular cultural initiatives rather than just spread high culture. But these projects were never well funded and did not have much of an impact. Indeed, culture lost its full ministerial status.

Giscard's conception of culture was much less ambitious than that of his opponent in the 1981 presidential election, François Mitterrand. Culture had played a central role in his remaking of the Socialist Party during the 1970s. After Giscard defeated Mitterrand in the 1974 election, Mitterrand developed a new cultural policy to win over artists and intellectuals to his new Socialist Party (which he had refashioned from the Old SFIO) and out of the orbit of the French Communist Party (where many had traditionally felt more at home). Mitterrand believed that culture must be expanded beyond the traditional concept of the arts and humanities to include mass media, popular music, films, video, advertising, and fashion.

Mitterrand's unexpected election as the first Socialist president in 1981 brought dramatic and ironic changes to French culture. A largely spontaneous (Jack Lang, whom we will soon meet, admitted later to giving it some push) celebration at the Place de la Bastille recalled the festivity that had erupted after the Popular Front's victory in 1936. To signal his seriousness, Mitterrand restored culture to full ministerial status, doubled its budget (and in both 1986 and 1993 came close to the 1 percent of government expenditure that Malraux had asserted was culture's due), and appointed an energetic and telegenic theatre director, Jack Lang, as its head. Lang under Mitterrand would take the Socialist Party through a dramatic series of cultural strategies to sustain and revive France's standing as a leading cultural center. It is debatable how much France's stature in the world increased under these leaders, but it is incontestable that Lang's influence has outlasted his tenure and is second only to that of Andre Malraux.

During the 11 years of Socialist government (1981–1986 and 1988–1993), with Mitterrand and Lang working closely together, government supervision and promotion of culture reached unprecedented and innovative heights. The legacy of these years is both paradoxical and ironic. On the one hand, the Socialists immediately gave workers more benefits and attacked American imperialism. As during the Popular Front, workers were given more leisure and vacation time, another week of paid holiday vacation was added, the workweek was cut to 39 hours, and the retirement age was lowered to 60. During the first years (1981–1982), Lang gained great international attention by visiting Cuba to chat with Fidel Castro. He was also noted for attacking capitalism in general and the United States in particular for threatening French and indigenous cultures around the world with the homogenizing "hegemony" of its Hollywood movies and television programs such as *Dallas.*

On the other hand, the Socialists deregulated much of the media, which had remained tightly controlled under previous conservative presidents. With television and radio deregulated, dozens of new radio stations and a variety of new television channels including cable television appeared by 1986. Taxes on cable television provided a new source of revenue for French cinema. Mitterrand paid particular attention to the creation of a series of architectural projects designed to add new luster to Paris's cultural clout and to inspire cultural creativity. Lang embarked upon the creation of a new set of festivals, the most successful of which has been the Fete de la Musique, and the acknowledgment and promotion of once marginal or new cultural forms such as rap, hip-hop, world music, graffiti, and comics. Lang's reaching out to new cultural forms during the 1980s coincided with the emergence of a first generation of children born of immigrants from North and sub-Saharan Africa, Asia, and the Caribbean. With their rise to cultural prominence France became a multicultural society; Lang acknowledged this with his development of the term and the promotion of the practice of the French *exception.*

In short, from 1983 Lang increasingly shifted his cultural policy from Malrauxian conservation, creation, and preservation to recognizing and promoting a broad range of contemporary cultural practices. Much of this cultural diversity and fusion between Western and world culture would be on display with the dramatic Marseillaise parade down the Champs Elysées on July 14, 1989, marking the bicentennial of the French Revolution and fusing national and multicultural themes. The animator of the parade, Jean-Paul Goude, claimed that the real revolution today was world music.

During his tenure Lang devoted much of his attention to expanding the conception of culture. Although he would try, especially when the Ministries of Culture and Education were amalgamated in 1992 and 1993, to coordinate education with cultural expression and appreciation, studies showed that the French had not become better read or more familiar with museums. What did change under Lang was an appreciation of how the French were increasingly consuming images and experiences rather than books and paintings in their moments of cultural consumption. Indeed, by the end of Lang's tenure, not only had innumerable Hollywood stars, such as Sylvester Stallone, Warren Beatty, and Martin Scorcese, been made Commanders of Arts and Letters by Lang but also a Euro, later a Paris, Disneyland had been created. Like French cinema directors before him Lang came to realize that it was sufficient for French cultural prestige to incorporate rather than to reject American culture—American culture could achieve a certain distinction and legitimation at the hands of the French. Lang, like Malraux before him, came to realize the "comparative advantage" that French culture continued to enjoy around the world, even in an increasingly globalized culture.

The power of the Socialist ideal of an expanded yet decentralized and more entrepreneurial conception of culture is measured in the fact that when conservatives won parliamentary majorities during Mitterrand's 14-year presidency (1986–1988 and 1993–1995), their ministers of culture merely refined rather than changed the direction set by Lang. Moreover, although the culture budget was cut, and the department for cultural development eliminated, the grands projects were not scrapped. Indeed, Lang's festivals and the policy of decentralization continued. By 1993, at the GATT meeting on international tariffs, the new conservative minister of culture, Jacques Toubon, carried the Langian mantle of French cultural exceptionalism by arguing that cultural products were not the same as soap, cars, grain, or other commodities and thus could not be subject to the same laws of the market.

The impact of the Lang years is also measured by the sharply divided assessments of his tenure by intellectuals. By the mid-1990s a substantial literature had emerged critiquing the Socialist conception of culture: Alain Finkielkraut's *The Defeat of Thought* (1987), Marc Fumaroli's *L'Etat culturel* (1991), Michael Schneider's *La Comedie de la Culture* (1993), and Jacques Rigaud's *L'exception culturelle* (1995). A key charge was that Lang has slighted high culture in favor of contemporary popular culture but had also replaced education and edification through the study and appreciation of art and culture with a facile and glib notion of cultural tourism and amateurism. Creation, in short, had been sacrificed to celebration.

French conservatives did not have much of a chance to address these issues, since the Socialists returned to power in 1997. After two governments in which a Socialist president had to "cohabit" with a conservative parliamentary majority (1986–1988 and 1993–1995) now the conservative Jacques Chirac had Socialist Lionel Jospin as his prime minister (1997–2002).

Under Jospin, two culture ministers—Catherine Trautman (1997–2000) and Catherine Tasca (2000–2002)—grappled with globalization of culture and the Lang legacy concerning tension between art and democracy. In 1998, at a meeting of the OECD (Organization for Economic Co-operation and Development), Jospin reiterated the position that culture should not be treated as just another commodity in the new global marketplace. In defense of their position Trautman and Jospin replaced the notion of the French exception with the idea of global cultural diversity as their primary rationale.

Here was a way to look forward, not backward, at the start of the twenty-first century.

Within France, Trautman again focused on changing cultural practice by educating the public. One of her favorite terms was mediation rather than animation. By promoting artistic education as much as artistic practices, she hoped to overcome the "sterile" opposition between creativity and democracy. But she had neither the time nor the funding to put this vision into practice. Tasca, her successor, had more of a chance when Jack Lang took over the education ministry and they jointly collaborated on a five-year plan to promote cultural education. Tasca was also inspired to extend Lang's gestures toward including new popular and mass cultural forms. She added techno, disc jockeying, and raves to the list of cultural forms sponsored by the government. Although a techno parade in Paris was cancelled in 2001 due to fears of disorder, it has taken place in the following years each September. In the run-up to the 2002 election Jospin raised funding back up to close to 1 percent, but this did not help Jospin win the presidential race. Subsequently Jospin lost his position of prime minister in the parliamentary election that followed closely on the presidential.

The new government of Jean-Pierre Raffarin appointed Jean-Jacques Aillagon minister for culture and communication. Aillagon's attempt to cut unemployment payments for around 100,000 self-employed artists and technicians, part of the larger spending retrenchment Raffarin attempted, led to protests and to his dismissal in March 2004. His replacement, Renaud Donnedieu de Vabres, has proven more adept at handling labor issues, compromising before the Cannes Film Festival opened in May 2004 with the strikers so that they would not disrupt the opening. He has since been touring the world in the name of French culture and global cultural diversity. In addition he has been working with President Jacques Chirac and the head of the French National Library to match the attempt by the American search engine company, Google, to digitize millions of book for use on the Internet. But he has offered no new vision of the culture ministry to supersede that of either Malraux or Lang.

For most of French history, political power and cultural development were intimately intertwined. State support declined after the French Revolution as the popular forces unleashed by the Revolution struggled to adjust to and also to define the relationship between artistic creation and a society based on the free and unregulated market. This laissez-faire approach (a term coined by the nineteenth-century French economic J. B. Say) lasted with little change until the 1930s and produced one of the great ages of French cultural expression. This is a legacy that France and its people live with today. We have seen how, since the 1930s, French government has become increasingly preoccupied with cultural life. The drive for economic modernization after 1945 broke the traditional bond between society and culture by creating unprecedented affluence and educational opportunities. First Andre Malraux and then Jack Lang tried to develop new relations between French society and culture, the former essentially disseminating high culture, the latter trying to expand and enrich the notion of culture by supporting new forms of culture. The irony is that as France has become a more modern society since 1939, the state has seen the need to return to cultural patronage in a fashion not seen since the age of Louis XIV. Naturally, however, the notion of culture has changed radically since the Sun King bestrode the Versailles Palace. Now a broad global tourist culture makes use of a site once reserved for the privileged few. With this sense of the broad landscape of French cultural history we can now plunge into the various territories and terrains of the culture and customs of France today. In the process we shall be true to the French mentality by seeing them in the light of a long and creative history.

The year 2005 will probably be known as a "dark year" in France. Public discussion revolved around France's decline, and palpable examples were easy to find: the division over ratification of a new European constitution and its eventual defeat in an election in May; Paris's failure to gain the 2012 Olympic Games in July; and then, in October and November, the worst rioting since May 1968.

The incident that lit the fuse occurred on October 27, 2005, when a group of youths playing soccer in the northern Parisian suburb of Clichy-sous-Bois fled when they saw police approaching to check their IDs. Controversy surrounds just how much the police pursued the fleeing teenagers, but in any case three of the youths, a 15-year-old of Malian origin, a 17-year-old of Tunisian origin, and another 17-year-old of Turkish descent (indeed a microcosm of Clichy-Sous-Bois's heavily immigrant population) climbed the fence surrounding a power station. Within the confines of this highly charged space two the youths were electrocuted and the other gravely injured and traumatized.

Upon hearing this news the largely unemployed and dispirited youth of France's impoverished suburbs (where unemployment, especially among youths, can run as high as 40 percent, compared to a national rate of 10 percent) began to riot. Even for second- and third-generation children of North African immigrants who have obtained a college degree, the rate of unemployment is 26.5 percent (compared to 5 percent for the French white population). In short almost everyone, especially those living in the suburbs, saw this simply as a spark that lit an already smoldering situation and turned it into a conflagration.

Riots in France over the past quarter-century have been marked by an almost ritualistic burning of parked cars. Even on a "normal" night in France in the past decade, about 80 are torched across the deprived suburban land-scape. Scholars and journalists view the burning of cars as a palpable mani-festation of rage on the part of impoverished children of immigrants who feel unable to afford such vehicles, which symbolize social mobility and inclusion in French society. They burn cars to demonstrate their exclusion from con-sumer culture. Many more cars usually go up in smoke during holidays (such as New Years and July 14, Bastille Day), but during the riots the numbers shot up to 1,000 on some night and 2,400 on the worst night.

Riots started on October 27 and quickly spread across the vast network of Parisian suburbs and across France by November 7. At their height over 274 towns and cities (indeed all of France's 15 major urban districts) were involved. Not only cars but also schools, gymnasiums, and hospitals were burned down if not badly damaged, hence rioters attacked symbols of state power along with the curfew then imposed based on law dating from the Algerian war. Use of such a measure enraged the French population of Algerian origin, who remembered how this draconian measure had originally been applied in Algeria during its struggle for independence.

This harsh measure may have helped to end the disturbances (which nev-ertheless probably would have subsided from sheer exhaustion) but not be-fore copycat disturbances erupted in neighboring countries. By November 17 the French government proclaimed order restored, but 10,000 cars had been burned, 2,888 arrests made, and 126 police injured, with scores of civilians injured and one civilian death. Since France strictly controls the ownership and possession of guns, unlike in the United States, little shooting occurred. Indeed even the hard-line minister of the interior, Nicholas Sarkozy, ordered police not to shoot even if shot upon.

We shall explore the origins and the ripple effect of these riots across al-most all of the chapters in this book. From the rage expressed in French rap to marriage and courtship patterns, to the state's administration of culture, to housing patterns, the riots illuminate both the failures and possibilities of French culture in the early twenty-first century. In the Spring of 2006, Chirac's protégé and Prime Minister, Dominique de Villepin, suffered a major defeat when a proposed measure to create more employment (without the usual guarantees of job security) brought strong protests from students and labor unions. Thus no easy or quick solution to youth unemployment has yet been found.

Thus France, even more than other European countries, faces a dramatic chal-lenge over the next century in regard to the developing world at its doorstep and economic and cultural globalization that are certain to increase. Even though the French proudly noted at the start of 2006 that the nation produced a record number of babies the previous year, the birthrate is still below replacement level (which is defined as a little over two children per woman). Even though birthrates are now falling around the underdeveloped world, the southern tier of Mediterranean nations has over 300 million young and largely under- or unemployed youths. Estimates predict that between 16 and 20 million more immigrants will come to France by 2050. Thus the tensions generated by high rates of immigration will continue to be a vital part of French culture for the next century at least. Perhaps it is thus appropriate that Jacque Chirac's biggest cultural legacy will be the Quai Branly Museum in Paris that strives to elevate the art of the non-European world to the same stature as that of the holdings of the Louvre. One hopes that this attempt to overcome "art-partheid" will inspire a fuller fusion of the cultural mosaic that is contemporary France.[13]

At the same time France is, as it always has been, at the forefront of a new cultural dynamic that affects all consumer societies today. The exact outlines and dynamic of this shift are still not fully known, but in general we can see that the age of the great patrons of the arts, such as the French kings were for centuries, and the great age of the heroic artist, which emerged after the Renaissance and became especially prominent between the French Revolution and World War II, have given way to an age in which the consumer, now increasingly the broad masses of affluent societies, sets the pace or is the target of the culture market and industry. From museums to world's fairs, festivals, and theme parks, the French are at the forefront of trying to define and profit from this new development in culture. We shall explore this dynamic throughout the following chapters.

NOTES

1. Eugen Weber, "In Search of the Hexagon" in *My France: Politics, Culture, Myth* (Cambridge, MA: Harvard University Press, 1992).

2. National Geographic Society, *The National Geographic Traveler: France* (Washington, DC: National Geographic, 2004), 274.

3. "French Clerics Oppose Scarf Ban," *BBC News*, Friday, December 12, 2003; also "French Scarf Ban Comes into Force," *BBC News*, Thursday, September 2, 2004, available online: new.bbc.co.uk.

4. Nicholas Ostler, *Empires of the Word: A Language History of the World* (New York: HarperCollins, 2005), 404.

5. Emmet Kennedy, *A Cultural History of the French Revolution* (New Haven: Yale University Press, 1989), 343.

6. For incident, see Jerrold Seigel, *Bohemian Paris: Culture, Politics, and the Boundaries of Bourgeois Life, 1830–1930* (Baltimore: Johns Hopkins University

Press, 1999); for quote see http://www.soupsong.com/flobster.html. Seigel is the main source for other points on Bohemia.

7. For café figure see Jean Dethier, *Cafes, bistrots et compagnie,* Catalogue d'exposition (Paris: Centre Georges Pompidou, 1977), 51.

8. Herman Lebovics, *Mona Lisa's Escort: Andre Malraux and the Reinvention of French Culture* (Ithaca: Cornell University Press, 1999), 99.

9. Michael D. Sibalis, "Gay Liberation Comes to France: *The Front homosexuel d'Action Révolutionnaire* (FHAR)" French History and Civilization. Papers from the George Rudé Seminar Vol. 1 (2005). These papers can be accessed at http://www.h-france.net/rude/2005conference/Sibalis2.pdf

10. Sibalis, "Gay Liberation Comes to France."

11. Sibalis, "Gay Liberation Comes to France."

12. For quote see womenshistory.about.com/od/france/.

13. Michel Daubert, "Quai Branly: le musée de l'autre," *Télérama hors série* (June 3, 2006).

2

Religion and Thought

FEW NATIONS HAVE AS rich and varied a religious and intellectual life and history as France. During the medieval period France was the most populous Christian kingdom, and during the Reformation France continued to be at the forefront of religious ferment. From the seventeenth century to the present this once-Christian nation has been at the forefront of modern science and the development of a nonreligious society. Since the age of Voltaire in the eighteenth century, French intellectuals have become a sort of worldly clergy upholding the values of tolerance, humanity, and mercy that once were the sole domain of the Catholic Church. Indeed, since the death of Jean-Paul Sartre in 1980, the French have continued to produce intellectuals that shake and shape the world's ideas. What has made the French world of ideas more important recently has been the confrontation between multicultural-ism and secularism in the light of a large Muslim immigrant population. The exchange of ideas on questions of religion and philosophy in contemporary France will have a central bearing on how the world will become a more global and inclusive society in the future.

A brief historical overview provides invaluable context for French religious and intellectual life today. Before the Roman conquest of Gaul a little over 2,000 years ago, a Druidic Celtic religion infused the semipastoral agricul-tural life of what is now France. Druid priests combined the role of priest, soothsayer, doctor, and magician and populated the Gallic landscape with sacred landmarks (for example, trees and mountains). Their ritual of human sacrifice would be ended by the invading Romans under Julius Caesar. The Romans, in turn, brought their own civic religion plus the wide variety of mysterious cults and mythologies of the Greco-Roman world to the imperial province of Gaul. In general the Romans were tolerant of religious belief as long as one honored the Roman civic rituals and did not connect religion to political revolt. In Gaul, as in the rest of the empire, the rise of Christianity after 50 C.E. or so often brought repression against the new religion, as the Romans feared the motives and effects of this creed, which claims to supersede all other religions and which kept itself apart from Roman civic rituals.

As the Roman Empire declined after 200 C.E., Germanic barbarian tribes brought their own religions and variants of Christianity to what was becoming France. One variant of Christianity common among these tribes was Arian Christianity (which rejected the doctrine of the trinity). As we have seen in chapter one, the Merovingian king Clovis brought a religious revolution to his kingdom when he converted to Roman Catholicism. From this point the French clergy and monarchy started to call itself "the eldest daughter of the Church."[1]

From the ninth through the seventeenth centuries, France was one of the most creative centers of Roman Catholicism. Two of the most important monastic orders of the medieval world, the Cluniacs and Cistercians, arose in France. Emphasizing piety and loyalty to the pope and engaging in agricultural development, spiritual counseling, and education, these two orders spread from Spain to Poland, and to the crusading kingdoms of the Middle East. Indeed, much of the impetus for the Crusades to retake the Holy Land of Jerusalem emanated from France. Pope Urban—who called for the Crusades, and Peter the Hermit, who helped spread the message across Europe, were both French, as were a large portion of the warriors who went (indeed, the Muslim world usually called the Christian Crusaders Franks). The military religious order set up for the Crusades, the Knights Templar, had its headquarters in Paris. Also in Paris was the leading university in the Roman Catholic West, the University of Paris. Here, during the twelfth century, the leading theologian of the medieval church, Saint Thomas Aquinas, developed and refined scholasticism, a synthesis of biblical and Greco-Roman philosophy, especially Aristotle.

In the fourteenth century, conflicts between kings and popes took their most acute form in France after Philip IV "the Fair" had one pope almost kidnapped and then had the papacy itself brought to the southern French city of Avignon (1309), where it would remain until 1378. The French monarchy thus played a central role in this age of the "Great Schism" in Roman Catholicism. During the subsequent Reformation France produced one of the most important theologians of Protestantism, John Calvin. The growth of Protestantism in France unleashed a barbarous civil war, with an almost gangland-like slaughter of Protestants in Paris on Saint Bartholomew's Day (1572). The aristocrat Michel de Montaigne, from the vantage point of his estate in southern France, penned profound reflections on the brutality that religious conflict could unleash and the rapacity that the discovery of the Americas could engender among Europeans. The "essays" that he would write on these and other subjects, such as cannibalism, mark the emergence of the modern essay. As the Catholic Counter-Reformation gained force during the seventeenth century, France again pioneered new forms of religious service with the work of Saint Francis de Sales, who created a new religious order to help the urban poor of Paris and other cities.

During the early stages of the Scientific Revolution, France again made major contributions. In Rene Descartes we see one of the major figures of this transformation in the theory and practice of expanding human knowledge. Descartes invented analytic geometry and he is generally considered the founder of modern philosophy. His radical questioning of all previous philosophical assumptions is based on his method of systematic doubt, a method which led to his famous first principle that he felt could not be doubted: "I think therefore I am."[2] Not only did Descartes turn doubt into a systematic tool for his deductive theory of the human mind, but he also showed how deduction was central to developing scientific models, which are at the root of the scientific method. Another French scientist and Catholic mystic, Blaise Pascal, made innovative discoveries about conditions in vacuums, built an early computer, and penned some of the most trenchant critiques of the scientific method from the perspective of his fervent Catholicism in his posthumously published penseés. These are merely two of the most distinguished French scientists who emerged after the 1600s.

Across the eighteenth century, however, Christianity in general and Catholicism in particular came into conflict with a rising new secular philosophy—the Enlightenment. Inspired by the ability of Sir Isaac Newton's physics to explain the laws of motion of bodies on earth and in the heavens, the *philosophes* (as they became known) campaigned to bring the scientific method to the study of society in order to find the "laws of motion" of society. The Catholic Church and the absolute French monarchy viewed much of their work as heresy, and a pitched battle between the forces of faith and reason developed across the eighteenth century. Indeed, this battle was more intense in France than in any other nation or region of Europe and led to a new type of philosophic activity. It is appropriate to use the French term for philosopher *(philosophe)* to describe a new type of activist thinker, such as Voltaire, Denis Diderot, or Jean-Jacques Rousseau, who diffused the ideas of Newton, John Locke, and other scientists and rationalist thinkers in compelling summaries and witty novels. These philosophes also participated in controversies. For example, Voltaire campaigned for the exoneration of a Protestant, Jean Calais, who was accused of killing his son because the son wished to convert to Catholicism. Voltaire joined Rousseau in aiding the middle class of French-speaking Geneva in their attempts to gain a voice in government. The growing number of philosophes saw it as their duty to change public opinion and could see success decade by decade as their ideas captured the venues of public debate: salons of upper-class women (where politicians, philosophers, writers, and the business elite gathered), cafés (brought to France and Europe by Turkish diplomats and businessmen in the sixteenth and seventeenth centuries), and provincial academies (created across France in the seventeenth and eighteenth centuries). By the time of the French Revolution much of the aristocracy and the upper bourgeoisie had become "free thinkers."

The French Revolution was a further stimulant to intellectual and philosophic innovation. During this turbulent period (1789–1815), the notion of the political spectrum and political ideology was born. The notion that politics, philosophy, and culture could be differentiated along a range of points from conservative to moderate to radical emerged at this time based on the seating of deputies in French political assemblies (conservatives sat on the right, moderates in the center, and liberals and radicals on the left). During the Revolution, the first radical dictatorship emerged (during the time of the Terror, when Robespierre was a member of the Committee of Public Safety from 1793–94), with the guillotine as the symbol of this new form of political organization striking fear across aristocratic Europe. Then, in 1796, the first Communist Party emerged in Paris with Gracchus Babeuf's Conspiracy of Equals (indeed, Communist parties around the world claimed this lineage). Across the nineteenth century, France continued to be a hothouse of ideas; notions of socialism and utopianism coursed through the radical circles of the Paris intelligentsia. By the end of the century, conservative thought had turned from royalism to nationalism, and the concept of National Socialism emerged. The political polarization of France reached a zenith in the Dreyfus Affair, during which the term intellectual was born. In his resolute defense of an innocent captain jailed more for his identity (being Jewish) than for his crime (espionage, of which he was innocent), Emile Zola carried on the tradition of intellectual activism pioneered by Voltaire and continued by such figures as Victor Hugo during the mid-nineteenth century. The leader of the French Socialist Party, Jean Jaures, put the concept of socialist humanism into action when he rejected calls from those within his party to abstain from this struggle over human rights (on the theory that legal niceties such as the guilt or innocence of a bourgeois army officer did not concern the struggle of the working class). Jaures argued that infringements of civil rights could hurt workers as much as groups in society and that Socialists must always stand for universal concepts of justice and due process.

The early twentieth century (1900–1940) saw an extraordinary imbrication of philosophical, political, and artistic thought. Philosophers such as Henri Bergson and novelists such as Marcel Proust explored the meaning of time with human psychology. They showed that the experience of time was vastly different from that of time as measured by the clock or by the calendar. While Andre Gide became one of the first writers to reflect upon his own homosexuality before World War I, calling for tolerance, Andre Breton explored the nature of art in a world shattered by the barbarism of war in an industrial age and demanded that society open itself to the healing currents found within the human unconscious and in non-Western cultures. Although France remained at peace between 1919 and 1939, its intellectuals became increasingly polarized. On the Right the journal *Action Française*, started during the Dreyfus Affair, argued that only a return to French "classical civilization" (after the fashion of the age of Louis XIV) could restore France to greatness. World War I veteran Pierre Drieu de la Rochelle embodied the rage felt by many veterans at the mediocrity and unheroic nature of the Third Republic after their sacrifices in the trenches. His right-wing political stance was close to that of many writers in Italy and Germany who joined the fascist or Nazi parties. From the left of center, Alain occupied a skeptical antiwar position that accorded well with the mentality of much of France's teaching and university communities. Disillusioned by the slaughter of so many of their own in World War I, they believed pacificism and socialism (of some sort or other) were the best ways to heal France's wounds. Farther to the left, socialism had an eloquent defender in the leader of the French Socialist Party, Leon Blum. Although committed to ending capitalism, Blum did not reject parliamentary democracy as the communists did. As did his mentor Jaures, he believed that only a society imbued with democracy and due process could truly become socialist. To the far left, late nineteenth-century anarchism, usually found among French artisans, had ceded place to the new French Communist Party, allied, as were all Communist parties, with the Soviet Union. This party, dazzled by Lenin's success in Russia, argued that a "vanguard" party should seize power, set up the "dictatorship of the proletariat," and transform France, stripping power from the "400 families" who ruled the nation and promoting a humane and egalitarian form of industrial society in which all basic human needs would be met. From the 1920s through the 1960s, the French Communist Party would wield a powerful attraction for intellectuals and artists. They seemed the one party strong enough to stand up to the fascist threat and the one that would provide intellectuals and artists with the tools needed to create a new type of truly democratic culture once they came to power. During the interwar period, writers such as Andre Breton and Andre Gide at some point joined or became "fellow travelers" with the French Communist Party.

France's intellectual class remained sharply divided during World War II. For the Right, in the words of the founder of Action Française, Charles Maurras, the collapse of the Third Republic within six weeks of warfare on the Western Front came as a "divine surprise." The time seemed to have arrived when the Right could implement their conservative agenda. Drieu de la Rochelle, Maurras, and a younger generation of journalists, such as Robert Brasillach, assumed positions within the new collaborationist Vichy Regime. At the same time, Catholics around Emmanuel Mounier and his philosophy of personalism and the journal *L'Esprit* tried to steer a path between the various ideologies on the Right and Left. Many future leaders of French intellectual life, such as the founding editor of the newspaper *Le Monde,* Joffre Dumazedier, and one of the pioneering students of leisure and recreation, were part of the Vichy leadership school at Uriage (but would join the Resistance by the end of 1942). On the Left, new currents of thought emerged and would become known after the war under the term existentialism. Jean-Paul Sartre, Albert Camus, Simone de Beauvoir, Maurice Merleau-Ponty, and others strove to find a third way between American capitalism and Soviet communism, a system that would be secular, socialist, and democratic.

The post–World War II era would prove to be one of the great eras in French thought. Seldom has France produced a greater variety of intellectuals who covered such a wide variety of topics on culture and society. To this day thinkers such as Jean-Paul Sartre, Simone de Beauvoir, Michel Foucault, Jacques Derrida, Pierre Bourdieu, and Bernard-Henri Levy continue to be at the center of debates on social theory, feminism, the relationship between power and culture, the role of the text in society, the power of family life and social class to shape economic and cultural life, and the role of terrorism in contemporary society. These thinkers, and many others that we will encounter below, have shaped such diverse schools of thought as existentialism, structuralism, feminism, poststructuralism, and postmodernism.

After its liberation in 1944, Paris again became the center of European culture. With Germany in physical and intellectual ruins following the fall of Hitler's "Thousand-Year Reich," there was no competitor for intellectual and cultural primacy. Although his career had started before World War II, Jean-Paul Sartre had come of age intellectually during the war. By writing novels, plays, and the philosophic masterpiece *Being and Nothingness,* along with his association with the Resistance, Sartre was at the center of a new generation of French intellectuals, writers, musicians, and artists who had made the Saint Germain des Pres neighborhood of Paris (to the north of Montparnasse and to the west of the Latin Quarter) the creative center of the France. The Golden Age of this area would extend into the early 1950s, and even to this day its cafés and bookstores are at the center of French intellectual life.

With fascism discredited, and Brasillach executed for collaborationism, the intellectual Right was virtually dead, and even parliamentary liberalism was in retreat. The future seemed to be on the Left as France struggled to create a truly democratic and affluent nation, and colonial peoples, many still under French domination, struggled for their own emancipation.

Existential philosophy can be seen as a logical outgrowth of the times in which it was born: Nazi domination and popular Resistance. Sartre posted a radical divergence between sentient and insentient beings. Rocks or animals lacked in his view a consciousness of themselves or of their relations with others (mediated through interpersonal perception, what Sartre termed "the gaze"). Sartre asserted that humans must create themselves through the choices they make; they cannot simply pretend to have some fixed identity (that is, an essence). In short, existence precedes essence. Even when one is imprisoned or living in an occupied city or country, a person can still choose their fate. Indeed, Sartre said that the occupation, when almost every moment was fraught with crisis and danger, was the time he had been the most free in his life. For Sartre, the worst thing a human can do is to not take responsibility for their actions, to pretend to be a mere pawn in the course of events. Such evasions he termed "bad faith." In his play *No Exit*, he penned the famous line, "Hell is other people," to capture the spirit of an environment in which a collectivity evades their duty to engage in the task of making the world a more humane place. Indeed, along with responsibility, engagement became one of the major themes of his writing. Because Sartre felt guilty over not having participated in the antifascist struggle during the 1930s and for remaining an aloof intellectual, he was determined during and after the fall of France in 1940 (when he was taken as a prisoner of war) never to be on the sidelines of history again. He called upon all writers also to be engaged in their age. For him, political commitment took the form of reformulating Marxism (the most important philosophy of the twentieth century, he believed) so that it could become more fully humanistic.

Often lumped with the existentialists, but never accepting the term, Albert Camus developed his own writings along similar yet distinctive lines from those of Sartre. His novel *The Stranger* dramatized the same sort of absurd universe and society that Sartre depicted in his novels, and in his philosophical essay, "The Myth of Sisyphus," he also emphasized that it was not the type of work or life that humans do or live but the attitude with which they engage in their labors that counts the most and makes them truly human. Thus in this essay, as often with Sartre, Camus drew upon Greco-Roman mythology to dramatize how the mythological character who had stolen fire from the gods and given it to humans and was thus condemned to roll a rock forever up a hill, only to have it always roll back down, could escape the wrath of the gods by endowing his labors with his own personal meaning. Camus, however, would break with Sartre on the question of Marxism and revolution. The son of a poor French family in Algeria, he could not support the drive by the indigenous population to free themselves from France. Along with his hesitation on anticolonial struggles (which Sartre and most French intellectuals supported), Camus also had qualms about whether revolutions would emancipate humanity or merely subject it to new tyrannies (see his other philosophical essay "The Rebel"). Camus would win the Nobel Prize for literature in 1957 and then die young and tragically in an auto accident in 1960. At Camus' death, Sartre brilliantly declared him within the long line of French moralists whom he felt "constituted what was most original in French literature."[3]

During the late 1940s, another member of the existentialist group, Simone de Beauvoir, would use the philosophy to analyze women's oppression. De Beauvoir had been among the first generation of French women to graduate from the elite and prestigious Ecole Normale Superieur and then to teach philosophy. As lover, collaborator, and confidant of Sartre throughout his life, de Beauvoir explicitly rejected marriage and forged what she believed to be a relationship that conformed to her philosophy of freedom. In *The Second Sex* (1949) she penned her most important book, one at the very center of the second wave of feminism that erupted around the developed world at the end of the 1960s. Women, she argued, had been made subordinate to men not by nature but by society. It was incumbent upon women to struggle against the definition imposed upon them by society in order to create their own existence and then overcome a stereotypical "essence" imposed by society but not mandated by nature.[4] Indeed, given the traditional injunction for women to bear children, especially in France due to its low birthrate, she advocated that women not become mothers. De Beauvoir also wrote other philosophical works on existentialist themes, as well as award-winning novels, but *The Second Sex* remains her great intellectual monument and one of the most influential works by a French intellectual in the twentieth century.

A third member of Sartre's inner circle, Maurice Merleau-Ponty, was also highly influential. Like Sartre and de Beauvoir, he was among the editors of *Les Temps Moderns* (*Modern Times*), the title inspired by the Charlie Chaplin movie, the journal founded by Sartre that would become one of the leading outlets for intellectual life in postwar France. Tragically, he died of cancer just as his productivity as a philosopher had become apparent. But in his books *Sense and Nonsense* (1948), *Signs* (1960), and *Phenomenology of Perception* (1962) he refined Sartre's existentialism and anticipated the emergence of the philosophical movement of structuralism. Merleau-Ponty replaced

Sartre's dichotomy of perceiver and perceived with the concept of the perceptual field. He then explored the dynamics of perception and space; that is, how space helps determine perception as we move through life. His emphasis on connecting the study of social space and social structure would be taken up by many later French thinkers. At the same time he was a pioneer in the study of the effects of linguist structures on human thought. But his work would not be at the center of structuralism.

During the 1950s, a relatively underappreciated French-speaking Swiss linguist, Ferdinand de Saussure, became the inspiration for a new intellectual approach to the study of culture and society. His key insight displaced the study of language from the meaning of individual words to studying relations between words and their connection to the overall structure of the language. In particular, he emphasized that all words fit into a set of binary oppositions (such as up or down), and that such oppositions are at the heart of how human beings make sense through language. One of the central insights that a series of French intellectuals would take from Saussure's work would be the idea that human cultures are structured like a language and should thus be studied according to Saussure's structural principles.

A wide number of intellectuals developed Saussure's method during the 1960s. In short, the age of Sartre, with his emphasis on action and choice, had passed, and the age of language and viewing culture as a set of linguist systems had arrived. The anthropologist Claude Lévi-Strauss viewed ethnographic reports on subjects from marriage strategies to cuisines and analyzed them in terms of their binary structure and how it related to such essential questions as, in the case of marriage, how the Oedipus complex or the taboo against marrying within one's immediate family functioned. The title of his study of cuisine, *The Raw and the Cooked,* provides insight into his method, which he related to the ways in which various indigenous peoples around the world situate themselves and others on a continuum between the human and the nonhuman. Perhaps the most important finding of Lévi-Strauss concerned the fundamental unity and equality of the human mind. In essence, structuralism buttressed his thesis that both "primitive" and "modern" humans think alike and that societies have a historical consciousness, which he called "hot," gave them no advantage over societies that lack a sense of history, which he called "cold."[5] He developed these points, in part, in a polemic with Sartre, for whom the Marxist sense of history (that is, the inevitable triumph of the working class) was the goal of human life (though it should be noted that Levi-Strauss considered himself a Marxist).

The literary scholar Roland Barthes developed another strain of structuralism, exploring the "myths" not among tribes outside of Europe but in his France of the 1950s and 1960s. Starting with a brilliant set of analyses of the seemingly banal objects and customs of daily life, from the drinking of wine or professional wrestling through advertisements and magazine covers, Barthes showed how the national identity was formed and reinforced. One of his most telling examples was of a magazine cover (before the process of decolonization had started in the 1960s) showing a uniformed member of the Foreign Legion saluting the French flag. This seemingly banal image had been turned into what Barthes called a "sign." How? Because the person in the photograph was of African descent, his allegiance to France provided the French populace with the reassuring notion that its colonial subjects remained loyal despite all the agitation for liberation. In general, Barthes used this type of analysis to show the way in which a society tried to portray its ideas and customs as the product not of a specific history tied to class struggle but of some timeless and "mythic" correct way to lead one's life.[6]

Yet, another variation on structuralist analysis emerged in the writing of Louis Althusser. This instructor at France's most elite preparatory school *École normale supérieure*, he used the epistemological break, a concept of one of the leading French philosophers of science, Gaston Bachelard, to argue that Marx's early writings on human creativity and subjectivity had no relevance for understanding Marx's "mature" theory of economics (centering on the inevitable disintegration of capitalism and its replacement by socialism). Althusser's thesis, that Marx's thought had changed radically from his youthful romantic emphasis on the power of the human will to a adult and mature realization that economic forces were larger than human volition, provides yet another example of how structuralism shifted analysis from human action to linguistic or social and economic structures.

One of the most controversial and influential of these structuralists was the Freudian psychotherapist Jacques Lacan. Until Lacan, Freud's theories, unlike those of Karl Marx, had not had much impact on French intellectual life. Lacan's confrontation with Freud would initiate many other French philosophers into the work of the Viennese master of the belle époque (the 1890s–1910 being his most creative period). In essence Lacan argued that the Freudian notion of the unconscious could most fruitfully be conceived of as like a language. Rejecting the Freudian-inspired ego psychologists of the United States, with their emphasis on willpower and adjustment to social norms, Lacan stressed the web of interpretation that surrounds the infant from the first time she or he sees themselves in the mirror (here we see his controversial mirror stage) and thus realizes that while they are a whole being (the assumption here is that infants first develop a consciousness via the individual part of their body that needs attention), there is a difference between the perception of their own existence and that others have of them. As a result, human beings always feel "split" between their subjective feelings and the perceptions of others. Since this division is built into the very structure of language, for example with binary oppositions between subjects and objects, Lacan counseled a creative exploration of one's mind (especially though language) rather than attempts to adjust to society. (Here we see the early influence of surrealism on his thought.)

Ironically, a dramatic and sudden event in May 1968 disrupted this search for the structural foundations of human life. The revolt on college campuses that turned into the largest strike in French history and almost brought down the government had a dramatic effect on intellectual life. Although students shouted the Marxist-Leninist slogans relating to the dictatorship of the proletariat and capitalist exploitation and imperialism, equal if not more emphasis was placed in psychological, sexual, and personal-identity issues. The failure of the French Communists to lead the revolution (it was their theory that this was merely an uprising of bourgeois students rather than a true crisis of capitalism) led many militants to brand the party "conservative." While state power and the industrial infrastructure may not have passed into the hands of the revolution (the traditional goal of Marxist revolutionaries, whether socialist or communist), society had been changed. Out of the turbulence of the late spring of 1968 emerged a series of new social movements related to issues heretofore not widely discussed in France: women's liberation, gay, lesbian, and transgender emancipation, and the need to preserve the environment in an age of rampant industrialization and consumerism. In short, notions of revolution shifted from political and economic change to cultural and behavioral transformation and from social class to personal identity.

No one philosopher or movement inspired the students of May 1968. But the one who was the most influential in an immediate sense, beyond the general tendencies of Marxism and a sort of grassroots surrealism, was Guy Debord and his Situationist International. Formed out of *lettrism*, an earlier philosophic movement in which he participated and which wished to transcend the distinction between art, literature, and life, Debord turned his attention to transforming the modern capitalist city. By traveling through the city on foot in spontaneous fashion and trying to inspire art and creativity, Debord hoped to disrupt the rationalist and consumerist rhythms of capitalist life and create a new type of freedom. He also advocated taking advertisements and other productions of a consumerist society and turning them away (his master verb was *detournement)* from the purpose of selling goods and showing how their images and rhetoric dehumanized rather than liberated people. The extraordinary explosion of poster and graffiti art that accompanied the May 1968 near-revolution was inspired by Debord's ideas.

One of the first fruits of this near-revolution was *The Anti-Oedipus: Capitalism and Schizophrenia* (1972) by two philosophers—Gilles Deleuze and Felix

Guattari. With an introduction by Michel Foucault, this book signaled an important shift in France's intellectual climate. To understand the failure of the near-revolution, these philosophers turned away from Marxism and toward psychoanalysis, but one that was far more radical than Lacan's. In essence, the revolution failed because the repressive forces of a capitalist society had been implanted at an early stage in the minds of almost everyone. Schizophrenia, traditionally viewed as one of the worst of the "mental illnesses," was instead a legitimate response to social control, because it could liberate the body and overcome "the cop within" imposed by a capitalist order.

The idea of the body as a potential site of social and cultural liberation was also prevalent among the French feminist movement. Like feminist movements around the world during this time, women chaffed at the Marxian idea that women's liberation must await the emergence of a socialist/communist revolution before being achieved. No longer would questions of class trump gender. Building on and surpassing Simone de Beauvoir's *The Second Sex,* a host of French feminist theorists, such as Luce Irigaray, in *Speculum of the Other Woman,* for example, and Helene Cixous, in her influential essay "The Laugh of the Medusa," argued that a liberation of women's power, rooted in their reproductive organs, would overcome the hierarchies, separations, and distinctions at the heart of "phallic" power and replace it with a power rooted in the liquids of a woman's body that could overcome such boundaries and limitations.

Another philosopher who turned to the body, in this case the relationship between power and knowledge in the case of modern prisons, asylums, and educational institutions, was Michel Foucault. Already associated with structuralism, a study on the linguistic breaks in the human sciences, Foucault published in 1975 and 1976, respectively, studies on the history of prisons and other carceral practices in education and the military, *Discipline and Punish*, and then on the emergence of the concept of sexuality in modern Western society, *History of Sexuality Vol. 1: An Introduction.* In what would become an especially influential thesis, Foucault argued that power and knowledge are not opposed but are intimately intertwined. Moreover, power does not repress, but rather creates our notions of individuality and the self. Indeed, sexuality had not been "repressed" but instead "produced" across the nineteenth and twentieth centuries. Although negative definitions of gay, lesbian, and transgendered people had emerged, the fact that society recognized these groups provided these groups with a stage upon which to fight for their liberation. For Foucault, the interaction between power, knowledge, and the body was complex and contradictory, and he credited the events of 1968 with orienting his work in these new directions. Tragically his life was cut short in 1984 when he died of AIDS. He would become a hero for gays around the world, especially with his call for a society in which "bodies and pleasures" could be emancipated.

While Foucault explored social institutions and discourses, another philosopher who came to prominence after 1968, Jacques Derrida, investigated the nature of reading and interpreting texts with unprecedented rigor. Even more than Foucault, Derrida would exercise an extraordinary international influence, especially in the United States in English and foreign-language departments. In his work, also, Derrida would best distill the notion of post-structuralism (a term that would become applied also to Foucault). Derrida's central argument was that texts always escape easy readings. Neither the author nor the reader can ever fully control the meaning of a text, which always refers to other texts and whose meaning is never final. The binary oppositions at the heart of the structuralist method—for example, culture versus nature in the work of Levi-Strauss—almost always privilege one at the expense of the other. Indeed, this had been common throughout Western Civilization, with the male predominating over the female. Derrida dubbed this linguistic male chauvinism *phallocentrism* (a concept developed by many feminists). Overall, to describe his method he developed the term deconstruction to denote the process of taking texts apart in order to show their lack of coherence. Ultimately Derrida counseled infinite care in the reading of texts rather than the nihilism his legion of critics charged. Derrida's productive career stretched from the mid-1960s through 2004 and included not only a vast array of books but also influential visiting-scholar appointments at a wide variety of American universities.

The growing disillusionment with communism received tangible and ample evidence with the publication in Paris in 1974 of Aleksandr Solzhenitsyn's *The Gulag Archipelago*. This three-volume examination of the forced labor camps in the Soviet Union turned many participants in the events of 1968 against the notion of revolution. Two of the most prominent of the "new philosophers" in this intellectual current were Bernard-Henri Levy (*Barbarism with a Human Face*, 1974) and Andre Glucksmann (*The Cook and the Eater of Men*, 1975, and *The Master Thinkers*, 1977). They argued that the totalistic thinking of German philosophers from Kant through Hegel and Marx (that is, the desire to bring all of human life under one all embracing explanation) had led to totalitarian dictatorships. Especially in Stalin's USSR (1930s through the early 1950s) or Mao's China (late 1940s through mid 1970s), living human beings had been sacrificed by the millions on the altar of a utopian ideal that excused any crime in the name of a higher ideal. By the late 1970s through the early 1990s, the historian and former Communist Francis Furet would apply a similar type of analysis to the French Revolution, arguing that it helped pave the way for totalitarian regimes in the twentieth century.

By the late 1970s, with Marxism in decline, with the French industrial plant becoming obsolete, and with the growing power of the media and new technologies, yet another philosophic movement arose: postmodernism. The two most important thinkers in this school of thought were Jean-François Lyotard and Jean Baudrillard. Indeed, Lyotard was the first European philosopher to use this term, and he did so in two memorable books, *The Postmodern Condition: A Report on Knowledge* (1979) and *Le Differend* (1983). In *The Postmodern Condition,* Lyotard argued that both the great narratives of history and progress in the twentieth century—the capitalist vision of mass affluence and the Marxist ideal of equality and freedom—had failed. Instead, he argued, local comities and subcultures were increasingly turning their attention to their own local conditions and stories. Mass culture was giving way to a widening variety of lifestyles. In *Le Differend* Lyotard explained that this growing diversity in culture and in the theories of the human and hard sciences could not be put into some overarching theory and that culture and science were increasingly fragmented, lacking the coherence found in the nineteenth- or early-twentieth-century thought and society. Jean Baudrillard focused more on the effects of the media in transforming the very nature and notion of reality. In *Simulacra and Simulation* and other works he argued that modern media and technology had supplanted ordinary reality and put in its place a hyperreality. A good example, he noted, was how the ancient cave paintings as Lascaux in the South of France had been deemed too fragile for tourists, so a virtually exact copy, a Lascaux II, had been built right next to the original. He cited the effects of Disneyland and computer games as other examples. *The Matrix* movies make reference to Baudrillard's work, and one of the main characters, Neo, has a copy of *Simulacra and Simulation* in his hand at one point. After the 1991 Gulf War, Baudrillard took this line of thinking to an astonishing end. In *The Gulf War Did Not Take Place*, he came close to saying that the war was closer to a computer-game simulation than to an actual war in the traditional sense.

By the late 1980s, however, French philosophy, like French politics, was losing some of its distinctiveness. With the Soviet Union in decline and other radical Marxist states withering, and with Francois Mitterrand's Socialist presidency unable to halt the rise in unemployment or transform society, some French philosophers returned to the virtues of traditional liberal thought. When the great liberal philosophic foil for Jean-Paul Sartre, Raymond Aron, died in 1983, there was much appreciation for his calm and steady advocacy of liberal humanism across a 40-year career that had seen so many left-wing philosophical fads come and go. Then, in 1987, Alain Finkielkraut, previously associated with the anti-Communist new philosophers, published *The Defeat of Mind,* an influential work arguing for the continued relevance of

Enlightenment ideas of rationality and tolerance as the best means of preserving minority rights and an open society in an age of growing ethnic and religious tension. Other philosophers such as Blandine Kriegel, in *The State and the Rule of Law,* and Pierre Manent, in *An Intellectual History of Liberalism,* tried to focus attention on the liberal foundations of a free society. The collapse of the Soviet Union in 1991 seemed to many to confirm this intellectual shift to the center.

Nevertheless, since 1991 liberalism has not achieved dominance in French thought. Problems with an increasingly global marketplace and the demands to cut the French welfare state to make the nation more competitive within Europe and the world have led to a vigorous response from both establishment intellectuals and new social movements. Although long a central thinker in French sociology, Pierre Bourdieu became, in the last decade of his life (1992–2002), one of the most eloquent defenders of European social democracy. Already having made contributions to the study of such important cultural institutions as schools, museums, and the French bureaucracy, Bourdieu now defended what he called the "left hand" of the government, its welfare wing, from assaults by "neo-liberals" who wished to strip the poor, the immigrant, and the marginal of many of the benefits they had enjoyed. Humanity, not economic efficiency, should be the guiding value in French society. France was far from perfect—he had shown how its educational system and its cultural institutions reaffirmed more than democratized its social and economic structure, because educational and cultural advantages gained at home while young were hard to overcome—but it offered a much better model, he believed, than the United States. Before Bourdieu died at the end of 2002, he had been perhaps the most influential living sociologist in the world. For example, his masterpiece *Distinction: A Social Critique of Judgment of Taste* had been voted the sixth most influential book of sociology in the twentieth century.[7]

At the end of his life, Bourdieu had become quite enamored, as had many intellectuals, with the emerging antiglobalization movement. Perhaps the most famous French critic of genetically modified crops and the "McDonaldization" of food is Jose Bove. This farmer from the French South, around Larzac in Provence, has destroyed the agricultural factory of a multinational seed producer and a McDonalds branch. He has been a staple at antiglobalization demonstrations and in 2003 helped stage a festival at Larzac that 300,000 attended and where they dedicated themselves to ensuring that "the world is not for sale." This movement has become influential because it attracts ecologists and farmers as well as the traditional French Left. By 2002 the movement has shifted from being "anti" global to a more positive "alternative" vision of global civilization (hence the shift from "anti" to "alter" in most statements).

So far this chapter has explored the dynamics of French thought and religion. Now we will turn to the ways in which it has taken root in French society across the centuries and through to today. Churches, monasteries, courts, salons, cafés, universities, streets, and private homes are some of venues in which religious and philosophic ideas have been spread, implanted, and internalized.

The Christian religious tradition sank deep roots in France. Supposedly the man Jesus raised from the dead, Lazarus, traveled with his sisters to live in the southern French city of Marseille. The great monk Saint John Cassian established a monastery also at this port city. As the Middle Ages progressed, two of the most important monastic orders, the Cluniac and the Cistercian, began in France and spread across the Roman Catholic West (900–1200 C.E. being these orders' greatest era of influence). On the one hand, Cluniac monks devoted themselves especially to an intense spiritual life in the service of the pope and to teaching. On the other hand, Cistercian monks were some of great agriculturalists of age, bringing much of Europe under plow and spreading new technologies and plants. France played an especially vital role in the Crusades. Thus in both secular and religious life monks played a crucial role in the daily life of the French population for centuries. Parish priests naturally were also highly influential, hearing confessions and recording marriages, births, and deaths for each parish in the kingdom.

Daily life was organized tightly by the Catholic Church through the eighteenth century. Church bells in both country and city announced the daily and weekly pattern of religious observance, and the calendar of saint's days and religious feasts in the Catholic Church created a religious rhythm to the year and for life. The enforced public display of religion is one reason why Jews in France, as in most of Europe, were restricted to living in ghettos. Although Protestantism would be tolerated after the end of the French Wars of Religion (1562–1598), the Edict of Nantes that granted such toleration mainly applied to Protestant fortified cites in which the reformed faith created its own daily routine. One reason Louis XIV revoked the Edict was to ensure that no aspect of French life would escape his control and that it moved to the rhythms he demanded.

Given the power of the Catholic Church in Old Regime France, it is not surprising that as the Enlightenment developed it tried to set up alternative institutions and spaces for its own ideas. The salons of aristocratic and upper-middle-class women (in essence their elegant living rooms), cafés (serving the new beverage from the East—coffee—and providing a place to read a new invention of the late seventeenth century—the newspaper), and provincial academies (created across the eighteenth century) were some of the places where Enlightenment thought took root and by the end of the eighteenth century had displaced Christianity in the minds of much of the French elite.

As the French Revolution unfolded (1789–1799), one of the major targets of the revolutionaries was the Catholic Church. (In his later life Voltaire ended his letters with the phrase, "Crush the infamous thing," referring to the Catholic Church.) The 1790 Civil Constitution of the Clergy was one of the most divisive acts of the Revolution, because it made the Catholic priests swear allegiance to the French state (interfering, many thought, with their allegiance to the pope). A popular movement spread aiming to de-Christianize France. The original Cluniac monastery was destroyed, and Notre Dame was at one point turned into a "temple of reason." Napoleon brought much of this conflict to an end when he signed a concordat with the pope in July 1801. But Catholicism was no longer declared the religion of France (only of the majority of its population); the registration of marriage, births, and deaths was to remain with local mayors rather than the parish priest, and Jews and Protestants gained full civic rights as French citizens.

Throughout the nineteenth century the tensions unleashed by the French Revolution resulted in an ongoing battle between secular and religious forces. Thus religious tensions exacerbated the political split between the Left and the Right. This conflict was often mirrored in French homes, with the women going to the church, the men to the café. Despite periodic attempts to create a liberal Catholicism, with such figures as Félicité Robert de Lamennais in the 1830 or Marc Sangnier's group Le Sillon at the end of the nineteenth and start of the twentieth centuries, the Church sided with the Right. The Catholic Church's political partisanship was especially manifest in their railing against the Commune in 1871 (the conservative leaders of the early Third Republic and the Church built the Basilica of the Sacred Heart at the top of Montmartre to "atone" for this revolt) and against Lieutenant Alfred Dreyfus (unfairly accused of spying for Germany) in "the affair" that divided France at the end of the nineteenth and start of the twentieth centuries. Indeed, the Radical Party that came to power to defend the Republic against the Right separated the Catholic Church from the state, in large part due to the Dreyfus Affair in 1905. (Dreyfus would finally be exonerated in 1906.)

The world wars of the twentieth century would highlight renewals in the Catholic Church and immigrations that made the nation more diverse. From the 1910s through the 1950s, French Catholics realized that much of the urban working-class population had so completely deserted the faith that these areas needed "missionaries." In order to reach the poor, priests and committed lay people, with Le Sillon still in the forefront, the Church sent "apostles" into working-class districts to live the life of the poor. Many priests used the café, once denounced by the Church as one of the centers of worldly sin, as a site to reach workers in their favorite place of recreation. The move-ment would culminate with the worker-priest movement of the post–World War II era that would last until banned by Rome in the 1950s. At the same time, a literary renaissance occurred among believing Catholics in France with such philosophers, novelists, poets, moralists, and activists as Charles Peguy, Georges Bernanos, Gabriel Marcel, Emmanuel Mounier, Paul Claudel, Francois Mauriac, and Pierre Teilhard de Chardin. These authors confronted all the major historical, philosophic, and cultural events and forces of the century: the modernization of French agriculture, the prevention of juvenile delinquency, existentialism, literary and artistic modernism, and war and the Holocaust.

During this same period, 1910–1950, France welcomed millions of immi-grants. Although many of them were from Catholic countries—Spain, Italy, Poland, and Portugal in particular—Jews and Muslims were also prominent. The first French mosque was built in the early 1920s in Paris. Most im-migrants came due to French labor shortages during World War I and the economic expansion of the 1920s. During the 1930s, German and Eastern European Jews came, despite the Great Depression, due to the rise of Nazism in Germany and anti-Semitism in other Eastern European nations. After the rapid defeat of France by the Nazis in 1940, the Catholic Church became two radically different churches. The hierarchy officially followed the Vichy col-laborationist government, because Marshall Petain and other leaders saw the Church as bulwark of tradition that could provide a basis for "regenerating" France according to the regime's ideals of "family, work, and country." At the same time, a set of Resistance networks developed among a large number of social and activist Catholic organizations. In some cases, for example that of Emmanuel Mounier, Catholics moved from collaboration to Resistance as the war progressed. By the time of the liberation, Catholic Resistance groups were among the most engaged in the struggle.

The intellectual energy and social commitment of French Catholicism between the 1910s and the 1950s ensured that the faith did not lose much of its base during these decades. For example, in 1872, 98 percent of the popu-lation was Catholic; as late as 1960 the figure still stood at 86 percent, with 89 percent affirming that they belonged to a religion and only 10 percent saying they were "nonreligious." At the same time, the first two postwar de-cades saw a growth in the population of Jews and Muslims. Jews often came to France due to the decolonization process in the French colonies (which essentially ended when Algeria received its independence in 1962) or due to the growing tension in Muslim countries between Jews and Muslims after the creation of the State of Israel (1948). The booming French economy of the 1950s and 1960s offered steady jobs and higher wages than could be found in North Africa and thus also attracted hundreds of thousands of Muslim immigrants. By the end of the 1960s France had the largest Muslim and Jewish populations in Western Europe.

During the 1960s, especially after the near-revolution of May–June 1968, French Catholicism began a steady decline. For one thing, after the 1960s no new generation of Catholic thinkers and activists emerged to rival the extraordinary dynamism seen in the first half of the century. By 2000 the percentage of the population declaring themselves Catholic had fallen to 69 percent. But this figure does not fully reveal the decline of Catholicism; while a majority of the French declared themselves to be without religious faith, the figure shot up to 63 percent for those between the ages of 18 and 24, in short, the children of the May 1968 generation.

Indeed, estimates are that for the first time in French history more people are outside rather than inside organized religion. For example, studies of the faithful who actually practice their religion (initiated by the pioneering religious sociologist Gabriel Le Bras) showed that in 2004, 10 percent of Catholics reported that they did not practice their faith, 49 percent said that they did so occasionally, for marriages, funerals, and major holidays, with only 10 percent saying that they attended mass at least one a month. For example, even baptisms, one virtually universal, have fallen dramatically: In 1960, 92 percent of the French had their children baptized, by 1980 the figure had dropped to 64 percent, and by 1999 it had fallen to just over half (52 percent).

Paralleling the decline of the faithful has been the retrenchment of the Church's infrastructure. The number of parishes in France in 1975 totaled 36,395, with 15,714 priests. By 2000 these figures were 22,491 and 8,278 respectively. In total, the number of priests is half of what it was in 1960 (26,000 versus 50,000). Ordinations of new priests has plummeted by 75 percent at the same time, and as a result priests under the age of 50 now compose only 11 percent of the total (after having been 34 percent of the total in 1975).

By contrast, both Protestantism and Judaism have remained relatively stable in their numbers. Today France has about one million Protestants and over 650,000 Jews. Although the percentage of Protestants regularly practicing their faith, 11 percent, is about the same as among Catholics, the more liberal stance of Protestant churches on birth control and abortion has resulted in less controversy and alienation with the faith. Among French Jews the rate of practice, although falling, is much higher than among Catholics or Protestants.[8]

While formal religious faith has declined, a personal quest for meaning in life with a religious tinge remains important. Often called "new age" spirituality in the United States, in France these often-diffuse ideas and movements are grouped under the French phrase "*bricoleurs du sens*" (in essence this colloquial expression refers to individual eclectic spiritual quests). But this characterization should not lead us to doubt the seriousness of these personal quests. Often inspired by Eastern religions such as Zen Buddhism, by the Dali Lama, or by various strands of Hinduism, spiritualism, telepathy, and astrology, those on a spiritual quest have greatly expanded religious options open to contemporary French society. For example, opinion polls have found that while belief in God has fallen from 62 percent in 1981 to 48 percent in 1999 among the French population, belief in an afterlife has risen from 35 percent to 42 percent and in reincarnation from 22 to 31 percent. Fearing that such unorthodox and often charismatic religious life might become more rampant in France, the National Assembly in May 2001 enacted an anticult law in order to prevent the sort of mass suicide that occurred at a Temple of the Sun in France in October 1994.

By the 1980s continuing immigration from Muslim nations resulted in Islam becoming the second largest religion in France. Indeed, in terms of weekly attendance at religious institutions Islam may well be tied with Catholicism. Overall the Muslim population of France has risen from about 1 million in 1970 to 2 million by the early 1980s to about 5 million today. It is hard to quote an exact figure since French census and population data, especially for citizens, is not allowed to record the race or religious affiliation of a person. A more precise gauge of the spread of Islam is to note the rise in the number of mosques. In 1970 France counted approximately 20 mosques, by 1980 the figure had risen to 250, and by 2000 it had blossomed to 1,535. Most of these, however, were not originally built for religious practice but were former stores or factories. At least 40 percent of French Muslims come from three former French colonies in North Africa: 1,550,000 from Algeria, 1,000,000 from Morocco, and 350,000 from Tunisia. In addition there are about 315,000 Muslims of Turkish origin and over 250,000 from sub-Saharan Africa. These figures, naturally, provide no sense of the depth of religious attachment among people from Muslim lands. Among French Muslims, an opinion poll from 2001 is telling: Only 36 percent said that they were both believers and observers of the faith, while 42 percent said they were simply believers. Thus, many Muslims lose much of their faith in France.

The growing secularization of Islam in France has been obscured by periodic incidents that have generated much media attention. The most consequential of these events occurred in October 1989 when three Muslim girls at a high school at Creil (a suburb north of Paris) were expelled for wearing a headscarf (the Islamic hijab). This incident sparked a wide-ranging debate across French society and government over the nature of French secular education and the concept of the separation of church and state. Over the past decade 100 schoolchildren have been expelled for wearing the head scarf. But in half of these cases courts annulled the expulsion.

Since 2000 the French state has tried to preserve the secular nature of the state's educational system while also incorporating Islam into French society. In 2000 the French president Jacques Chirac met with the leaders of Islam in France and pledged to create favorable conditions for the religion in France. Towards this end, in 2002, the French government established the National Convention of French Muslims (CFCM). The aim of this organization is to facilitate the development of Islamic schools and religious institutes in France so that a moderate "French" form of Islam can develop. The hope is that French Islam will be able to train its own religious leaders rather than having to import them from the Middle East and will thus prevent the spread of more radical forms of Islam.

Two events in 2004 have put the notion of a French Islam to the test. In February 2004 the National Assembly passed a law banning headscarves in schools. Before passage of this law, the French secured the acceptance of this law from the Grand Sheik of the al-Azhar Mosque in Egypt. French Muslim opinion is divided evenly on whether this law is appropriate. This split is yet one more indication of the secularizing trend among French Muslims. Then in August and September of 2004 the new law was put to an agonizing test when militants in Iraq kidnapped two French journalists and demanded that the headscarf law be repealed. If France failed to do so, they warned, they would execute the two journalists. In the face of this crisis French Muslims rallied with the government and in opposition to the extremists. Clearly French Muslims wish no outside help in defining their place in French society in the early twenty-first century.[9]

Could we be witnessing the birth of a European version of Islam? This is one of the questions that make the study of religious life in France today both fascinating and important. How will Islam interact with an increasingly individualistic society that sees religion in terms of a personal quest rather than the following of a set of moral laws? This will be a central question well into the future.

France is now a laboratory for a set of dramatic changes in religious observation that have worldwide implications. On the one hand, the Catholic Church continues to lose ground steadily; on the other hand the immigration from Muslim nations has meant a steady increase in believers in Islam. Since the late 1980s, indeed, Islam has become the second religion of France, surpassing the number of Protestants and Jews. At the same time a growing individualism and eclecticism in religious observation and practice has meant that religious affiliation is now much more diffuse. The biggest change, however, is the fact that shortly after the year 2000 pollsters found that a majority of the French, roughly 52 percent, do not belong to any religion and class themselves as being without religion.

While the power of organized religion may be waning in France, the influence of the intellectual remains strong. Commentators thought that after the death of Jean-Paul Sartre in 1980 the reign of Parisian intellectuals had come to an end. But since then the deaths of Michel Foucault (1984), Simone de Beauvoir (1986), and Pierre Bourdieu (2002) have been major news items around the world, and the French president usually reflects upon the death of these important figures in French culture.[10]

When Jacques Derrida died in early October 2004, President Jacques Chirac issued this statement: "With him, France has given the world one of its greatest contemporary philosophers, one of the major figures of intellectual life of our time." American presidents have not generally been so effusive on the deaths of great American thinkers. This is a good indication of just how valued intellectual ideas remains in France. (We shall see this too when we examine French television in chapter seven.)[11]

The riots of October and November 2005 have already spawned much reflection. Whether French society can overcome the distance between religion and secular rationality is in the balance. Virtually all observers and experts agree with Olivier Roy, one of the leading experts in France on Islam, that the riots were sparked not by religion but by the urban alienation and high rates of unemployment that can be found around the developed world. But many fear that Muslim organizations, such as the Tabligh sect or the association Jeunes Musulmans de France (JMF), which they see as dedicated to promoting an Islamic more than a French national identity, may be gaining ground.[12] Whether such groups are helping to develop or undermine French national identity when they try to quell riots in the name of Islam is a complex and debatable issue. What cannot be denied is that the French police, both local and national, have spawned great enmity among Muslims who perceive the police as there to repress rather than to protect them. "If you practice your religion, you're dangerous; if you don't drink alcohol, you're dangerous," said a man in suburban café in the Parisian suburb of Evry recently. (This certainly provided a historical irony in that a century ago the police feared drunken workers in cafés rather that sober Muslims.) This resident and others in the café went on to say, "At dusk, they put on their helmets and as soon as they do that the kids say, great, there's going to be a party tonight," the result would be "an often destructive game of cat-and-mouse."[13]

NOTES

1. See the overview of France's relationship with the Catholic church in the following article in the online *Catholic Encyclopedia,* "Nobilissima Gallorum Gens, On the Religious Question in France His Holiness Pope Leo XIII," February 8, 1884; www.newadvent.org/library/docs_le13ng.htm.

2. John Cottingham, ed., *Reason, Will, and Sensation: Studies in Descartes' Metaphysics* (Oxford: Oxford University Press, 1994), 744.

3. Jean Paul Sartre, *Situations IV Portraits* (Paris Gaillmard NRF, 1964), 127. Translated by author.

4. Simone de Beauvoir, *The Second Sex,* trans. unknown (New York: Vintage, 1989).

5. Claude Lévi-Strauss, *Structural Anthropology,* trans. Claire Jacobson and Brooke Schoepf (New York: Basic Books, 2000).

6. See especially Roland Barthes, *Mythologies,* trans. Annette Lavers (New York: Hill and Wang, 1972).

7. International Sociological Association. See their 1998 survey on the most influential sociological books of the century chronicled on their website, http://www.ucm.es/info/isa/, under ISA-Books of the Century which contains a list of all the votes for all the books.

8. Data on religious observance in France today can be found in the following article: Frédéric Lenoir, "Religion, croyances et spiritualité," in Serge Cordellier, ed., *L'état de la France 2004: un panorama unique et complet de la France* (Paris: Editions La Découverte, 2004), 146–152.

9. Bruce Crumley, "Showing Faith in France," *Time Europe Magazine,* September 13, 2004.

10. "Radical Agonized over Society's Ills: Pierre Bourdieu," *The Australian,* February 6, 2002.

11. Patricia Sullivan, "Jacques Derrida Dies; Deconstructionist Philosopher," *Washington Post* Sunday, October 10, 2004, Page C11. Accessed online: www.washingtonpost.com/wp-dyn/articles/A21050–2004Oct9.html.

12. John Carreyrou, "Culture Clash: Muslim Groups May Gain Strength From French Riots; Islamists Try to Mediate Peace but Encourage Isolation From Secular Society; A Minister 'Plays Rambo,'" *Wall Street Journal,* November 7, 2005, A-1.

13. Craig S. Smith, "Inside French Housing Project Feelings of Being the Outsiders," *New York Times,* November 9, 2005, A-1 and A-11.

3

Gender, Marriage, Family, and Education

How can a country have among both the highest birthrates and the highest labor-force participation rates for women in Europe during the first decade of the twenty-first century? Historical trends and cultural traits relating to gender relations, marriage patterns, and educational opportunities explain why this seemingly anomalous case is reality.

The unique demographic experience of France after its great Revolution of 1789 continues to influence questions of gender, marriage, family life, and education in ways not found in other European societies. Throughout most of its history, until about 1640, France had the biggest population in all of Europe; and then, until the mid-nineteenth century, in all of Western Europe.[1] The French army, from Charlemagne through Napoleon, relied upon a large reserve of manpower to dominate Europe. When Napoleon created a new code of laws for France, he intended to ensure that French women would continue to produce soldiers.

However, in one of the great silent revolutions of modern times, by the 1850s French women became the first in the modern world to lower their fertility to little more than replacement level. Within 20 years (1870–1871) Prussian victory on the battlefield and an expanding German population (as opposed to a stagnating French one) led to increasing anxiety in France about its population. This anxiety took many forms, one of which was an attempt through education to inculcate patriotism and, it was hoped, a higher birthrate. Complementing education was repression, in the form of harsh laws outlawing contraception and abortion. When it became apparent by the late

1930s that neither education nor repression worked, the French embarked on system of welfare and education benefits for those families that had numerous children. Even partial implementation in the midst of war brought a rise in the French birthrate for the first since the eighteenth century.

After World War II, the most generous system of family allowances for children in the world was implemented, and the French population grew as it had not since the middle of the eighteenth century. But in the wake of the near-revolution of May 1968 and the rise of the women's movement, the French birthrate declined by half by the early 1980s, the divorce rate rose dramatically, and cohabitation (living together outside of marriage) became common. Much of this change can be attributed to the rise of the "second wave" of feminism and the great gains women achieved in education after the 1960s.[2]

Nevertheless, the stern admonition to populate has not been forgotten by the French. The French birthrate has not fallen as far as in such countries as Germany or Italy. Moreover, since the 1990s, despite less-generous family allowances than in the post-1945 era, the French fertility and marriage rate is among the highest in Europe (although low by historic standards) and French women, more than any of their European counterparts, have combined work outside the home with raising children. Nevertheless, the relative neglect by the French state of young French families in favor of middle-aged workers and retirees could produce problems in the coming decades, as is revealed in opinion polls of French youth today. In the short term soaring rates of youth unemployment have been mitigated by growing rates of college attendance since 1980 (see data later in this chapter).

GENDER, MARRIAGE, AND POPULATION

The institutions of gender, courtship, and marriage in France have for millennia been rooted in the Catholic Church. At least in theory Catholicism prohibited premarital sex, abortion, and sex outside of the function of procreation. In practice, sexual and matrimonial mores were quite diverse. For example, to ensure the fertility of the couple and thus the reproduction of the family, for centuries peasant couples in particular went to the altar after pregnancy was underway. The Church usually overlooked such sins in the name of the greater good of the faith and its expansion. (Especially in the light of the Protestant Reformation, the Church enjoined its faithful to have large families.)

After 1789 Catholic morality was tempered by the new republican tradition. Although praising motherhood, fatherhood, and devotion to the children, and as recent historical work shows creating a more open and equal family life, the revolutionary decade would inaugurate a century-and-a-half decline in the French birthrate. Historians still puzzle over the reason for this unprecedented drop. Some argue that the denial of the right to vote to women in the new republican regimes (Olympe de Gouges, the woman who would pen a Declaration of the Rights of Women to supplement the absence of women from the Declaration of the Rights of Man, would go to the guillotine) was important, others that laws requiring equal inheritance among all children encouraged farmers to limit family size to keep their holdings viable. Napoleon, after seizing power following 10 years of revolutionary turmoil, kept two gains won by women during the Revolution—equal inheritance and the right to divorce. But he made gender relations dichotomous and draconian. The influence on women of his Civil Code would not be fully erased until the 1970s:

the husband must possess the absolute power and right to say to his wife: Madame, you shall not go out, you shall not go to the theater, you shall not visit such and such a person: for the children you bear, they shall be mine.[3]

This statement of Napoleon's provides a good idea of his conception of ideal gender relations. He rounded out this image of the fertile and submissive wife when, in answer to a question by the famous writer Madame de Staël—"Who is the most important woman in France?"—he quipped: "She who bears the greatest number of children."[4] On the question of homosexual relations, however, Napoleon followed the revolutionary legislation in not criminalizing such sexual acts undertaken in private. Naturally, the Catholic Church continued to condemn any form of sexuality outside of procreation within the context of marriage.

Under Napoleon's Civil Code women were French nationals only after marriage, and they could not be witnesses in courts or to civil acts such as marriages, births, and deaths. Moreover, all property women inherited passed to their husbands, as did their salaries. Only late in the nineteenth century did women win the right to open bank accounts on their own. Sexual promiscuity on the part of a wife could land her in jail, but a husband's sexual escapades would land him in trouble only if he tried to have his lover live in the family home. Men were not liable to be sued for paternity or the maintenance of illegitimate children. If a husband allowed his wife to go into business, he had a right to the profits she made and to distribute her property as he chose.

Women did not take kindly to this mistreatment. They expressed their anger in women's magazines and in their diaries. Across the nineteenth century, a domestic civil war would rage in many French households as men went to cafés and other secular institutions while women remained more committed to the Catholic Church. Examinations of anticlerical literature of the nineteenth century reveal deep anxiety among French middle-class males that their wives were being seduced by the clergy. It would certainly be rash to say that women's anger explains a drop in the birthrate after 1790. Nevertheless, along with a desire to save and achieve upward mobility among the urban middle class and to prevent the fragmentation of farms into smaller and smaller plots on the part of the peasants, this has to be considered as a reason for the declining birthrate. After reaching 36 million in the 1860s, the French population would only reach 39 million by the start of World War I. Despite the low birthrate, the French marriage rate continued to be high. Families with one or two children had become the norm in much of French society.[5]

Gender and population issues came to a crisis point after the Franco-Prussian War of 1870–1871. French politicians, generals, and intellectuals threw their hands up in despair as the French population stagnated and the German population soared to 67 by 1914 (in 1815, at the time of Waterloo, the population of the disparate German states has only been about 22 million). Although the new Third Republic (republicans having replaced monarchists as the conservatives in power in 1879) committed itself to secularizing society, it also dedicated itself to raising the birthrate. The right to divorce was restored in 1884 (after having been abolished following the fall of Napoleon by the governments of the Restoration, 1814–1830). The Third Republic also created a system of universal free primary education for all French youth (to counter the traditional role of the Church). While Christian morality may have given way to secular values (laïcité) on matters of religion, on matters of fertility and family life the Republic remained committed to the Napoleonic paradigm in the Civil Code (which was only marginally amended to give women such rights as being able to open a checking account).

Due to it smaller population, French women had to shoulder more of the burden of running civil society and war production during World War I than in other combatant nations. During the first two years of the war, with the husbands in the trenches, the French birthrate fell to then-historic lows (which would come back to haunt France when the children of these "hollow years" reached the age of military service in the late 1930s, just in time for World War II). Not only did the French birthrate fall, but women (men thought) had become much more masculinized due to having worked in war factories and being out in public more, and especially having experienced the new syncopated jazz dances and smoking and drinking more freely in that new site of liberation, the night club.

Continuing fears about its population in the light of massive losses during the bloody conflict made France, unlike other Western nations, decide not to give women the right to vote after World War I. Moreover, the French parliament strictly prohibited the rising family-planning movement from distributing literature or setting up offices (even though American activists such as Margaret Sanger had, in part, utilized techniques developed by French women in their grassroots birth-control movement). Although French people continued to be enjoined to have large families, the birthrate rose only for a few years during the early 1920s and then fell to all-time lows during the Great Depression of the 1930s. In 1939 the French government finally instituted a system of government subsidies for families that had more than two children.

During the dark days of World War II, a period not only of increasingly economic scarcity but also of growing intolerance of all forms of promiscuity, the birthrate started to rise. To what degree this was due to new measures enacted by the Third Republic to provide financial assistance to large families or to the propaganda of the collaborationist Vichy regime is still hard to tell. Vichy was the first French government to enact a law against homosexuality since 1789. After the liberation of France, the Resistance-inspired government of Charles de Gaulle confirmed the Vichy laws against homosexual acts, especially in the case in which one of the participants was under the age of 21 (no such regulation applied to heterosexual sex).

After the war ended, the birthrate continued to rise. The Fourth and Fifth Republics (between 1945 and 1960) implemented a much more comprehensive system of allowances for large families. Indeed, by 1950 a working-class family would have their income double if they had two or more children. At this point the French had the most bountiful family subsidy in the world. It would remain so until the late 1960s, when greater attention began to be paid to the plight of poverty among senior citizens.

By the time the baby boom ended in the late 1960s, the French had seen the largest surge in French population since the late eighteenth century. The population had increased from about 40 million to 55 million, and the average number of children per family between 1945 and 1975 was three. The French nuclear family seemed stronger than ever. Aiding this domesticity was the emergence of a consumer society and an unprecedented array of consumer durables for care, nurturing, and entertaining family members (from cars, to dishwashers, to television, to refrigerators, to washing machines). Within this short-term context, neither the granting of the vote to women in 1944 nor the publication of Simone de Beauvoir's *The Second Sex*, an indictment of women's second-class status in society, caused much of a controversy. The legalization of contraception (loi Neuwirth), however, in 1967, pointed towards a new society.

Within a year, the social, economic, and generational tensions of French society burst to the surface. The "events" of May–June 1968 brought the youth and countercultures that were sweeping the developed world fully into French life. At the center of this attempt to rethink the very foundations of modern life was a questioning of traditional family and sexual roles. The contemporary concept of gender emerged at this time not only out of the thoughts of intellectuals but also the actions of ordinary people. The aftershocks of this earthquake are still felt today.

May 1968 also created a "second wave of feminism" and the emergence of gay, lesbian, and transgender liberation. Young French women had been especially militant during the events of 1968, but often felt pushed to the sidelines or into the kitchen by male radicals. In the months following May and June 1968, women met in small groups along the lines of the consciousness-raising groups then forming in the United States. The main organization to emerge was the Women's Liberation Movement (Mouvement de libération des femms, MLF). Also, like their transatlantic sisters, French women soon engaged in media-focusing events such as placing a wreath at the Arc de Triomphe in Paris at the tomb of France's unknown soldier "in remembrance of someone more unknown than the soldier—his wife." Such actions helped launch the French women's liberation movement. In April 1971 France's newspaper of record, *Le Monde,* along with the leftist *Nouvel Observateur,* published a "Manifesto of 343" women, both prominent and ordinary, who noted that they had had an abortion. Under then-current laws, these women could have been prosecuted. Their act, however, lent immense publicity to the prochoice movement in France. This movement would score a major victory in 1975 when abortion was legalized (the Veil law of 1975). However, by the early 1980s internal fighting led to the MLF splintering into many factions.

Nevertheless, the French women's movement, along with the gay and later transgender liberation organizations, helped spread the idea that sexual identity is as much social as biological. Following on the work of such French psychiatrists as Jacques Lacan and such philosophers as Michel Foucault and Jacques Derrida, feminists argued that humans beings were not rigidly and universally destined for one function in life—women to breed and men to work—and that indeed all people were composed of both male and female elements and desires and that desire could not be easily contained in the male/female dichotomy of traditional morality or psychology. The study of gender has come to denote the study of the infinite variety of human sexuality and marriage forms across cultures and history.[6]

Gay liberation in France has had an exceptionally distinguished literary pedigree. Dating especially from the essays, novels, and plays of, for example, Andre Gide and Marcel Proust during the first decades of the twentieth century, through to Jean Cocteau and Jean Genet during the 1930s and 1940s, a foundation had been laid for the explosion after 1968. After the spring events of that year, philosophers such as Roland Barthes and Michel Foucault, especially, explored their sexual orientation. Tragically, Foucault would die of AIDS in 1984 just as he was in the course of developing an encompassing exploration of the history of sexuality. His partner, Daniel Defert, would be one of the founders of Aides, an organization that linked gay activists and the medical establishment in fighting this new scourge.

French gay and lesbian liberation has also been inspired by Anglo-American models. Although there was no pivotal moment such as the Stonewall riots in New York City in 1969 against police harassment of gay bars, grassroots action were taken against police repression. One of the French pioneers of "coming out" was the philosopher and novelist Guy Hocquenghem. Born in the working class in the Parisian suburbs, he joined the Communist Party during May 1968 but was subsequently expelled due to his homosexuality. He then became one of the founders of the Homosexual Revolutionary Action Front (Front Homosexuel d'Action Révolutionnaire) in 1971. He went on to write many important works on gay desire, which have not been as full appreciated outside of France as they should be.[7] In 1989 another activist, Didier Lestrade, created a French version of Act Up (Act Up-Paris), which engaged in the same creative forms of debate to capture media as did the Anglo-American original. Among theorists of lesbian identity and sexuality, few are as influential as Monique Wittig. In her novels, such as *Les Guérillières* (1969), concerning a feminist Amazon society, and *The Lesbian Body* (1973), she became one of the pioneers of lesbian and transgender thought and a brilliant innovator in the French language. The gay and lesbian press has also been vital to these movements, as it provides a forum for expressing and elaborating upon gay and lesbian identity, not only in words but also in space; these publications list the locations of bookstores, cafes, and clubs in which sociability can happen. *Gai Pied* (1979–1992) was especially vital in the formative years of the gay movement, and *Lesbia Magazine* (founded in 1982) continues to be so to this day. The Internet has increasingly also become important to the elaboration of alternative sexual identities. Perhaps the best benchmark for the acceptance of diversity in gender is the tremendous success of Paris's annual Gay Pride Parade and Festival. Occurring at the end of each June, this festival of gender openness and tolerance is one of the largest in the world.

This explosion of sexual freedom, variation, and creativity in attitudes quickly became translated into a new set of behaviors. The statistics on nuptuality, fertility, divorce, and cohabitation all show dramatic changes since 1970. While in 1969 over 380,000 marriages took place, only 253,000 were celebrated in 1994. The decline in marriage is revealed in even starker terms in the decline in the rate of marriages per 1,000 people, from a rate of 8 to 4.4 per thousand between these two dates. Then in 1996 the number of marriage rose: to 280,000. This was due, in part, to a tax reform that allowed cohabiting couples who married to gain tax advantages from having children if they tied the knot. The number continued to increase to over 300,000 in 2000 before falling back some in subsequent years (to 295,882 in 2001 and 266,300 in 2004). Nevertheless, this is significantly above the figure for 1994, and there are now close to 5 marriages per thousand. Two trends that have not altered are the increasing age at the time of the first marriage and the increase in the number of divorces. Between 1970 and 2002, the average age at marriage rose: from 22 to 29 for women and from 24 to 31 for men. Between 1945 and 1965, the divorce rate had held essentially steady at 9 percent of marriages. But between 1968 and 1980, the rate jumped to 22 percent. By 1990 the rate had continued to increase to 32 percent, and it hit 40 percent in 2000. The trend in divorces has held essentially steady. But then from 1965 to 1980 it jumped to 22 percent and then to 32 percent in 1990 and almost 40 percent in 2000. The trend is still going upward, with 125,175 in 2003 as compared to 112,631 in 2001.[8]

Accompanying the decline in marriage and the rise in divorce was a shift to cohabitation and to out-of-wedlock children. In 1970, 3.6 percent of couples lived together outside of marriage. The rate grew but not by much during the 1970s and stood at 6.3 percent in 1980. But in the next 20 years the rate tripled—to 18.1 percent by 2002. This type of lifestyle was so new in 1970 that statisticians did not record the number of out-of-wedlock couples with children in 1970, but by 1980 the percentage stood at 31 and by 2002, 47.7 percent of cohabiting couples had children. Logically, thus, the number of births outside of marriage jumped from around 6.8 percent in 1970 to 11.4 percent in 1980 and then to 43.7 percent in 2002. This upward curve follows almost precisely the curve in cohabitation.

Not surprisingly, amidst all of this change, the French birthrate fell. In 1970 it was not far from the figure for the baby boom era, 2.47 (as opposed to 3.0 or above between 1943 and 1965). During the 1970s, however, the French birthrate fell decisively, to 1.94 by 1980 and then to around 1.7 by the mid-1990s (and thus below the replacement level of around 2.1 children per woman). From 1995, though, the birthrate has rebounded back up to almost 1.9, with the number of births in 2004 at almost 800,000 (as compared to 760,000 in 2000).

Another factor in the decline of the birthrate is the growing number of people remaining single. While the overall growth may not seem that great, from 26.5 percent in 1970 to 27.7 percent in 1980, and then, as in the case of cohabitation, a more substantial jump to 34.4 percent in 2002, these figures are much more substantial for those in the peak years of raising a family (25 to 49 years of age). Here we see the percentage of single men going from 16.8 in 1970 to 18.0 percent in 1980, but then leaping to 39.7 by 2002. Although from a lower percentage, the trend is the same for women over this period: 10.4 percent in 1970, 12.2 percent in 1980, and 31.1 percent in 2002. Deterioration in the labor market can certainly account for much of this change—but not divorce. The divorce rates in these age groups for both men and women have not changed radically over the past 30 years. For example, in this age group in 1970 only 2.2 and 3.0 percent respectively of men and women were divorced; the percentage increased slowly to 3.3 and 4.8 percent respectively by 1980, and then only to 6.6 and 9.0 percent by 2002 (again respectively).

Recognizing the changed gender relations since the 1960s, the Socialist government in 1999 passed the Civil Solidarity Act (Pacte civil de solidarité, PACS). This act provides legal recognition and tax benefits to cohabiting heterosexual coupes and to gay and lesbian couples. Since its implementation in October 1999, over 120,000 couples have taken advantage of this new legal union. The rate of dissolution has been about 10 per year. In the spring of 2004, in the wake of the gay marriages in San Francisco, a French mayor and member of the Green Party, Noel Mamère, conducted the first gay marriage in France, in the southwestern town of Bègles. This act crystallized the growing debate in France over this issue, with the conservative president Jacques Chirac favoring a revision of the PACS and the Socialist Party advocating legalization of same-sex marriage, but the former Socialist Prime Minister who passed PACS opposing his party's stance. Public-opinion polls show that a strong majority of the population favors gay marriage, at 58 percent (as opposed to a European Union average of 57 percent and 42 percent in the United States, in 2004 data).

Several contemporary facts highlight the state of gender relations in France today. The percentage of women in the workforce has continued to grow. It is now at 80 percent for women between the ages of 25 and 49.[9] Nevertheless, France's population has continued to internalize long-standing fears of population decline. This is one reason why the French fertility rate (1.9 children per woman) is the second highest in Europe (just behind Ireland at 1.99).[10]

Families in France can afford to have more children than other European nations in part because its system of childcare is more extensive than that in most other nations.

The condition of women today remains mixed, in some ways liberated while in others still tied to a greater share of domestic duties than are men. One of the key changes that has helped to liberate women had been the tremendous changes in the French education system over the last century, as outlined below.

EDUCATION

Until the French Revolution (1789) the Catholic Church was intimately involved in every level of education. The Revolution itself, following the impetus of the Enlightenment, wished to make education both more secular and more scientific. Grand plans were sketched for a comprehensive education system, but the rapid turnover in governments prevented a new system from emerging. In 1793, with the radical Jacobins in the ascent, the National Convention created a Committee of Public Instruction in order to transform the educational system. After the fall of the Jacobins, and their leader Robespierre, the more conservative government of the Directory established the Conservatoire des Arts et Métiers (Conservatory for Arts and Crafts) and the Ecole centrale des Travaux publics (Central School for Public Works) for scientific and industrial fields, and the Ecole Normale Supérieure (1795) to train college teachers. Napoleon brought these and other universities under centralized control with his Université de France. He also created 30 high schools (*lycées*) in order to train a new administrative, military, and industrial elite. Primary education, however, remained largely in the hands of the Church. Indeed, despite some innovations, such as the 1833 law requiring local communities to build primary school and *the creation of ecole normales* in each department to train local teachers, no national and mass system of education would exist in France until the late nineteenth century. The Falloux Act of 1850 required most localities to create schools for girls, but the results were not substantial in a society that still severely limited women's options.

During the early 1880s, Jules Ferry created the foundations of the modern French primary education system. Across France by the 1890s a network of free, obligatory, and secular primary schools had emerged for children between the ages of 6 and 13 (raised to 14 in 1936). Religious instruction was banned and no one belonging to an order of the Roman Catholic Church could be a teacher. Ferry and his fellow republicans intended this education to transform French culture from one based on Catholicism to one based on reason, science, and nationalism. But little hope existed for members of the lower classes, much less women, to go to high school, much less college. The *lycée* system was left virtually untouched, and only a few of the most gifted members of the lower classes or women were able to study at universities (although ecole normales to train women school teachers did emerge after 1879). Primary school teachers become known as the "hussars of the Republic" and were often in tension if not conflict with priests in local communities, as secular and clerical culture squared off against each other. Although predominantly filled by males, the post-primary school teacher position did become open for women.[11]

Not much change then occurred until after World War II. After 1900, women started to enter French universities in some numbers, and after World War I, with the decline in fortunes in many middle-class French families putting an end to the ability to provide a dowry, an increasing number of women did attend college—among them Simone de Beauvoir. During the late 1930s the same tiny percentage of the national budget, 7 percent, was devoted to education as had been in 1900. Jules Ferry had anticipated education's share of the budget reaching one-sixth. With the rapid industrialization and urbanization of France from the late 1940s, a consensus developed that major changes would be needed in the education system, but these changes still had not emerged during the 1950s at a time when just a million or so students attended high schools and about 200,000 reached the collegiate level.

Dramatic changes started during the early years of de Gaulle's Fifth Republic. In 1959 the Berthoin reform moved the age of compulsory school up to 16 and created a new sequence in schooling: primary education, then a lower, and then an upper secondary school to prepare larger number of students either for college or for technical training. A network of technical middle schools replaced the earlier apprenticeship centers. Another innovation in 1963, the Fouchet Reform, refined and rationalized this new French middle-school system. The result was unprecedented: The percentage of French primary-school students starting high school jumped from 50 percent to 95 percent within a few years. The vast majority, however, still did not attain the prized *baccalauréat* exam, which was essential for college admission. Nevertheless, the number of college students also increased dramatically, from 175,000 in 1958 to over 500,000 at the time of the student revolution 10 years later.

The transformation of the French economy during the 1970s and 1980s prompted the socialist government to initiate another expansion of the system of higher education. The 1989 Orientation Law was designed to increase the number of students taking the baccalauréat exam to 80 percent. Although this target was never met, the percentage of students taking the various forms of the *bac* (the colloquial expression) rose from 39 percent in 1986 to 70 percent in 1994. By 1995 63 percent of those taking the exam passed (compared to a mere 24 percent in 1975).

As a result of these reforms from the late 1950s to the late 1980s, the number of students attending secondary schools has increased over 400 percent, and the number of those attending college has increased by 700 percent. The aging of the French population and a resulting decline in the number of school-age children had meant a stabilization or decline in these numbers since the late 1990s.[12]

One of the most dramatic developments in these soaring college enrollments has been the growth in prominence of women. Starting in the early 1970s, more girls than boys *passed the* baccalauréat (in 1998 the rate stood at an 81.2 percent success rate for girls as opposed to 76.5 percent for boys), and by the late 1970s more girls were graduating from college (currently for every 100 boys there are 120 girls in college). From the late 1990s more women had attained a master's degree than men.[13]

Nevertheless, women are still a distinct minority in most of the elite *grandes ecoles.* More so than any other European country, France continues to train its directing class separate from ordinary universities and colleges. The grandes ecoles number around 150 and include specialized schools for academics (such as the Ecole Normale Superior formed during the French Revolution) and engineers (such as that for bridges and roads, the Ecole des Ponts et Chausses, dating from the 1740s). There are as well L'Ecole des Hautes Etudes Commerciales, the schools for political science, and the most famous and influential, created just after World War II, the National School of Administration (Ecole Normale d'Administration, known as ENA). Graduates of these schools monopolize the top positions in French society to an extraordinary degree. A 1993 study found that 73 percent of the upper-level executives in the top 200 companies are graduates of the ENA, as are most of the recent prime ministers and the current president.

Lack of women at these schools is one of the major reasons there is a "glass ceiling" in France, as in most countries that prevent women from reaching the top positions in society. For example, in the late 1990s women composed only 5 percent of the top 5,000 executives in France, and more broadly only 27 percent of women were in high-wage jobs while 85 percent were in the low-wage jobs. Part of this stems from the fact that 71 percent of women work in the lower-paid service sector (and not the higher-paid commercial or industrial sector), as opposed to 47 percent of men, and compose a majority of the part-time and temporary workers. Overall, women earn 25 percent less than men and have a higher rate of unemployment—for example, in March

2001, 10.7 percent as opposed to 7.1 percent. In short, neither the Socialist Francois Mitterrand nor his conservative successor Jacques Chirac has been able to narrow the gender gap in wages. Indeed, the gap remains as wide in 2005 as it was in 1980.

Moreover, women still carry the majority of the burden of housework and childcare. A 1999 study showed that women still spend on average almost four hours on domestic work each day (down just 14 minutes from 1986) as opposed to men whose time doing these same tasks has increased by only 2 minutes (from 1 hour 22 to 1 hour 24 minutes) between 1986 and 1999).[14] This is probably why fathers with children have a lower unemployment rate than do mothers with children. Indeed, the more children a woman has the more likely she is to be unemployed. This is especially true of young mothers with children under three years of age. Only about 10 percent of children in this age group were in nursery schools; almost 80 percent were at home being cared for by a parent (usually the mother), grandparent, or a neighborhood babysitter.[15]

We will conclude this chapter by exploring the implication of these changes in women's education and work by exploring the condition of French youth in the early part of the twenty-first century and especially how they view their society. Naturally, the condition of those under 30 today will greatly determine the condition of France well into the twenty-first century and is thus crucial in understanding questions of gender, marriage, and the family.

The condition of French youth today is cause for serious concern. While French senior citizens and those in the working class born between 1940 and 1955 are living better than any previous generation, those born after the middle of the 1950s face much bleaker prospects. This is a radical departure compared to the generation that came of age after World War II. Between the 1950s and the early 1970s workers in the age bracket 18–40 saw their income double. Moreover, the benefits of family allowances provided half of the income of families with at least two children. By the early twenty-first century this system provided less than 20 percent of such a family's income. A big reason for the declining fortunes of youths is the fact that real wages for workers under 40 have at best stagnated since 1980 and that the youth unemployment rate climbed steadily to 25 percent during the late 1990s. Even those with employment faced a precarious situation, since more than half of the jobs created during the 1980s and 1990s were temporary. It is thus no wonder that France has one of the highest rates of youth unemployment in Europe.

As we have seen, the rising number of youths in college helped offset this rise in unemployment and created a skilled work force that would eventually be integrated into society. To what degree has the greater education been a boon to French youth? Sadly, the answer is, not that much. For example the percentage of French college graduates who worked in unskilled occupations doubled between 1986 and 1995. Although 70 percent of high-school students may now go to college, only one-third get a degree. Part of the reason why college may not be as effective as it once was in educating and motivating students stems from the fact that spending on education has declined as a percentage of the total budget (while spending on health and pensions, for example, have increased).

Given these statistics it is not surprising that French youths in the late twentieth and early twenty-first century are anxious. For example, a survey in November 1999 found that unemployment and violence were the greatest fear for 15–24-year-olds. Most did not see much opportunity for upward social mobility and looked more to find a permanent job than one that would be interesting. (Young women, it is interesting to note, were more concerned about finding fulfillment at work than were young men.) Bleak job prospects may be one reason why youths rated family and friendship more important than work, or love for that matter. Society is viewed as corrupt, with money having too much influence. Unlike the 1960s generation, the turn-of-the-century generation is not turning to politics to solve their problems. Nevertheless, they see the benefits of associations and led the protests against the far-right politician Jean-Marie Le Pen when he made it into the presidential run-off in 2002.

Despite these problems, the ordinary French youth in the first decade of the twenty-first century is not on the verge of staging a new May 1968. In most opinion surveys, 70 percent or so do not wish to alter society radically. Indeed, the student demonstrations of Spring 2006 against a new law— (*Contrat première embauche*, CPE: First Employment Contract or Beginning Workers Contract) that would have eased restrictions on hiring young workers but provided none of the traditional guarantees about being easily fired—centered on conserving, not changing, French labor law. Most youth focus their attention upon the new leisure products of the digital age—from cell phones to music and video CDs—and the youth culture—from baggy pants to rap music—with a heavy American accent. Yet, as we shall see in the chapters on music, literature, and theater, French youth are putting a distinctive French spin on the global youth culture.

In short, on matters of gender, marriage, education, and youth, French society has become more open and flexible. Though serious problems must be faced, as was clearly evidenced during the riots of October and November 2005, the strong and generous welfare state has helped preserve family cohesion and has muted protests on family issues. Contemporary France's increased tolerance was apparent when conservative accusation that the wayward children of polygamous Sub-Saharan African families were primarily to blame for the riots was met with disdain by public opinion. The question of improving and expanding education opportunities for marginalized youth remains a serious problem, but is one that virtually the entire political spectrum recognizes must be addressed.[16]

Notes

1. See the poignant reflections of Fernand Braudel on the fact that if the nation's population had continued to be as big in relation to its neighbors today as it was in the seventeenth century, France would have over 200 million inhabitants. Fernand Braudel, *The Structures of Everyday Life: The Limits of the Possible* (Civilization and Capitalism: 15th–18th Century), trans. Sian Reynolds (Berkeley: University of California Press, 1992).

2. See http://www.insee.fr/en/home/home_page.asp., the website for the French National Institute for Statistics and Economic Studies (INSEE), which contains an English language portal that supplied all the relevant data discussed in this chapter.

3. Felix Markham, *Napoleon* (New York: Mentor, New American Library, 1963), 73.

4. http://www.historyguide.org/intellect/lecture15a.html and http://www.old-andsold.com/articles06/draperies-14.shtml.

5. E. A. Wrigley, "The Fall of Marital Fertility in Nineteenth-Century France: Exemplar or Exception?" *European Journal of Population* 1 (January 1985):31–60.

6. Mary Louise Roberts, *Civilization without Sexes: Reconstructing Gender in Postwar France, 1917–1927* (Chicago: University of Chicago Press, 1994).

7. For example, Laura Lee Downs, *Writing Gender History* (London: Hodder Arnold, 2005).

8. Data on Marriage and the birth rate in France today can be found in the following articles: Laurent Touleman, "Population, Grandes tendances," 61–65, and Claude Martin, "Familles et générations, Grandes tendances," 75–81, in Serge Cordellier, ed., *L'état de la France 2004: un panorama unique et complet de la France* (Paris: Editions La Découverte, 2004).

9. See "Hocquenghem, Guy (1946–1988)," *glbtq: an encyclopedia of gay, lesbian, bisexual, transgender & queer culture.* Available online: www.glbtq.com/literature/hocquenghem_g.html.

10. All statistics from previous paragraphs from Serge Cordellier, *L'état de la France 2004: un panorama unique et complet de la France* (Paris: La Découverte, 2004).

11. Anna Willard, "Experts Ponder France's High Birth Rate," *Reuters* (April 26, 2006). Accessed online: news.scotsman.com/latest.cfm?id=625012006.

12. Robert Gildea, *France Since 1945,* 2nd ed. (Oxford: Oxford University Press, 2002).

13. For data on gender and academic success see www.sfc.fr/Societes Savantes/2%20-%20Bac%20g%E9n%E9ral.PDF.

14. Serge Cordellier, ed. *L'état de la France 2004: un panorama unique et complet de la France* (Paris: Editions La Découverte, 2004), 154.

15. All statistics in the previous paragraphs from Serge Cordellier, ed. *L'état de la France 2004: un panorama unique et complet de la France* (Paris: La Découverte, 2004).

16. Elaine Sciolonio, "Gaulist Says Polygamy by Immigrants Is Factor in French Riots," *New York Times*, November 18, 2005, A12.

4

Social Customs: Leisure, Holidays, Sports, and Festivals

THE TREMENDOUS INCREASE IN wealth and technology in France since World War II has transformed the daily life and customs of France in an unprecedented fashion. One of the casualties of this dramatic transformation is the many stereotypes we have come to believe about the French. The image of France as a land of leisurely paced meals and café conversations, of a people who smoke more than they exercise and spend more time strolling and socializing on their picturesque streets than in their homes or cars, needs to be seriously revised. The France of the magisterial photographer of the 1930s through the 1980s, Robert Doisneau, whom we shall explore in chapter ten, had ceded place to that of the world-champion soccer player of Algerian heritage, Zinedine Zidane, whom we shall cover shortly.[1]

No Western nation moved so quickly from a society with a large rural farming sector to one with a dense urban industrial concentration and then to a service economy as the French between the 1940s and the 1990s. Today the French are six to seven times wealthier than they were in 1950, and they enjoy a lower rate of income inequality than that found in the United States.[2] An urban worker today labors 1,600 hours annually, compared to his or her counterpart a century ago, who worked 4,000 hours each year.[3] Finally, the image of French leisure in the early twenty first century has to take into consideration the following two facts: (1) The number of cafés, one of the most iconic symbols of French "joie de vivre" has declined precipitously since 1940;[4] and (2) French workers are the second-most-productive labor force in the world today (even though they work many fewer hours than the first-place Americans).[5]

In 1900, France still had almost half its population working in agriculture and society was sharply polarized. While the lower classes had their cafés and the café concert (a cross between the English music hall and American vaude-ville), the upper, or "leisure," classes had their salons (upper-class intellectual suppers and gatherings in the home), teas, receptions, such urban institutions as the opera and the symphony, and such rural retreats as water spas, the beach, and country homes. In between these classes and institutions were the cabarets (incipient night clubs) of Paris, which would first become world famous with the singer Aristide Bruant (especially as painted by Toulouse Lautrec in his fa-mous posters) and would help spawn imitators around the world. Lautrec and Bruant helped make Paris "the capital of the nineteenth century," the home of the arts, a central place in the bourgeoning tourist trade, and the site of two of the greatest world's fairs ever, in 1889 and 1900, for which the Eiffel Tower was built and became a icon of the modern world. But beneath the glittering society of the Parisian haut monde were the congested and deprived quarters of the working class and the often medieval conditions of the peasants. One measure of France's poverty and desperation was that its people, by the 1870s, consumed more alcohol than any other nation in the world and would con-tinue to do so until the end of the twentieth century.[6]

Although the French Revolution had introduced the concept of the na-tional holiday, with Bastille Day celebrating July 14, 1789, when the people of Paris conquered the royal fortress on the eastern edge of town, and the Third Republic had perfected the concept of the world's fair, with one in 1889 celebrating the centennial of the French Revolution and one in 1900 ringing in a new century, the French had few days off. When in, 1879, July 14 become the formal national holiday, the modern vacation was still virtually un-known for the toiling majority. For laborers in town and country it was hard to get out of the town, village, or much less the neighborhood in which they worked or lived because they still worked between 40 and 50 hours a week. For this reason the café was central to leisure activity. Across the nineteenth century the number of cafés had grown dramatically, from 280,000 in 1828 to close to 500,000 on the eve of World War I. French parliamentarians increasingly railed against the immorality, vice, and drunkenness of café life, but only in 1906 did they start to provide an alternative to this form of daily recreation sandwiched between long working hours when they mandated a week-long holiday.[7]

Even the Herculean efforts of the French workers during World War I did not win them much new leisure time. In a spirit laced both with gratitude and fear, the French parliament following the war enacted the forty-hour work-week. But this law was dead virtually from the start due to the fragile state of the French economy and to receding fear that the Russian Bolshevik Revolution would spread to France. The arguments of French workers, that they would be more productive and better consumers if they did not have to work long hours, fell on deaf ears among France's employers, bureaucrats, and politicians. During the 1920s, ironically, as more and more workers worked indoors rather than outside, the economic and artistic elites consolidated the development of the French Riviera as a recreation and tourist center and made getting a suntan chic. The upper classes also pioneered automobile tourism.

The onset of the Great Depression, hitting France later than elsewhere, in 1931 rather than 1929, resulted in a renewed push for a shorter workweek. The Popular Front government that came to power in 1936 brought major innovations in the leisure patterns of the working classes. Not only was the eight-hour day restored, but two weeks of paid vacation for all workers was won. The summer of 1936 saw an unprecedented popularization of camping and sunbathing. Parisian workers for the first time discovered the delights of the French south and of that southern drink, *pastis*. Workers started to save their earnings for their vacations and thus cut back on the amount of time spent in cafés. But the number of cafés in France hit an all-time high of over 500,000 on the eve of World War II. With growing political polarization, the Popular Front government lasted little more than a year, and with the onset of rearmament for the upcoming war, workers' gains in leisure and vacation time were frozen. Due to occupation by the Nazis, the war years proved to be among the bleakest eras in modern French history in terms of leisure. Even that traditional staple of French recreational life, the café, saw a dramatic diminution in number: from 508,000 in 1938 to 315,000 in 1945.[8]

The first 15 postwar years (1945–1960) saw the French hard at work rebuilding and modernizing their society, and the next 15 (1960–1975) saw an explosion in leisure and consumption. The gains made by the Popular Front were reinstated and workers enjoyed the 40-hour week and two weeks of paid vacation. A third week of paid vacation was added in 1956, and a fourth in 1963. By the 1960s a "fun morality" began to emerge, fuelled not only by increasing leisure time but also by the dramatic increase in purchasing power, essentially doubling in real terms between the late 1940s and the late 1960s. In particular, between 1960 and 1975 consumer society arrived in France with a suddenness and thoroughness not seen in other Western societies. Car ownership over this period jumped from 30 percent to over 60 percent, and the number of televisions rose from over one million to over 11 million (thus including 85 percent of French households). In 1960 only 40 percent of French families had a refrigerator; by 1975, 90 percent did. The car was a vital tool of leisure because it expanded people's horizons outside of the neighborhood and city and into the countryside, beaches, and mountains of France. By the 1970s automobile tourism had been democratized. TVs and refrigerators meant that one no longer needed to go out to cafés either for entertainment or for a cold drink. As a result, the number of cafés in France, even in an age of prosperity, continued to decline to around 200,000 by 1980.[9]

Despite economic turbulence, the past 30 years (1975–2005) have seen a consolidation of the postwar leisure society.[10] When the Socialists won the presidency and the parliament in 1981, they immediately cut the workweek by one hour (to 39 hours) and provided a fifth week of paid vacation. When they again came to power in parliament in 1998 they legislated a further reduction in the workweek, to 35 hours. The rationale for these measures continued to be the Popular Front assumption that a truly democratic society would expand the leisure opportunity of its citizens plus in the hope, born of the high unemployment of the post-1973 oil shock era, that freeing up of work time would provide additional jobs. This law has become an integral part of French society and has proven popular even among managers and employers because it allows for more flexible schedules. Thus a worker might work her or his 35 hours over the course of four rather than five days and then take a three-day weekend or take more days off at another time. A year after the law's implementation (2001) the national planning agency asserted that its findings proved that the law had helped reduce unemployment. Subsequent studies have found that roughly 60 percent of French workers believe that their leisure time had improved, with only 15 saying no. But only half of the respondents felt that their work time had benefited. In any case, the café did not benefit from this reduction in the workweek, with numbers in France falling to about 46,000 in 2005.[11]

After the reelection of conservative Jacques Chirac as president in 2002 and legislative elections that gave him a parliamentary majority, the new center-right government began to retrench on questions of work and vacations. A rise in unemployment after 2001 provided the pretext for this retrenchment. The most dramatic development so far has been the attempt to abolish the 35 hour law. In March 2005 the parliament passed a law allowing employers to add 220 hours per year if they compensated workers via higher salaries. Contrary to the Socialists, Chirac argued that the 35-hour week had put a brake on French economic growth. Nevertheless, this law remains in force and it seems unlike that Chirac's government will succeed any better than any previous center-right government in increasing the work week.[12]

What do the French do with their leisure time? Here one must distinguish between daily leisure activities, those reserved for the weekend, and those undertaken on vacations. The French government has done extensive research on daily leisure patterns and produced a splendidly detailed survey. Recreation during the weekends and on vacations is best studied in terms of the destinations and tourist institutions that have become so popular over the past 50 years.

In essence French daily leisure habits since World War II have increasingly shifted from the public face-to-face ambiance of cafés, cinemas, theaters, music, and dance halls or the intimate act of reading to home-centered entertainment ranging from watching television or listening to music, puttering around the home and garden, and surfing the Internet. Ironically, now the most homebound social group is the working class. During the nineteenth century middle-class moralists condemned laborers for wasting their lives in front of the café bar; now the cultural elite berates them for spending too much time on the couch in front of the TV rather than taking cultural excursions or reading (although the French have not yet developed an equivalent term for couch potato). In contrast, the French professional class of engineers and technicians, known as *les cadres,* is praised for all their cultural activities outside the home, for going to restaurants and museums, and for their high rates of reading.[13]

Despite the cadres, the French in general have increasingly shifted their daily leisure activities to audiovisual activities in the home and away from social and cultural outings in town and country. This shift has been made possible by the dramatic increase in the number of private homes and spacious apartments that have been created since 1945. In 1962, of the 14,538,500 principal residences in France, 6,041,640 (41.6 percent) were owner-occupied. By 1999, of the 23,810,161 residences, 13,034,632 (54.7 percent) were owner-occupied.[14] More-spacious and well-equipped domestic interiors have allowed for a steady accumulation of televisions, stereos, VHS and now DVD players, and computers (first with the Minitel and now with the Internet).

The growth in car ownership has allowed for the growing number of residences outside the old city centers and has also dramatically impacted daily leisure patterns. Even since the mid-1960s, when the percentage of car ownership jumped from 30 percent to 50 percent between 1960 and 1966, the number of cars in France had increased by 440 percent. The rise in the use of the car, as in the United States, has been accompanied by the shift from shopping in the city centers to traveling to large malls (known in France as *centres commercials*) just off of highways.

Thus the French closely associate affluence and mobility (both social and physical) with the automobile. The deep bond of the French with their cars is probably the reason, according to researchers, that youths living in deprived and isolated neighborhoods have turned to burning cars as their chief means of protesting their exclusion from the mainstream of French society. This is logical given how central the car has become to French life; most of the population has moved from old city centers in which pedestrian traffic was predominant to new housing complexes connected by highways.[15]

The French now buy 60 percent of their food and 30 percent of their other household items at such supermarket and "hypermarket" (a unique French term) chains as Carrefour, Auchan, Promodès, and Leclerc (the biggest super-market chain). Conversely, the number of traditional small commercial estab-lishments has fallen precipitously: from 302, 600 shops in 1966 to 128,400 in 1999, a drop of 58 percent.[16] Thus during daily life the French are now much less likely to stroll and browse along picturesque streets and have a refreshment in a café before returning home. Now all of this is done with a car at a shopping mall (or increasingly at the computer, with online purchases from FNAC—the home entertainment, computer, music, and book chain—or Amazon.fr).

This shift to life centered in the contemporary home is illustrated in con-sumption figures for the average French family. French consumption since 1960 has become steadily more focused on home life: In 1960 the average family spent 23.2 percent of their yearly expenditures on food and only 10.7 percent on housing, heating, and lighting. By the year 2000, while food had fallen to 11.4 percent of the average French budget, housing had risen to 18.8 percent. At the same time, spending on other home-related activities also in-creased: Health spending rose from 1.5 percent in 1960 to 2.9 percent in 2000, telephone and Internet expenses went from .5 percent in 1960 to 1.7 percent in 2000, and transportation spending from 9.3 percent in 1960 to 12.2 percent in 2000. During the same period the percentage spent on alcoholic drinks and tobacco (goods especially associate with café life) has been cut in half: from 5.4 percent to 2.7 percent. But the percentage devoted to hotels, restaurants, and nonalcoholic beverages in cafés has held steady (dropping only slightly, from 6.5 percent in 1960 to 6 percent in 2001). Finally, the percentage devoted to leisure and culture, after jumping from 6.2 percent to 6.8 percent during the 1960s, has remained virtually constant at around 7.1 percent.[17]

Table 4.1 allows us to explore in great detail the various leisure patterns of the different social classes in France today.

Television ranks number one by far among leisure activities. Indeed, when a cross section of the French population filled out a sheet on their daily leisure activities, television came in at 78.3 percent, compared to the next two, reading (at 35.1 percent) and semileisure activities around the house (at 32.4 percent). In 1975 the French watched on average one hour and fifty minutes of television daily; by the millennium this figure had almost doubled, to three hours and nine minutes. Workers are now the social group most glued to the television set: 80.7 percent listed this as their number one leisure activity compared to the lower percentage, among the professionals (cadres), of 58.3.

The second-most-popular leisure activity is reading. The professional classes of France—cadres and middle-range professionals *(profession intermédiaries)*—are the most assiduous of readers by far, listing reading as their second-most-favorite activity (with both having rates above the average

Table 4.1
Leisure Activities in Daily Life by Occupations

Activity	Agriculture	Artisans, Shopkeepers, Entrepreneurs	Professionals (Cadres)	Intermediate Professions	White Collar	Workers Total
Television	60.4	67.4	58.3	71.0	73.4	80.7	78.3
Reading	21.8	21.6	44.0	35.8	25.8	17.9	35.1
Semileisure	23.2	23.3	23.7	29.9	25.8	38.8	32.4
Trips (besides shows)	12.5	13.9	15.0	20.4	20.2	25.3	24.8
Hiking	6.1	8.6	12.5	13.5	12.9	13.3	18.8
Relaxing	3.3	12.5	15.9	17.5	14.5	13.9	15.6
Games	4.1	3.3	12.1	12.6	8.2	10.6	14.4
Sport	1.4	4.7	11.5	8.8	6.7	6.2	8.1
Radio, Hi Fi	3.1	3.0	4.9	3.2	3.6	4.7	7.0
Other cultural trips	0.0	16.9	9.1	7.1	11.6	8.8	17.2
Movies	0.0	0.5	3.1	1.8	1.1	0.2	1.3
Sporting events	0.9	1.0	0.7	1.0	0.8	1.2	0.8
Hunting/ fishing	1.4	1.4	0.2	0.3	0.4	1.6	0.8
Amateur art	0.0	0.0	0.8	0.6	0.2	0.2	0.6

Adapted and translated by author from table "Pratiques des loisir quotidienes par professions et categories socials (PCS)" in Serge Cordelier, ed., *L'état de la France 2004: un panorama unique et complet de la France* (Paris: Éditions La Découverte, 2004), 157.

of 35.1 percent, at 44 percent and 35.8 percent, respectively). On the contrary, workers are the least likely to read (17.9), with artisans, small shopkeepers, employers (21.6) and farmers (21.8) are only slightly more likely, and white collar workers remain at 25.8 percent, at least ten percentage points below the professional classes. The connection between television watching and reading is obvious when we see that some of the most popular magazines in France cover weekly television broadcasts. The connection between television watching and reading is intimate when we see that some of the most popular magazines in France cover weekly television broadcasts. The major television magazine are consulted by an astonishing 52 million readers: the leader is *TV Magazine* with 14.2 million readers, *Télé Z* with

8.7 million, *Télé 7 Jours* with 7.9 million, *Télé Loisirs* with 7.9 million, *Télé Star*, with 6.7 million, and *TV Hebdo* with 5.8 million. By contrast even the popular glossy pictorial magazine *Paris-Match* has a readership of only 4.5 million.[18]

Some of the other most popular magazines lead us into the third-most-popular daily leisure activity, home renovation and repairs. Here again workers lead all other social groups, and by a wider margin than in television watching (at 38.8 percent compared to 29.9 for the intermediate professionals, 25.8 for white-collar workers, and 23.7 for cadres). Here again we see an historical irony. By tending their gardens at such a high rate, today's workers are doing exactly what prewar moralists hoped they would do with greater affluence: desert the café, become more rooted in family life, and return to the soil.

The other major leisure pursuits of daily life—neighborhood and cultural outings, hiking, and relaxation—show the growing complexity of the behavior of social classes in an age of mass leisure. This is highlighted when we look at the two types of outings listed: local and cultural. On the one hand, neighborhood outings (activities ranging from club meetings to dances, parties, and fairs) are most prevalent among the lower classes— workers, white-collar employees, and even the intermediate professions. Thus the lower class is not completely housebound by television. On the other hand, the bosses of French society, ranging from skilled trades people to merchants and CEOs, are most likely, by a wide margin, to attend cultural sorts of outings (such as the theater, ballet, museums, the circus, and expositions). High culture is thus still very much associated with the upper classes. But when we look at the cadres, in many ways the group that is increasingly gaining prestige and status due to their technical knowledge, they are much more likely to socialize in the neighborhood than go to a cultural event.

The distinctive behavior of the upwardly mobile cadres is also seen in lesser daily leisure pursuits such as sports, movie-going, and amateur artistic expression. In each of these categories these highly skilled professional lead other social groups by a wide margin. But these leisure activities, along with listening to radio and music, are minor pursuits.

The decline of cinema attendance is especially striking. This used to one of the most popular recreations for the French. In 1947, for example, with a population of a little over 42 million, French cinemas had 432 million ticket buyers; in 2003, with a population of over 61 million, this number had fallen to just 174.2 million.[19]

The recreation that unites all classes of the French equally is listening to the radio. This is highly appropriate in an age of walkmans and iPods as well as car radios and home stereo systems.

Weekly leisure patterns, already growing in popularity over the past 30 years with the mass ownership of cars, have become much more popular with the advent of the 35-hour workweek. The 35-hour week has led many to distribute their weekly work schedule so as to take three-day weekends. In short, the French are trying to separate work and leisure time more clearly—to cram five days of work into four—in order to take more trips and vacations rather than have more hours after work in the home or the neighborhood during the workweek. Sadly this law, while indeed providing more free time, has benefited men more than women, especially in the familial context, because women, as noted in chapter 3, still do most of the house work.

Two of the most popular activities to do on long weekends are to go to country homes or to visit the growing number of amusement parks. France has led the world in the development of second homes and has led Europe in theme parks. The number of second homes has increased dramatically: from 330,000 in 1954 to 1.7 million in 1975 to over 3 million by 2001.[20] France pioneered the development of European theme parks in the early 1960s with the modest Sea of Sand (built in Ermonville outside of Paris in 1963), which still draws a respectable 450,000 annually, despite stiff competition. Since 1977 a whole series of theme parks have been built, the most popular one in the early twenty-first century being Euro Disney, outside of Paris.

The first fully developed theme park was Puy du Fou (1977), created in the Vendee region of the northwest and dedicated to tell the story of a family in the region across 700 years of history. It also illuminates the larger saga of France from the Middle Ages through the region's revolt (the Vendee Revolt) during the French Revolution through the traumas of World Wars I and II. This *cinéscénie* employs 2,600 actors, mostly volunteer locals, on an expansive 23-hectares stage (probably the largest in the world) to recreate this sage 28 times a year. This is now the fourth-largest park in France and is especially well connected to France's highway system.

The second, Futuroscope, was created a decade late (1987) also in the northwest (around Poitiers). It is not a French version of Disney's Tomorrowland, but instead is dedicated to special effects and wide frame cinemas (such as IMAX), and as the name implies takes its customers on a journey into the future. Futuroscope draws not only on a regional but also on a national audience with its connections to the French bullet train system (TGV). In 2003 it trailed only the Disney Parks and Parc Asterix in attendance, with 1.5 million paid entrants.

Asterix Park opened two years later, in 1989, and is based on the popular comic book about crafty Gauls outwitting their Roman colonizers after Caesar's conquest. Attendance lagged at the park for a decade, then picked up after the big-budget French Film *Astérix and Obélix against Caesar* (1999) brought new attention to the comic strip and to the theme park. Often seen as a riposte to Americanization (the Romans being surrogate Americans), it is now the third-most-popular theme park in France (with 1.8 million visitors in 2004).[21] Other French parks include Vulcania (opened in 2003), in the mountainous Auvergne, the first volcanic theme park in the world, and Space City near the southern city of Toulouse (France's aerospace capital).

In 1992 Euro Disney opened south of Asterix Park in the Marne La Vallee (on the eastern side of Paris). After a slow start, and although still problematic in its profitability, Euro Disney has become the most-attended theme park in Europe. For example, in 2003, 10.2 million passed through its turnstiles, which represented approximately 37 percent of the total attendance for French theme parks. Moreover, Walt Disney Studios Park, which opened in 2002, now has the second highest attendance of French theme parks at 2.2 million in 2003. The attendance at these two Disney parks is more than double the number that of that traditional icon of France, the Eiffel Tower.[22]

Weekly or monthly vacations have steadily become more common since the Popular Front. By 1982 half the population took vacations. The Socialist government of the early 1980s provided new subsidies for those in the lower income brackets with the establishment of the National Agency for Vacation Checks in 1982. By 2002, the percentage of those traveling during their six weeks of paid vacation had jumped to two-thirds. Not only do more people take vacations, but the way in which they do so has also changed. Through the 1950s, state-run summer camps or union-inspired package deals were common. After 1960, individuals increasingly planned their own vacations through private companies. By the mid 1970s, they increasingly took vacations outside of the traditional period of July and August. By 2003, 47 percent of French adults took at least part of their vacation in the winter.[23]

The evolution of France's most famous and distinctive travel agency, Club Med, provides a good example of a tourist organization shifting from public service to profit and then to second-tier status in an age of globalization. After World War II, initially dedicated to facilitate working people going to Mediterranean beaches, by the 1960s it was profitably tapping into the baby boomers' love of sun, fun, and food with its concept of rustic and all-inclusive vacations in which tourists could leave their wallets and cares behind and live a life of simplicity and sport on the beach. Although it remains the largest travel company in France, it does not have the cachet it did in the 1970s and 1980s. AIDS, the rise of sex tourism in Asia and ecotourism around the world, and the aging of the baby boomers have blunted its novelty, and it has now fallen far behind its European and American rivals. After the merger of American Express and Havas, this conglomerate has become the largest travel agency in the world, showing that American and French cultural and corporate culture can work together in harmony.[24]

Although Club Med is truly global in offering dozens of vacation sites on every continent, over 90 percent of the French population still stays within the hexagon. Moreover, of those traveling beyond the nation, two-thirds stay in Europe. Those under 30 and the ranks of upper management compose the groups most likely to travel overseas. Regardless of where they go, half of all French tourists list exercise as one of their primary objectives (climbing, tennis, golf, mountain biking, trekking). This fact allows us to conveniently segue into the subject of sport.[25]

SPORT IN FRANCE

A land known in the Middle Ages for the physical prowess of its mounted warrior-knights and for probably being the site of the creation of one of the greatest sporting events of the age, the tournament, and in the early modern period for developing the game of tennis, France felt itself fall behind England by the late nineteenth century in the development of modern sport. Modern soccer, rugby, and track and field are just some of the sports that the English spread around the world during their imperial days. Today the United States basks in its sporting prowess and has seen basketball in particular, but baseball to a lesser degree, become an international sport.

France nevertheless has produced the two sporting events with the greatest rate of participation and spectatorship in the contemporary world: the Olympic Games and the World Cup of soccer. Moreover, in both sporting events the hexagon has been one of the leading competitors since the mid-1990s. Today France has achieved a fascinating hybrid between the state-centered sports machines of the old Soviet bloc and Western entrepreneurial efforts. Moreover, sport is one of the truly comprehensive national phenomena in France, since Paris does not dominate in this sphere as it does in so many others.

Sports has become one of the primary means by which a wide cluster of identities—national, racial, regional, gender, and class—are displayed, negotiated, and articulated in today's increasingly globalized world.

The concern for sport in modern France can be traced to the defeat in the Franco-Prussian War in 1870–1871. Many reformers felt that French soldiers in particular and the French population in general were not as physically fit as the enemy across the Rhine and that this was one of the principal reasons for defeat. Indeed, many reformers offered the evidence of what they considered the high number of rejections of young male conscripts into the army as proof. Some looked to Britain's burgeoning athletic tradition (and imported soccer, rugby, rowing, and track and field) for inspiration in general and for the integration of sports into its elite boarding schools as a model France should follow. Others turned to the example of German gymnastics and shooting societies for inspiration. Although shooting, gymnastic, and soccer societies subsequently emerged and bicycling became the major commercial and spectator sport (starting in Paris in 1868), France lagged behind their late nineteenth century rivals.

None of these sporting organizations achieved national reach or state subsidies and none was integrally integrated into the school curriculum. Moreover, compared to England and the United States, neither amateur nor professional sports flourished in the late nineteenth and early twentieth century in France.

By the 1880s, surveying what he believed to be French national and racial degeneration and athletic underdevelopment, a French aristocrat, the Baron Pierre de Coubertin, would launch his successful crusade to recreate the ancient Greek Olympics in modern times. Inspired by the ideals of the ancients and the practice of the modern English, de Coubertin hoped that international competition would inspire his people to become a leading athletic nation. Sadly for him, he would not see this in his lifetime.

Jules Rimet, unlike de Coubertin, came from the Parisian working class and was a staunch Catholic. In 1897, at the age of 24, he created the Red Star soccer club for blue- and white-collar worker in the Gros Caillou neighborhood on the Left Bank of Paris. This visionary hoped thereby to bring workers out of the cafés and back into the Church and more generally to unite all of the world's people though athletic competition. He is one of the best examples of the Social Catholic Movement that created a wide range of sporting clubs across France during the first half of the twentieth century. By 1910 he had launched a national soccer league, and in 1919 he reorganized it as the French Federation of Soccer (Fédération française de foot-ball). His greatest accomplishment, however, would come when as president of the World Soccer Federation (FIFA, itself founded in France) between 1921 and 1954 his internationalist vision would lead him to create the World Cup competition (first held in 1930). By his retirement the number of nations in the organization had soared from 20 to 85, and in 1946 the World Cup trophy was named after him.

Another influential French sporting innovation was the cross-country cycling race, the Tour de France. Created by journalist Henri Desgrange (editor of the sporting newspaper *L'Auto*) in 1903, this annual sporting event covers a 4,800-km course across France over a three-week period. Ideally suited in its origins to bring a palpable and visceral sense of French nationhood to a still largely rural society, it has today become an international venue. The success of Americans such as Greg Le Mond (Tour de France winner in 1986, 1989, and 1990) and Lance Armstrong (Tour de France winner seven consecutive times from 1999–2005) has inspired many American states and regions (literally from Georgia to California) to set up their own tours. The race covers three weeks, with each day ending with the awarding of the yellow jersey (instituted in 1918). The competition not only rewards endurance but is also a contest between those who are good on mountains *(grimpeurs)* and those good on flat surface *(rouleurs)*. One sad aspect of the internationalization and commercialization of this sport is the controversy over the use of performance-enhancing drugs (especially during the 2006 race when the winner Floyd Landis failed the drug test).

All three of these events reflect that private initiative so prevalent in the development of French sport through the early 1930s. Only with the Popular Front government (1936–1938) and then especially with the collaborationist Vichy regime (1940–1944) did the French state become extensively involved in sport. The Popular Front government created an undersecretary of state for sport and leisure, a school for skiing, and an athletics program open to all from which it awarded sporting licenses *(brevet sportif populaire)*. The fall of the Popular Front prevented these initiatives from receiving much funding, but when France fell little more than two years later to the Nazis, the Vichy regime quickly picked up and enhanced these initiatives. Within three days of assuming power, Petain appointed the former international tennis star Jean Borotra as head of the Commissariat Général de l'Éducation générale et sportive (EGS) in the ministry of family and youth. By December, Vichy had promulgated a sports charter, and all sports were grouped into federations. More importantly, spending rose dramatically: 20 times as much money went to sport as had been the case under the Popular Front. At the same time Vichy, while continuing the *brevet sportif populaire* under a new name—Vichy's *brevet sportif national*—also dramatically increased the number of hours devoted to athletics in the schools and interscholastic competitions. Much of this increased funding went to the construction of athletic fields, stadiums, swimming pools, and sports centers. By 1943, France had over 30,000 sports clubs, with over three million members. Moreover, 2 national and 15 regional athletic training centers had been established.

The Resistance-inspired governments of the Fourth and Fifth Republics, although also placing sport at the center of their plans to regenerate France, were slow to add to this organizational infrastructure. De Gaulle was enraged at the poor showing of France's athletes at the 1960 Rome Olympics but, outside from pushing for and receiving the 1968 Winter Olympics in Grenoble, did not accomplish much. The major innovation would come in 1975 with the creation of the National Institute of Sport and Physical Education (INSEP). The creation of this body led to a much more educated and sophisticated generation of coaches that has been at the heart of France's rise in athletic prominence since the mid-1990s. Let us first look at sports at the grassroots level.[26]

By 2003 close to a quarter of France's 730,000 associations were dedicated to sport. The number of sporting licenses has steadily risen since 1945: from 1,864,518 in 1949 to 12,022,170 in 1985 to 15,128,632 in 2003. An inquiry by the Ministry of Sports in 2000 found that 36 million people (aged between 15 and 75) said they engaged in some form of sports. Of those, 26 million said they did some type of sport at least once a week, and more than half of those belonging to sporting clubs said that they were active competitors. The most favorite sporting activities are walking, swimming, and cycling. Women are twice as likely as men to hold a sporting license, but the biggest French sporting federation, with more than two million members, is soccer, in which less than 2 percent of the membership is female. The second-biggest federation, tennis, has over a million members, of which about one-third are women. The other major federations, with memberships running between half a million and 400,000 members, include judo, horseback riding, basketball, and petanque (somewhat similar to lawn bowling) and other provincial games and have widely varying gender ratios. For example, horseback riding is almost 75 percent female, while petanque is only a little over 14 percent. Basketball, on the contrary, is highly popular among women. Indeed, at 40 percent it contains a higher percentage of women than golf (29.5 percent). Women are found especially in gymnastics (78.4 percent) and swimming (55.3 percent). Not surprisingly, rugby has the lowest percentage. What is most surprising, from the vantage point of the United States, is the lack of women's participation in soccer.

France's success in elite athletic competition often goes unrecognized. For example, France ranks fifth in total Olympic medals won since 1896.

Across French history, as is true of many other nations, sport has been a means by which people from impoverished or marginalized backgrounds can gain upward social mobility. This has been especially the case for women. From the time of the tennis champion Suzanne Lenglen during the 1920s to the gold-medal sprinter Marie-José Pérec at the 1992 and 1996 Olympics to the current tennis star Amélie Mauresmo, women athletes have expanded the definition of both women's accomplishment and identity. For example, Lenglen's domination of women's tennis made her France's first true sporting "superstar," Pérec's three gold medals, among the most of all French Olympians, underscored the emergence of people of color from France's periphery (in her case, Guadeloupe) to athletic immortality, and Mauresmo's courage in breaking gender stereotypes by acknowledging that she is a lesbian and refusing to play in a "feminine" fashion.[27]

In the case of men, soccer has been an especially fruitful avenue for social mobility. This can be seen in successive generations stretching back to the

1950s. During this decade the son of a Polish immigrant miner, Raymond Kopa, led the French national team. He guided the great Spanish team (Real Madrid) to several European Cups and the French national team to third place in the 1958 World Cup. In that same year he was named European Footballer of the Year. Michael Platini, the grandson of Italian immigrants, grew up around soccer, since his father was a coach. Playing for the Italian team Juventus during the 1980s, Platini helped win three Italian titles in four years. In 1984 he broke the French national record for goals and helped the French national team win the European Championship. In 1986, under his inspiration, France again finished third at the World Cup. Overall, he won three awards as European Footballer of the Year.

Most recently, Zinedine Zidane, born in 1972 at Marseille of Algerian immigrants, has continued and augmented this legacy. He helped lead the French team to its first World Cup championship in 1998 and then came back two years later to lead the team to another European Cup title. In 2004 and 2005, he made a switch from Real Madrid to Juvenus for a unprecedented European contract worth $68.6 million. At the 2006 World Cup in Germany, Zidane both enhanced and complicated his legacy. On the one hand, he led France to another final and won the coveted Golden Ball as the best player in the tournament. On the other hand, in the waning minutes of overtime in the championship match, he head-butted a member of the opposing Italian team and was ejected from the game. As a result, the French lost their best penalty kicker; the match then went into a shootout to break the tie. Controversy quickly swirled as to whether the Italian player had hurled religious and ethnic slurs at Zidane. The controversy has still not been fully resolved by the time of this writing in August 2006. Both players have been suspended for future matches, however this ruling will never really apply to Zidane, who had declared his retirement even before the championship game began.[28]

Television has made Zidane a true national (even international) icon. The synergy of television and sports developed much later in France than in the United States, in the 1980s rather than the 1960s. The vehicle of this transformation was cable television, in particular the company Canal Plus. In 1984 the rights to televise soccer games went for about $1 million, by 1999 this figure had risen to about $150 million, and in 2005 the figure hit $600 million.[29]

When France won the 1998 World Cup almost half the population was watching on television. The spontaneous joy and celebration that erupted in every French city led to the declaration of a national holiday the following day. As one historian noted: "The government shrewdly declared the day following the victory a public holiday, effectively linking the celebrations to the annual national festivities on *le 14 Juillet.*" We shall now see that this move fits into the vibrant history of French festivals.

FESTIVALS

A nation steeped for centuries in the ritual calendar of the Catholic Church, France, after its 1789 Revolution, pioneered in creating the modern secular holidays, and over the last 30 years it has pioneered in the development of a wide variety of cultural festivals.

In the Middle Ages and through the eighteenth century, French society was intimately connected to the liturgical calendar of the Catholic Church. Over the course of centuries Rome had consecrated a large number of holy days not only for the major events in the life of Christ (Christmas and Easter in particular) but also for the Virgin Mary and John the Baptist, and saints' days, and to celebrate the new year. The Catholic Church still celebrates many of the moveable feasts dating from the medieval period: Good Friday, Easter, Easter Monday, Ascension, Pentecost, and Whit Monday.

Overlaying the Catholic calendar is the republican one dedicated to the great moments in the creation of the modern secular nation state. These holidays include May 1 (Labor Day), May 8 (Victory in World War II), July 14 (Bastille Day), and November 11 (Armistice Day for World War I).

The contemporary national holiday calendar blends both secular and religious holidays as follows:

January 1: New Year's Day *(Jour de l'an)*

May 1: Labor Day (*Fete du premier mai*)

May 8: World War II Victory Day (Fete de la Victoire, Fete du huitieme mai)

July 14: Bastille Day (Fete nationale)

August 15: Assumption of the Blessed Virgin Mary (Assomption)

November 1: All Saints Day (La Toussaint)

November 11: Armistice Day (Jour d'armistice)

December 25: Christmas Day (Noel)

December 26: Second Day of Christmas (in Alsace and Lorraine only)

Unlike in the United States or Great Britain, where public holidays usually are moved to a Monday or Friday to create a long weekend, in France national holidays are celebrated on the day on which they fall. But when a holiday occurs on a Tuesday or Thursday, the French often forgo work on the Monday or Friday next to the holiday (known as *faire le pont,* making the bridge).

In addition to the holidays listed above, over the last 20 years the French government and local groups have sustained or created a wide variety of festivals of three types: art, local and regional, and national. In 1993, at least 500 festivals happened during the summer; by 1997 the number had grown to 800, and by 2000 topped 1,000. In addition, a wide variety of festivals occur throughout the rest of year. Some of the most important were created or inspired by Jack Lang, minister of culture, under the Mitterrand Socialist governments of 1981–1986 and 1988–1993. Since 1998 the Office of Music, Dance, Theatre, and Spectacles in the Ministry of Culture and Communication has overseen the festivals (in conjunction with the National Education Ministry).

The most famous of all the arts festivals is the Cannes International Film Festival. Begun haltingly just as Europe went to war in 1939, it became an annual event (except for May 1968) after 1951. It has been famous not only for showcasing French film but also for promoting the works of a diverse number of international directors and stars, including Luis Buñuel, Frederico Fellini, Quentin Tarantino, Mike Leigh, and in 2004, Michael Moore. The most famous theater festival is at Avignon, created in 1947 by Jean Vilar. This director became legendary for sparking a provincial renaissance in French theatre and staging plays in unorthodox locations, such as the courtyard of the papal palace at Avignon and now across the breadth of the city. Since 1970 an alternative festival has been held at the same time for young, innovative, and nonprofessional theater groups and directors. Finally, the Bourges Spring Festival, started in 1977, has become a venue at which French song can both relive its great legends, such as the 1930s star Charles Trenet, or find new ones, such as Renaud.

A flavor of the wide diversity of regional festivals is captured in the following examples: the Salon of Creative Leisure at the Nice acropolis (late September through early October), Music of the Basque Coast, Saint-Jean de Luz (from late August to the middle of September), and the Festival of the Cathedrals of Picardy (early September to early October).

Bastille Day is the most famous of the national festivals but has been augmented by a wide variety of others in recent years. For example, the celebration of the annual Beaujolais Nouveau in November has become an international event. Another festival that has achieved international prominence, but not necessarily American attention, is the Festival of Music. This celebration of the world's music on the summer solstice (June 21) was conceived by Jack Lang in 1982 based upon research that showed that over five million French played a musical instrument. Since its inception it has grown dramatically within France and is now also celebrated in 80 other nations. Another of Lang's efforts, a summer Cinema Festival in Paris, has not been as successful.

The development of national holidays and the growth of a wide variety of national, local, and artistic festivals reveal the creative collaboration existing in France today between the government, artists, and local communities and entrepreneurs. Many former activists of May 1968, such as Lang, have seen festivals and holidays as a way to achieve the goals of this movement: community participation, spontaneity, creativity, and sociability. Moreover, in an age when many French fear the homogenizing effects of globalization, these festivals seems to show that French identity, at the national, regional, and local levels, continues to thrive.

There are so many festivals in France today that if Hemingway were alive he would have to modify his famous saying to "France is a moveable feast."[30]

NOTES

1. One of the best evocations of Paris before the post-1945 modernization is Elliot Paul's *The Last Time I Saw Paris*. A classic study of the changes that swept over French rural life after World War II is Henri Mendras, *The Vanishing Peasant: Innovation and Change in French Agriculture* Trans. Jean Lerner (Cambridge; MA: MIT Press, 1970).

2. See Henri Mendras and Laurence Duboys, *Fresney, Francais comme vous avez change: Historie des Français depuis 1945* (Paris: Tallandier, 2004).

3. See Bertram M. Gordon, "Leisure," in Hugh Dauncy, ed., *French Popular Culture: An Introduction* (London: Arnold, 2003).

4. See statistics through late 1970s in Jean Dethier, *Cafes, bistrots et compagnie*, Catalogue d'exposition, Centre Georges Pompidou, 1977, p. 51, and for today my entry on French cafes titled "Drinking Establishments (France)" in Jack Blocker, et al. eds., *Alcohol and Temperance in Modern History: An International Encyclopedia*, 2 vols. (Santa Barbara, CA: ABC-Clio, 2003).

5. See the CNN article on the UN's International Labor Organization findings: archives.cnn.com/2001/CAREER/trends/08/30/ilo.study.

6. Michael R. Marrus, "Social Drinking in the Belle Epoque," *Journal of Social History,* 7, no. 4 (Winter 1974), pp. 115–141.

7. On Bastille Day and the 1889 Paris World's Fair see Rearcik; for cafés see my article, *The World of the Paris Café: Sociability among the French Working Class, 1789–1914* (Baltimore: Johns Hopkins University Press, 1996).

8. For Popular Front see Julian Jackson, *The Popular Front in France: Defending Democracy, 1934–38* (New York: Cambridge University Press, 1988). For data on drinks and café life, these points are based on my oral histories of Parisian area cafes currently underway and the statistics cited in Jean Dethier, *Cafes, bistrots et compagnie,* Catalogue d'exposition, Centre Georges Pompidou, 1977, p. 51.

9. For statistics, see W. Scott Haine, *The History of France* (Westport, CT: Greenwood Press, 2000), 184–185; for café statistics, see Dethier, as cited in the previous note.

10. Jacques Marseille, *Le guerre des deux France: Celle qui avance et celle qui freine* (2004; Paris: Perrin, 2005) provides compelling truth on this point.

11. Anders Hayden, "Europe's alternative work-time," www.commonground. ca/iss/0410159/cg159_Europe.shtml. Also, see W. Scott Haine, "Drinking Establishments (France)" in Jack Blocker, et al., eds., *Alcohol and Temperance in Modern History: An International Encyclopedia*, 2 vols. (Santa Barbara, CA: ABC-Clio, 2003), 203–205.

12. A good overview of this debate can be found at www.timesizing.com/gts0407a. htm.

13. Nicholas Hewitt and Rosemary Chapman, eds., *Popular Culture and Mass Communication in Twentieth Century France* (Lewiston: The Edwin Mellen Press, 1992).

14. Homeownership data from INSEE data found at www.demographia.com/ db-frhomeown.htm.

15. Mark Landler, "A Very French Message from the Disaffected," *New York Times International,* November 13, 2005, 6.

16. Bruno Lutinier, "Les petites enterprises du commerce depuis 30 ans, Beaucoup moins d'epiceries, un peu plus de fleuristes," *INSEE Premiere,* 831 (Février 2002). For period up to 2003 see Nicolas Cochez, "L'évolution du petit commerce en France entre 1993 et 2003." www.pme.gouv.fr/essentiel/etudesstat/pdf/evol_ commerce_fr.pdf.

17. *L'état de la France 2004: un panorama unique et complet de la France* (Paris: La Découverte, 2004).

18. Data is from the handy online site Discover France, www.discoverfrance.net/ France/DF_media.shtml.

19. For 2003 see Janine Cardona and Chantal Lacroix, *Statistiques de la culture: Chiffres clés 2005* (Paris: Documentation Francaise, 2005).

20. See W. Scott Haine, *The History of France* (Westport, CT: Greenwood Press, 2000), 184. See also the website of the French Embassy in the United States: www. ambafrance-us.org/atoz/housing.asp, and La France en bref—France in Facts and Figures, www.insee.fr/fr/ppp/publications/intfrcbref.pdf.

21. Websites of French theme parks are as follows: Figures, including attendance figures: www.merdesable.fr/parc/histoire.php; Asterix at www.parcasterix.fr/en/park/ theme-park-france.htm; and cultureetloisirs.france2.fr/loisirs/9729459-fr.php; Puy de Fou at www.puydufou.com/; Futuroscope at www.futuroscope.com.

22. PricewaterhouseCoopers, *Hospitality Directions, Europe Edition 9* (March 2004), www.themeparkdenmark.dk/Downloads/Artikler/pwc_ThemeParks.pdf; for Eiffel Tower figure (6 million), see the French Embassy in the United States web site http://www.ambafrance-us.org/atoz/culture.asp#10.

23. Lydie J. Naenlin, "Leisure," in Wayne Northcutt, ed., *Historical Dictionary of the French Fourth and Fifth Republics, 1946–1991* (Westport, CT: Greenwood Press, 1992), 260; also, Gérard Mermet, *Francoscopie: Pour comprendre les français 2005* (Paris: Larousse, 2004), 507.

24. For the rise of Club Med, see Ellen Furlough, "Packaging Pleasure. Club Mediterranee and French Consumer Culture, 1950–1968," in Richard Golden, *The Social Dimension of Western Civilization*, vol. 2, 5th ed. (Boston: Bedford/St. Martin's Press, 2003); for Club Med at the turn of the twenty-first century see Gordon, "Leisure," in Dauncy, and for recent statistics on Club Med and other travel agencies see Dominique Frémy and Michèle Frémy, eds., *Quid* (Paris: Robert Laffont, 2006), p. 1844.

25. Northern Ireland Tourist Board, French Visitors, www.nitb.com/articlePrint. aspx?ArticleID=351.

26. Richard Holt, *Sport & Society in Modern France* (Oxford: Oxford University Press, 1981) remains the best introduction to French sport history; see too the chapter in Robert A. Nye, *Crime, Madness, and Politics in Modern France: The Medical Concept of National Decline* (Princeton: Princeton University Press, 1984), and the chapter by Philip Dine on sport in Hugh Dauncy, ed., *French Popular Culture: An Introduction* (London: Arnold, 2003).

27. For Pérec and Mauresmo, see brief comments by Philip Dine, "Sport" in Hugh Dauncy, ed., *French Popular Culture: An Introduction* (London: Arnold, 2003), 173.

28. See Zidane's profile online at Zinedine Zidane at worldsoccer.about.com/cs/soccerstars/p/zizou.htm.

29. See archives of Soccer Europe.com at soccer at europe.com/Archives/News/2004/December.html.

30. Of course this refers to Ernest Hemingway's classic evocation of the Paris of his youth (the 1920s), from his *A Moveable Feast* (New York: Charles Scribner's Sons, 1964).

5

Cuisine and Fashion

PERHAPS NO OTHER TWO facets of French culture are more synonymous with the nation's fame and greatness than the food and fashion industries. Both embody French flair and creativity at their finest, and both industries remain world leaders and trend setters. The French have been especially ingenious over the last century not only at adapting but also marketing these two industries (so intimately tied to health and appearance) to an international audience. In recent decades the French have developed different strategies to defend and expand their influence. The integrity of a growing number of food and wine products has been carefully regulated in terms of production, preparation, and distribution to ensure France's distinctive alimentary contributions and heritage. In fashion, however, France has increasingly opened its venerable sartorial tradition to an international galaxy of designers and to the mass market. These two divergent strategies have proven able to sustain French primacy in both fields and show the creative specificity and adaptability of French culture in the early twenty-first century.

FOOD

Elite French cuisine (known as haute cuisine) is famous throughout the world and is perhaps the most dominant aspect of French culture today. As noted food historian Stephen Mennell has noted, what the world thinks of as "nouvelle cuisine" is but the most recent revolution/renovation in French food. Not only has French cuisine been extraordinarily innovative and reflective (note the tremendous number of cookbooks, restaurant guides, and philosophical reflections on eating and drinking) but a unique synthesis between foods and wines and a creative tension between Parisian and provincial cuisine has also developed.

The origins of French cuisine's diversity and complexity, as we shall see more fully below, can be found in the nation's unique geographical position. France is the only nation that spans both northern and southern Europe, and it contains an extraordinary richness in local dietary practices. At the same time, the long tradition of a strong centralized state has ensured an overall coherence through a steady interaction between its capital, Paris, and its diverse hinterlands.

The first great renovation in French cuisine occurred in the mid-seventeenth century. In 1651 one of the principal chefs at the kitchen of Marie de Medicis, La Varenne, wrote his *Le Cuisinier François*. This was the first cookbook to list recipes in alphabetical order and to provide instruction in the preparation of vegetables. Cooking meats in their own juices and the deft use of mushrooms and truffles replaced the emphasis on heavy spicing of medieval kitchen. Although natural flavors and the use of chicken, meat, or fish stock were emphasized, sauces were also stressed.

Another great renovation occurred during the French Revolution. Although the first restaurants had opened before the great explosion in 1789, many great chefs moved from palaces to open restaurants in the aftermath of the aristocracy's decline. The middle classes of France increasingly made the consumption and discussion of food and drink a public affair not only in restaurants but also in newspapers and books. Alexandre Grimod de La Reynière (1758–1837), wrote his *Almanach des gourmands* in 1803, Anthelme Brillat-Savarin's (1755–1826) *Physiologie du Gout* (Taste) appeared in 1826, and the highly influential chef Antonin Careme's (1784–1833) *L'Art de la Cuisine Francaise au Dix-Neuvieme Siecle* arrived in 1833. At the end of the nineteenth and start of early twentieth centuries, Auguste Escoffier (1846–1935) updated and simplified this cuisine for the growing hotel restaurant trade.

After 1900, with the rise of the automobile, regional French cuisine achieved unprecedented prominence. The *Michelin Guide* (known also as the *Guide Rouge),* appeared after 1900 and evolved into a vast compendium of restaurant rankings. Adding to the luster of so-called gastronomadism was the work of Austin de Croze in *Les Plats régionaux de France* (1928) and Curnonsky in *Le Tresor Gastronique de France* (1933), which elaborated on the genius of regional cuisine, especially that of Lyon and the southwest. The 1931 Colonial Exposition exposed a large audience to the foods of the French Empire, especially those of Vietnam and North Africa, including couscous. Another monument of French gastronomy (culinary customs) was Prosper Montagne's (1865–1948) *Larousse Gastronomique,* an encyclopedia that covered the history and practice of eating and restaurants and appeared just before the outbreak of World War II in 1938.

Although the privations of World War II forced a return to the basics of cuisine and enhanced the value of simple vegetables and salads, the real renovation in French cuisine happened only after the dramatic modernization of the French economy was well under way, during the early 1970s. As was the case before the war, Lyon remained a gastronomic powerhouse, producing Mother Brazier (who would help train one of the nouvelle cuisine's most famous chefs, Paul Bocuse). Another chef in nearby Vienne, Fernand Point, would also train many of the chefs who would become part of this new school. Moreover, from the early 1950s, the new medium of television played a vital role in renovating *cuisines bourgeois* (cooking in the home). Chefs such as Raymond Oliver, the owner of *Le Grand Vefour* in the Palais Royal of Paris, became household fixtures as they showed French housewives new recipes and cooking styles.

Within a year of the dramatic near-revolution of May–June 1968, in March 1969, H. Gault and C. Millau brought out their *Le Nouveau Guide*. By 1972 they were lauding what quickly became known as "nouvelle cuisine." This new movement took advantage of postwar advances in farming and refrigeration by stressing freshness and the variety of French regional products. Improvements in ovens and steamers resulted in meat and vegetables that retained more of their original flavor and were not overshadowed by the heavy sauces of nineteenth- and early-twentieth-century cuisine. Here the influence of the cuisines of Japan and China were felt. Moreover, artistic presentation of small portions replaced the large plates favored previously. Some of the bibles of this new cuisine were the works of chef Michel Guérard, *La Grande Cuisine Minceur* (1976) and *La Cuisine Gourmand* (1978).[1]

The receptivity of nouvelle cuisine to Asian cooking signaled a large shift in French taste that paralleled the increasing role of immigrants and the growing power of multinational corporations in French life. Immigrants from former French colonies from the Caribbean to Algeria to Vietnam brought their distinctive cuisines. By the mid-1970s, Chinese, Vietnamese, and North African restaurants had spread throughout most of France. Couscous and other North African dishes became a hearty and spicy alternative to French food in much the same way that Mexican food did in the United States. By the 1980s, Thai and Indian cuisine had also become popular. Americanization came to France in the 1970s in the form of McDonalds. By 2005, McDo's (as it has become known in French youth slang) had over 1,000 restaurants and served one million people daily. Nevertheless, the appeal of hamburgers has leveled off: The French now eat eight times more sandwiches than the McDonald's staple, and over the last decade French fast-food outlets have overtaken McDonald's (totaling 1,521 outlets by 2004). In any case snacking or grazing (the French words are *grignotage* and *nomadisme*) at work, at home, or on the go about town has become more fashionable than fast food in recent years among those under 25.[2]

With the traditional three-course meal now accounting for only about 17 percent of dinners and lunches (and mostly among those over the age of 50), it is not surprisingly that recent cuisine trends in France have striven to return to the basics. Over the past 20 years a style of cooking dubbed grandmother's cooking, or country cooking *(cuisine de terroir)*, has become a staple of French cookbooks. The traditional peasant and proletarian soup and stew is at the heart of this cooking. To preserve family recipes across France, Mitterrand's Socialist government created the National Center for Culinary Arts (initials CNAC in French) in the early 1990s. By 1998 the CNAC had published numerous volumes on regional cooking before being closed by the center right government of Raffarin, which came to power in 2002.

Food fears have also been at the heart of some political and cultural movements. The alternative globalist Jose Bové in 1999 gained publicity and immense popularity across France when he attacked a new McDonalds not far from his home in southern France. For Bove and other activists, McDonalds symbolizes and epitomizes the corporate takeover of the world's food supply, with genetic modifications and standardization as the end result. Also current in France today is the slow food movement. Although started by the Italian Carlo Petrini in 1986, the movement became international after the signing of the slow food manifesto at the Opèra Comique in Paris in 1989. Like alternative globalizers, the slow food movement strives to protect biodiversity and sustain local food production and traditional cuisines through the creation of vegetable gardens in schools and the promotion of restaurants that eschew fast food and high prices.[3]

The tensions in French cuisine today revolve around accepting or rejecting the increasingly porous national borders. Philippe Faure, president of Gault Millau, and restaurateur Alain Ducasse have often taken opposite positions. Faure wishes to protect and Ducasse to open up the French palate. The latter has advocated the fusion of cuisines and the restaurateur as a culinary ambassador, the former the maintenance of French tradition.

Perhaps the most famous French chef today is Alain Ducasse; he embodies many of the tensions and opportunities of French cuisine in a global age. This son of the French-peasant South now has a world wide network of twenty plus restaurants and inns and cooking schools, as well as his own publishing imprint *(éditions Alain Ducasse)*. Ducasse is as much a CEO of a corporation as a chef of a traditional restaurant. His restaurants—found not just in France, but in the United States, Europe, Asia, and in North Africa—combine elements of the Nouvelle Cuisines of the 1970s and 1980s with the heartier regional dishes of the 1990s through the early twenty first century, incorporating international influences from Asia, to the United States, to North Africa, or wherever one finds his restaurants (He insists on the freshest local ingredients). In short his restaurants display eclecticism and embrace globalization. Nevertheless, Ducasse continues the French tradition of excellence in cuisine with his school Alain Ducasse Formation (ADF) in the Parisian suburb of Argenteuil, and his annual event Fou de France (literally, mad about French food), for which Doucasse and a committee choose five young chefs to cook for two weeks at his restaurant, Le Relais Plaza in the Hotel Plaza Athenée Paris.

At age 33, Ducasse was the youngest chef to receive Michelin's three stars for a restaurant and later became the first to have three, three star restaurants. By 2003, his global empire employed over 950 people and earned 21 million euros with 20 restaurants world wide. In December 2003 Forbes magazines placed him among the 100 most richest celebrities of world (the only French person on the list) at 91st place with a revenue equivalent of 5.5 million dollars.[4]

Amidst these changes in theory and practice among haute cuisine, ordinary French people dine in an increasingly dichotomous fashion in an increasingly harried world. On the one hand, for ordinary meals during the workday they may have fast food, snack, or prepare simple meals at home. On the other hand, on weekends they tend to prepare more elaborate meals for family gatherings. With busy working schedules, however, French women no longer have time for the long preparations in the kitchen that once were a hallmark of French food: Time spent preparing food fell from 42 minutes in 1998 to 36 minutes in 2001 and for weekend meals dropped from 60 minutes in 1988 to 44 in 2001. Women remain (at 91 percent of the time) the overwhelming cooks in the home, with 72 percent saying they work alone in the kitchen. This is one reason why by 2005 one in every five meals in France is eaten outside the home.[5]

In general, French food consumption has become lighter and more discriminating as the country has modernized and moved from an agricultural to an industrial and now a service and information-based economy. With the reduction in manual labor the number of calories needed per day has dropped from an average of 3,000–3,500 in 1900 to between 1,700 and 2,000 today. Food now plays a much less prominent role in the average individual and family budget, accounting for only 14 percent of expenses today as compared to more than double that amount (28.6 percent) in 1960. Between 1970 and 2001, moreover, the French increased their consumption of fresh fruit and vegetables and decreased their consumption of bread, meat, and potatoes. Indeed, the French eat more fresh fruit than any other nation in Europe. By 2005 the nouvelle cuisine values of freshness, presentation, and taste topped the list of the qualities the French found most appealing about food. Moreover, by 2005 the French drank almost as much Appellation of Controlled Origin (AOC) wine—the rate had more than tripled between 1970 and 2001—as they did the lesser qualities—whose rate of consumption had declined by two-thirds. The Appellation of Controlled Origin (Appellation d'Origine Contrôlée) is a French wine classification system by which wines are produced under rigorously controlled guidelines to maintain consistent levels of quality.

Overall, between 1960 and 2001 wine consumption fell from 174.3 to 78.9 liters per year per individual, and the number who considered themselves regular consumers of wine plummeted from 47 percent of the population in 1980 to just under one-quarter by 2000. During these same years the French doubled their consumption of sodas and mineral waters and saw an even higher rate of increase for fruit juices. One trend that France has not followed is vegetarianism or veganism. While the United Kingdom counts 6.1 percent of its citizens and the United States 2.5 percent of its as vegetarian or vegan, France has just a little under 1 percent.[6]

Tracing the culinary geography of France today concretizes the above generalizations and illuminates the interaction between cultures and classes across centuries. France can be divided into five regions and explored via some of the most characteristic foods, wines, and dishes. France was an early pioneer in essentially copyrighting its regional products. As far back as 1415 King Charles VI defined the burgundy wine region by dividing it into an upper and a lower portion (from the bridge in the city of Sens); in 1666 the high court (called a *parlement* in Old Regime France) of Toulouse codified the composition of Roquefort cheese. In 1855 at the International Exposition in Paris, Bordeaux's leading wine merchants categorized the region's leading wines into 61 varieties. Burgundy's wine regions received a similar sort of classification in 1905. But only with the law of May 1919 did the complete system of regulated wine districts (that is AOC) come into being law for the protection of place of origin, and then in July 1935 the National Institute of Place of Origin (INAO, Institut national des Appellation d'origin) was formed. The reach of this law has been steadily expanded from wine to a wide variety of other products, all of which carry a seal of authenticity and have become icons of regional identity.

The northwest, especially Brittany and Normandy, is famous for dishes involving seafood, cream, crepes, and apples. The French believe Breton lobsters to be the best in the world, and one of the great specialties is lobsters in tomato-cream sauce *(homard a l'armoricaine)*. Some say that this dish is really *a l'americaine,* either from the United States or from the Caribbean, but like many recipes the exact history is not known. That is not the case with *sole Normande,* sole with shellfish and mushrooms in a cream sauce, which was developed in the early nineteenth century in Paris and is now a staple in the cooking schools. Cream is central to northern cooking, and there is an AOC for cream and butter in this region, the only place in France. Breton crepes are distinctive due to use of buckwheat (brought back to France by the crusaders who found this fruit, which is related to sorrel and rhubarb, in the holy land). Once the food of the poor, buckwheat is now a gourmet delicacy at upscale creperies.

Northeast, in terms of cuisine often is taken to include the arc that moves from Flanders on the English Channel, to Paris, then to Alsace on the German border. As one would expect this large area contains a rich and diverse set of dishes, from the mussels and French fries (the potato was first eaten in France here) of Flanders, Picardy, and Artois; to the onion soup of the Parisian food markets; to Alsatian sauerkraut, which was especially prominent in Paris after the province was annexed by Germany (1871–1918). These are foods that appeal to all classes, for example the legendary gourmet Jean Anthelme Brillat-Savarin called sauerkraut, along with foie gras, the "gastronomic litmus test of gentlemen."

The Center is France's great pasture for cattle and pigs. The cattle of Charlolais are considered France's best and this locality is the home of beef burgundy, a hearty meal for farmers and workers that has also become an elite dish when the best cuts of meat are paired with the best wines. Lyon competes with Paris for the right to call itself the capital of French cuisine. This city on the Rhone and near the Alps counts Paul Bocuse among its many distinguished chefs, who was proclaimed by Gault Millau as best chef of twentieth century. The Massif Central's plateau also features hearty dishes, but even here in heart of France, fish can be found. For example, Estofindo, in the Aveyron region is a dish featuring dried cod. Few women have the time to prepare this dish in the home so it has become a restaurant and café staple and is still usually served on Sundays. Other Averyronais specialties include *aligot* (pureed potatoes with cheese) or *truffade* (sautéed potatoes with melted cheese and cream). Michel Bras, at his world renowned restaurant atop the Laguiole highlands, takes the diner through an "aligot journey" of over a thousand years of variation in this dish. In the neighboring Auvergne region, Potee Auvergne, which is pork and cabbage in bullion, is another fortifying meal beloved since the time of Vercingetroix, and dear to generations of the region's peasants. These dishes, like so many in France began as staples of the working class diet but steadily moved upscale as they were brought to Paris by immigrants and became featured in cookbooks.

In the southeast we find the cuisine of olive oil, citruses, and garlic. There is much diversity here too. On the one hand there is the famous Marseille fish stew, bouillabaisse, which began as a fisherman's snack. By time of the belle époque, however, it had become a fixture of upper class restaurant tourist trade. On the other hand, there is the fondue of the Savoy region which also began as a peasant food; it was brought down from the mountains by some of the first waves of tourists in the eighteenth century. Even though fondue is now world renowned, it is still usually consumed in a family setting, rather than in restaurants. The southwest is also famous for its AOC chickens of Bresse and the great dish, *poulet à la crème bresse.* The fame of these chickens goes back at least to the time of Henry IV (who promised to ensure that every French family had a chicken in their pot on Sunday), and on to the great gourmets Brillat-Savarin and Curnonsky, who in 1933, praised one of Bresse's restaurateurs, Marie Blanc, as the best cook in the world. Her grandson, Georges, continues to serve this dish to international acclaim even now in the early twenty first century. This region's chickens—perfect national icon with their red crests, white plumage, and blue feet—are celebrated in annual autumn festivals, known as the *Glorieuses,* in such towns as Bourg-en Bresse, Louhand, Montrevel, and Pont-de-Vaux. Moving further down the south eastern coast to Nice, one finds the pissaladiere tart (onion olive oil and anchovies), which is something like a pizza. The AOC olives also used in this region have been renowned since Roman times. Finally, the island of Corsica is especially well known for its *fiadone,* a flourless cheese and lemon cake. The island also boasts some AOC cheeses and the famous Corsican lemon, with its distinctive hearty luminous yellow appearance.

The southwest contains more AOC and IGP products than any other region; IGP stands for *indication géographique protégée* (protected geographic designation). The rise to prominence of this area can be tied to European encounters with the Americas, in particular in the use of corn, but also tomatoes and pimentos from the "New World." Corn products make its chickens and geese so flavorful. Classic dish like confits and cassoulets abound, the latter cooked slowly in special pots in which the interaction between beans and meat transforms both into one of the great French dishes. Prosper Montagné, who started the *Larousse Gastronomique,* summed up both the power of this dish and its regional variations: "Cassoulet is the God of Occitane cuisine; God the father is the cassoulet of Castelnaudary, God the Son comes from Carcassonne, and God the Hold Ghost emanates from Toulouse." For centuries, dating again to the Romans, the foie gras of this region has been cherished by the European elite; its production now centers in the town of Gers. While Bresse may be famous for its chickens, the *poulet au pot* of Béarn of his native province is what Henry IV had in mind. Here, too, fall festivals celebrate this regional chicken. Finally, along the border with Spain the Basque tart combines onions, tomatoes, and sweet pimentos—a synthesis of the oldest people of Europe with innovations from afar.

French cuisine today presents not only the diversity we have seen above but also tragedy and paradox. Tragedy in that the "diamond of cookery," according to Brillat-Savarin—the truffle—has become so much harder to find. This dark and pungent tuber, rooted out by specially trained dogs and pigs, two centuries ago cost less than a tomato, and just a century ago had an annual harvest of 1,320 tons, with 60 percent coming from the southwest. Today harvests average little more than 30 to 40 tons.[7] Damage due to wartime decimation of southern forests, land clearing due to acid rain, and a decline in farming are the usual explanations for this tragic collapse. The paradox of French cuisine, most famously propounded on the news show *60 Minutes,* is that a nation that consumes so much saturated fats (in the form of foie gras and confits, for example) has such a low rate of coronary heart disease. An initial hypothesis held that drinking red wine thinned the blood and prevented high cholesterol. Although many researchers are now dubious of such an explanation, since the obesity rate in France is climbing, the hypothesis, nevertheless, demonstrates the intimate link between food and wine in the French diet.[8]

No consideration of French cuisine would be complete without an overview of French wine. In no other cuisine has the melding of wine and food become so sophisticated. After Italy, France produces the most wine in the world. The immense varieties of grapes grown in France are now, due to the AOC, arranged into the following four classifications:

AOC (wine of precise origin): most elite wines; grapes raised in meticulously graded *terroirs* (based on soil and microclimates); grape type and level of alcohol very much tied to French chateau mode of production; especially found in Burgundy and Bordeaux.

AOVDQS (wine of high-quality origin): regulated by the INAO; emphasis more on zone than a specific plot of ground.

Vin de Pays (country wine): emphasis on using just one type of grape rather than a specific plot or zone (regulated by the Conseil Interprofessionnel organization of the wine growers in this category).

Vin de table (table wine): remainder of wine production; about 70 percent of production specially regulated; alcohol content must be between 8.5 percent and 15 percent.

The first two are the elite wines and the second two are ordinary wines. Over the last 40 years, two vital trends in French wine consumption have been noted: a growing consumption of higher-quality wine and a steady decline in overall consumption.

A regional tour of French wine regions illustrates these changes. The two leading regions, Bordeaux and Burgundy, have remained as powerful as ever and have not suffered much due to high quality and an assured export market.

Although trailing Burgundy in the number of AOC wines, Bordeaux has the lead in elite wine exports. Although this southwestern region facing the

Atlantic contains over 7,000 chateaus, it is renowned especially for the "big five" chateaus of Lafite Rothschild, Mouton Rothschild, Lafite, Latour, and Haut-Brion. Most wine tasters still consider the red wines of this region to be the best, or at least the standard by which all other red wines are measured. (But the region also produces such varied and classic white wines as the sweet Sauternes, its name classified in 1855, and the dry Graves.) The most important grape is cabernet sauvignon, which is usually mixed with Merlot and in smaller amounts with Cabernet Franc, Malbec, and Petite Verdot grapes. The region currently contributes 34 percent of the total value of all French wine exports.

The golden hills (hence the name *cote d'or)* of Burgundy deserve the name because this area produces more AOC wines than any other region (180 as compared to 84 in Bordeaux). This diverse region's most famous grapes are Pinot Noir for Reds and Chardonnay for whites. The most famous vineyard is Clos de Vougeot, known for its extraordinary variety in wines, with 80 producers. The largest number of Grand Cru reds are found in the vineyards of Gevrey-Chambertin: Chambertin, Chambertin-Clos de Beze, Chapelle-Chambertin, Charmes (or Mazoyeres)-Chambertin, Griotte-Chambertin, Latricieres-Chambertin, Mazis-Chambertin, and Ruchottes-Chambertin. Elite Burgundy vintners perfectly embody artisanal and specialty wine-making, since many vintners produce only 1,000 bottles annually.

Just south of Burgundy is the Beaujolais region. The principal grape in use is the gamy, which goes into its light red wine (Beaujolais); its wines of a higher quality are known as Beaujolais-Villages. It has 41 AOC wines, including Chenas, Fleurie, Chiroubles, Morgan, Brouilly, Cote de Brouilly, St-Amor, and Julienas. Perhaps the most famous moment of any year for this region is when its internationally known first harvest wine, Beaujolais, comes on the market in the third week of November. This ritual first spread to Paris after World War II, and by the 1960s the now famous marketing phrase "Beaujolais has arrived" *(Le Beaujolais Nouveau est arrive)* emerged. Today this phrase is heard around the world.

Moving south, the Rhone Valley also contains much diversity. While the red Syrah and the white grape Viognier prevail in the more temperate north, the red Grenache grape becomes prevalent in the hotter south, along with the white Marsanne and Roussanne grapes. In total there are 40 AOC wines in this region, the most famous of which is Chateauneuf de Pape (which includes 13 types of reds and whites) and is named after the vineyard that supplied the papacy when it was located in nearby Avignon. It was one of the first wines consecrated when the AOC was established.

The southeast coast of Provence and the island of Corsica have not traditionally been a center of fine wine production, but this has been changing recently. The region has only 17 AOC delimited wines, and 80 percent of the wine produced is the underrated rosé (half of all the rosé produced in France). Recently, with the decline in wine consumption in France and with stiff international competition, Provençal vintners have planted Syrah and Cabernet Sauvignon grapes.

To the west is the Languedoc Roussillon region, one of the largest in the world and the traditional home of *vin de table* and *vin de pays*. The Grenache grape is dominant. Recently this region has achieved much success in upgrading its quality to meet shifting French tastes and a more competitive international market. Now there are 48 wines with the AOC mark, including Corbieres, Cotes du Roussillon, and Cotes du Roussillon-Villages. The region also produces sweet dessert wines such as Muscat de St-Jean de Minervois.

North of Bordeaux is the Loire Valley, essentially the northern limit of French wine production today. Home of popular red and white wines, the region has 68 AOC wines. Its white wines are especially well known and include Sauvignon Blanc, Chenin Blanc, Vouvray, Sancere, Muscadet, and Pouilly-Fume. These moderately priced wines have become a staple of restaurants in France and around the world.

The Paris region once had a vigorous wine production before the railroad brought the bulk production of the south to the capital. Today the small vineyard behind the Sacred Heart Basilica on Montmartre is just about all that is left of the capital's wine-making tradition, although some intrepid Parisian wine lovers do grow grapes on their balconies. There is even an AOC available for these small scale balcony wines!

Moving across France from west to east we come to the Champagne region. It should first be noted that this word originally meant chalky soil. This type of soil is found not only in the home of sparkling wine production but also in the brandy-producing region north of Bordeaux known as Cognac. This why on Cognac bottles you see the term fine champagne; it refers to the soil and not to the drink. Chardonnay and the red wine grape pinot noir are the main grapes used. Champagne gains its bubbles by undergoing a secondary fermentation when yeast and sugar are added. Much care is then need to remove sediment of the dead yeast. The capital of the Champagne region is Reims (Rheims). The most famous names are Dom Perignon, Taittinger, Veuve Cliquot, Mumm, Mercier, and Perrier. Historians have shown recently that champagne makers were as skilled as manufacturing the myth of the blind monk Dom Perignon, who supposedly created the first bottle, as they were at persuading the Anglo-American elite after the fall of Napoleon that no party, wedding, or celebration would be complete without this "natural" symbol of festivity and sophistication. Labeling can be confusing, because the terms demi-sec (literally half-dry) and extra dry refer to varying degrees of sweetness. Brut (literally raw or unrefined) is the driest of champagnes.

East of Champagne are the wines of Alsace. The wines of this region, of largely German ethnicity and French heritage, provide a palpable taste of cultural synthesis. Its wines have an unmistakable German taste, due to the use of Riesling and Gewurztraminer grapes, but have a drier taste than is found among German wines. These two grapes are the most elite and compose most of the 61 AOC wines of the region. Pinot blanc and pinot gris grapes are used for the more simple wines.

With the sharp decline in French wine consumption, the nation's wine industry is at a crossroads. Increasingly it must turn to the global marketplace. In recent years much effort has been expended on opening up the wine market in India and China. Nevertheless, much wine is also being turned into industrial alcohol, and French wine producers, outside of the most famous vineyards, periodically demonstrate against the decline in their fortunes.[9]

FASHION

Although not as dominant as a century ago, French fashion is still at the top of the clothing industry around the world. This follows a tradition of sartorial splendor dating especially from the age of Louis XIV. From the Sun King's reign through to France today, Paris has especially dominated women's fashions, the most important part of the market, though often having to take a backseat to England, Italy, or recently the United States in men's fashions. A constant stream of innovators in haute couture (whose customer base for handmade and individually crafted clothes totals only about 3,000), a steady democratization with ready-to-wear *(prêt a porter),* and more recently leisure wear has ensured that France remains the formidable presence in the fashion world. The ability to combine elegance with social relevance is still being shown as a new generation of designers has recently reenergized the fashion industry and put Paris back on top in the middle of the first decade of the twenty-first century.

Under Louis XIV (ruled 1643–1715) France became the arbiter not only of diplomacy but also of fashion. Even when the French Revolution (1789–1799) toppled his descendants, the nation still set the fashion patterns. It would be in France that a revolution in men's fashion, the adoption of the pant and the discarding of the knee britches as standard wear, would first take place and then spread around the world. But across the nineteenth and twentieth centuries, London, Rome, Milan, or New York would vie or overtake Paris in men's fashion.

The nineteenth century witnessed the consolidation of France's dominance of women's fashion. Under Napoleon's rule (1799–1815) women's fashion revived. Joseph-Marie Jacquard's eponymous loom, which was in use by 1801, allowed for a greater diversity in the color, patterns, and ornamentation in women's clothes. As machine production progressed, fashion houses invented ready-to-wear outfits. The Parisian firm Gagelin innovated in this market, which was still rather restricted in the mid-nineteenth century. One of their designers, a young English émigré, Charles Worth, created his own "house" at the end of the 1850s, becoming the first fashion designer to sign his products. His innovative grasp of design and production would result in a new word being invented for his work: "couturier." Despite these mid-century innovations, women's fashion during the nineteenth century was tied to the corset and to an opulent use of fabric, making women's clothing ornamental rather than utilitarian (as were men's fashions). Indeed, seldom if ever in the history of human fashion have gender differences been as complete as they were during the nineteenth century.[10]

One of the most perceptive observers of the Paris fashion system of the late nineteenth century was the novelist Emile Zola. In *The Ladies' Paradise* he opulently observed how the modern department stores of Paris had become theaters of fashion in which upper-class women competed with each other not only in the art of conspicuous consumption but also in competitive display. Novelists such as Marcel Proust and Henry James elaborated on how the system had become refined and internalized as thousands of tourists flocked to Paris in the belle époque.[11]

A revolution in women's fashion emerged at the start of World War I (1914). It is ironic that French women would win their freedom from the corset long before they would gain the vote in France (1946). Designers Paul Poiret, Madeleine Vionnet, and Coco Chanel all rebelled against the corset. Opening his fashion house in 1904, Poiret created a revolution in women's fashion by discarding the multiple petticoats and creating a "straight-line" dress that virtually ended the need for a corset, the staple of nineteenth-century women's fashion. (He advocated substituting the girdle and brassiere.) With his tightly cut "hobble skirts," Poiret created a scandal by displaying women's legs. Poiret also drew upon contemporary artists such as Paul Iribe and Georges Lepape as illustrators and worked with painter Raoul Dufy at art exhibitions. In 1912 he produced the first modern fashion show. In the same year he introduced "harem pants," which women could wear in the home, inspired by the fashions of Asia, especially Turkey and Russia (in an age when Stravinsky's music for Serge Diaghilev's *Ballets Russes* had whetted Parisian taste for the exotic). With his use of non-European motifs and by putting women in pants, Poiret pointed the way to the future of twentieth-century fashion. Right before World War I, Madeleine Vionnet's house consolidated Poiret's revolution by creating women's clothes tailored to the body. The natural, rather than the artificial, would become another motif of twentieth-century fashion.

Although starting on the eve of World War I, Coco Chanel would come into her own after this terrible bloodletting and would merely be the most prominent among a large number of women fashion designers. Chanel would add an elegant and daring touch to the casual and simpler styles of women's dress that emerged as social constraints fell after years of privation and slaughter. Moreover, she ventured into perfume with her classic Chanel No. 5, launched in 1922. In 1925 she introduced her inimitable cardigan jacket, and in 1926 her "little black dress." Like her perfume, these clothes have become classics, even though in their own time they blurred gender boundaries (women wearing jackets) and social customs (the long dresses of the prewar era).

Although dominant, Chanel's influence did not inhibit other French fashion designers in the 1920s. While Jean Patou was another designer innovating in casual clothing in the interwar period, Madelein Vionnet sustained her own line signature style of elegant dresses. The most serious challenger to Chanel's elevated status was Elsa Schiaparelli. One of Schiaparelli's first innovations was to upgrade the fashion status of the sweater. Fascinated by the iconoclastic artistic movement surrealism, she became especially famous for using such colors as "shocking pink," "ice blue," or for creating a hat shaped like a shoe. She was also the first designer to use the zipper and synthetic fabrics in haute couture fashion. Like Chanel, Schiaparelli, too, would branch out into perfumes as well as jewelry and swimwear.

World War II, resulting in the Nazi occupation of France for four years, made French fashion unavailable. Moreover, the protofascist and puritanical Vichy collaborationist regime frowned on the innovations that had made France famous in the interwar period. The rationing and shortage of the immediate postwar era made some doubt the ability of French fashion to rebound.

Christian Dior, however, emerged in 1947 as French fashion's "savior." He would also be part of a new generation of prominent male designers. Subsidized by a major textile manufacturer, Marcel Boussac, Dior's "new look" brought elegance and opulence back to women's fashion. Dior's dresses deemphasized the shoulders but showcased the hips and legs and brought back into fashion corsets (built into the dresses) and petticoats. One of his new look dresses could use up to 30 yards of cloth. Throughout the 1950s his style would achieve dominance across the developed world. For example, in 1954 his sales accounted for two-thirds of French fashion's total exports. Dior's fashions, originally intended for elite fashion, became by the end of the decade the style of middle-class housewives and would inspire dozens of imitators who mass-produced his clothes for the growing number of affluent consumer during the post–World War II boom. This highly feminine look was also developed and tied to the world of cinema through such designers as

Hubert de Givenchy and Pierre Balmain. De Givenchy became famous for dressing Audrey Hepburn and Balmain for dressing Marlene Dietrich.

But Dior did not totally set the pattern for high fashion in the 1950s. Returning to favor in 1954, after controversy over her actions in German-occupied Paris in the early 1940s, Coco Chanel reasserted her style with the Chanel suit. Before her death in 1971 she would also revolutionize women's fashion with pea jackets and bell-bottom pants. Thus she set in place many of the fashion accessories that would become central to women's increased role in business and leisure outside of the home.

The long-standing fashion designer and Spanish émigré Christóbal Balenciaga by the 1950s had turned his emphasis on the woman's silhouette into a series of long flowing chemise dresses that deemphasized the curves central to the new look. In the last years of the 1950s he would come out with dresses that looked like Japanese kimonos and a "sac" dress. In the last year of his life, Dior shocked the fashion world by also coming out with a "sac" dress that seemed to contradict his previous emphasis on femininity but was a harbinger for the 1960s fashion revolution.

Yves Saint Laurent, who would take over the House of Dior after the master's death, anticipated much of the transformation that the turbulent 1960s would bring. For example, in 1961 he would move his headquarters from the traditional home of couture, the Right Bank, to the Left Bank, the center of intellectual life and artistic creation. He would also develop a mass-produced ready-to-wear collection of clothes in 1966 with his business partner Pierre Berge. This line would spur an unprecedented democratization of high fashion that almost all other Parisian couturiers would follow. He opened his own retail stores and sold the rights to sell his clothes to a number of department stores. Across the 1960s and 1970s, Saint Laurent would integrate abstract art—with his "Mondrian" dress (named after the abstract artist Piet Mondrian)—youth culture, pop art, political protest, and gender bending, such as his tuxedo suit, into women's fashions.

The 1960s also became know for its attention to the rapidly grown-up baby boomers, its emphasis on revealing the body with miniskirts, and its use of synthetic materials. André Courrèges was one of the first to design the miniskirt, in 1961; he would bring out bell-bottom pants in 1962, and then a pantsuit. In 1964 he launched a futurist "Moon Girl" line, with a signature white minidress and white vinyl boots. Michelle Rosier received the nickname "vinyl girl" for her innovations with that and other new materials that transformed clothing manufacture. Spanish émigré Paco Rabanne and Pierre Cardin also drew upon motifs from the space age. While Rabanne used plastic and metal in his dresses. Cardin experimented with one-piece jumpsuits. Cardin, like Yves Saint Laurent, would turn his name into a brand. Finally, a more political twist was found in the work of Emmanuelle Khanh, who designed clothes inspired by the "Mod" London's Carnaby Street and Kings Road—in part inspired by Beatlemania and by the "street." She wished to create "a socialist kind of fashion for the grand mass."

Following the events of May–June 1968, high fashion found itself out of fashion. Indeed, despite the continued importance of fashion in French life, the percentage of the family budget devoted to clothing has fallen steady since the 1970s: from 9.7 percent in 1960 to 8.1 percent in 1970, 6.1 percent in 1980, 5.4 percent in 1990, and 3.8 percent 2001. (Expenditure over the same period for hotels, cafés, and restaurants has held steady.)

A French variant of Anglo-American "hippie" styles became popular. Known as "baba cool," blue jeans, shawls, and dresses from Third-World countries were some of the favorites of a generation that rejected consumer society with its ever-shifting fashions. Not surprising, sharp criticism greeted the attempt by French fashion designers in 1970 to end the reign of the mini-skirt. Although hemlines would drop over the succeeding years, women increasingly adopted the pantsuit as they increasingly went into the workforce. Saint Laurent once again capitalized with a new line, but one of the most emblematic of designers in the 1970s would be Sonia Rykiel, dubbed the "Coco Chanel of the 1970s" for her creative knitwear that was relaxed and casual, yet distinctive. Also in the 1970s, the immigrant Japanese designer Kenzo Takada would blend the traditions of peasant clothing of both the West and the East into a distinctive earthy but elegant style. By the late 1970s and early 1980s a French protoyuppie style emerged know in French by the initials BCBG (bon chic, bon genre; or good style, good sort). Agnès Troublé filled the same niche in France that Ralph Lauren occupied in America, in terms of a subdued yet standard appeal to tasteful elegance.

The next major wave of French fashion, however, would begin in the mid-1970s, especially with such figures as Jean Paul Gaultier. Influenced both by British Punk and by the emerging gender-bending potential in the gay, lesbian, and transgender liberation movements, Gaultier created clothing that mixed the traditions of male and female fashions into a new synthesis. For example, his coats for men included corset lacing, and the brassiere he created for Madonna's 1990 Blond Ambition tour included metal pointed cones. Gaultier proved that his provocations could have long-lasting appeal, and he helped restore the luster of French fashion in the 1980s. By 2004 Gaultier had breathed new life into another French fashion institution, Hermes.

Two other central designers showed the growing multiculturalism of haute couture: Azzedine Alaïa, from Tunisia, and Karl Lagerfeld, from Germany. Like Thierry Mugler and Claude Montana, Alaïa designed close-fitting clothing that emphasized the body. According to fashion scholar Valerie Steel, his "dresses fit like a second skin." What made him so central was not only his genius at design but also his ability to use new materials, such as Lycra and viscose. Karl Lagerfeld, already famous at the couture house Chloé since 1964, moved to the slumping house of Chanel in 1982. His opulent revival and updating of the Chanel suit, a ready-to-wear one costing over $3,000 and a custom-made one going for as much as $16,000, was in perfect synchronicity with a "decade of greed."

The apogee of 1980s fashion in France perhaps came in 1987 when Christian Lacroix opened his own fashion house with skirts that recalled Dior's "new look." The media buzz indicated that fashion had regained the luster that had been eclipsed in the 1970s. Like Saint Laurent and Cardin before him, Lacroix soon created his own mass-market brand.

Lacroix's new company anticipated a feature that would become common in the 1990s through to the early twenty-first century, the growing incorporation of fashion houses into multinational corporations. Bernard Arnault, chairman of LVMH (Louis Vuitton, Moët Hennessy) not only bankrolled Lacroix but would go on to buy the Givenchy and Dior houses. In the late 1990s Yves Saint Laurent's house would be bought by the Gucci Group (much to Saint Laurent's chagrin), and in 2004 Gucci was bought by the French conglomerate of Pinault-Printemps-Redoute. Today, of the 20 top haute couturiers, only Alaïa remains independent.

At the same time as powerful, large corporations had made themselves felt, a growing globalization of French fashion has also been in evidence. In recent years, the American Marc Jacobs at Luis Vuitton, the Britons Stella McCartney and then Phoebe Philo at Chloé, Roberto Menichetti at Celine, Alexander McQueen at Givenchy, John Galliano at Dior, Stefano Pilati at Yves Saint Laurent, the Belgian Oliver Theyskens at Rochas, and the Israeli Alber Elbaz at Lanvin have rejuvenated these storied French houses. Like so much else in French culture, these designers draw upon the fashions of the past century in an eclectic and creative mix. Fashion today, like so much else in contemporary culture, seems scattered and variegated, suiting the tastes of an increasingly global marketplace. Through adaptation and flexibility French fashion seems well set to continue to be a major if not the central player in world fashion for the coming century.

Paris fashion in the middle of the first decade of the twenty-first century has been able to utilize all the strengths of its surroundings. French intellectuals continue to explore, in the tradition of Roland Barthes, the meaning of fashion in contemporary life. One of the most challenging analyses is by Gilles Lipovetsky in his book *The Empire of Fashion: Dressing Modern Democracy*. Here he explores the paradox of fashion in an age growing simultaneously both more culturally diverse and more individualistic and builds on his previous work on how notions of identity and character of become increasingly diffuse in modern society (see his earlier book *The Era of the Void*). While the city's monuments and museums ground its designers in a broad artistic tradition, its multicultural population has now fully internalized the tolerance and informality of the 1960s and 1970s without losing a keen appreciation for elegance and display. As a result, both designers and the city's population have embraced clothes that are simultaneously haute-couture elegant and ready-to-wear practical. Marc Jacobs attributes much of his success to being out and about in Paris and not "living in a bubble." For Anna Wintour, editor of U.S. *Vogue*, "Marc's genius is to show that luxury can be young, fun, and cool. It's not about looking rich. It's about the most luxurious version of your most wearable pieces."

The city's fashion-concept stores and cafés can become an extension of the runways of the fashion shows, because these are the venues upon which the fashions of the day, much as in the ages of Louis XIV or Emile Zola, are displayed and evaluated. Opened eight year ago, the Right Bank shop Colette is, according to the *New York Times*, "where the chic" roost. But the same sort of "human peacocks" can also be found at Mona on the Left Bank, Erotokritos in the Right Bank Marais district, and in the stores in the Maria Luisa and L'Eclaireur chains that dot Paris. These small-scale shops must be acutely attuned to the latest fashion trends to survive.

Indeed the French are keenly aware in an age of growing globalization in general and Chinese domination of the textile industry in particular that they must be ever more creative. As Didier Grumbach, president of the Chambre Syndicale, charged with directing French fashion, remarked, even after the hugely successful 2005 March fashion week: "Our own market is much too small to survive without export; if we don't export we die." Realization that creativity must be constantly stoked has led to a dramatic increase in innovative textile designs. One entrepreneur, Lucien Deveau, has noted: "New fashion must be delivered faster to avoid becoming out-moded by the passage of time or by copies, since China—on its domestic and regional markets—can quickly copy our creations." As a result, "today we bring out 5,000 designs a year, 20 a day. Formerly 200 to 300 designs a year already had seemed enormous."[12]

To retain or gain global market share French fashion designers now sell online and have opened designer boutiques in such American chains as Neiman Marcus (for example, Yves Saint Laurent, Chanel, and Christian Dior). Estee Lauder, already present in 130 countries, has recently brought American fashion designer Tom Ford in to create a line of products that will synthesize the fashion and beauty industries.

Thus French fashion, like its food and wine industries, is keenly aware of the new rules of a global marketplace and at least for now has adapted brilliantly.

Even if success does not remain as palpable in later years, Lisa Armstrong, fashion editor of the *Times* of London, correctly notes the decisive role the French have played in creating an international code for both food and fashion:

Just as the original principles of French cuisine mean you can now dine like a king in Sydney and get a decent meal in London, the obsessive, sometimes indulgent but always technically brilliant creative outbursts of French couture mean that what we buy in Zara, Gap or Holt Renfrew are that much better than they would have been without couture at an apex.[13]

NOTES

1. John Marks, "Food" in Hugh Dauncy, ed., *French Popular Culture: An Introduction* (London: Arnold, 2003), 178–192.

2. For recent data see French data from the hotel industry: www.coachomnium. com/presse/chainesrestau2005.htm.

3. For an overview of Bove and the slow food movement, see Jose Bove and François Dufour, *The World Is Not for Sale: Farmers against Junk Food,* trans. Anna de Casparis and interviews by Gilles Luneau (London: Verso, 2002); for slow food manifesto see the numerous slow food websites, such as www.slowfood.com/eng/sf_cose/ statuti/sf_statuto_manifesto.lasso; for an overview of the movement including activities in France, see Carl Honore, *In Praise of Slowness: How a Worldwide Movement Is Challenging the Cult of Speed* (San Francisco: Harper San Francisco, 2000).

4. Paul Lewis, *Alain Ducasse: histoire d'un succès mondial* (Paris: Saint Honoré Media, 2005), 157

5. For data, see Gérard Mermet, *Francoscopie: Pour comprendre les français 2005* (Paris: Larousse, 2004), 187 and 197.

6. "Global News Round Up," The International Vegetarian Union (IVU): http://www.ivu.org/news/95-96/general.html. also see the European Vegetarian Union's site: www.europeanvegetarian.org/lang/en/info/howmany.php.

7. For a range of figures on yearly truffle harvest see Hannah Beech Hama, "Truffle Kerfuffle, Chinese 'Pig-Snout' Fungi Are Flooding Gourmet-Food Market, and the French Are Not Amused," *Time Asia Magazine,* February 21, 2005; *The Truffle FAQ: The Basics,* members.tripod.com/~BayGourmet/trufflebas.html; and Rosario Safina and Judith Sutton, *Truffles: Ultimate Luxury, Everyday Pleasure* (New York: Wiley, 2002).

8. One of the first books on the subject was Lewis Perdue, *French Paradox and Beyond: Living Longer with Wine and the Mediterranean Lifestyle* (Sonoma, CA: Renaissance Pub., 1992), appearing in the same year as the *60 Minutes* report. The following year Gene Ford applied it to wine drinking in *The French Paradox & Drinking for Health* (San Francisco, CA: Wine Appreciation Guild, 1993). The publishing trend continues with Will Clower, *The Fat Fallacy: The French Diet Secrets to Permanent Weight Loss* (New York: Three Rivers Press, 2003) and most recently the best-selling

Mireille Guiliano, *French Women Don't Get Fat: The Secret of Eating for Pleasure* (New York: Knopf, 2004). On the rise of the obesity rate in France is Celestine Bohlen, "French Diet Advice Book, U.S. Bestseller, Is Ignored at Home," November 4, 2005, Bloomberg.com/Europe. It is generally agreed that the obesity rate is rising as the French and other southern Europeans move away from their traditional cuisine. Charles Bremner, "Ooh la lard! Now even the French are getting fatter" *The London Times*, April 11, 2005. Accessed at http://www.timesonline.co.uk/article/0,,8122-1563822,00.html

9. For recent alcohol consumption statistics see H. Leifman, "Alcohol Consumption in the European Union," 26th Alcohol Epidemiology Symposium of the Kettil Bruun . . . , 2000; sofi.su.se/EUPRES7.PDF. For French efforts in India see the website for the India Brand Equity Foundation (http://www.ibef.org/aboutus.aspx) and see especially the article on December 16, 2005, "Food and wine: The French target India." For French and their "active offices" in China see *Wine Business Online—News & Information for the Wine Industry* (www.winebusiness.com) and especially see the article by M. David Levin, "China Wants Wine: Shanghai-Brush Up on Your Chopsticks Technique."

10. The following narrative draws heavily upon Valerie Steele, *Paris Fashion: A Cultural History*, 2nd rev. ed. (1988; New York: Berg Publishers, 1998).

11. Emile Zola, *The Ladies' Paradise*, trans. unknown (Berkeley: University of California Press, 1992); see especially the superb introduction by Kristen Ross.

12. Guy Trebay, "Paris Is Entitled to Sniff" *New York Times*, March 13, 2005, section 9, p 1.

13. For all points about Paris fashion in 2005 see Guy Trebay, "Paris Is Entitled to Sniff." *New York Times*, March 13, 2005, section 9, p 1. See also the article in *Time Europe* (April 14, 2002).

In the shadow of the Eiffel Tower, we see the extensive nature of the museum and conference complex that surround the Tower, whose shadow is visible. This is the Trocadero, a site that was at the center of the 1937 Worlds Fair. © Daniel Colagrossi. Used by permission.

This photograph shows the way in which modern sculpture surrounds the Eiffel Tower. We also see some graffiti, which has become much more common in France since the early 1980s. © Daniel Colagrossi. Used by permission.

Saint Germain des Près is the famous church that anchors the neighborhood famous in the 1950s for its cafes, such as the Flore, Deux Magaux and the Brasserie Lipp, and is now increasingly known for its luxury stores such as Cartier and Armai. © Daniel Colagrossi. Used by permission.

This photograph of the Louvre Museum shows the blending of classical and contemporary architecture. © Daniel Colagrossi. Used by permission.

This ferris wheel on the Place de la Concorde is an example of the mix of high culture with popular culture that emerged during the Lang years. © Daniel Colagrossi. Used by permission.

Now an opera house, Place de la Bastille intends to bring culture to the people. It has also brought higher property values and trendy stores. We also see in this picture an example of the new trend for installation art as has been practiced by Christo and Daniel Buren. © Daniel Colagrossi. Used by permission.

Centre Pompidou, shown here, is a center of cultural animation on both the interior as well as on the exterior. © Daniel Colagrossi. Used by permission.

Affluent suburbs, such as Issy-les-Moulineaux, which is just west and south of the Bois de Boulogne, feature custom made homes and upscale apartment houses. © Daniel Colagrossi. Used by permission.

A perennial classic of Paris, along with the Louvre and the Eiffel Tower, Place des Victoires is among one of most visited sites in France. Also we see here the assiduous attention to cleanliness that has marked Paris over the last quarter century: from scrubbing monuments of dirt to keeping streets free of litter with a fleet of specialized vehicles. © Daniel Colagrossi. Used by permission.

Luxembourg Gardens and Palace. These magnificent gardens are set amidst the place created for Catherine de Medici during the French Renaissance. It is at the heart of the Left Bank of Paris. A favorite space for young children who sail miniature boats in the great fountain, to tennis players, and bibliophiles who read among the lawns, statues and gardens, the park has universal appeal. © Daniel Colagrossi. Used by permission.

An original Metro sign. The Paris Metro dates from 1900. The first stations, of which this is an example, were designed by the Art Nouveau architect Hector Guimard. © Daniel Colagrossi. Used by permission.

Pont Neuf. The most famous of the many bridges of Paris, these thoroughfares through the century have been the center of almost every type of cultural activity, from the now famous book sellers and landscape and portrait painters to less savory activities such as prostitution. © Daniel Colagrossi. Used by permission.

This café patron is playing a pinball game, exotic now in the age of computer games but a big part of café life among the young during the 1950s through the 1980s. © Daniel Colagrossi. Used by permission.

Youth of the suburbs playing in the central courts of housing projects. The drab quality ally ways and streets contrasts with streets named after great French writers. © Daniel Colagrossi. Used by permission.

French shopping malls (known as centres commerciales) are an attempt to inject some small more personal commerce into the district. © Daniel Colagrossi. Used by permission.

Café life today. A modern gargantua in a world that is increasingly gender inclusive. © Daniel Colagrossi. Used by permission.

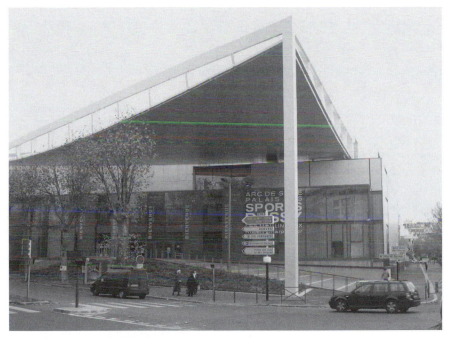

A sport facility in Issy-les-Moulineax. Such centers can be found through France since the 1950s. © Daniel Colagrossi. Used by permission.

Pictured here is the interior of a North African café. We can see the flags of France and Alegeria hanging, as well as citations from the Koran, illustrating the strong influences between France and northern Africa. Courtesy of the author.

This mural found in a Turkish coffee house shows the landscape of Turkey. Through buildings and images such as this, we can see the way in which immigrants in Paris create spaces that recall their native countries. Courtesy of the author.

This is the exterior of a Turkish coffee house in Paris. Courtesy of the author.

Suburban towers in one of the first and most famous and notorious of the French new towns dating from the 1950s, Sarcelles. Its 50th anniversary was in 2005, and we see the ways in which TV satellite discs sprout from housing towers and cafés and other small commerces dot the bottom floors. © Daniel Colagrossi. Used by permission.

Issy-les-Moulineaux is also home to high tech companies such as Hewlett Packard, banking, and entertainment. Shown here is the building for France's channel 5 station. © Daniel Colagrossi. Used by permission.

Advertisement for online chat groups have become as big in France as they are in the United States, combined with irreverence for publicity so common in France. © Daniel Colagrossi. Used by permission.

Designed by one of the same architects as the Centre Pompidou, Renzo Piano, the Lyon Museum of Contemporary Art shows the attempt by Metterrand's government to spread culture and contemporary architecture throughout the provinces. © Daniel Colagrossi. Used by permission.

6

Literature

ONE OF THE MOST VENERABLE of world literatures has been transformed over the last few decades by new currents both within and outside of France. French literature entered the twentieth century "trailing clouds of glory" from the extraordinarily creative nineteenth century.[1] Across the twentieth century, writers infused their work with such philosophies as Freudianism, Marxism and existentialism, as well as various linguistic theories. New schools of writing such as surrealism and the new novel emerged. Moreover, since the 1920s a steadily growing stream of colonial and now postcolonial writers has created a French literature beyond the nation's borders (Francophone literature) that is enlarging and transforming the august literary tradition within the hexagon. At the end of the twentieth century, a new generation of writers had incorporated such new (or "postmodern") themes as mass culture, popular culture, and tourism into French literature. Not only the types of authors but also the kinds of writing considered literature have been steadily expanding. Moreover, French writers are producing literature at an unprecedented and steadily expanding rate. Considering that there are about 170 million people speaking French around the world and that 500 million people inhabit the 63 member states and governments of the International Organization of the Francophonie (OIF), there is no doubt that French literature will remain a major force in the emerging global culture of the twenty-first century.[2]

Although complaints are constantly heard about the decline of literature, France remains a country committed to it, whether in the form of books or, as the Internet takes over, the printed word. France remains much more tied to the printed word than does the United States. While the United States has a population that is five time as large as France (300 million as opposed to 61 million), the annual number of its published books is only three times as large (175,000 books in 2003 compared France's 60,000 books in 2002). Moreover, French television devotes much more space to book reviews than U.S. television does. C-Span in the United States has recently inaugurated a book-review program, but none of its reviewers have gained much national prominence. This is very different from France where the main channels have book review shows.[3] The main innovator of the television book review, Bernard Pivot, has indeed become a household name and a legend in France and is a cross between the American talk show personalities Oprah Winfrey and Charlie Rose.

Starting out as a journalist and then becoming editor of the newspaper *Le Figaro,* Pivot left journalism for television in 1973 and started his first TV hit, *Apostrophes,* in 1975. This show quickly became one of the main venues at which to debut a new novel. Indeed, an appearance on his show is credited with having made such books as Marguerite Duras's *The Lover (L'Amant)* a best seller and perhaps the most influential novel of the 1980s. After ending *Apostrophes* in 1990, Pivot created a new show that had a similar level of success until he ended it in 2001. The name of this show, *Bouillon de Culture,* literally means cultural soup, but can better translated as cauldron of culture. Pivot explored the dynamics of culture creation not only among writers, but also among filmmakers, musicians, and artists in an informal yet intimate way that won millions of devoted viewers. Not surprisingly, *Bouillon de Culture* was sponsored by FNAC, the largest retailer of books in France. (Indeed, only one-third of the books bought in France are from traditional book store rather than from large chain stores, news vendors, or book clubs.) In 2002 Pivot returned with a new show, *Double Je* (translated as the double "I"), which explores the lives of writers, artists, and scholars who have learned French and added French culture to their lives. Since the 1960s, French market research has shown that television viewers and book readers tend to overlap, and the success of Pivot and other reviewers continues to prove the complementarity of word and image. (We shall see this below when we note the number of writers who have had success as both novelists and screen writers.)[4]

To foster the love of reading and books the government and publishers mount a series of book fairs and festivals each year. Each spring since 1981, a *salon du livre* takes place in Paris. Thousands of authors show up to do interviews, sign books, and mix with over 1,200 publishers who span every form of book from poetry to comic strips, from detective stories to essays. The success of the Paris event has led 10 other French cities, including Strasbourg, Lyon, and Bordeaux, also to mount salons. Since 1988 there is a reading festival *(lire en fête)* held in October to try to infuse the sense of the adventure that reading holds across France. This festival has now spread to 91 countries. Events range from simple readings to "reading challenges" to theatre pieces enacted by grammar- or high-school students.[5]

The post–World War II paperback revolution has helped spread literature at an unprecedented rate. In February 1953, Henri Filipacchi, one of the directors of Hachette who had started a successful series of detective novels with the *série noire* in 1945, launched the modern French paperback (known as *livre de poche*, or pocketbook). This was not the first paperback edition in France, however. Since even the eighteenth century book-hawkers had gone throughout France selling almanacs and popular tales, and the late nineteenth and early twentieth centuries had seen the French equivalent of dime novels for the mass market. What Filipacchi brought to the business was corporate muscle that could produce popular and classic texts in unprecedented numbers and could market and distribute them across France. Despite the misgivings of intellectuals, most prominently displayed in a debate in Jean-Paul Sartre's journal *Les Temps Modernes* (1964–1965), paperback sales skyrocketed from 8 millions copies sold in 1957–1958 to 28 million in 1969. By the late 1950s, other large French publishing houses followed suit: Flammarion with *J'ai lu* (1958), Presses de la Cité with *Presses-Pocket* (1962), and Gallimard's *Folio* (1972). By the early twenty-first century one book in three was a paperback, with more than 18 million copies sold in 2002 and close to a billion sold since 1953.[6]

Despite the continued prominence of literature in French culture and the wide distribution of paperbacks and an abundant production of novels, French publishing, like that of other nations, is increasingly concentrated in fewer and fewer companies. This trend started in earnest in the early 1980s and has accelerated ever since. Especially since the late 1990s, French publishing has been a constantly mutating monopoly as the major publishers, both international and French, play a game of corporate musical chairs, buying and selling companies almost on a yearly basis. For example between 1979 and 1981 a duopoly emerged with Matra and Havas dominating publishing. Then, by the mid 1980s Hachette and another consortium known as Éditis emerged as the preeminent book conglomerates. By 2006, they had regained that status, but in between such giants as Vivendi (which had, among other acquisitions, obtained Havas) and Lagardère (which once controlled Hachette) had risen and fallen. In 2006 the twelve biggest publishing houses controlled virtually 80 percent of the publishing market (three percentage points higher than in 2003) with Hachette Livre and Editis almost as big as the next ten groups combined. Increasingly the French consumer buys books in large stores such as FNAC (which also sells high volumes of musical and video recordings, as well as audio-visual and computer equipment). For example, between 1998 and 2001 the percentage of books bought in traditional book stores declined from 30 to 27, or 1 percent of the total sales. On the other hand, sales at large outlets, such as FNAC, have jumped from 15.2 percent to 20 percent (and by 2004 had reached 21.8 percent).[7]

But corporate consolidation in publishing and book selling has not slowed the production or sales of new literature, especially novels, and comic books, known in France as *bande dessiné* (BD), or drawn strip. These types of books often have a much wider French audience than they do in the English speaking world. In 1980, 5,032 new pieces of literature appeared (the vast majority of which were novels); by 2002, this number had swelled to 7,0357. Even though this is an extraordinary proliferation, most publishing houses still reject a majority of the manuscripts submitted; for example the prestigious Gaillimard receives 6,000 manuscripts per year and even smaller ones such as Éditions Paul Otchakovsky-Laurens are sent over 3,200 annually. Much of this literary vitality can be ascribed to the rise of new voices in French literature: women, gays and lesbians, immigrants, and members of the greater Francophone world. But the increase also reflects a larger trend, whereby the number of writers has increased but the number of readers has diminished. Since 1975 the number of new books has virtually tripled but the average number copies printed has fallen by almost half (usually novels are printed in runs of 3,000). The *band dessiné*, with the French comic character Asterix, and the British Harry Potter have been the only sectors of the book industry to show growth rather than stagnation. The last section of this chapter explores the dynamic role of this unique French cultural product. Indeed; the French have dubbed the BD as the "ninth art" and consecrated it with a museum.[8]

HISTORY (ORIGINS TO 1900)

French literature's greatness in part rests upon an ongoing tension between a sprit of classical (that is Roman Latin) order and an earthy and ribald freedom (that many be attributed to the original Gauls and their *esprit gaulois*). For centuries, too, the French have laced their prose and poetry with philosophic and political implications, which has put them in the vanguard of European literature. Indeed, the notion of a literary avant-garde first developed in France in the mid nineteenth century.

The tension between order and disorder was first played out in the medieval world as the Late Latin writings of the French Church fathers contrasted with the raw physicality of the poems of French warrior knights. Saint Gregory of Tours in his *History of the Franks* provides one of the first great works by a French author (even writing in a Late Latin that in some ways anticipates French). His work details the miracles and pious devotion of the churchmen and women of France and its kings. The first great work in early French is *The Song of Roland,* a heroic poem concerning the victory of Christians under the leadership of Charles Martel over Muslims at the Battle of Poitiers. This is merely the most famous of a larger literature exalting heroic prowess—the well-known French writer Chrétien de Troyes reworked the Arthurian legend into French. A very different side of aristocratic culture, courtly love, emerged in the poems of the troubadours of southern France (Provence), who had assimilated the erotic and sophisticated culture of Muslim Spain.

Francois Villon (1431–1465?), one of the most distinctive and historically influential French poets, would emerge in Paris in the fifteenth century. This son of a poor but pious family and an alleged thief and murder who roamed the Paris region with a criminal gang in the generation after the burning of Joan of Arc, he wrote poems on the themes of the tensions between the heat and the body, a ballad of the hanged (a fate he narrowly missed), and "Ballade de la grosse Margot," about a prostitute. There is an enduring and well-known line in his "Ballade des dames du temps jadis": "But where are the snows of yesteryear?" Nineteenth-century French lyric poets, as we shall see, saw him as a fellow "accursed poet" *(poet maudit).*[9]

When the Renaissance arrived in France, this tension between order and spontaneity took on a new form. A self-conscious school of writers, La Pléiade, promulgated a doctrine in 1550, in one of the first literary manifestos ever penned, based upon what they perceived to be the "classical unities" of time, place, and action and a strict hierarchy of poetic and dramatic form. The leading member of this school was Pierre de Ronsard (1524–1585). The influence of this school would be felt especially upon the greats of seventeenth-century French classical drama (as we shall see in the chapter on the theatre). But during this same era two mavericks put an indelible stamp upon French and European literature: François Rabelais (1490–1553) and Michel de Montaigne (1533–1592). In one of the first novels, *Gargantua and Pantagruel,* in a language so uniquely earthy and erudite that it would inspire its own adjective (Rabelaisian), Rabelais told of the adventures and mishaps of the two giants whose names grace the title. Rabelais's capacious imagination juxtaposed the low language of the marketplace with the high diction of the university lecture hall to produce one of the most comprehensive imaginings of any society. Montaigne, in contrast, stayed above the fray of the French wars of religion and culture and contemplated the weakness and vanity of all human societies. His cultural relativism anticipated what was to emerge in both the Enlightenment and the late twentieth century and was expressed through his own unique creation, the modern essay.

French classicism reached its apogee with Nicholas Boileau-Despreaux (1636–1711) in the age of Louis XIV. His *The Art of Poetry* gave definitive expression to European classicism for the coming centuries with his emphasis that all great art should aspire to the nobility and universality of the ancient Greeks and Romans and avoid the vulgar, the plebeian, and the contemporary. His theories, in short, would provide a foil for all future rebels in literature and art. In matters of French Counter-Reformation of Catholic orthodoxy, Jacques-Benigne Bossuet (1627–1704) set an incomparable oratorical tone with his great funeral orations and his universal history written for the heir apparent to the throne *(dauphin)*. His contemporary, Blaise Pascal (1623–1662), is often considered the greatest stylist of French prose. Pascal combined the talent of a great scientist (discovering the nature of the vacuum) with a profound skepticism about the ability of science to unravel the mysteries of the world more successfully than Catholicism. Rounding out this golden age of French prose were Jean de La Fontaine (1621–1695), whose explorations into the folklore of his era inspired his *Fables,* which have become a staple of children's literature around the world, and François de la Rochefoucauld (1613–1680), whose maxims perfectly encapsulated the wit and repartee of French aristocratic court and salon life.

After being the epicenter and epitome of classical order during the age of Louis XIV (who had lavishly subsidized writers), France during the eighteenth century became the center of a new subversive school of literature and thought, the Enlightenment. Advocating a critical and empirical reason, this movement, perhaps the first modern counterculture, aimed to reform if not revolutionize French society through a transformation of public opinion. The Catholic injunction to know God was replaced with the Socratic injunction to know thyself and the imperative, inspired by Newton's physics, to find the "laws of motion" of society. Voltaire (1694–1778), the original and archetypal *"philosophe,"* was a combination of writer and agitator determined to change the climate of opinion of his age from religion to science. His short novels, such as *Candide,* proved potent weapons against what he saw as the source of so much evil, the Catholic Church. Charles de Secondat Baron de Montesquieu (1689–1755), especially in his *Persian Letters,* raised to high art the popular genre of depicting the foibles and irrationalities of European society through the eyes of outsiders. Dennis Diderot (1713–1784) wrote penetrating art and theatre criticism and innovative novels on such issues as fate and hypocrisy, but achieved his greatest fame by composing an *Encyclopédie* that summed up the Enlightenment viewpoint on virtually every subject. Perhaps the greatest writer of the age, however, was also a great contrarian. Jean-Jacques Rousseau, born in Geneva and never really at home in the cosmopolitan Paris of the philosophes, questioned the Enlightenment assumptions concerning the superiority of European urban civilization over rustic, rural, or non-European civilizations and called for a return to a more simple and emotional lifestyle attuned to the joys of nature and human camaraderie. His novels such as *Julie, or the New Heloise* and *Emile,* helped launch, respectively, romanticism and modern children's education, while his autobiographies *The Confessions and Reveries of a Solitary Walker* turned earlier spiritual quests for personal understanding in a more secular and psychological direction.

French literature languished during the periods of the French Revolution and Napoleon (1789–1815). It seemed that great actions have been substituted for great words. Many early nineteenth-century novelists, such as Stendhal and Balzac, would reflect on this fact in their novels. Nevertheless, during the Revolutionary era writers such as Francois-Rene de Chateaubriand (1768–1848) heralded the return of Christianity to intellectual favor, and he thus anticipated the Restoration with his *Genius of Christianity,* and helped consolidate an age of romantic inner self-disclosure with his *Memoirs beyond the Grave (Memoires d'outre tombe).* Madame de Staël (1766–1817), was in some ways a feminist pioneer as we have seen as well as one of the first to detail the new romantic literary movement in Germany. She also helped sustain salon life across the Revolutionary period, an invaluable institution for writers.

By the 1820s, romanticism emerged fully in France with a new generation of poets. It is not surprising that they considered themselves a generation, since they had lived through the searing events of the previous 20 years. Alphonse de Lamartine (1790–1868), in his *Poetic Meditations* (1820), saw the poet as replacing the theologian as the one best able to decipher the symbolic meaning of life. While Alfred de Vigny (1797–1863) searched for the poetic essence in his work, Victor Hugo (1802–1885) began an extremely long and creative literary life that would be devoted to championing the cause of the underdog by attempting to develop a new poetic language drawn from the heart rather than from classical models. A second generation of romantic authors would appear during the 1830s who would produce, as we have noted in the introduction, an edgier and more combative poetry that proclaimed the power of the poet in particular and the artist in general to create a new and more genuine existence through their work than that found in an increasingly utilitarian middle-class society. The most important writers in this generation were Alfred de Musset (1810–1857), Gerard de Nerval (1811–1872), and Théophile Gauthier (1811–1872).

Many of these romantic writers, especially Hugo, would also write novels. But there are other romantic writers who were primarily novelists. Among these were the fantastically popular Alexandre Dumas, père (1802–1870), writer of such popular classics as *The Three Musketeers* and *The Count of Monte Cristo,* the short-story writer Prosper Mérimée (1803–1870), most famous for *Carmen,* upon which Bizet based his opera. The most iconoclastic of the French romantics was the woman writer George Sand (1804–1876), whose cross-dressing, cigar-smoking, and love affair with Chopin pointed towards the counterculture of the 1960s. Finally, Charles Augustin Sainte-Beuve (1804–1869), proved to be the greatest literary critic of the age, embodying the romantic virtues of empathy and openness to new literary styles.

Some of the greatest writers of the period 1820–1850, however, do not fit easily into the romantic framework. The great novelists Stendhal (Marie-Henri Beyle, 1783–1842), writer of *The Red and the Black* and *The Charter House of Parma,* and Honoré de Balzac, with his novel series *The Human Comedy,* were much more like the realist school of painters that emerged around Gustave Courbet than the romantics. (Indeed, Balzac was Karl Marx's favorite novelist.) The poet and literary and artistic critic Charles Baudelaire, as noted earlier, in many ways can be termed the writer who pioneered what would be aesthetic modernism.

Inspired by Théophile Gautier and Baudelaire, a new poetic movement known as the Parnassians emerged in the 1860s. Named after their epony-mous journal, which ran between 1866 and 1876, the poets in this school, such as Leconte de Lisle, Banville, Sully-Prudhomme, Verlaine, Coppée, and J. M. de Heredia, rejected romantic effusions in favor of a more rig-orous and symbolic poetry that drew upon both classical and exotic sub-jects. They embraced Gautier's ideology of art for art's and helped lay the groundwork for going beyond sense perception in poetry and art. Indeed, Verlaine would become the lover of Arthur Rimbaud, one of the premier symbolists and a child prodigy who would cease writing poetry at the age of 19. Unknown at the time, a young poet by the name of Isidore Ducasse (1846–70) would live a reclusive life in Paris during the late 1860s but cre-ate poetry that the later generation of the surrealists would proclaim as their model (*Poésies* and especially *Les Chants de Maldoror* under the pseudonym Comte de Lautréamont).

By the 1860s, French novelists also began to move away from the concern with realistic depictions of society to explore the ways in which literary style or biological forces shape human beings. Gustave Flaubert's *Madame Bovary,* like Baudelaire's *Flowers of Evil,* caused a scandal in Second Empire France and led to a trial on charges of obscenity. Yet Flaubert merely tried to em-body in description and literary style the life of a frustrated provincial woman without assigning any moral value to her life. Flaubert's method of rigorous, ruthless observation, rejecting all past presuppositions as he looked at the events of life, was passed down to his young protégé Guy de Maupassant

(1850–1893). Emile Zola, on the contrary, would embrace the injunction of the literary critic and historian Hippolyte Taine (1828–1893) to explore the interaction between heredity and environment in human life in his expansive 20-novel Rougon-Macquart series (1871–1893), chronicling the life of a family across the Second Empire. Alphonse Daudet (1840–1897) created a more sentimental variant on naturalism, especially in such famous stories as "The Last Lesson," in a school in newly annexed German Alsace.

Late nineteenth-century French poetry of the 1880s and 1890s has become known primarily as symbolism, but in many ways it anticipates developments 50 years later. Verlaine continued to write in this genre, as did the Belgian Maurice Maeterlinck (1862–1949), whose poetry would influence the great French composer Claude Debussy (who created an opera out of Maeterlinck's *Pelléas and Mélisande*). The most innovative of the symbolists was Stéphane Mallarmé (1842–1898), who pushed the movement into an exploration not only of the symbolism of words themselves but also of their sonority and rhythm without any necessary reference to the outside world. In short, a poem became a self-contained referent only to its own inner dynamics. In this fashion Mallarmé was exploring in poetry what the French Swiss linguist Ferdinand de Saussure was doing: showing that language was a system of signs with no necessary relation to external reality. These ideas received much greater elaboration during the era of the new novel and structuralism during the 1950s and 1960s.

The years between 1900 and World War I (1914) are best seen through the lens of three towering figures of modernism: Andre Gide, Guillaume Apollinaire, and Marcel Proust. Their respective works, Gide's novel *The Immoralist*, Apollinaire's poetry collection *Alcools,* and Proust's first volume of *Remembrance of Things Past, Swann's Way,* provided benchmarks for subsequent twentieth-century fiction. Andre Gide brought a psychological and sexual dimension to French literature by wrestling with his cultural heritage as a strict French Protestant and the realization that he was a homosexual (at a time when the concept was just becoming a topic of artistic and medical discourse). Gide also grappled with the iconoclast philosophy of Friedrich Nietzsche and the injunction to create new values. All this played out in Gide's novels and journals, which also became landmark works.

In 1908 Gide also helped found *La Nouvelle Revue Francaise,* the most influential literary journal for most of the twentieth century. One of its great errors was to reject Proust's first volume. Gide believed that the observations of a socialite such as Proust on high society would have little merit. Naturally, Gide later repented of this judgment, and of course Proust's eventual seven-volume series would be recognized as one of the great literary achievements of the century. In essence Proust explored regions of memory, time, and experience to an unprecedented degree, complementing what the French philosopher Henri Bergson and Sigmund Freud were doing at the same time.

Finally, Guillaume Apollinaire (1880–1918) not only continued and expanded poetic experimentation but was also an impresario who popularized painters such as Pablo Picasso and Marcel Duchamp and helped shift the site of French artistic creativity from the Right Bank hilltop of Montmartre, where it had flourished since the 1860s, across the Seine to Montparnasse, where it would develop from the early 1900s through the 1930s. His experimental poetry played with new offbeat forms of presentation on the page (calligrammes) and with expanding the references to include the symbols of painters and the conversations of café customers. In 1913 an essay on Picasso and other "cubist" painters helped define the movement. Apollinaire would later also coin the term surrealism for art that went beyond symbolism to get to the inner workings of artistic imagery. Tragically he would die of Spanish influenza after surviving World War I in the trenches, on Armistice Day, November 11, 1918.

Although not considered an exemplar of stylistic modernism, Colette must also be cited. Her popular novels concerning the coming-of-age and sexual exploits of young women (with both men and other women) mark an important development in the emergence of French literary feminism. Seldom before her *Claudine* novels or her short stories had women's desire been so candidly discussed. Although not a feminist per se, her ability to win independence from her first husband, who had published her novels under his name, and to become one of the leading writers of France provided a role model for the generation of women who came of age after 1900.

The interwar period (1919–1939) marked a continuation of French literary genius. The rise of the surrealist movement and the Communist Party and the emergence of fascism across Europe politicized poetry and prose to an unprecedented degree. Henri Barbusse, a veteran of trench warfare and author of the searing and best-selling indictment of the War, *Fire,* became a communist shortly after the formation of the French Communist Party and helped organize a group of writers who followed the party line. On the right, another veteran, Pierre Drieu de la Rochelle, came to the opposite conclusions of Barbusse after his experiences in the trenches. His books and novels would glorify the heroic action and camaraderie of the trenches and would call for a strong government in France after the fashion of Mussolini in Italy or later Hitler in Germany. Andre Breton's surrealist movement would include, at one point or another, many of the most creative poets and novelists of twentieth-century France: Philippe Soupault, Paul Eluard, Louis Aragon, Robert Desnos, René Crevel, Benjamin Péret, Antonin Artaud, Georges Bataille, Michel Leiris, and Raymond Queneau. The sheer diversity of their output prevents any easy generalizations, but all were moved by Breton's call for a reinvigoration of art through a rejection of middle-class notions of morality and beauty (often held to be the cause of World War I) and an embrace of the emancipator impulses to be found in the human unconscious (after the fashion of Freud) and the cause of the workers and the peoples of Africa and Asia oppressed by European colonialism (after the fashion of Marxism and the Russian Revolution). The human unconscious, Breton argued, was the ultimate source of artistic creativity and could be tapped by free association by writers and artists. Perhaps the most notable achievement was Jules Romains's ambitious series of novels, *Men of Goodwill,* which chronicled French society after 1900 in ways similar to Zola and Proust. André Maurois and Francois Mauriac were best-selling authors. While Maurois chronicled World War I and the lives of a host of famous figures in best sellers, Mauriac chronicled the provincial middle-class society of his native Bordeaux. Both wrote in the style of their great nineteenth-century forbearers.

While the onset of the Great Depression in France in 1932, a few years after the onset in the United States, threw the nation into turmoil, it only stoked the creative literary fires of the nation. Perhaps the most creative new voice to emerge in French literature in the early 1930s was Louis-Ferdinand Céline, a writer trained as a doctor. In *Journey to the End of Night* (1932) and *Death on the Installment Plan* (1936) Celine for the first time incorporated working-class slang into a major novel and combined this stylistic innovation with a deft touch for atmospheric description that produced a forlorn feeling about the fate of modern society. Céline's despair would end in his becoming a fascist and collaborationist during World War II. The turbulent decade also saw the rise of what would be called existentialism after 1945. The first writer to gain fame who was termed an existentialist was Andre Malraux. In his adventures around the world he would become a sort of French Hemingway, exploring and pilfering artistic treasures in Cambodia, writing abut the Chinese Revolution (in *Man's Fate* in 1934), and fighting in Spain against the fascists during the nation's civil war in the late 1930s (which led to *Man's Hope* in 1938). A young lycée professor, Jean-Paul Sartre, also covered the topic of the nature of human identity in relation to actions and consciousness in his 1939 novel *Nausea,* which was hailed as a masterpiece. But Jean-Paul Sartre would remain above politics during the 1930s and into the start of World War II—but not for long thereafter. Finally, 1939 also saw the publication of a first novel, *Tropisms,* by the young woman writer Nathalie Sarraute. This novel would be an early harbinger both of postwar women's writing and of the new novel of the 1950s and 1960s. This title defines her essential quest: to explore how this biological term (which means how an organism responds to changes in its environment) could be applied to human society, especially the unconscious and instinctual ways in which humans adapt to their environment.

The sudden defeat in World War II, the Nazi occupation and resistance struggle that then emerged, liberation, and the immediate onset of the Cold War challenged and renovated French literature. Much of the writings of the 1940s and the 1950s are best termed existentialist. Jean-Paul Sartre, Albert Camus, and Simone de Beauvoir, although beginning their careers before or during the war, emerged after 1945 as the leading literary lights of continental Europe. These and other French writers had been heavily influenced by the German philosopher Martin Heidegger, who had been one of the first to explore the nature (ontology) of human existence and being beyond traditional theology and metaphysics. Following Heidegger, Sartre saw the mere existence of human beings, much less the attempt of humans to communicate with one another, as deeply mysterious. Although Camus, unlike Sartre and de Beauvoir, was not trained in philosophy, he too grappled with the sheer majesty and terror of human consciousness in a seemly indifferent universe. What made these writers so great and their influence so pervasive around the world was their ability to translate philosophical problems into literary masterpieces.

After World War II, Sartre was determined never again to be oblivious to politics. Towards this end he develop the concept of "engaged literature" and called upon writers to not only bear witness to their age but also to change it. He would devote the rest of his life to causes such as trying to prevent or end the Cold War, to dismantle France's colonial empire, and to win equality and dignity not only for the working classes in the developed world but also for the rising peoples of the Third World. Following his first novel, *Nausea,* Sartre wrote a trilogy about the start of World War II, the *Paths of Liberty,* and studies of writers such as Baudelaire and especially Gustave Flaubert (indeed this latter multivolume study is one of the longest ever written). He also championed the work of African and Caribbean writers who wished to create a new kind of French writing based on placing the African at the center of the text rather than the white (negritude). He would also write an introduction to the highly influential study of anticolonial revolt, *The Wretched of the Earth,* by Frantz Fanon (raised in the Caribbean, schooled in France as a psychologist, and a partisan in the Algerian liberation struggle, 1954–1962).

The full measure of Sartre's engagement comes through in the following quote from the introduction to an anthology of negritude poetry (1948):

When you have removed the gag that was keeping these black mouths shut, what were you hoping for? That they would sing your praises? Did you think that when they raised themselves up again, you would read adoration in the eyes of these heads that our fathers had forced to bend to the very ground? Here are black men standing, looking at us, and I hope that you—like me—will feel the shock of being seen. [10]

The passion of this quotation gives some idea of the electricity that Sartre communicated to a French society still reeling from the aftershocks of a world war. Sartre would set the tone for the politically engaged writer until at least the events of 1968.

Though a fellow in the Resistance, Albert Camus would not follow Sartre into a strong leftist stance after 1945. The two writers came from very different backgrounds. Sartre, on the one hand, came from an intellectually prominent family (which included Albert Schweitzer) and went to the elite schools of France. Camus, on other hand, was born into a poor white settler family in Algeria. Although he joined the Communist Party at a young age, he steadily drifted away from it (in the very years Sartre was becoming the classic fellow traveler and a partisan of the Communist position, but not formally joining and keeping a critical distance). Camus's novels, such as *The Stranger, The Plague,* and *The Fall,* dealt with the absurdity of human intentions in a world deprived of God, but the nobility of human actions when harnessed to struggle against barbarism and brutality. Camus, as a native of Algeria, could not reconcile himself with the nation winning its total independence from France. Towards the end of his life he despaired of a just and equitable solution for both native Muslim and colonial settler. He broke with Sartre over the questions of Algeria, the Soviet Union, and the Cold War. Camus had been the youngest winner of the Nobel Prize (at 44) in 1957 and delivered an address that tried to speak for the generation that had come of age during World War II. Jean-Paul Sartre would also receive the Nobel Prize (in 1964) but rejected it as both superfluous and as a protest against so few Soviet writers having received the award. Here we see the fascinating dialectic of Sartre, the French-born intellectual, rejecting his heritage to live life on the edge and Camus, the born outsider, embracing the West at a time when it seemed to offer a more humane alternative than the Soviet system.

Simone de Beauvoir, along with her groundbreaking contribution to feminist theory, also became a highly influential novelist. Her greatest success as a novelist was *The Mandarins,* which won the highest French literary award, the Goncourt Prize (1954). This novel traced, in fictional form, the intricate literary, political, and personal lives of a literary intellectual group that was very similar to the one to which Sartre, Camus and de Beauvoir belonged.In this novel, as in others, she did not portray women as what she hoped they would become—their own autonomous subjects free of male domination— but as they were in a sexist society dominated by middle-class morality. Her subsequent novel, *The Beautiful Images (Les Belles Images)* did not achieve much critical success but was a pioneering novel in exploring the postwar affluent society, and especially the world of advertising. Perhaps her greatest contribution to literature was her multivolume autobiography *(Memoirs of a Dutiful Daughter, The Prime of Life, The Force of Circumstances,* and other volumes). In these richly detailed volumes she explores her coming-of-age as a philosopher, a feminist, and a socialist. These books have been as important for the women's movement in France and around the world as her philosophical study, *The Second Sex,* because she personifies and exemplifies the difficulties and rewards of living a life free of male domination and shows how she created a unique lifelong relationship with Sartre outside the boundaries of marriage.[11]

From the mid 1950s a new trend developed in French literature that became known as the "new novel." A new generation, including Nathalie Sarraute, Alain Robbe-Grillet, Marguerite Duras, Claude Ollier, Michel Butor, and Claude Simon, emerged wishing to explore alternate avenues from the existentialists. Rather than political engagement, they explored the nature of language and its relation with literature. The literary critic Émile Henriot first used the term "new novel" in a review in the newspaper *Le Monde* in May 1957 to describe the innovations in language in which these novelists seemed to be constantly engaged. These writers were part of a new concern with language that developed in France during the 1950s with the diffusion of the work of Ferdinand de Saussure. In his essay collection, *For a New Novel* (1963), Robbe-Grillet asserted that novelists must unsettle the reader and call into question the traditional notions of the narrator, the plot, and the coherence of lived experience. Not surprisingly, these writers shared more in literary method than they did in political philosophy. Nevertheless, most hoped that their linguistic explorations would help produce a new type of human being. In the words of Robbe-Grillet "New Novel, New Man."[12]

Though these writers have been highly productive and have won numerous awards, they have never achieved the level of international success of the existentialists. Robbe-Grillet's most important novels were *The Erasers* (1953), *The Voyeur* (1955), and *Jealousy* (1957). In 2004 he was elected into the "immortals" of the French academy (Academie Française). Claude Simon won the Nobel Prize for literature in 1985 for novels such as *The Wind* (1957) and his four-novel sequence *The Grass* (1958), *The Flanders Road* (1960), *The Palace* (1962), and *History* (1967). Through a combination of stream of consciousness and various narrative styles he tried to bring coherence to twentieth-century life. Along with *Tropisms,* Nathalie Sarraute would write *Portrait of an Unknown* (1948), a reworking of a Balzac's novel *Eugénie Grandet,* and *The Planetarium* (1959), which is written without a narrator. In a collection of essays, *The Age of Suspicion* (1956), Sarraute wished to see narrative and "characters" eliminated from novels to be replaced by "a matter as nameless as blood, a magma." In a collection of essay *The Age of Suspicion* (1956) Sarraute desired a literature that removed all of the old certainties:

Suddenly the reader is on the inside; exactly where the author is, at a depth where nothing remains of the convenient landmarks with which he constructs the characters. His is immersed and held under the surface until the end, in a substance as anonymous as blood, a magma without name or contours.[13]

Michel Butor has been the recipient of such awards as the Prix Renaudot and has published novels that often have a science fiction motif, such as *Passing Time* (1956) and *Second Thoughts* (1957). Although she started publishing novels in the early 1940s, Marguerite Duras did not achieve her greatest fame until her Prix Goncourt–winning *The Lover* (1984), which is now generally considered to be the most important French novel of that decade. Duras also wrote important screenplays, made movies (which will be covered in the chapter on cinema), and experimented in a variety of styles. After the events of May 1968, for example, she tried to change her style completely and develop a writing style closer to women's life experiences. In short, she became part of the new wave of French feminism.

During the 1960s, new schools emerged that also focused on the nature of writing, including the Tel Quel group, named after the eponymous journal edited by Philippe Sellers and Jean-Edern Hallier, which was published from 1960 until 1982. These editors enjoyed a distinguished group of writers, which included Roland Barthes, George Bataille, Michel Foucault, Jacques Derrida, Julia Kristeva, Jean-Joseph Goux, and the composer Pierre Boulez and the filmmaker Jean-Luc Godard. The authors in this journal would help to define the nature of what became known as poststructuralism. By 1967 their more literary and theoretical essays gave way to praise of Mao's Cultural Revolution in China. By 1968 Roland Barthes would proclaim the "death of the author" following Michel Foucault's earlier pronouncement of the "death of man." The work of a young psychoanalyst originally from Bulgaria, Julia Kristeva, is especially representative of this group. Her work on the role of body (especially women's) in literature and the sciences and her exploration of the mother and pre-oedipal stages in the development of human consciousness and the role of what she calls matricide (death of the mother) as the means by which society has constructed the development of the adult personality exemplifies this group's tenets. Not surprisingly, her work has been highly influential with feminists. In 1990 she published her first novel, *The Samurai,* a novel in the tradition of Simon de Beauvoir's *The Mandarins* in that it portrays the intellectual landscape of Paris during the era of Tel Quel's prominence in the late 1960s.

Another group of avant-garde novelists became known by the French acronym Oulipo (what meant in English "workshop of potential literature"). The founders of the movement in 1960 included the former surrealist Raymond Queneau, one of the most earthy and productive of French novelists between the 1930s and the 1970s, along with the novelist François Le Lionnais. Other members included the Italian Italo Calvino and the American Harry Matthews, both writers, and the mathematician Jacques Roubaud, thus giving the group an international and interdisciplinary cast. In essence this group believed that constraints in writing could produce innovation and creativity.

The most important and innovative novelist to emerge from Oulipo was Georges Perec. This son of a fallen French soldier during World War II, he was able to survive in occupied France despite the high risk that he would be sent to the death camps because he was Jewish. Living life on the edge from the very start may have honed his creativity with literary experimentation. For example, in his novel *A Void* (1969), Perec did not use the letter "E," and in one piece of less than 500 words he used only one vowel: A. He was also fond of palindromes—words or sentences that read the same backwards or forwards. Indeed, he wrote what is considered to be the longest one ever, composed of over 5,000 words. In his most famous novel, *Life: A User's Manual,* Perec used the logic of the chess board to structure this tale of daily life in an apartment house. This novel is one of the most perceptive works on the emergence of French consumer culture during the 1950s and 1960s and details the central role that the modern home and consumer durables played in the lives of postwar France. Perec's exploration of consumer culture and urban daily life had been encouraged and inspired by Roland Barthes, who had himself pioneered the study of the symbology of daily life in his series *Mythologies.*

Although highly innovative and used across the world in literature and French language classes, the postexistentialist generations have never received the popular acclaim of Sartre, Camus, and de Beauvoir. Many novelists noted above were criticized for engaging in language games and interior monologues rather than confronting history (such as World War II or the Cold War) or firing the imaginations of their readers with great love stories or heroic adventure stories. Such criticisms, however, fail to understand the dramatic changes brought about by the events of May–June 1968 to French culture, and especially literature. This near-revolution profoundly shook up cultural categories in France. Distinctions between high and low culture and high and low literature became less pronounced as the emergence of a variety of liberation movements transformed, and in part dissolved, the notion both of established and avant-garde literatures. In the wake of this volcanic cultural eruption, the literary landscape was transformed: women's, lesbian, gay, postcolonial (literature written in French but outside of France), and immigrant literatures all emerged. Moreover, by the 1980s virtually all novelists writing in French were as likely to draw their inspiration and reference from popular or mass culture (television, comic books, or popular music) as they were from the literary canon.

Almost every women writer was deeply affected by the events of May 1968. As we have seen in the chapter on French thought and with women writers such as de Beauvoir, Duras, and Kristeva, these dramatic events transformed women's writing, producing a new utopian vision of a world in which women have gained their full voice. Below the plain of high philosophy and literature, May 1968 led to a range of new publications that gave a broader range of women than ever before the chance to write. Out of the first of these grassroots publications was *The Burning Rag (Le Torchon Brule),* which appeared in 1971. By the end of 1974 Simone de Beauvoir and a women's collective published a column in the monthly journal *Les Temps Moderns* (which de Beauvoir edited with Sartre) on "everyday sexism." By 1974 a publishing house, Editions des femmes, had opened and another would in 1977 (Tierce). But Editions des femmes was more than just a publishing house; it strove to be a "sphere of creativity," and towards this end included a bookshop and an art gallery. Moreover, to spread the women's voices, Editions des femmes also set up a library of voices *(la bibliotheque des voix),* which was a collection of tape recordings of the women writers they published reading their novels and essays or of prominent stage and screen actors reading women's classics such as those by Madame de Staël, Colette, or Madame de Lafayette. Such grassroots action helped produce the largest generation of women writers in French history in the succeeding decades.

By the 1970s the already-developing literature in French produced around the world among French speakers was achieving growing prominence. The geographic and cultural range of this literature is fantastic: from the Antilles in the Caribbean, to West, Central, and North Africa, the Indian and Pacific Oceans, Vietnam, Quebec, Belgium, Switzerland, and France. Pioneers of Francophonie included the creators of the negritude movement among African students and the African diasporas who attended college in Paris during the 1920s, 1930s, and 1940s. They included Léopold Sédar Senghor, from Senegal, later president when it became an independent nation, Aimé Césaire from the Antilles, and León Damas from French Guyana. In essence they asserted their identity as Africans within the French language and explored historically, literarily, and linguistically the paradoxes and possibilities of this dual identity, "assimilating, not being assimilated."

Over the past 15 years, Francophone writers have often won prestigious literary honors. For example, Moroccan-born Ben Jelloun Tahar won the most honored French literary award, the Prix Goncourt, in 1987 for *The Sacred Night*, the Antilles writer Patrick Chamoiseau won the Goncourt prize for *Texaco* (1992), and the Lebanese-born Arab Catholic Amin Maalouf won the following year for *The Rock of Tanios*. Francois Cheng, born in China and elected to be among the "immortals of the Academie Française" in 2002, won the Prix Feminia award for women's literature in 1998 for *The One Know as Tianyi,* and in 2001 Marie Ndiaye, daughter of a French mother and a Senegalese father, won for *Rosie Carpe.*

The past 20 years have not seen the emergence of any literary schools such as the ones in the previous periods. If any one term summarizes recent trends in French literature, that term would be postmodernism. In France this movement has taken on the form of a distrust of grand literary gestures, in particular, the notion that writing can save or change the world. Colin Davis and Elizabeth Fallaize, in a study of recent French fiction, argue that since the 1960s, the "era of suspicion" that Nathalie Sarraute illuminated in her novels and criticism towards all traditional literary forms has given way to what the philosopher Gilles Lipovetsky calls the era of emptiness *(l'ere du vide)*. In essence this means that what we see in recent French literature is a shift away from the hope that some ideology (such as Marxism) or critical method (such as structuralism or poststructuralism) can achieve human emancipation and towards a more modest hope that ordinary individuals working on their own amidst the spaces of daily life can piece together some sense of meaning and purpose in their lives. Gone are the grand themes of revolution and a break from history and society and instead there is an attempt at accommodation with history and mass media and consumption culture that allows individuals to forge some sort of meaningful life.

Towards this end, novelists since 1980 have increasingly turned to the genre of detective fiction to illuminate individual strategies of daily life. Sebastien Japrisot and Daniel Pennac have been especially adept at this style. Japrisot created dramatic story lines in such novels as *The Sleeping-Car Murders* and *Trap for Cinderella,* and Pennac, in his series of novels on the Belleville district of Paris, in particular *The Scapegoat,* developed highly detailed descriptions of the effects of shopping malls and the mass media on contemporary culture.

Marguerite Duras's *The Lover* (1984) marked an important turning point not only in her own work but also in the French novel. After great skepticism about love as a literary subject, her novel reinstated this seeming eternal theme to centrality in French fiction. Moreover, like many of the new novelists, the novel marked a return to autobiography. But in Duras's case, and in that of most postmodern writers, this is an autobiographical quest laced with both irony and modesty, and in the case of *The Lover,* framed within the context of postcolonial reflection. (The novel explores her sexual coming-of-age as a youth in pre–World War II French Indochina.) Duras's success was also "postmodern" in the sense that it was greatly aided by her brilliant interview on Pivot's television show *Apostrophes,* which sent sales soaring.

Among the most innovative but characteristically understated explorations of love by a women writer are those by Annie Ernaux. Especially in *Simple Passion* (1991) we see a writer whose seemingly spare prose and plot line contain profound philosophic and literary ruminations upon the nature of love and social class in contemporary French society. Coming from a working-class background, Ernaux is acutely aware that her novels could not be produced and most likely will not be read by those with whom she grew up. This perspective has honed her postmodern irony about the ability of individuals to create coherent narratives of their lives, since life, unlike literature, cannot have a "plot." These vantage points, both social and literary, led her to argue that love is not, as has been traditionally conceived, the fusion of two souls and bodies in a perfect harmony, but, instead, following the work of Kristeva, a revolutionary act of individuality in which the person in love gains greater insight into his or her own personality.

The renunciation of the revolutionary utopia of politics or language has also led to a new engagement with history. One of the most important writers dealing with a central topic in French culture, the legacy of the occupation, Resistance and the Holocaust of World War II, has been Jorge Semprun. In such novels as *The White Mountain* (1986) he has traced the fragility of culture and its inability to prevent the Holocaust. Rather than a condemnation of culture, as found in the work of Andre Breton, Semprun's is more of a meditation.

Of the novelists who explore the nature of contemporary culture, none has been more accomplished than Jean Echenez. In *Chopin's Move,* for example, the whole panoply of artifacts of consumer culture, from cars, to radios, to furniture, to hi-fis, to shopping malls permeate the characters and their actions. The result is a literary demonstration of Jean Baudrillard's concept of the hyperreal, with unexpected parallels drawn between the cultural and natural worlds giving the novel a sense of Darwin's evolutionary struggle.

During the late 1990s and early 2000s, the highly regarded novels of Michel Houellebecq have gained worldwide attention. For example *Platform* has been translated into 25 different languages, in part because the novel was seen to contain a premonition of the September 11, 2001, attacks on the World Trade Center in New York. In brilliant and belligerent prose Houellebecq exposes virtually every social group and institution in the contemporary world, not from the position of some ideal political philosophy, but rather from one that endears him to the world youth, as summed up in the title of one of his novels: *Whatever.*

A *New York Times* review of *Platform* provides a fitting overview and a summary of much of the cultural interaction between the various levels and types of culture within and outside of France that characterize the best of French fiction in the early twenty-first century:

MICHEL HOUELLEBECQ is an ugly writer, vulgar, often silly, sex-obsessed. His heroes are unprepossessing loners, eaters of junk food and watchers of far too much television, and generally, egotistically, they are named Michel. His settings are dreary suburban offices and studio apartments, with the addition, in the present novel, of airports, planes and holiday resorts in Thailand. The sex, the politics, the theorizing are inexorable, and often unpleasant and extreme: in his current volume, strong views are expressed on topics like interracial sexual attraction, Islam, Cuba and leisure marketing in developing countries. "All humanity instinctively tends toward miscegenation"—this is one of the more striking aperçus in "Platform"—and "the only person, however, to have pushed the process to its logical conclusion is Michael Jackson." "What does God compare to?"—and here is another one. The answer: a woman's private parts, of course, "but also perhaps the vapors of a Turkish bath."[14]

Houellebecq's 2005 novel, *The Possibility of an Island,* however, did not sell at the blockbuster rates in France that most publishers and critics anticipated, especially given the tremendous publicity on all media venues from television to the Internet. (While only about 180,000 copies have been sold in France, the publishing run was up around 250,000.) Indeed, for many French critics, his biting satire seemed little more than cynicism. But in the United States the dust jacket of the book proclaimed him as the "the most famous French novelist since Camus. Regardless, Houellebecq's career shows the ever-growing synergy between print and electronic media.[15]

Although no French novelist can currently compare to Proust or Sartre in international reputation, the new generation of writers both within and beyond France ensures the dynamism and vitality of French literature. Certainly in the coming decades some of the writers mentioned above will achieve the status of classics.

Comic Books (*Bande Dessinée*)

No survey of French literature today would be complete without some mention of the prominent role of the *bande dessinée.* The American concept of the comic book has been transformed by the French, especially since the 1950s. Today in almost all bookstores there is a section devoted to the BD. Moreover, this literary form has been labeled the "ninth art" and given its own museum and festival at Angoulême each January since 1974.

Although French comic books can be traced back to the nineteenth century, the genre first emerged in its modern form during the 1930s after the Belgian comic-strip writer Hergé invented the character Tintin in 1929 and after the export of Disney cartoons from the United States. But the biggest success for French comics came with the creation of the witty and tricky Gaul, Asterix. As we have seen, this comic strip inspired a major French amusement park. This is not at all surprising, given the fact that the adventures of this clever Gaul against the plodding Roman conquerors sold over 22 million copies between its appearance in 1961 and 1974. A measure of Asterix's success is found in the fact that this figure is about the same for all the Tintin comics sold between 1946 and 1974.

Comics in France have explored political and social questions much more freely than most of their American counterparts. Not surprisingly they flourished in the aftermath of May 1968 and have remained a staple of French literature ever since.

NOTES

1. This line is from William Wordsworth's poem "Intimations of Immortality" in *Recollections of Early Childhood*. In William Wordsworth, *The Major Works: including the Prelude* (Oxford: Oxford University Press, 2000), 299.

2. The rise of a vigorous and extensive literature beyond the hexagon is one reason why Peter France, ed., and Oxford University Press brought out *The New Oxford Companion to Literature in French* (Oxford: Oxford University Press, 1995), making the distinction between French literature and literature in French. See too Oxford online resources at www.library.uiuc.edu/mdx/bibliogs/French/frelitadv.htm and Laila Ibnlfassi, Nicki Hitchcott, Sam Haigh, Rosemary Chapman, Malcolm Offord, and M. H. Offord, eds., *Francophone Literatures: A Literary and Linguistic Companion* (London: Routledge, 2001).

3. See Sabine Rougeron, *Le Livre de poche a 50 ans: histoire Livres*, available at: www.fluctuat.net/379-Le-Livre-de-poche-a-50-anson, for example. Also, on channel France 3, see the brief presentation *1 Livre Jour,* which takes place in the Café Rostand near the Luxembourg Gardens, available at unlivreunjour.france3. fr. Finally, see *Le Bateau Livre* on channel France 5, available at http://www. france5.fr/bateau-livre/archives/20186776-fr.php.

4. See Hélène Michaudon, "La lecture, une affaire de famille," INSEE Premiere, No 777, Mai 2001, 1–4.

5. For the Internet site of the Salon du Livre see salondulivreparis.com. For the Reading Festival see the official government site, Lire-en-Fete, www.lire-en-fete. culture.fr/.

6. See Rougeron, *Le Livre de poche a 50 ans: histoire Livres*

7. Christian Robin, *Le livre et l'édition* (Paris: Nathan, 2003), 24–25, 120–121. For a visual flow chart, see pp. 154–55. Also, "Le marché du livre 2006" *Livres hebdo,*

sup. 637 (March 17, 2006), 8. For a visual flow chart, see pp. 16–17. Finally, Jannine Cardona and Chantal Lacroix, *Chiffres clés 2006: Statistiques de la culture* (Paris: La Documentation Française, 2006), 79.

8. Christian Robin, *Le livre et l'édition* (Paris: Nathan, 2003), 27. Also, Oliver Bessard-Banquy, ed., *L'édition littéraire aujourd'hui* (Bordeau: Presses Universitaires de Bordeaux), 80, 96, 217. Also, Gérard Mermet, *Francoscopie: Pour comprendre les français 2005* (Paris: Larousse, 2004), 458. Finally, "Le marché du livre 2006" *Livres hebdo,* sup. 637 (March 17, 2006), 5 and 42.

9. See the recent overview of Villon and his life: Jane H. M. Taylor, *The Poetry of François Villon: Text and Context* (Cambridge Studies in French) (Cambridge: Cambridge University, 2001).

10. Jean-Paul Sartre, *"What Is Literature?" and Other Essays,* trans. Steven Ungar (Cambridge, MA: Harvard University Press, 1988), 289–332.

11. Claudia Card, ed., *The Cambridge Companion to Simone de Beauvoir* (Cambridge: Cambridge University Press, 2003).

12. Alain Robbe-Grillet. *For A New Novel: Essays on Fiction.* trans. Richard Howard (New York: Grove Press, 1965), 133–142.

13. Nathalie Sarraute, *The Age of Suspicion: Essays on the Novel,* trans Maria Jolas (New York: George Braziller, 1963), 71.

14. Jenny Turner, "'Platform': Club Bed," *New York Times,* July 20, 2003; see also the collection of reviews at www.arlindo-correia.com/061105.html.

15. Michel Houellebecq, *The Possibility of an Island.* Cover. Trans Gavin Bowd. American ed. (New York: Knopf, 2006). See also "Perspectives et lignes de fuite editorials, en guise de conclusion" in Olivier Bessard-Banquy, ed., *L'édition littéraire aujourd'hui* (Bordeaux: Presses Universitaires de Bordeaux, 2006), 222–223.

7

Media

FRANCE HAS ALMOST ALWAYS been at the forefront of new media and visual arts. Here we will consider the question of the modern media that have transformed the relationship between image and word in constantly more complex ways. The French have been at the center of numerous new media creations, from photography, to movies, to the Minitel (a forerunner of the Internet). One of the most fascinating aspects of French media creativity is the varying degree of individual, corporate, or state initiatives in these various ventures across the past few centuries and through to today. The imperatives of expression, censorship, and subsidies have all played a role in the fast-changing media world of France. This nation that once was at the forefront of the revolution in print and journalism is now witnessing these older media decline rapidly as the Internet quickly becomes adopted with an alacrity that some doubted the French possessed just a few years ago.

Here we will trace the modern media in order of their development: newspapers and magazines, cinema, radio, television, and the various types of Internet. Due to its special hold on the world's imagination, we will consider French cinema in depth in its own chapter, which follows. But the full contemporary story of French cinema cannot be known without situating it within the context of these other media. For example, in the first decade of the twenty-first century much of the subsidy and impetus for French film-making now come from cable television. Naturally, too, the Internet may soon play a crucial role in film distribution. It is thus vital to see the synergy of the contemporary and fast-moving media universe.

NEWSPAPERS AND MAGAZINES

The French press has always been intimately related to the government. Early centralization of the monarchy ensured that new media such as the press were carefully policed and regulated. Printing developed not far from France, first along the Rhine River in Mainz (with Johann Gutenberg's first printed book in 1455). Publishing in France began shortly thereafter, in the 1470s, but really came of age after the onset of the Protestant Reformation (started in 1517 by Martin Luther). By the 1570s a short-lived French Protestant surge of publishing was overtaken by a militant Catholic Counter-Reformation press spearheaded by the crown.

Paris (1631) had its first newspaper a few decades after Strasbourg (1609) and was the first European city with a newspaper. (This city on the Rhine was then not yet part of the kingdom.) In 1631 two Parisian booksellers brought out a publication entitled *Ordinary News of Diverse Places* (*Nouvelles Ordinaires de Divers Endroits*), but the ever-watchful prime minister Cardinal Richelieu quickly had the named changed to *La Gazette* and found a new publisher, Théophraste Renaudot. This event illustrates the tight control that the French monarchy maintained over the publishing and newspaper industry through the Old Regime. Paris would not have its first real modern daily newspaper until *Le Journal de Paris* in 1777. Although the number of periodicals grew across the eighteenth century, the censorship of crown and church remained pervasive. Sweden would be the first nation to declare freedom of the press with a law of 1766.

The revolutionaries who remade France after 1789 initiated the first great age of the French newspaper and periodical. Then number of pamphlets published jumped notably from 217 in 1787 to 819 in 1788 and then exploded to 3,305 in 1789 and 3,121 in 1790. Even this efflorescence paled next to the rush to publish newspapers: 184 new ones appeared in 1789, then 335 more in 1790, and then almost 800 more by 1799. Most of these papers and pamphlets became part of the "opinion press," meaning that they eschewed objectivity for partisan politicking. They remained a staple of French journalism for much of the nineteenth century.[1]

Starting with the Terror during the mid-1790s through the age of Napoleon, the Restoration, and the July Monarchy, the press was rigorously controlled. After Napoleon came to power in 1799, for example, he closed 60 of Paris's 73 newspapers. One of Napoleon's most famous quips also concerned newspapers. Asked by his aide if he wished to know what was in the papers, he is said to have demurred: "Skip it, skip it, . . . I know what is in them, they only say what I tell them to."[2]

Across the nineteenth century French journalism made impressive innovations. One of the first examples of the modern popular press was *La Presse* (1836) brought out by an early incarnation of the modern press lord, Emile de Girardin. This ambitious publisher had already amassed 120,000 subscriptions for his magazine *Useful Knowledge (Connaissance Utiles),* and he was also one of the most successful publishers of almanacs (one of the staples of French journalism from the very beginning) with his *Almanack de France* (1834), which sold more than a million copies. But Girardin also appealed to the Parisian upper crust in *La Mode. La Presse* was targeted at a mass audience, cost half of what other newspapers did (the difference being made up in advertising revenues), and emphasized such attention-grabbing items as serial novels, such as those by the best selling Alexandre Dumas. This enabled the daily press run to expand to over 20,000 copies. Like many French journalist of the age, Girardin also became embroiled in duels and played a central role in King Louis Philippe's abdicating in 1848.[3]

But the most durable innovation and institution created by French journalists in this period was by Charles-Louis Havas. In 1835 he created the first international news agency. This filled an important need: a means by which small regional papers could have access to major stories. In essence Havas became the "father of global journalism" and the creator of the first real journalistic monopoly in France (which lagged on this score behind the Anglo-American world). In another innovation, in 1852 Havas created an advertising arm of his international agency. Here again he was way ahead of most French newspaper owners, who did not include as much advertising as found elsewhere. One area in which Havas lagged in innovations was in shifting from carrier pigeons (between London, Paris, and Brussels) to the telegraph. (Here one of his former employees, Paul Julius Reuter, would be the great innovator, first in Germany and then in London.)[4]

During the Second Empire (1852–1870), journalism took new directions, both literary and popular. After the Tanguy Law (1850) required writers to sign their names to articles, poets and novelists became more infatuated with the press as a means of enhancing their reputations. A good example of this was a new newspaper, *Le Figaro* (founded in 1853, published as a daily by 1866), which tapped the talents of Charles Baudelaire, Alexander Dumas, and Henri Rochefort. The editors of another new paper, *Le Petit Journal* (founded in 1863) followed a strategy aiming at mass appeal over politics or literature. Eschewing all attempts to lead the public politically, the editors of *Le Petit Journal* wished to be "expressing what everyone is thinking." Its dramatic success by 1880 resulted in its having a daily press run of 583,000, four times its closest competitor and composing one-fourth of all Parisian papers printed each day.[5]

It was the founder of *Le Figaro,* however, who best expressed this ideology of mass circulation. Henri de Villemessant compared *Le Figaro* to a department store, in essence a Paris innovation that came of age during the same Second Empire:

Like a well-stocked store, a newspaper should offer in its different departments, known in the profession as columns, everything that its clientele could need. It is necessary that I please serious people; it is also necessary that I am agreeable to light-hearted people or those who wish to refresh their spirits for a while.[6]

Mass newspaper publishing in Paris achieved a true "golden age" under the Third Republic. Along with the United States, France had the highest distribution of newspapers in the world (250 copies per thousand inhabitants). In 1881 the young Third Republic ushered in freedom of the press with the Law of 29 July 1881. This measure ended the various restrictions on the press dating from the latter part of the French Revolution: licenses and caution money (in essence deposits given to the government to pay for legal expenses in case of law suits and governmental crackdowns). The growing literacy of the population and the centrality of Paris made its four biggest dailies— indeed known as the "Big Four"—*Le Petit Journal, Le Petit Parisien, Le Matin,* and *Le Journal*—some of the most widely read papers in the world. On armistice day ending World War I, November 11, 1918, *Le Petit Parisien* set the French newspaper circulation record with over 3 million copies printed.[7]

The press helped make the Dreyfus Affair (1894–1906) not only a national but an international media event. But with the growing power of the media a question arose that has become all too common today as digital media increasingly blur the already distorted distinction between reality and reporting. During the "apache" events of the early 1900s (apaches being in essence some of the first modern juvenile delinquents), a writer in *Le Gaulois* worried that "it seems impossible to determine if the recent emergence of the Apache has inspired a genre of writing, or if it is the genre that has created the Apache."[8]

The end of World War I (1918) started the long decline of the French press, especially the mass-circulation dailies of Paris. Total war and mass slaughter brought a general disillusionment with authority, compounded by the discovery that not only politicians but also foreign governments, such as that of Czarist Russia, had subsidized the press. As a result circulation declined, never again to reach the figures noted above. Moreover, the status and pay of journalists also deteriorated, resulting in unionization (with the Syndicat des journalists in 1918). Soon radio began to challenge the dominance of the papers. To try to blunt the rise of radio and cash in on the profits, some papers, such as *Le Petit Parisian,* created their own radio stations.

The industry as a whole, however, pressured the French National Assembly to impose restrictions on radio news and grant print journalists perquisites in news gathering. Not surprisingly, a growing groundswell of opinion demanded an end to the close connection between politicians and the press.

France's startlingly sudden defeat in June 1940 and four years of collaboration brought a profound revolution to the press. For one thing, with France divided into occupied and unoccupied zones, Paris papers could no longer have an easy national distribution. Consequently, regional papers continued to expand their circulations. By the Ordinance of June 22, 1944 the newly installed Resistance government of de Gaulle mandated the takeover by the Resistance press of the papers that collaborated with the Nazi occupation and the Vichy collaborationists. Moreover the Havas and Hachette empires were also dismantled. De Gaulle appointed a young idealist intellectual, Hubert Beuve-Méry, to transform *Le Temps,* perhaps the most serious of the prewar dailies, into a world-class paper that could be the conscience of the nation. The result would be *Le Monde,* to this day the leading journal of record in France (fulfilling a role similar to the *New York Times* and *Time* magazine in the United States).

Initially, in the immediate postwar years the press enjoyed its greatest circulation ever, but by even the late 1940s many of the new papers were bankrupt. Between 1946 and 2003 the number of French dailies plummeted from 203 to 86, and the diffusion of papers shriveled to 164 copies per thousand inhabitants. Steadily the Parisian press lost ground to its regional rivals (who had been gaining steadily across the century). By the late 1960s even the regional press's reach was contracting. Though the events of May 1968 produced a spate of new newspapers, such as *l'Enragé* and *Action,* only *Liberation,* founded by Jean-Paul Sartre and then Maoists, has survived. Indeed, *Liberation* is the only major newspaper in France created in the last 50 years.[9]

In the 1970s through the early 2000s the French press would be beset by further problems, including a dramatic drop in readership: Between 1970 and 1990 the number of readers fell by half. This continuing slide in readership has dropped France far behind most other nations; for example, the French read newspapers at half the rate of the British and a quarter of the Scandinavians. France is not currently even in the top 20 nations in terms of national circulation, after having been world leader a century ago with daily circulation twice that of the British. Moreover, French papers have not kept pace with the rate of technological innovation and consolidation found in other nations. As a result, outside of Agence France-Presse, the old Havas, France is not a major player among the world's press conglomerates.[10]

The most dramatic decline in newspaper readership has been suffered by the great Parisian dailies, and the one that has suffered the most is *France*

Soir. Created in 1923 as *Paris Soir,* it was a fast-paced and photogenic paper following the latest trends in crime and celebrity. Recreated after the liberation of France in 1944 as *France Soir* by Pierre Lazareff, one of the most successful press magnates in French history, the paper reached over 1,500,000 in circulation in the 1960. Over the past decade, however, its readership has been steadily falling and is now below 70,000. In September 2005, *France Soir* published the notorious caricatures of Muhammed that caused an international furor. This bold move led not to an increase in ratings, but instead to the removal of the paper's editor.[11]

In the early twenty-first century the French press presents a complex portrait. On the one hand the Parisian press still retains much cachet, both domestic and international, but has seen its press runs steadily fall. Increasingly the regional press, catering to local concerns, dominates. On the other hand, the rise of free newspapers and the increasing recourse papers have had to Internet sites offers hope for future increases in press distribution. (These points will be further discussed shortly.)

In 2004 the French press had its biggest drop in sales since World War II. This affected the Paris press in particular. *Le Monde* saw its circulation drop by 4.1 percent (to a circulation of 330,768). *Le Figaro's* drop was slightly less: 3.1 percent (to 329,721). *Liberation* and *France Soir* fell by even greater rates: 7.8 percent for the former and 11.6 percent for the latter. On the contrary, the Paris regional edition of *Le Parisian (Aujourd'hui)* increased its circulation by 3.1 percent, the financial *Les Echos* by 2.1 percent, and the Communist daily *L'Humanite* and the Catholic *La Croix* by smaller percentages. These latter papers have seen increases in circulation recently also after languishing during the 1990s. The national sports daily, *L'Equipe,* however, had the most impressive increase, raising its circulation by 8.6 percent (with 355,135 daily readers).[12]

The following table, based on newspaper cirulation in 2004, provides a dramatic example of the contemporary dominance of regional newspapers among the top French dailies.

Quest-France (Rennes)	762,000
Le Parisien and *Aujourd'hui* (Paris and provinces)	356,000
Le Monde (Paris)	345,000
Le Figaro (Paris)	340,000
Sud-Ouest (Bordeaux)	318,000
Le Voix du Nord (Nord, Pas-de-Calais, and Aisne)	305,000

Le Dauphiné Libéré (Rhone, Alpes, and Burgundy)	250,000
Le Progrès (Lyon)	249,000
La Nouvelle Republique du Centre-Ouest (Tours)	234,000
La Montagne (Clermont-Ferrand)	204,000
L'Est Républicain (Nancy)	203,000
La Dépêche du Midi (Toulouse)	201,000
Dernières Nouvelles d'Alsace	196,000
Le Télégramme de Brest	190,000
La Provence (Marseille)	161,000
Midi Libre (Montpellier)	156,000
Le Republicain Lorrain	153,000
Liberation (Paris)	151,000
Nice-Matin	128,000
L'Union-L'Ardennais (Reims)	116,000
Les Echos (Paris)	114,000

Source: Gérard Mermet, *Francoscopie: Pour comprendre les français 2005* (Paris: Larousse, 2004). 448.

Since 1999 a series of free newspapers, usually weeklies, have become a part of major French cities. Usually distributed at subway, bus, and train stations, these have a wide appeal to an especially younger audience not being reached by what they perceive as the "boring" traditional press, with its long and detailed articles. These papers can be free due to funding by the already established press and companies wishing to find new sources of advertising. The oldest is *A Nous Paris,* which distributes 400,000 copies each week in the Paris region. Two of the other most important, *20 Minutes* and *Marseille Plus,* are part of international chains started by ex-Maoists in Sweden and Norway. *Marseille Plus* distributes 100,000 in this Mediterranean port, and *Métro* reaches Marseille, Paris, Lyon, Lille, Toulouse, Toulon, Aubagne, and Bordeaux, with over half a million total circulation for all these cities. The biggest is *20 Minutes,* with a total distribution of 675,000, of which 450,000 is in the Paris region. Much of the success of these papers resides not only in their being free but also in their being handy and available in convenient places and having attractively laid-out short articles, especially on cultural issues and coming events.[13]

France over the past 40 years has become much more of a magazine-reading than a newspaper-reading nation. Each day 64 percent (almost

31 million people) read at least one magazine as compared to only 33 percent who read at least one newspaper. France has more than 3,000 magazines and adds more than 300 new ones each year. Another important indication of France's strong magazine-reading habit is that the magazines of many of the national dailies—such as *L'Equipe Magazine* at 3,862,000, *Le Figaro Magazine* at 2,054,000, *Le Monde diplomatique* at 1,626,000 and *Le Monde 2 magazine* at 839,000—have subscription rates far higher than their newspapers.

Currently all the top-selling magazines in France date from the post–World War II era. Venerable nineteenth-century institutions such as *Le Revue des Deux Mondes* or satirical twentieth-century staples such as *Le Carnard Enchaniné* have much lower numbers of subscribers than the following list of the top 20 French magazines:

TV Magazine	14,164,000
Version Femina	9,230,000
Telé Z	8,695,000
Telé 7 Jours	8,384,000
Telé-Loisirs	7,957,000
Femme Actuelle	7,654,000
Télé Star	6,745,000
TV Hebdo	5,768,000
Art et Decoration	5,540,000
Santé Magazine	5,041,000
Géo	4,604,000
Top Santé	4,590,000
Paris Match	4,536,000
Notre Temps	4,360,000
Voici	4,272,000
Maison et Travaux	4,121,000
L'Equipe Magazine	3,862,000
Parents	3,812,000
Modes et Travaux	3,722,000
Science et Vie	3,689,000

The key point about this list is the domination of magazines devoted to television, then to women's issues, then to health, family, and home decoration. Outside of these issues we see just two magazines: one devoted to geography and the other, *Paris Match,* a photo journal of daily life in the vein of the old *Life* magazine in the United States. None of the famous intellectual journals—*Le Nouvel Observateur* (on the left), *L'Express* (modeled on America's *Time* magazine and in the center), *Le Point* (a rival to *L'Express*), or

Le Figaro Magazine—is on this list. Nevertheless, with their circulation figures (for example, *Le Nouvel Observateur* at 2,571,000, *L'Express* at 2,181,000, or *Le Point* at 1,530,000) we see that their circulation is much higher than the newspapers whose position they share. Opinion surveys have found, as these surveys would tend to indicate, that most French readers now pick up their information more from magazines than from newspapers.[14]

One reason why the political press may now do so poorly compared to technical and entertainment magazines stems from the education of most journalists. A common argument is that because there are so few journalism programs in France, and because most journalists are frustrated in their literary or academic careers and turn to journalism as a secondary choice, they may lack the professional pride and sense of objectivity found more in other nations with a stronger tradition of journalistic objectivity.

In general, French newspapers may be doing poorly vis-à-vis magazines due to lack of advertising and lack of home delivery. As compared to the magazines, the French newspaper industry has not been successful in attracting advertising. Moreover, most newspapers are not delivered at home but are sold (in order of prevalence) in press and tobacconist stores, specialty stores devoted to books and magazines, bars, and, book and magazine stores in shopping malls, train and bus stations, and kiosks. There is thus no tradition of a large Sunday edition in France that bundles extra news with large amounts of advertising before being dropped on the doorsteps of residences.

As we shall see below, when we look at the Internet, one of the ways that newspapers are now entering French homes is through online editions. It is too soon to tell whether this development will lead to a renaissance in the French newspaper. In any case it seems hard to believe that newspapers in the hexagon can ever regain the glory they enjoyed early in the last century.

RADIO

Although France was not home to this invention, it was quickly part of this new technology as it developed before World War I. France continued to be among the leading radio countries during the Interwar period (1920–1930s). The start of World War II and France's stunning and immediate defeat ushered in a golden age of radio (initiated by broadcasts from Marshal Petain and Charles de Gaulle), which would last into the early 1960s (until the rise of television). Since the 1970s French radio has been deregulated and has become more diverse and is now also moving onto the Internet.

Within a year of Guglielmo Marconi's path-breaking first radio transmission (1896) a Frenchman, Eugene Ducretet, sent radio message from the Eiffel Tower to the Pantheon four kilometers distant. By 1899 Marconi had moved from his native Italy to England, set up a factory, and created a radio connection between England and France. At the first International Conference on Radio in 1903 the French system developed by the companies Ducretet-Popoff and Rochefort was used in the militaries of Russia and the United States and had gained a foothold in Spain. (In short, the radio, much like the Internet 60 years later, had military origins.) Thus the hexagon was imbricated early into this new media.

Although as early as 1903 the minister of the postal service wished to impose a government monopoly on radio, this did not happen. By 1908 an American radio pioneer, Lee de Forest, was broadcasting opera from the Eiffel Tower and predicting that opera would one day be heard in every home. But it would only be after World War I that radio transmission would begin in earnest. In 1920 the General Company of Wireless Telegraph emerged (Compagnie Generale de Telegraphie Sans Fil), a corporation that would fill the role in France that RCA did for the United States or Telfunken did for Germany or Marconi Wireless Company did for England.

The year 1921 brought the birth of both public and private radio in France. The central government put a station on top of the Eiffel Tower (Radio Tour Eiffel) and the private Radio Paris was also set up. In 1921 stock-market quotes and weather reports began to be read from a studio at the Eiffel Tower (with the first report read by a fireman). The following year, a few days before the creation of the BBC, the first French private radio service, Radiola, commenced broadcasting such staples as news and sports and reporting discussions among journalists. The first radio announcer to achieve celebrity was Marcel Laporte, who took name of Radiolo. Concerts, talent shows, and singing competitions hosted by, among others, soap companies (Dop, Monsavon) emerged along with advertisements (at first usually sung but by the late 1920s spoken). To compete with radio, the French press launched its own stations. The most important example is *Le Petit Parisien*, which created *Le Poste Parisien* in 1923. Nevertheless, French newspapers succeeded in banning radio announcers from the 1924 Olympic Games staged in Paris. One inventive radio reporter, Raymond Dehorter, found a creative way to evade this restriction by renting a dirigible so that he could report from over the stadium. By 1928, sport would be the occasion for more innovation when radio broadcast the Tour de France bicycle race using mobile transmitters over the thousands of miles covered. During the mid-1920s, two major private radio stations came on the airwaves: Radio Luxembourg (1925; which become Radio Paris) and Radio LL (1926) created by Lucien Levy, inventor of the superheterodyne receiver. During these years advertising (temporarily banned in 1925) emerged on Radio Paris and then in the first provincial radio stations (Radio Toulouse and

Radio Lyon, for example) as the chief source of funding. A young Marcel Bleustein, who would go on to create the first modern advertising firm, Publics, became famous for his catchy efforts on provincial radio. Due to the growth of private stations, the government created a more systematic regulatory system in 1929 with the National Office of Radiodiffusion. By 1930, 13 private radio stations had emerged, and the government capped the private sector at this number.

After being a curiosity in the 1920s, radio became a commodity in the 1930s despite the onset of the Great Depression (which hit France later than other industrialized nations). By 1932, when the bad economic times started, one French home in five had a radio. The following year (1933), with the downturn in full progress, the government levied a tax on radios to aid government broadcasting and bought the private Radio Paris. In 1934, after right-wing demonstrations toppled the ruling coalition and threatened, it seemed to many, to bring fascism to France, the Minister of the Interior (in charge of state security) George Mandel created Conseil Superieur de la Radio to monitor radio programs more carefully. The following year (1935) Marcel Bleustein bought Radio LL and created Radio-Cite. He set about recasting the station to appeal to the youth audience by creating Youth Music Hall (Music Hall des jeunes) with an American format that launched the careers of such teen idols as Charles Trenet and his swing music hit "Here's the Joy (*Y a d la joie*)," which won the 1937 competition. Bleustein's station also introduced in 1937 one of the longest-running and most successful French radio dramas, the *La Famille Duraton* which would run through the mid-1960s. Despite the hard economic times and due to the relatively cheap price and appeal of the youth market and the need for diversion, radio ownership continued to spread: By 1936 the number of families with radios doubled, now one French home out of every two. As war approached, the public continued to buy radios at a fast pace, with about 1,500,000 purchased by 1939 (when the total in the nation stood at 5,200,000).

French radio in the 1930s was caught in the middle over controversies concerning public versus private ownership and commercialization versus politicization. The city of Lyon was one of the most volatile venues on these issues, as its liberal radical mayor Edouard Herriot supported public radio against his rival, the increasingly reactionary Pierre Laval, who bought his own private radio station. During the short-lived Popular Front (1936–1937) the government increased the number of documentaries and news shows to raise public political and cultural awareness. But in 1937 the National Press Federation still had sufficient power to limit the amount of news broadcast on the airwaves. By the start of World War II (September 1939), French radio was evenly split between public and private radio, with 12 public and

14 private stations. As war approached, regulation of radio passed from the postal to the information ministry.

Some of the most dramatic moments in French radio history occurred in the opening months of World War II, when war was not merely reported but also fought on the air waves. On June 17, as the Nazi military machine rolled across northern France and into Paris, one of the great heroes of the Great War, Marshal Petain, announced on the radio that he was taking charge of the government and asking Hitler for an armistice because the French cause was "hopeless." His most memorable phrase was the "making a gift of my person." All private broadcasting was immediately taken over by new Vichy "state" (as opposed to a republic) to be used in service of a "national revolution." The day after Petain's speech his former subordinate and recently elevated general Charles de Gaulle's appealed over the BBC from London to the French to continue the fight and to look to the resources of the overseas French Empire as well as to England and eventually the United States. Throughout the war Vichy and the BBC would take the war to the airwaves. BBC devoted a daily half-hour show—the French speaking to the French—which not only provided moral support but also contained coded messages for resisters. In 1941, for example, Operation V called for the letter, standing for victory, to be written or displayed in any manner possible in France. A rumor and whisper campaign also spread whereby the German station Radio Paris was renamed "radio-Paris ment," meaning Radio Paris lies. In the southern unoccupied zone the Vichy authorities controlled radio on their own. By 1943 Petain and Laval allowed the creation of a new station, Radio Monte Carlo, under the direction of the financial holding company SOFIRAD. Both would survive the liberation and the purge and continue into the postwar era.

De Gaulle and the Resistance movement that took over at liberation (August 1944) and kept radio under government control. First as Radiodiffusion de France (RDF, 1945) then as Radiodiffusion Television France (RTF, 1949) and finally as the Office of France Television and Radio (ORTF, 1964). After seeing the effects of radio propaganda under the Nazis and the Vichy and fearing the potential domination of the United States, de Gaulle and a generation of administrators across the political spectrum believed it was essential to keep radio, in the words of one historian, free of "private capital and foreign influence." The RDF quickly authorized a network of both national and regional stations. National stations included Programme National (1945–1957), Programme Parisien (1945–1957), Club d'Essai (1946–1947), Paris-Inter (1947–1957), Paris-Etudes—Paris IV- Radio Sorbonne (1947-to the present), and in 1954 the first FM station, Réseau FM—Programme Spécial (1954–1960). These stations tried to raise the cultural level of the French public with classical music and documentaries on literature and art. Only seldom did new radio "personalities" emerge.

Under this system private transmitters were banned, but private radio stations beyond French borders still broadcast and carried on the commercial traditions of the 1930s. These stations included Radio Luxembourg (RTL, dating from 1933), Radio Monte Carlo (1943), Radio Andorra (broadcasting from the tiny principality on the Spanish border), and Europe No 1 (1954). Although beyond official government control, these stations were majority owned and operated by French capital (SOFIRAD and Havas). Radio dramas (such as *The Family Duraton*), quiz shows (*Quitte ou Double,* Double or Nothing), talent shows, and fund raisers produced radio "stars"—such as Zappy Max, the most popular radio host of the era, and Pierre Bellemare, whose "*Vous etes formidables*" (You are great!) produced a seductive appeal to both fun, solidarity, and generosity that rivaled those of the movies. (Later Bellemare transferred this concept to television with the show *Téléthon.*) Europe 1 had great success bringing the American formula of music/news to France. Not surprisingly the national stations lost market share to more dynamic commercial peripheral stations broadcasting from outside France.

In response to declining market share, in 1963 the government created a station on the model of Europe No. 1, France Inter, and two high-culture channels, France Culture (specializing in drama and discussion) and France Musique (mainly classical). Thus when the ORTF emerged in the following year it was a formidable force in broadcasting, especially when it turned its financial investments in Europe No. 1 into a controlling interest. Although it had regained audience share and tailored shows for specific audiences at specific times, the ORTF came in for sharp criticism for its national- and Parisian-centric bias at the expense of regional concerns (usually allotted just 15 minutes a day on 15 regional channels).

The period between 1944 and the early 1960s was the golden age of French radio. By 1953, 90 percent of the population had one and it held a central place in every family residence and had become a national ritual. Moreover, radio continued to be an integral part of national events. At the start of the 1960s Europe 1 debuted a show that sparked the introduction and development of rock 'n' roll *Salut les Copains (Hi There Pals!)*. The hosts, Frank Ténot and Daniel Filipacchi, set the cool and hip *(jeune et décontracté)* style and inspired the emergence of the disk jockey in France. Soon all of France was talking about the generation *yéyé* (from the English yea-yea). The transistor radio (based on the 1948 invention) played a vital role not only in the spread of a new youth culture but also in French politics by subverting official broadcasts. In 1961, at the height of the Algerian conflict, French generals in Algiers opposed to de Gaulle's plan to grant independence staged a coup and took over the airwaves and tried to confiscate all transistor radios. But military opposition to the coup rallied when unconfiscated transistors confirmed that de Gaulle remained in power and denounced the general's actions. Soon the general's plan fizzled. Again at the end of the decade, during the events of May 1968, when government radio refused to report on breaking events, the students and workers found out the news from the peripheral stations Europe 1 and RTL. During these fateful weeks the ORTF faced its own identity crisis as workers went out on strike and challenged the entire structure of the organization.

The spirit of youth and rebellion of the 1960s and early 1970s was best captured, however, in the emergence of a free radio movement and the creation of pirate and anarchist radio stations. The first pirate station was Radio Veronica, broadcasting from 1960 from a boat in the North Sea off the Dutch coast, and then the even more popular Radio Caroline (off the English coast) debuted and gained an audience in excess of 50 million over its five-year life span (1964–1969). After May 1968 anarchist stations emerged and waged a legal and often physical war versus state monopolies. In 1974 a wide variety of dissidents created the France Radio Club to liberate the French airwaves. Inspired in part by similar movements in Italy and the United Kingdom, militants in the feminist, ecology, labor, and regional movements created radio stations within France. Their provocative stance can be seen even in some of the names of the hundreds of radio stations that opened during the 1970s—Radio Verte, Radio Riposte, SOS Emploi, and Radio 25—and in their goal to "give voice to those who have never had one, to favor the renaissance of local and regional life anchored in social and cultural life and the social movements of the region."[15]

Despite the strike at the ORTF, de Gaulle and his successors in the Elysée did not change the basic fact of government control. A few new shows aired, such as *Listeners have the mike (Les Audieurs ont la parole)* on France Inter, but no attempt at freeing up radio occurred. Even after Giscard D'Estaing became president in 1974 and reconfigured the ORTF and allowed new local radio stations to open (such as Radio Mayenne; Fréquence Nord; Melun FM; a station for "youth," Radio 7; and a station for seniors, Radio Blue) critics remained unimpressed because the government vigorously prosecuted the new independent stations both inside and outside France. For example, Radio Paris 80, Radio Pomarède à Béziers, Radio Ivre (Paris), the CGT labor union's Radio Quinquin in the Nord department, and the new peripheral Radio K in San Remo, Italy, all faced police action and judicial proceedings. Critics hoped the 1981 elections would bring change if Mitterrand fulfilled his promise to open up the airwaves.

After his victory in May 1981 Mitterrand immediately took steps to liberalize radio. Regional radio stations, due to the strong support they give Mitterrand and the Socialists, were the first to benefit even before the passage of the 1982 law on liberty of communication (with its new Superior Council of the Audiovisual—CSA—to oversee French media). Within the first few months of his presidency 500 new regional stations received authorization, and by the end of 1982 more than 2,000 had come into being. FM was now the growth area in French radio due to its greater bandwidth and better sound. In 1985, the new radio stations had gained a quarter of the French audience. Their growing power was aided by the government's dropping restrictions on advertising (1984) and allowing the stations to be part of national networks (1986).

The new stations organized themselves into national networks from the mid-1980s. The big new Paris stations dominated: NRJ, which had captured the youth audience, along with Hit FM, Kiss FM, Skyrock, RFM, and Chic FM. Radio Nostalgie created its own network based in Lyon and Lille. The large provincial stations carved out their own local niche: Radio L in Lorraine, RVS in Normandie, Alouette in the west. Deregulation led to domination by these commercial stations over local and regional radio, which remained viable only with the help of the CSA. By the 1990s, three major players had emerged among the new commercial stations: NRJ, the old peripheral Europe 1, and RTL. The development of cross ownership of media ensured that Matra-Hachette and CLT-UFA now own much of French media.

Along with deregulating the radio industry, Mitterrand also divested the state of much of its holdings. Government interest in such peripheral stations such as Europe 1 was sold to the Matra-Hachette conglomerate in 1986, and RTL gained independence when Havas was privatized in 1987 (under Chirac's tenure as prime minister). By the end of the 1990s RMC had fallen on hard times and was bought out and is now part of one of the largest of the post-1981 private networks, NRJ (indeed pronounced in French like the English word energy).

Opening up the radio market brought increased competition and market segmentation. Aiding in the process was the growth of stereo systems in car radios. All-day stations developed, and stations honed their particular niche audience (radio thematique). Usually stations segmented by age: Skyrock, Fun, and NRJ for under 25; Chérie FM, Europe 2, RTL 2 for 25 to 45; and Nostalgie for over 45. Even within such a competitive market thousands of the new stations survived. Local private and noncommercial stations strong only in the Paris region (even with government assistance)—Radio Notre Dame, Fréquence Protestante, Radio Shalom, Radio FG (gay), Beur FM, and others—often change format to draw better ratings. Fun Radio recently experimented with a U.S. talk-radio format.

To keep up with the competition, the remaining radio stations run by the government moved onto FM and also became more attuned to audience segmentation. Radio France developed a network of local radios *(radios decentralisées)*, which is currently at 39 stations and services half of France, and in 1987 a 24-hour news station, France Info, was added. France Musique Traditional, catering to European classical music, would in the 1990s add an "s" to its name and add jazz to satisfy the increasingly diverse French radio audience. Other national stations included FIP for music and traffic and Radio Blue for older listeners. The station RFI (Radio France Internationale), like BBC Radio, has an international reach and has 30 million listeners world wide. Anxiety that Radio France did not attract the youth audience led to the development of a new pop music channel, Le Mouv' (which would later add, in the 1990s, a website and chat room).

The 1990s and early 2000s brought increasing concentration, commercialization, and technological innovations. Satellite, web, and digital broadcasting came into use as well as the potential radio service with WAP (wireless application protocol) portable phones. Digital radio, for example, allowed one to listen to a number of stations via satellite. Companies such as TPS and Canalsatellite offered packages of stations to their subscribers. The RDS (Radio Data System) improved the quality of sound in car stereos. With the growth of the Internet more than 30 stations are now available, and some, such as NOPROBELMO and NETRADIO, were created specifically for the Internet. By 1990 France had achieved virtual radio saturation, with more than 98 percent of the population having one, and by 2000 families often had more radios than rooms in their homes. (This was a higher rate of distribution and ownership than with televisions.) Each day 83 percent of the population listens to the radio for an average to three hours. The peak hours of radio listening are in the morning between 6 and 9 A.M. A steady decline then sets in with two smaller peaks, the first between 12 and 1 P.M. for lunch, and second during the commute home between 5 and 7 P.M. Moreover, 80 percent now have a car radio and 27 percent have a walkman (known as a *baladeur* in French). As of 2005 France ranked ninth in the world in number of radios (with 55.3 million) and had 41 AM stations and about 3,500 on the FM band.[16]

TELEVISION

France was not as innovative in the development of this media as with others. Indeed, not only are there fewer French names associated with television's development, but it also came later to France, as with the rest of continental Europe, than to the United States or England. One can argue that even in the early twenty-first century French television is not as all-encompassing as elsewhere, judging by the lower number of stations available even today as compared to the Anglo-American world, although it is, as we have noted, the most popular leisure activity in France.

Nevertheless, the term "television" was first made public in Paris at the 1900 World's Fair. Russian physicist Constantin Perskyi used the term for the first time in a paper on the subject of future scientific breakthroughs, and his term became the source of the word in all European languages. Russians and immigrants in the United States after the Russian Revolution, along with the English and the Germans, played a more central role in television development than did the French.

Two of the few French developers, engineers René Barthélemy and Henri de France, with so-called radiovision in the early 1930s, initiated a distinctly French approach to television development—meaning that their systems transmitted a different number of lines than other national systems—that would continue to be seen in later decades. A few years later, in April 1935, the nationalist politician George Mandel, a protégé of George Clemenceau, who had led France at the end of World War I, helped initiate the first French radio transmissions, indicating the immediate interest that the French state took in the new medium. The following year (1936) the government created the French Radiodiffusion (RDF in French initials) with a monopoly over television broadcasts. A pavilion of radio and television was set up at the 1937 Universal Exposition held later in that year, and in 1939, 15 hours of shows each week were broadcast from the Eiffel Tower (which was also used for the radio) to the 200–300 sets then in use in the Paris region. When war was declared in September 1939, television operations ceased.

For the most part television languished during the occupation. But the Nazis did set up their facilities in Paris, on Rue Cognacq-Jay, to broadcast shows to their war wounded (using the German system of 441 lines). This system was largely intact at the time of liberation in August 1944 and provided the foundation for the new French system. The liberation government, based on the decision of the young minister and future president, François Mitterrand, adopted a system of 819 lines, making France the only nation with this system. This system would remain in place until late 1967 when the French shifted to the color television system developed by Henri de France known as SECAM (but using the same 625 lines as English and German TV). (The U.S. system is based on 525 lines.)

In 1949 the French state created the R.T.F. (Radiodiffusion et Télévision Française) by decree (thus it did not go through the parliamentary process that a law would have). Television, along with radio, would in essence remain a government monopoly closely monitored until the early 1980s. The fact that television was placed second indicated its still second-rate status within the nation. This was not at all surprising, since there were still only about 3,000 sets and only 10 percent of the national territory could get television (still coming from the Eiffel Tower).[17]

However, 1950 brought the precocious development of television in the northern departments of Nord and Pas de Calais. Centering in the city of Lille and with the nearby Beffroi mountains as the transmission site, Henri de France's company Radio Industry (Radio Industrie) put in place the first comprehensive television network. By 1958 these departments had over 200,000 television sets—when the entire nation had just 988,000. Even though the number of televisions was clearly growing rapidly, only half the nation was connected to television transmission. Moreover, government control remained tight and advertising was strictly limited to just five hours annually. The French were not exposed to much American television during this period. In the late 1950s, with a mere 50 hours of television per week (60 percent of it live), it is not surprising that only two half-hour American programs were shown. The United States had a much greater penetration with its films: Of the average 160 films that aired annually, 70 or so were usually dubbed American ones.[18]

In short, unlike in the United States, France's baby boom was not saturated with television shows and ads during the 1950s. Even in 1966 only half of French homes had television as compared to 92 percent of American homes in 1965. Even in 1968, after the creation of a second channel and sharp criticism by young revolutionaries of a "society of the spectacle," the American entertainment newspaper of record, *Variety,* lamented: "it feels that in France today one could live without television but it would be impossible to in other big countries, especially the U.S., where television teaches, reveals, instructs and has become a necessity."[19]

The pace of television development picked up in the 1960s. For example, while the number of televisions rose across this raucous decade from 2 to 10 million, the number of hours broadcast more than doubled: from 2,300 hours in 1958 to 6,000 in 1968. In 1960 the French versions of *TV Guide* (which had debuted nationally in the United States in 1953), *Télé 7 Jours* and *Télérama,* appeared (with another one, *Télé Poche,* added in 1966). A second channel, Antenne 2, was added in 1964 and a general reorganization of radio and television undertaken. A new governing body emerged: ORTF (l'Office de la radiodiffusion-télévision française). Under the watchful eye of de Gaulle, who saw television as a "magnificent instrument to support public opinion," the new service was given the following four tasks in its mission statement: "inform, distract, educate, and cultivate." By 1965 these two stations were showing 200 films per year (all pre-1958 films following an agreement with the movie industry not to compete with contemporary releases). By this date the percentage of American films was on the rise, with 100 or so usually being dubbed American efforts. By 1970, belying the statement in *Variety* cited above, French television had increased its showing of American films to 170 annually (now more than French films, 130 that year) and was buying 75 percent of its foreign shows from the United States (and 20 percent from the United Kingdom).[20]

Although government-controlled television had presented a highly sanitized version of the Algerian war for liberation (1954–1962), during the 1965 elections French television preformed its civic function objectively. All candidates received television time, and this exposure helped to push de Gaulle into a run-off election against Mitterrand. But government manipulation of television again became glaringly obvious three years later with the May 1968 events. None of the events appeared on television, and de Gaulle manipulated the medium, at the start of the events poorly but by the end brilliantly, to maintain power. Even so the staff and journalists of the ORFT went out on strike themselves and demanded major changes in a system that they found oppressive.

The liberation of television from government control, one of the demands of the young revolutionaries from the start of the revolt and an imperative for the ORFT that went on strike during the events, became all the more pressing after de Gaulle had used television not only to hold onto power but also to gain a dramatic victory in parliamentary elections in late June. But television could not convince the French electorate the following April (1969) that de Gaulle's proposed constitutional changes would benefit the nation. With the defeat of his referendum to give more power to the regions and to occupations, de Gaulle retired.

The two center-right successors as president after de Gaulle tried to liberalize French television. Georges Pompidou tried to bring autonomy and competition to the two already-existing channels and added a third under his presidency (FR3, created in 1973). (One of the impetuses for this shift was a controversy over sub rosa advertising on television via product placement.) Programming became more diverse, with more dramas, variety shows, and movies. After Pompidou's illness and death while in office (1974) his successor Valery Giscard D'Estaing did more extensive alterations. Giscard knew well the power of the media, since his performance, which seemed more from the "heart" in a televised debate with his opponent, François Mitterrand, was considered to be one reason he won. Moreover, Giscard wished to blunt left-wing criticism that the media remained in government control and to assume the mantel of a liberal reformer.

In 1975 Giscard's government reorganized French television with profound but not long-lasting or efficacious (for him) results. The ORTF was dissolved and split into seven separate companies: the three television channels,

French radio, two new production companies—TDF (Télédiffusion de France) and SFP (Société française de production)—and an institute—INA (Institut national de l'audiovisuel). As a result of these shifts the overall amount of airtime rose almost 200 percent, but funding for programs did not. More advertising was allowed, in part to raise revenues, but this did not raise the revenues of the stations by much. Even though Giscard's government demanded that more documentaries, fictional series, and local programming be created, the stations found American imports cheaper and thus more profitable. One of the biggest sensations on French television for the year 1980–1981 was the American prime-time soap opera, *Dallas*. The trend toward increased use of American material continued into the 1980s. Between 1980 and 1985 French television production dropped 30 percent, and foreign television transmission jumped by 75 percent. In part this was due to the economics of production: While a French television show cost about $4,000,000 to produce, an American production ran around $350,000.[21]

Giscard's liberalization did not blunt Mitterrand's call for a thorough overhaul of the system during the 1981 presidential campaign, one that was filled with accusations of bias concerning television coverage. Television debates figured even more prominently in 1981 than they had in 1974, with an audience of over 25 million. This time Mitterrand seemed the more sincere and warm compared to a "royal and aloof" Giscard. Accusations of media bias again surfaced from the camps of both candidates. During the night of Mitterrand's victory at a party at the place de la Bastille celebrants jeered TV journalists considered biased against their victorious candidate.

After Mitterrand's election, as part of his media revolution, television was deregulated decisively and an attempt was made to limit American penetration. As in radio, one of Mitterrand's goals was to place television in the hands of regional groups, and by 1985 over 128 regional groups had applied for channels. At the same time the first Socialist president in French history wished to limit foreign programming to 30 percent. To facilitate deregulation, regionalism, and limitation of foreign shows, Mitterrand set of a series of regulatory bodies: the law of July 29, 1982 created a foundation, High Authority of Audiovisual Communication, to promote greater diversity in television programming. In 1986 this body was replaced by a National Commission of Communication and Liberties (CNCL), which was succeeded in turn in 1989 by the Superior Counsel of the Audovisual (CSA). These organizations essentially failed in their missions: The percentage of American shows was not held to 30 percent, especially during prime time, and many of the local stations became more commercially than regionally oriented. In line with his goal of great liberty and diversity in broadcasting, but in this case through governmental control, in 1984 Mitterrand launched a station, TV5, dedicated to serving the world's

Francophone community and launched a telecommunication satellite, Telecom 1A, in 1986 for both national and international broadcasts.

The biggest impact of the Mitterrand presidency on television would be in opening up the private sector and inaugurating the age of cable and satellite television. In 1984 Canal Plus opened for business and quickly became dominant in subscription cable television. (Other stations, Canal J and Paris Première, also opened.) In 1986 two new network stations, TV5 (Cinq)—a general commercial station owned by the Italian media magnate Silvio Berlusconi—and a music station, TV6, were opened. TV6 lasted just a year in its original format and then became M6 in 1987 and adopted a more American-style MTV format. After the center-right won the 1986 parliamentary elections and Jacque Chirac became prime minister (the first cohabitation government), Chirac privatized the oldest station, TF1, by selling 50 percent of its stock to the French media conglomerate Bouygues.

During the 1990s and in the early years of the twenty-first century, no further radical restructuring of French television has occurred. The two most important events continue to unfold. First, television stations have been reorganized and transformed due to commercial pressures. For example, in 1992 TV5 went bankrupt and was replaced by a French-German joint-venture cultural channel, Arte; channel Antenne 2 became France 2; and FR3 became France 3. Then in 1994 a channel devoted to education and employment, La cinquième, broadcast during the day (while Arte filled the evening hours).

The most dramatic commercial story in French television has been the rise and fall of Jean-Marie Messier. This brash entrepreneur, a graduate of the Ecole Polytechnique and the ENA, had steadily risen through the ranks of both French government and enterprise through the 1980s and 1990s. By 1995 he was transforming a utility company, Vivendi, into an international media titan (at its height with assets of over 51 billion) including Canal Plus. But in 2002 the company reported the biggest loss, $14 billion, in French corporate history. A year later Messier was fired but claimed that the company's problems were not his fault (a point somewhat confirmed by the fact that Vivendi had an even bigger loss in 2003 of $25 billion and sold off Canal Plus to another French company, the computer and appliance giant Thomson). The following year Vivendi merged with the American media giant NBC and continues to play a major role in many aspects of French television and computer-game media.

Despite the growing power of the private sector and the growing global interpenetration of television and the media, virtually all shades of French opinion remained committed to preserving French cultural distinctness in television. One of the most stinging criticisms of Messier was that he was "too

American" in his behavior and mentality, especially in his advocacy of entertainment over educational values in the media. Fear of American domination
of French television had its first great moment shortly after Mitterrand started
his tenure. In the fall of 1981, a Committee for National Identity, including a
plethora of prominent writers, directors, and actors, placed a statement in *Le
Monde* demanding that American domination be reversed. Ultimately few were
satisfied with the policies of Mitterrand and Lang (his culture minister) in practice within France. But Lang took a strong stand when European government
officials and broadcasters called for limiting American penetration of the European market during the late 1980s. At the 1993 GATT talks concerning world
trade, the French spearheaded a successful drive to get cultural productions (including television) excluded from the general agreement that promoted a low-
ering of barriers to international trade. As noted in the introduction this victory
in the spirit of Mitterrand and Lang was won by a center-right government.

Half way through the first decade of the twenty-first century, French television is holding its own if not gaining back some ground on American
television. In part this is a result of the French, and other European nations, beating America at its own game, for example, with reality television,
which scored a major hit in 2001 with the *Loft Story,* or such talent shows as
Star Academy. In 2003, *Julie Lescaut,* a detective series—a staple of French
television—was the highest rated show. Indeed, in 2003 France, along with
Italy, imported fewer American television fiction shows than other European
nations. Admittedly the French still import a majority of their foreign shows
from the United States (68 percent of television features and 67 of films
as opposed to 77 and 80 percent in Germany, Spain, and England, for example). Moreover, American shows are increasingly being shown outside of
prime-time hours.[22]

Overall, in 2003 the major channels, although they continued to lose
viewers to cable and satellite television, still have the highest rating. Table 7.1
indicates ratings:

Table 7.1
French Television Stations Ratings: 2003 and 2001

TF1	31.5	32.7
France 2	20.5	21.1
France 3	16.1	17.1
M6	12.6	13.5
France 5 Arte	4.7	3.4
Canal Plus	3.7	3.6
Others	10.9	8.5

If we go beyond ratings to examine public-opinion polls about French perceptions of television in daily life we find much ambivalence. On the one hand, though the French spend more time watching television than in any other leisure activity, 60 percent of them are unsatisfied with the programming. Indeed, the channels that the French are most satisfied with are not the ones with the highest ratings: Thus France 3 finds the highest rate of satisfaction, with Arte second at 65 percent, followed by France 5 at 60 percent, M6 at 56 percent, with TF1, the leading channel by ratings at 49 percent (followed at a long distance by the cable station Canal Plus at 36 percent). The French often find the shows they watch superficial and stereotypical and, indeed, trust the news they hear on the radio a bit more than what they see on TV. On the other hand, the culture of celebrity that has emerged in France, almost as much as in the United States, has created a new set of heroes such as soccer player Zinedine Zidane or the star of *Loft Story* Loana, whose public exploits and emotions permit an accessibility millions identify with much more than with the programs of politicians.[23]

FRANCE ONLINE: FROM THE MINITEL TO THE INTERNET AND BACK?

Paradoxically, France came late to the World Wide Web/Internet precisely because it had been, unlike in television, a pioneer in computerized communication. The sector of the media that drove France's early entry into electronic networking was also an unexpected source, the national French telephone company (France Telecom).

Until the 1970s France, like other continental nations, lagged far behind the United States in installing phones in private homes. In 1970 the figure stood at a mere 6 percent. But across the 1970s the rate of home installation skyrocketed to 54 percent, and by 2000 France had equaled the United States in the density of its phone network. Cell phones achieved much more rapid diffusion: going from 11 million *portables* (as they are called in France) serving 19 percent of the population in 1998 to 43 million cell phones in 2004 serving 70 percent of the population (Italy has the highest concentration in Europe with nearly 90 percent).[24]

It was in the course of increasing its phone network and trying to save money on printing phone books that France Telecom hit upon the idea of an electronic directory. In 1979 the general director for telecommunications, Gerard Thery, launched the concept, and the following year a small version of the system began a small-scale test in the provincial town Saint-Maio, 46,000 in the Ille-el-Vilaine department, with the whole department (with its population of 250,000) using the system by February 1983. The following

February (1984) the system went national as France Telecom distributed terminals to subscribers for free (the rational being that the Minitel would replace paper telephone directories and thus cut down on the need to publish and distribute them annually). For nonsubscribers a pay-as-you-go system was developed. All transactions on the Minitel were added to the phone bill.[25]

Between 1985 and 1994 growth was phenomenal. From a million terminals in 1985 the number shot up to over 6 million by 1991 and then plateaued. The number of companies doing businesses on the Minitel leapt from about 2,500 in 1985 to 25,000 by 1994. This growth occurred with few glitches, the most famous one happening in June 1985, when the system crashed due to traffic outstripping the capacity. The perception that sex sites *(messageries roses)* had caused the crash hurt the image but augmented the national and international visibility of the system. In April 1989 new simplified and more powerful terminals came out, which had to be bought or leased. Only in 1997 did the value of American Internet commerce catch up with the $750 million the Minitel system handled. By 1997, 6 million French were using the system.[26]

In 1998, by contrast, only 2 percent of the population went onto the Internet, which greatly worried the government. Due to the earlier success and the rapid rise of the Internet no government had formulated a policy on the information and communication technologies (ICT). Thus in 1998 Prime Minister Lionel Jospin developed a Programme d'action gouvernementale pour la societe de l'information (PAGSI), which laid out a plan to connect France to the emerging World Wide Web. Just two years later the Jospin government put up one of the most convenient Internet sites (www.service-public.fr) for its citizens to facilitate administrative matters and handle questions and complaints. By 2005 this site was receiving 600,000 hits monthly. By 2000 all high schools and 65 percent of middle schools had Internet connections. Then in November 2002 the new center-right government of Jean-Pierre Raffarin introduced the Plan RE/SO 2007 *(Pour une République numérique dans la Société de l'information)* (in essence a Digital Republic in an Information Society), which aims to overcome the French "digital divide" *(fracture numérique)* by joining with local government and private industry to facilitate each family acquiring a computer, and a laptop for each student, and becoming computer literate.[27]

After a slow start, France has rapidly caught up with the rest of the developed world. By the end of 2000 the percent using the Internet in France had jumped to 10 percent. But the number of businesses on the Internet (2000) and the number of buyers lagged far behind the United States (15 percent versus 44 percent). However, by October 2004, France had 24,352,522

Internet users, or 40.6 percent of the population; this represents one of the fastest increases in the world. Indeed, between September 2004 and March 2005 France moved from ninth to sixth on the list of the top 15 countries with PCs in use. Purchases on the Internet have jumped dramatically between 2004 and 2005, by 97 percent between the first quarters of these two years. Some of the lowest Internet access fees in Europe have helped this dramatic growth.[28]

Growth in PC use is expected to continue to be strong for another decade, though naturally nations with larger populations will eventually surpass France and other Western nations with relatively small or slowly growing populations. As seen in Table 7.2, as of February 2005 France had a higher average rate of Internet use per month than did the United States, trailing only Hong Kong and Japan, and had the second-highest online year-to-year growth next to Hong Kong, with 25 percent compared to 19 percent.[29]

Table 7.2
Average Time Spent a Month Online: February 2005

Country	Time Spent Online	Year-to-Year Growth
Hong Kong	21:53:24	25 percent
Japan	14:50:42	12 percent
France	14:25:38	19 percent
United States	13:44:04	−2 percent
Brazil	13:13:58	6 percent
Germany	12:31:22	4 percent
Australia	11:39:06	10 percent
Spain	11:36:56	5 percent
United Kingdom	11:20:34	8 percent
Switzerland	10:52:28	7 percent
Sweden	10:29:33	8 percent
Italy	7:59:57	15 percent

What do the French do online? The French rating service Ipsos and the journal devoted to the Internet in France *(Le Journal du Net)* provide revealing answers. In January 2005 the French went online especially for news (64 percent)—this is a big jump, since in ratings from July 2003 this activity did not even rate in the top 10. Here we see how the French are moving from newspapers to the Internet as their primary source of news. Banking comes in second (53 percent), followed in third place by instant messaging (42 percent); in fifth is listening to radio online (34 percent), with exchange of photographs (33 percent), online purchasing (30 percent), consulting movie listings (28 percent), participating in a chat (24 percent), or a discussion group (21 percent), and sharing files (19 percent) all bunched closely together. At the bottom are the following activities: buy music online, MP3 (15 percent), consult videos (14 percent), play computer games (13 percent), buy games (12 percent), or videos (11 percent). This list has not changed much since December 2003 or even from July 2003 except for the rise of news.

As the French have increasingly gone online, the corporate servers benefiting have increasingly been American companies. This information is summarized in the Table 7.3.

Table 7.3
Top Ten Domains in France

	April 2005			July 2000	
Company	*Audience*	*Reach percent*	*Company*	*Audience*	*Reach percent*
Microsoft	12,160,000	75.39	Wanadoo.fr	1,760,000	52.65
Google	10,467,000	64.89	Voila.fr	1,384,000	41.40
Wanadoo	10,064,000	62.40	Yahoo.fr	1,213,000	36.29
Iliad–Free	8,591,000	53.26	Free.f	1,124,000	33.61
Yahoo!	7,182,000	44.53	Multimania.com	977,000	29.21
PagesJaunes	5,730,000	35.52	Microsoft	945,000	28.25
PPR	5,111,000	31.69	Yahoo.com	878,000	26.25
Time Warner	4,998,000	30.98	Multimania.fr	866,000	25.91
Lycos Europe	4,729,000	29.32	MSN.com	780,000	23.34
Tiscall	4,352,000	26.98	Chez.com	766,000	22.91

After 2000, as the Internet took off, the Minitel system went into a seemingly permanent decline. A big problem was that Minitel, in contrast to the Internet, was a closed system rooted in the France Telecom and could not be immediately connected internationally. By 2002 Minitel commerce was down one-third from the 1997 figure (to $500 million) and with a decline of 19 percent in the number of hours spent on it (47 million hours) as compared to 2001. As of 2003 the number of terminals had also declined, to 4.8 million.[30]

Nevertheless 32 percent of the population is still connected to the system and can now download an attachment (an "emulator" version, i-Minitel) to run on their PCs. Hundreds of thousand have signed up for this service, and it is estimated that Minitel service currently contributes about 50 percent of the income of French ISPs. France Telecom hopes that the Minitel, with its uncomplicated and direct means of accessing information, can make a comeback as the Internet and cellular phone service increasingly integrate. (Indeed, the Minitel was the specific inspiration for Japan's I-mode, its hybrid Internet and cellular phone service.) This is the strategy of a new system entitled *"et hop Minitel"* (roughly translates as "off we go, Minitel") to integrate the Minitel into the wide range of new applications that are developing.

As one *New York Times* columnist noted about the riots of October and November 2005, "The banners and bullhorns of protest are being replaced in volatile French neighborhoods by cell-phone messages and Skyblog, a Website that is host to messages inflammatory enough to prompt three criminal investigations this week." Indeed a common observation was that cell phones and text messaging allowed groups to form quickly and move swiftly to avoid police repression. For example, a 14-year-old in the southern city of Aix-en-Provence was detained, but then later released due to violations of due process, for advocating that police stations be targeted, and sites on the popular Skyblog exhorted "Unite Ile-de-France, and burn the cops" . . . "Go to the nearest police station and burn it."

Skyblog is the highly popular Internet site of the national radio station Skyrock. With four million people listening each day, it has the biggest market share of all French radio station for French youths (13– to 24–year-olds). The Skyblog site has over three million blogs, with additional blogs opening at the rate of 20,000 a day. It is probably the preferred Internet site for French youth. As the riots continued Skyrock vowed to police its sites more closely. Whether this had any impact on the course of the riots is now moot.

One thing that is certain is that many official French government Web sites were disrupted by what is known as "bombing," rerouting users on Google when they type in an address to another site. Thus, for a few days during the rioting, Google France displayed the home page for President Chirac's political party when users looked up the key words Paris, riot, or suburb in French.[31]

The new media in France today, as newspapers did before and during the French Revolution of 1789, are transforming the political landscape.

Notes

1. Antoine de Baecque, "Pamphlets: Libel and Political Mythology," pp. 165–166, and Jeremy D. Popkin, "Journals: The New Face of News," pp. 9–10, 150? in Robert Darnton and Danel Roche, eds., *Revolution in Print: The Press in France 1775–1800* (Berkeley, Los Angeles, London: University of California Press with the New York Public Library, 1989) and Jeremy D. Popkin, *Revolutionary News: The Press in France, 1789–1799* (Durham, NC: Duke University Press, 1990).

    2. Felix Markham, *Napoleon* (New York: Mentor, 1963), 76.

    3. Theodore Zeldin, *France 1848–1945 Vol II, Intellect, Taste and Anxiety* (Oxford: At the Clarendon Press, 1977), 495–496. Also see the important work of Jeremy D. Popkin, *Press, Revolution, and Social Identities in France, 1830–1835* (University Park: The Pennsylvania State University Press, 2002), which covers the development of the press in France's second largest city, Lyon.

    4. See the French Press Agency's website: www.ixiasoft.com/default.asp?xml = / xmldocs/customers/CUSTOMER-AFP.XML.

    5. Theodore Zeldin, *France 1848–1945 Vol II, Intellect, Taste and Anxiety* (Oxford: At the Clarendon Press, 1977), 526.

    6. For quote and overview of de Villemessant and *Le Figaro* see *History of International Newspapers: Le Figaro in France,* www.trivia-library.com/a/ history-of-international-newspapers-le-figaro-in-france.htm.

    7. Christian Delporte, "Maillons de la chaîne," in Jean-Pierre Riouw and Jean-François Sirinelli, *La culture de lasse en France: de la Belle Époqe à aujoud'hui* (Paris: Fayard, 2002), 307. Also, Clyde Thogmartin, *The National Daily Press of France* (Birmingham, AL: Summa Publications, 1998), 93.

    8. Cited by Robin Walz in his review of *L'Encre et le sang: recits de crimes et sociéte à la Belle Epoque,* Dominique Kalifa, *H-France,* July 1996 (Society for French Historical Studies). Available online: www.h-france.net/.

    9. Gérard Mermet, *Francoscopie: Pour comprendre les français 2005* (Paris: Larousse, 2004), 446.

    10. For above statistics see Mermet, *Francoscopie,* 446.

    11. Jean-Claude Sergeant, "The Mass Media" in Nicholas Hewitt, ed., *The Cambridge Companion to Modern French Culture* (Cambridge: Cambridge University Press, 2003), 93. Also, Gérard Mermet, *Francoscopie: Pour comprendre les français 2005* (Paris: Larousse, 2004), 448.

    12. Doreen Carvajal, "Top Editor Resigns at le Monde" *International Herald Tribune* November 30, 2004. See their online site, www.iht.com, for circulation figures. Also, Mermet, *Francoscopie,* 448.

    13. See M. Bernard Spitz, "Les Jeunes et la Lecture de la Presse Quotidienne d'information politique et général," *Rapport de mission remis par M. Bernard Spitz au Ministre de la culture et de la communication* October 6, 2004, www.culture.gouv.fr/ culture/actualites/rapports/spitz/rapport.pdf and Mermet, Francoscopie, 449. Also Jean-Marc Chardon and Oliver Samain, *Le journaliste de radio* (Paris: Economica, 1995), p. 25 for graph of hourly listening.

    14. Mermet, Francoscopie, 449–453, especially the list on p. 450.

    15. See *Petite histoire de la radio,* available: artic.ac-besancon.fr/college_de_ mouthe/radio3.htm.

    16. Mermet, *Francoscopie,* 417–18.

    17. Statistics and story from *MSN France; Encarta: télévision française,* fr.encarta. msn.com: encyclopedia_761590986_2/télévision_française.html.

    18. Kerry Segrave, *American Television Abroad: Hollywood's Attempt to Dominate World Television* (Jefferson NC: McFarland & Company, 1998), 48.

19. For the number of televisions in France see Colin Jones, *The Cambridge Illustrated History of France* (Cambridge: Cambridge University Press, 1994), 102, 312.

20. Kerry Segrave, *American Television Abroad,* 102.

21. Kerry Segrave, *American Television Abroad,* 200–201.

22. Debra Johnson, "Auds prefer local flavor over U.S. fare: Studios tailor shows to Euro tastes," March 23, 2003. Available: www.variety.com/index.asp?layout=miptv2 003&nav=features&content=story&head=preview&articl. Also, Neal Gabler, "The World Still Watches America," *New York Times,* January 9, 2003, 27.

23. For ratings, see Mermet, *Francoscopie,* 423 and for polls, 424–426.

24. For cell phone penetration, see Mermet, *Francoscopie,* 472 and 474.

25. See the homepage for The Hong Kong University of Science and Technology. Available: www.ust.hk/-webiway/content/France/history.html.

26. James Arnold, "France's Minitel: 20 years young," *BBC,* May 14, 2003. Available: news.bbc.co.uk/2/hi/business/3012769.stm.

27. Stephanie Hutchison and Stephen Minton, "France has some of the fastest growth rates for Internet usage," http://www.cid.harvard.edu/cr/profiles/France.pdf. See the report by the French prime minister's office, Information Service of the Government, "Four years of government measures to promote the information society." Available on the Ministry of Culture Web site: www.ddm.gouv.fr/article.php3?id_article=841.

28. For Internet usage and penetration statistics see www.spreadfirefox.com/?q=node/view/4812.

29. For these figures based on Nielsen/Net ratings see IT Facts mobile edition, for March 2005 see blogs.zdnet.com/ITFacts/wp-mobile.php?view=archives, under the heading, "Americans spend 13 hours 44 minutes a month online" (03–21).

30. See *Le Journal du Net,* http://www.journaldunet.com/ under the rubric "Les usages du web par les internatures by month and year."

31. Thomas Crampton, "French Police Fear that Blogs Have Helped Incite Rioting," *New York Times,* November 10, 2005. A12.

8

Cinema

ONE OF THE GLORIES of contemporary French culture is cinema. Paris witnessed the first public showing of a movie in 1895, and French entrepreneurs quickly dominated not merely their own market but that of the world. Only with World War I did France lose its primacy to the United States. Nevertheless, from the 1920s through to the present only American cinema rivals the French in influence or in the richness and complexity of various styles and periods. At the start of the twenty-first century France remains one of the most important movie producers in the world and the most important in Europe. Although in decline there as in the rest of the world, movie attendance in France remains comparatively robust. The ingenious means of financing (through a tax on cable television), publicity (such as with Cannes and other film festivals), and an openness to multicultural filmmaking within France and the Francophone community ensure that French cinema will continue to be at the center of world production and film theory.

Unlike other French media, cinema developed initially outside of government control or funding and unlike photography had little immediate connection to the world of art. (This is ironic for a nation that has become famous for its "art movies.") Cinema emerged from the efforts of scientists and entertainment entrepreneurs and only by the 1910s became associated with art. In short this was a technology before it was an art (though it quickly became dubbed the seventh art) and brought a new public into contact with a new type of visual culture. Virtually every decade since 1895 has produced its own distinctive style and sensibility, assuring French cinema a richness and complexity that is second to none. Moreover, few national cinemas are as key to the elaboration, development, and study of a national culture as the French film industry.

ORIGINS

Cinema's origins are found primarily in three nations: the United States, England, and France. The role of Edison is well known in the English-speaking world, but not as well known are the French contributions. E. J. Marey, a French doctor, created the first motion pictures made with a single camera during the 1880s, in the course of his study of motion. In France, the Lumière brothers created the first projection device, the *cinématographe* (1895), which combined the tasks of camera, projector, and printer simultaneously. They were also the first to show a movie in public, on December 28, 1895, in the basement of the Grand Café on the Paris boulevards (Bd. des Capucines). They showed 10 shorts lasting 20 minutes, including such banal subjects as *Feeding the Baby, The Waterer Watered,* and *A View of the Sea,* but the short *The Arrival of a Train at the Station* terrified the audience and made them jump out of way because they feared that the train was coming straight at them. Thus within the seeds of seemingly ordinary "realism" the flower of movie magic first flowered. Ironically, though the Lumière brothers made 1,452 shorts, even filming from the air before the invention of the airplane, they did not believe that cinema had much future, because it merely recorded what could be seen in daily life.[1]

The work of George Méliès (in the audience at the Café de Paris) is usually and rightfully seen as the antithesis of that of the Lumière brothers. This trained magician was the first real movie director (in French the word is auteur, and we shall see this has an especial resonance in France) and the first to fuse imagination with the seeming "realism" of the cinema. Méliès created the first film studio, introduced the use of artificial light and specially designed sets and special effects and produced the first fantasy and "science fiction" films. The year after the Lumière brothers debuted their first short documentary films, Méliès produced *The Conjuring of a Woman at the House of Robert Houdin* based on the camera trick of substitution (filming a woman, then taking her out of the scene, and then continuing to film), the result being that it appears that the person just vanishes (the technique known as stop-motion). In 1900 he was the first to adapt a text to the screen with *Cinderella,* and then in 1902 his *A Trip to the Moon* paved the way for future filmmakers such as Stanley Kubrick, Steven Spielberg, and George Lucas. In creating the first real French film, Méliès utilized motifs from the work of novelist Jules Verne and worked on this 11-minute film for three months (an extravagance for this early period). He also injected a sense of humor into this movie: After a cannon shoots a spaceship to the moon, we see a picture of the man in the moon grimacing as the spaceship gets lodged in his eye. On a more serious note, Méliès also pioneered in contemporary historical documentaries with a movie on the ongoing Dreyfus Affair (1899).

Tragically Méliès was neither able to capitalize nor sustain his innovations. He was not able to prevent bootleg copies of his films from proliferating across Europe and the United States and thus lost vast amounts of revenue. Méliès was also unable to continue to innovate: He never used mobile cameras, and thus his last film *The Conquest of the [North] Pole* (1912) was as static as *A Trip to the Moon* at a time when other filmmakers were discovering that a mobile camera brought greater excitement to the new medium. As a result Méliès went bankrupt by the end of the year and ended up as a toy seller at the Montparnasse railroad station through the 1930s.

Unlike other media and arts, French cinema innovated as much and as quickly with its commercial organization as with its technical and artistic. In the same years that the Lumière brothers and Méliès innovated in making films, Leon Gaumont and the Pathé brothers laid the foundation for production and distribution companies that in one form or another are still in existence. In 1895 Gaumont founded a film camera, projector, and phonograph distribution company and quickly went into movie production. The following year (1896) the four Pathé brothers, who had begun selling phonographs, created their own film-production company (Societe Pathé Freres) and rapidly surpassed Gaumont. By 1900 other cinema companies had emerged, including the following major ones: Eclipse, Lux, and Éclair (which went bankrupt by 1919).

In the age of Henry Ford's assembly line for automobiles, the Pathé brothers created a similar process for the cinema. They immediately gained European patents for the Eastman film process and by 1909 produced their own film. Film production, distribution, and projection quickly became vertically integrated as Pathé gained control over all aspects of the cinema industry. Before 1906 Pathé studies produced 6 films a week, after this date through 1914 the studio turned out 10 per week.

The Pathé system produced the first international film star, Max Linder, whose fast-paced visual slapstick humor (especially in the dozens of films that appeared between 1905 and 1914) anticipated Chaplin, Keaton, and other American stars. Along with humor, Pathé also brought melodrama to the cinema, especially with the Corsican director Ferdinand Zecca and his *Histoire d'un Crime* (1901) and *Les Victimes de l'alcoolisme* (1902). Pathé also brought the newsreel to *France (Pathé Journal)*.

Gaumont did not match Pathé in film production, but was still powerful and was especially pioneering in installing film equipment in theatres and building some of the first great movie palaces. The company's head of film production and a director in her own right, Alice Guy, made 200 films between 1896 and 1920—the first powerful woman in film history. Gaumont's most influential directors were Victorin Jasset and Louis Feuillade. While Jasset pioneered the serial detective thriller, based on the American comic strip detective Nick Carter (1906–1911), Feuillade is best remembered not only for his own crime series (with detective Jean Dervieux) but also for his mystery series *(Fantômes,* based on a series of popular French adventure books). Overall, Feuillade made more than 600 films before World War I. Finally, Gaumont would also take in the animator Emile Cohl. Cohl's *Fantasmagorie* (1908) and *The Joyous Microbe* (1909) were acknowledged by Walt Disney as pioneering work in the animated film and helped inspire the surrealists during the 1920s. Along with installing film and sound systems, Gaumont would also build one of the first movie "palaces," the 5,500 seat Gaumont Palace in Paris.

As the French film industry developed in its first decade, it increasingly expanded its audience from the lower classes of the urban and rural areas to the upper classes. The legendary French stage actress and perhaps the most famous actor of the nineteenth century, Sarah Bernhardt (1844–1923), quickly saw the importance of film and made a version of *Hamlet* as early as 1900. Her most famous film roles would come around 1910—Tosca, Camille, and Queen Elizabeth. To satisfy the growing desire of the upper classes for high-quality films, the company Film d'Art, created in 1907, used much of the directing and acting talent of the national landmark theater the Comedie Francaise. Its 1908 hit *The Assassination of the Duke de Guise* caused Pathé, Gaumont, and Éclair to create their own quality cinema production companies.

As film became a more established art in France it also became more anchored architecturally. Films had first been shown not only in cafes but also at fair grounds and amusement parks, as well as in theatres and music halls and café concerts. Often individuals peered into nickelodeon machines permitting only one viewer at a time. After 1907, cinemas built specifically to show films, rather than converted from theaters, erupted across Paris and France. By 1918, France had 1,444 cinemas. Two years after the end of World War I (1920), the number had jumped to 2,400. By 1929, this number almost doubled to 4,200, but then by 1937, it declined to 3,700 towards the end of the Great Depression.[2] With their elaborate architecture and ornamentation (often recalling exotic locations such as Muslim palaces and Asian temples) and large organs (especially during the silent era) these spaces truly became the magic and dream spaces of modern secular life.

French cinema between 1895 and 1914 contained an almost ideal combination of large companies and fervent competition that resulted in innovations that laid the foundation for modern cinema. Indeed, France dominated world cinema production and distribution: By 1910 two-thirds of the world's cinema production occurred in France.[3]

The 4 1/2 years of bloody hell that was World War I radically changed the French film industry. Although film was harnessed for the war effort, with thousands of propaganda films and newsreels produced, the French state did not take over control of the industry. With all of France's energies directed to survival and with the emergence of Hollywood, after a brief spell of East Coast dominance, French cinema found itself after World War I dethroned from not only world dominance but also national prominence, with American films now predominating even within the hexagon. Although still in existence, Pathé, Gaumont, and most other prewar companies no longer dominated French cinema.

Due to the rise of American dominance and the decline of the French studio system, the 1920s became the first great age of the French art film and also initiated modern film criticism. The literary and artistic avant-garde, especially drawing upon the painting schools of impressionism through expressionism along with the new surrealist movement and new decorative school that would become known as art deco, played a central role in French cinema. While World War I may have radicalized all aspects of culture, the conflict produced great vigilance in the French government. In 1919 the government imposed new regulations on the film industry, which often resulted in innovative films being banned.

At the center of postwar cinema, both its theory and practice, was Louis Delluc. University educated and working in journalism as book reviewer, Delluc initially disdained movies. He overcame his prejudice against the seventh art when he met (and later married) the former muse of the poet Paul Claudel, Eve Francis. During the first years of World War I, she introduced him to film. Delluc was first spellbound by the American film *The Cheat* by Cecil B. DeMille. As a result Delluc turned his critical acumen to film. Indeed he invented the word *cinéaste* for those who followed and critiqued films, and he laid the theoretical foundation for such future French film writers as Andre Bazin and François Truffaut. After serving in the army late in the war (he had initially been rejected as physically unfit by the military) Delluc created the first important film club and film journals *(Le Journal du Ciné-club* and *Cinéa)* in France. Included in this network were the great directors of the 1920s: Abel Gance, Marcel l'Herbier, Germaine Dulac, and writers Colette and Andre Gide.

Delluc would also direct seven films, two of which are considered masterpieces. *La Femme de nulle part (The Woman from Nowhere)* and *Fièvre (Fever)* were both filmed in the open air with a spare and minimal plot and acting. Delluc brought a painterly avant-garde impressionism and naturalism to the screen. These films, along with his criticism, inspired the 1920s avant-garde. Delluc died tragically while shooting *L'Inondation (The Flood)*. The inclement weather produced a fever and lung congestion and led to his untimely death at the age of 33. To honor his central role in the development of French film, the "Prix Louis Delluc" was founded in 1937 for the best annual French film.

The most ambitious and innovative of all 1920s French filmmakers was Abel Gance. Inspired from childhood by literature, he worked as a scenario writer and then director for Gaumont. In one of his first films, *The Madness of Doctor Tub (La Folie du Docteur Tube,* 1915), he used the recently invented anamorphic lens to distort objects and thus vividly portray the power of a mad scientist to alter the world. Then in the tragic drama *Mater Dolorosa* (1917), his camera work focused on the character's inner world through a series of flashbacks and montage sequences. After being inducted into the army and almost dying in a gas attack, Gance returned to the trenches in August 1918, bringing a camera crew with him. The result would be *J'accuse!* (1919) the story of a love triangle in the midst of the war in which actual soldiers are used as extras and, in one of the most powerful sequences in movie history, rise from the dead to ask the living if their sacrifices have been worth it. (Many of these soldier-actors later died in combat.)

This searing film was an international hit and inspired Gance into epic cinema. In *The Wheel (La Roue,* 1922) he again used the love triangle and framed it within a retelling of the Oedipus and Sisyphus myths set among railroad workers. The most innovative moment occurs when one character falls to his death and his entire life flashes before him. Critics have argued that "Gance had discovered 'Russian editing' before the Russians did."[4] Though popular, the film barely recouped its immense budget, so for his next film Gance turned to a winning formula: Max Linder in a comedy *(Help,* 1923). (Tragically Max Linder committed suicide shortly thereafter.) With his reputation for making hits restored, Gance turned to his grandest project: an epic life of Napoleon Bonaparte and the French Revolution (1926). This vast six-hour film included unprecedented camera techniques: cameras attached to horses, cable that brought the camera right into the middle of the crowd and into battle scenes, and the use of three screens to create wide panoramic shots (which he dubbed polyvision). The finished film was a critical but not a commercial sensation across Europe. During the early 1930s, with the advent of sound, Gance experimented with an early form of a stereo system. (Only in the 1980s would a restored and shortened version of this classic be available.)

Gance would live into the early 1980s but completed only a few more movies. His next epic, *The End of the World* (1931), failed in part due to the fact that it had not been shot as a talking picture (on the belated arrival of sound in France, see below). In the late 1930s he made a sequel to *J'accuse* in which all the war dead of the Great War rise up in an attempt to prevent a second mass slaughter. Abel Gance personifies the visionary ambition of much of French avant-garde cinema in the 1920s. He could not adapt to the constricted budgets of French film in the 1930s, as did the following generation of French filmmakers.

The French filmic avant-garde of the 1920s, however, more characteristically focused on human psychology and creatively fused cinematic technique and avant-garde painting. Marcel l'Herbier, a poet and dramatist, for example, in *The Inhuman* (1924) and *The Late Mathias Pascal* (1925) used sets created by the artist Fernand Leger and architect Mallet-Stevens, and both incorporated the emerging art deco style of architecture and interior design as well as Leger's own emphasis on the dignity of the worker. One of the most fruitful collaborations grew out of the new surrealist movement when the Spanish expatriates Luis Buñuel (director) and Salvador Dali (painter) made the short film *An Andalusian Dog (Une Chien Andalou,* 1929). The most dramatic and famous scene involved a razor seemingly cutting an eye, suggesting the power of cinematic images to radically alter perception. Buñuel's radical politics—as with many surrealists he was attracted to the Communist Party—led the Parisian Right to destroy the theater when his next film, one of the first French talking pictures, *The Golden Age,* debuted. Moreover, the prefect of police then banned future showing under the censorship laws.

Another innovator in surrealist filmmaking was Germaine Dulac, because she fused Buñuel's avant-garde stance with feminism. She had honed a feminist perspective as both writer and photographer with two of the most important women's journals of the prewar period, *La Front* and *Le Francaise.* After she became part of Dulac's circle she turned one of his novels, *Fête espagnole* (1919) into what is usually considered to be the first impressionist film (one focusing on atmosphere and psychological impressions rather than a strong story line). Then in 1923 her film *Souriante Madame Beudet* (1923) pioneered feminism on screen, and her film *Coquille et le Clergyman* (1927)—with a script by d'Antonin Artaud (see the next chapter on this central figure's contributions in the theater)—is the first surrealist feature film.

The genius of René Clair resided in his ability to combine surrealist and avant-garde sensibilities in commercial feature films but also to make the transition from silent to talking films and from the avant-garde sensibility of the 1920s to the poetic realism of the 1930s. During the 1920s his movies combined atmospherics with science fiction in *Paris Qui Dort,* another movie about a scientist controlling ray beams (1923), *Le Fantôme du Moulin-Rouge* (1924), and *Le Voyage imaginaire* (1925). He also produced an experimental avant-garde short piece, *Entr'acte*. But it was his talking movies *Sous Les Toits De Paris* (1930), *Le Million*, and *A Nous La Liberté* that brought him international acclaim. *Under the Roofs of Paris* was a classic evocation of the ordinary but picturesque lower middle classes of Paris, *Le Million* was one of the few successful French musicals, and *Liberty for Us* anticipated Charlie Chaplin's *Modern Times* in satirizing the degrading dullness and repetition of assembly-line work and the conformity and rigidity of office work in large offices.

During the 1930s French cinema entered a complex and highly creative period. At the start of the decade the nation's film industry found itself playing catch-up. Talking pictures came late to France, after both the United States and Germany had pioneered this new process. As a result French directors frequently went either to Hollywood or Berlin during the early sound period to do their films. In the early years of French talking cinema, dramas predominated, to be followed at the end of the decade by the school of poetic realism that most critics consider the classic, indeed, golden age of French cinema. The seeming contradiction in the term poetic realism captures well an agonizing age, on the verge of another war, that struggled between the political extremism of communism and fascism.

The emergence of sound made the theater actor and the sound director key to the movie industry. Much of the movie production of the early 1930s has thus received the title "filmed theater." Playwrights such as Marcel Pagnol and Sacha Guitry translated their stage success to film. Pagnol in particular achieved film immortality, despite criticism by many cineastes that he lacked the innovative flair of 1920s directors, by turning hit plays about his native Marseilles into film classics. His trilogy about a café owner, his son, family, and community—*Marius* (1931), *Fanny* (1932), and *César* (1936)—showcased the comedic talents of such actors as Raimu and Pierre Fresnay. Later Pagnol films about the French south, with screenplays by novelist Jean Giono—*Harvest* (1937) and *The Baker's Wife* (1938)—were also well received and popular and helped launch Fernandel as one of the enduring comedic and cinematic stars over a career extending through 150 movies until his death in 1971. Sacha Guitry, son of great actor Lucien Guitry, also transferred many of his plays to the screen and directed 12 films during the 1930s, the most famous being *The Story of a Cheat* (1936).

With the onset of the Great Depression (1929), followed by the rise of Hitler and Nazism to power in Germany (1933), first France's economy (by 1932) and then its politics (especially with riots near the National Assembly in February 1934) became turbulent and polarized. By 1935 a politically engaged cinema had emerged (paralleling the rise of the Popular Front). Its origins are found in Ciné Liberté, created to defend French cinema amidst the economic crisis. By November 1935 the French Communist Party formed its own organization, the ACI (Alliance of Independent Cinema) and hired the Jean Renoir, son of the impressionist painter August, to direct the film *People of France (La Vie est à Nous,* 1936). Subsequently Renoir received financial backing from the largest French labor union (CGT) to direct a film celebrating the 150th anniversary of the French Revolution, *La Marseillaise* (1939). Both these films were filled with an optimism that was not always prominent in this "devil's decade" that started in world economic depression and ended in world war.

The most characteristic mood in French cinema by the second half of the 1930s, found abundantly in "poetic realism," was a hopeful but resigned fatalism. An extraordinarily talented cluster of directors emerged including Marcel Carné, Jean Vigo, Jean Gremillon, Jacques Feyder and Julien Duvivier and perhaps the greatest screen writer in French cinema history, Jacques Prevert. Most of their movies expertly explore the physical and sociological shadows and corners of French society, especially of working-class neighborhoods. Many films took up such dark themes as night and fog. These directors could draw upon some of the first and greatest of French movie stars, Jean Gabin, the archetypical worker, and Arletty, the quintessential female seductress.

From 1933 to 1939 an extraordinary series of films emerged from these directors, screenwriters, and actors. Son of an anarchist writer and publisher Jean Vigo only completed one film in this genre, *Zéro de conduite* (1933), but it is generally regarded as one of the finest achievements of French cinema for its searing and haunting portrayal of the inhumanity of the French school system (which led to the censors banning it through the 1930s and World War II). The following year Vigo began working an unconventional love story, *L'Atalante,* but died before he finished. Despite having less then three hours of film, Vigo's two films are considered to be two of the greatest in world cinema. Along with the films listed above, Renoir's antiwar film about World War I (*Grand Illusion,* 1937) and his devastating satire of French decadence on the eve of World War II *(Rules of the Game,* 1939) are also among the most important French and international films. The third greatest director of an era filled with masterpieces is Marcel Carné. His *Port of Shadows* (1938) and *Daybreak* (1939) perhaps best embody the moody atmospheric of black and white dramas and show both Jean Gabin and Arletty in some of their greatest roles. Like *Rules of the Game, Daybreak* was banned by the censors for being too pessimistic on the eve of a new war effort.

One of the most important developments in France in the 1930s concerned not film production but conservation. Unlike in the United States, where little concern was taken to preserve the silent film heritage as the genre was replaced by talkies, French cinema was lucky to have Henry Langlois, who created Cinémathèque Française in 1936. Growing up in a Turkish city looted during World War I may have motivated this collector to amass as big a collection of films as possible. From an original collection of 10 in 1936, his collection grew to over 60,000 by the 1970s. His collection of Louis Delluc and other film pioneers made his library a center of French filmmakers from the 1940s. Eventually the French government would help fund and then take over his collection.

The outbreak of World War II and the French sudden and almost immediate collapse radically altered French cinema. Surprisingly, French cinema emerged stronger rather than weaker from the agony and oppression of Nazi occupation. First, American films, which had gained almost half of the French market during the 1930s, were banned by the Nazis. Thus French cinema lost one of its main competitors. Second, French cinema, after being in chronic economic difficulty during the 1930s, received funding and direction with a new government agency under the collaborationist Vichy regime. The COIC (Comite d'Organization de l'Industrie Cinématographique) brought uniformity to ticket prices, rationed the limited supply of film stock, required everyone in the film industry to be part of their organization, and provided financial assistance for films. The Vichy regime also set up a large production company, Continental, that made more films during the period (20) than did either Pathé (14) or Gaumont (10). Then in 1944 Marcel L'Herbier created the IDHEC (the French Institute for Advanced Film Studies), an institution that has also become central to French cinema. Among its students we find such central figures as Alain Resnais, Louis Malle, Costa-Gravas, Claude Sautet, and Patrice Leconte.

Third, under German occupation, when few material goods remained abundant—for example, fuel for home heating was scarce—the cinema became one of the most important refuges for a devastated population, offering warmth both for mind and body. French theatres that showed French films, theatres showing German films being shunned, were almost always filled, and thus due to such prosperity could afford to be heated. It is in this context that a new generation of cineastes developed, such as young Parisian by the name of François Truffaut.

French cinema between 1940 and 1944 was surprisingly free of Nazi and collaborationist propaganda and was much less politicized than the press and the radio. Naturally, newsreels carried a heavy does of fascist rhetoric, but it is revealing that the police had to monitor theatres during their showing because of the pervasive booing and catcalls that occurred. The Vichy regime did remove and imprison Jews in the film industry and also imposed new censorship provisions, which largely removed 1930s poetic realism from the screen. For example, no explicit representations of the working class or references to the Nazi occupation, contemporary events, and "vulgarity and slang," were allowed, but each film was not required to follow a strict ideological formula. Indeed, some censorship provisions, aimed at protecting minors under the age of 16, continued in force after the war. Aside from a few anti-Semitic, anti-Masonic, anti-communist, and anti-republican productions arranged by the Nazi occupiers, such as *Les corrupteurs* (1942) and *Forces occultes* (1943), cinema production was oriented to entertainment rather than political mobilization. Comedies, historical dramas, thrillers, and fantasies dominated French production.

Although producing films at only half the rate of the 1930s, and seeing many of it greatest directors and stars leave for Hollywood, French cinema unexpectedly flourished. Some of the 200 films made during the occupation era rank among the best ever made, and one, *The Children of Paradise,* is usually considered the greatest of all French films. Directors such as Jean Renoir, Rene Clair, and Juliven Duviver, and actors such as Jean Gabin and Michelle Morgan left, but directors such as Marcel Carné, Sach Guitry, Jean Delannoy, and Marcel L'Herbier, and actors such as Raimu, Fernandel, and Arletty remained. Moreover, some of French film's greatest script writers, Jacques Prevert and Jean Cocteau, were at the height of their powers. Finally, the dislocations of the era gave birth to a new generation of directors and actors who would play a vital role during the coming decades, among them directors Jacques Becker, Robert Bresson, and Henri-Georges Clouzot, and actors Jean Marais, Gerard Philipe, and Maria Casares.

An overview of some of the most important films of the occupation revel the complexity, escapism, and genius of the era. The complexity of the era is perhaps best summed up in Henri-Georges Clouzot's 1943 film, *The Raven (Le corbeau),* and two films by Jean Delannoy, *Pontcarral* (1942) and *The Eternal Return* (1943). *The Raven* was a mystery and thriller about the effects on a provincial city of a set of anonymous letters (signed simply, "the Raven") that accused respected members of the community of murders, abortions, and other crimes. Both the Vichy government and the Resistance denounced the movie as undermining French morale. In the case of Delannoy, while *Pontcarral* seemed to celebrate the Resistance, *The Eternal Return,* with is main characters with shining blond hair, seemed to be a myth of Nazi racial purity. The escapism of the era is well attested by L'Herbier's film *The Fantastic Night.* This film, *The Raven,* and Carné's *The Devil's Envoy* (1942) were the biggest hits during the occupation. The *Devil's Envoy* also contained an ambiguity that French audiences embraced: the effects of two emissaries of evil spreading havoc across fifteenth-century France. Carné's masterpiece, *The Children of Paradise,* made during the war but only premiered at the end of the conflict when France was liberated, best shows how genius can flow from adversity. A four-hour epic made on a shoestring budget, this film embodies

the resilience and courage of the French people and synthesizes the achievements of the national cinema. The movie combines the broad focus and scope
of Gance with the intimate portraiture of Renoir, along with dazzling pantomime recalling French street theater and the silent film era, and also a cast of
characters, a beautiful actress (Arletty) with a circle of admirers—a man about
town, a count, and an actor. In a time of crisis the film celebrates the human
imagination and the ability of the various arts to create beauty amidst a world
filled with misery and tragedy.

The postwar era (1944–1958) contained many continuities and contrasts
with the previous two eras. Although often derided by the film-critics-turned-
directors of the new wave generation that followed as a cinema for old fogies
(cinéma de papa) in reality this era contained many currents, some of which
helped produce the new wave. This 14-year period was an age of rising incomes
but continued material shortages, especially apparent in France in the lag in
television distribution. The result was a period of prosperity for the film industry, as cinemas recorded their highest ticket sales, with a record that still stands
of 400 million viewers in 1957. Such assiduous cinema attendance helped
blunt what many believed would be an American takeover of the French film
industry. At the time of liberation more than 2,000 American films from the
previous period of prohibition (effectively 1940 to 1945) were available for distribution. At meetings in Washington, DC in May 1946 concerning American
assistance in rebuilding France, Leon Blum signed an agreement with the
American secretary of state Byrnes that effectively opened France wide to this
backlog of American film. Indeed, cheap (because it had already been produced and distributed) American films captured more than 60 percent of the
French market in the late 1940s. To counter this seeming American cinematic
tsunami, French directors and actors formed a Committee for the Defense of
French Cinema in 1947, which succeeded in diminishing the presence of U.S.
film on French screens.

French governments of the Liberation and the Fourth Republic, however,
took major steps to sustain a national cinema. In 1946 the COIC (Comite
d'Organization de l'Industrie Cinématographique) became the CNC (Centre
National du Cinéma) and took a series of measures to ensure the production
and innovation in French film. A 1948 Loi d'Aide created funds for film production derived from a tax on the sale of movie tickets, and the following year
the state created UniFrance, an agency dedicated to the international distribution of French films. The 1948 law was subsequently supplemented by
a 1953 measure providing for development funds (fonds de développement),
which in turn was supplemented with a 1959 system of "advances on ticket
sales" (avances sur recettes) that helped launch successive generations of filmmakers, starting with the new wave. This was the most innovate aspect of

postwar government financial assistance, as it allowed directors and producers to receive loans that would be paid out of the future profits generated by their films. As a result of all these measures, French film was not as overwhelmed as British or Italian cinemas (where the U.S. share of the market often topped 75 percent of film revenues annually).[5]

France also was blessed with a number of dedicated intellectuals who wished to bring a love of movies to the entire population. André Bazin, affiliated with a governmental organization Travail et culture, toured the country showing films and lecturing to students and white- and blue-collar workers at public meetings. Bazin, in short, continued the mission he had been imbued with from his days in the 1930s Popular Front of bringing culture to the masses. The Cinematheque Francaise expanded its holdings and attracted a growing number of students and scholars. Finally, a number of new film journals emerged that placed film study on a much more solid intellectual footing and helped spawn the new wave. These journals included *L'écran française* (1943), *Image et son* (1946), *Les Cahiers du Cinéma* (1951) and *Positif* (1952). It would be in *Les Cahiers du Cinéma* that the young François Truffaut in 1954 would launch a critique of contemporary cinema that would also prove to be a manifesto of the new wave. Perhaps the greatest French action to restore itself as a center of international cinema was the launching of the Cannes Film Festival in 1946. (The festival was cancelled due to the onset of World War II.)

By the late 1940s French cinema was healthier than it had been in decades. The vitality of the postwar period is best seen in the sheer diversity of genres and styles in which French directors worked. One of the first great works, in a heroic realistic style, was Rene Clement's *La Bataille du rail* (1946). This film used both wartime footage and additional filming to narrate the heroic actions of French railroad workers in sabotaging the system in the period leading up to and including the Allied landing in Normandy in June 1944. In contrast, Marcel Carné in *Les Portes de la Nuit* (1946), despite a meticulous recreation of a Paris metro station in a sound studio, failed to hold his audience because the film's wistful and world-weary tone did not fit with the postwar emphasis on vigor and reconstruction. Perhaps due to the great events that it had just survived, French audiences became infatuated with grand historical epics. The director most famous for making this "quality cinema" was Claude Autant-Lara, and one of his greatest triumphs was the brilliant cinematic rendering of Stendhal's classic novel of the post-Napoleonic period, *The Red and the Black* (1954). Another adapted classic novel, Raymond Radiguet's, *The Devil in the Flesh*, showcased Gérard Philipe, who with his smoldering good looks and simmering rebellion became a rough equivalent to the American James Dean. While a new generation was coming of age, Jean Gabin successfully switched from playing workers and adventures to solid bourgeois and gangster roles. One of his greatest successes was in Jacques Becker's film of the Parisian criminal underworld, *Grisbi* (1953). Fernandel continued to have a deft comedic touch with audiences and enjoyed a continuous run of hits, as did Louis de Funès and another singlenamed comedian, Bourvil. The most successful comedy of the 1950s, and in terms of ticket sales still, was Julien Duvivier's *The Little World of Don Camillo.* For the historian the comedies of Jacques Tati—*Mr. Hulot's Holiday,* 1953, and *My Uncle,* 1958—are especially revealing because of their caustic but loving take on the travails of modernizing the French economy and society during the 1950s.

Although not as overtly revolutionary as the films of the new wave, some directors and films did cut a trail into the future. Roger Vadim's *And God Created Woman* (1956) was one of the first French films in Technicolor and introduced the world to Brigitte Bardot. Her frank relatively unbridled sensuality and animal magnetism made the reigning sex goddess of the period Martine Carol seem suddenly old fashioned. More cinematically exciting were the films of Henri-Georges Clouzot—with gripping thrillers such as *Wages of Fear* (1953) and *Diabolique* (1954)—the gangster and period pieces of Jacques Becker *(Golden Marie,* 1952) and the probing of loss in the mind of a child in Rene Clement's *Forbidden Games* (1952). All of these films contained moments of dark brooding atmospherics that new wave theorists would label film noir. The period's most influential director, however, was Robert Bresson. His films such as *Diary of a Country Priest* (1951) and *A Man Escapes* (1956) are among the most analyzed films around the world. They reveal great range: *Diary* is an adaptation of a literary classic while *A Man Escapes* derives from a prisoner's memoir. Bresson was less concerned with action or resolution than with "interior movement" and "spiritual outcome" and thus created new layers of psychological depth and added range for an actor's performance.

Even though the above directors anticipated the new cinematic style, the "new wave" of young directors that burst upon the French and international cinema scene in 1959 revolutionized cinema. Never before or since has such a large generation of young directors brought out so many films so quickly. Thirty new directors debuted their first films around 1959. The exact composition of this group varies according to the text, but virtually every scholar includes François Truffaut, Jean-Luc Godard, Agnès Varda, Claude Chabrol, and Alain Resnais at the center of this cinematic ferment. Directors such as Louis Malle, Eric Rohmer, and Claude Lelouch are best seen as precursors or sympathizers rather than as members. This new wave of directors also helped launch a new generation of actors, which included Anouck Aimee, Michel Piccoli, Alain Delon, Jean-Paul Belmondo, Catherine Deneuve, and the full blossoming of such established actors as Jeanne Moreau and Yves Montand. The actor that most embodied the new wave sensibility was Jean-Pierre Léaud, who appeared in numerous films, especially those of Truffaut. The new wave, however, had an undertow, and after the mid-1960s big-budget commercial productions and comedies made a strong comeback. Nevertheless, the director-centered improvisational style that the new wave developed has become a part of the international cinematic language and is the foundation and inspiration of the independent film industry.[6]

Most of the new wave directors started as cinephiles, carefully studying the history of cinema. Indeed, out of their efforts, based on utilizing the *cinématheque* and writing articles in the *Cahiers du Cinéma,* the term film noir has entered film vocabulary for the style of American cinema of the 1940s and early 1950s often found in murder mysteries, crime thrillers, and to some degree in westerns. Alfred Hitchcock was a particular hero to Truffaut, to Chabrol, and to Rohmer, who wrote the first book ever about Hitchcock. From this study of cinema, the new wave directors developed the theory of the "auteur." This word can be translated as director, but this misses the vital creative control that this young cohort wished to invest in their own hands. In essence they called for directors to steep themselves in cinema and their own experience rather than in literary classics. They also called for a film logic freed from nineteenth-century novelist procedures of clear plot, story line, and resolution New, more portable and quieter hand-held cameras allowed them to film outside and more cheaply and spontaneously. They would also add freeze-frames and jump cuts as standard techniques to express psychological and social dislocations. All of this innovation demanded a more attentive and creative reading on the part of the audience. No longer could an audience expect a predictable unfolding of a narrative by a collage of images and impressions that unfolded according to a visual logic. Not surprisingly, this self-conscious and open-ended approach to moviemaking had many affinities to the new novel that developed at the same time. Indeed, some members of this literary school, including Alain Robbe-Grillet and Marguerite Duras, also made films. What is perhaps most fascinating but still wanting detailed study is the fact that the new wave cinema was much more influential and popular in France and around the world among move goers and makers than the new novel was in the French or international literary world.

Indeed, almost from the start the new wave cinema received both critical and popular acclaim. The term was first coined in an article written by Francoise Giroud, which appeared in the French weekly *L'Express* in 1957 before the first films of Chabrol, Truffaut, Resnais, Godard, and Varda had made an impact, but after the first film of Jacques Rivette. Chabrol brought out two films in 1958, *Bitter Reunion* and *The Cousins,* and won both the

Jean Vigo Prize and the Golden Bear award at the Berlin Film Festival the following year for these efforts. In 1959 the new wave also triumphed at Cannes, with Truffaut's *The 400 Blows* winning the award for best director and Resnais's *Hiroshima Mon Amour* (1958) taking the critic's prize. In the fall of 1959 Godard brought out *Breathless,* which is usually considered to be the most innovative of the school as it combines in almost emblematic form all of the stylistic innovations noted above. While Chabrol, Truffaut, and Godard's films plumbed personal and familial memories and traumas, Resnais, in a movie based on a screenplay by the novelist Marguerite Duras, was more literary, having an almost Proustian sensitivity to the question of time, space, and memory. Subsequent new wave films did much to help French society to think in new ways about sexuality, gender, and commercialization. Truffaut's *Jules et Jim* (1961) returned to one of the great motifs of French film, the love triangle. In this film Jeanne Moreau displays not only a sexual but also an emotional and intellectual emancipation that would anticipate the coming assault on gender stereotypes. Agnès Varda's *Cléo from 5 to 7* explores, especially via visual image and juxtapositioning the day of reckoning of a fading Parisian female pop singer who has to go for a cancer test. Just as Varda explores the relationship between success, gender, illness, and identity in this film, so Godard meditated upon the compromises necessary for commercial filming in *Contempt* (1963), which starred the great German expressionist Fritz Lang as an agonized director.

Despite new wave attacks, commercial cinema scored some impressive successes across the 1960s. One of the best syntheses between innovation and commercialism was Claude Lelouch's *A Man and a Woman* (1966), which featured a seductive film score and an endearing love story filmed in the flowing and intimate style of the new wave. (It is interesting and important to note that Lelouch was one of the first of an increasing number of French directors who rose through the ranks directing advertisements.) Jean Gabin again had a big hit in an adaptation of a George Simenon detective novel, *Any Number Can Win* (1963). Although not esteemed much by critics, Gerard Oury's comedies with Louis de Funès and Bourvil, *The Sucker* (1965) and *Don't Look Now—We're Being Shot At* (1966), the first about the vexations of daily life and the second about the Nazi occupation of Paris, remain as of 2005 the fifth and the first most watched French movies in the history of the cinema. Clearly the French of the mid-1960s wanted a break from the rush of economic modernization and filmic innovation. This pause would not last long.

In the wake of the new wave, the events of May 1968 brought a fundamental reappraisal of contemporary society and the role of the cinema within an affluent capitalist consumer society. The near-revolutionary events of

May 1968 were foreshadowed by controversy concerning the direction of the Cinematheque Francaise in February of that year. The French government, which had steadily increased its subsidies to this largest film archive in the world, gained control by this date and decided to replace its founder, Henri Langlois. The response from the film community was swift and decisive, and over 300 filmmakers, including Jean Renoir, Marcel Carné, Truffaut, and other new wave directors, formed a Cinematheque Defense Committee. Faced with such virtually unanimous resistance on the part of the film community, the government retreated, reinstating Langlois and eventually building a film museum at the Palais de Chaillot (1972), thus fulfilling Langlois's long-held dream. When the events of May did erupt, members of the film community formed their own Estates General du Cinema and demanded a revision of the state's role in cinema. Such actions contributed to government reforms of the ORTF in 1974, which resulted in the television channels producing more movies and an end to censorship. As a result, French film became and remains much more frank in its images and language in terms of both sexuality and profanity.

No director, and few artists, mirrored the increasingly militant and radical nature dynamics of French society more fully than Jean-Luc Godard. Since he increasingly eschewed any commercialization, however, his films became increasingly hermetic. His increasing radicalism was also mirrored in *Les Cahiers du Cinéma,* which, as it moved farther to the left, alienated its old stalwarts François Truffaut and Eric Rohmer. One of the enduring legacies of this time was the creation of the politically militant organization Societe des Realisateurs de Films (SRF), which created a film festival (*La Quinzaine des réalisateurs*) in 1969 that is still going, serves as a preliminary to the Cannes Festival each year, and has spotted much new talent.

One of most vital developments in the wake of May 1968 was the fusion of filmmaking and the new feminism. Chantal Ackerman brought a deconstructive sensibility and a mordant wit to the industry with such films as *I You He She* (1974), which rejected traditional pacing and focused on interior monologue. Her production of *Jeanne Dielman, 23 Quai du Commerce, 1080 Bruxelles* (1975) was judged by *Le Monde* as "the first masterpiece of the feminine in the history of cinema." She continued to explore her childhood and adolescence in *Portait of a Young Girl of the 1960s in Brussels* (1993). Then in the mid-1990s, she ventured into the world of commercial cinema with *A Couch in New York* (1996), starring William Hurt and Juliette Binoche. Since then she has also explored the interconnection between cinema and art by creating documentaries and video installations at the Venice Art Biennale (2001) and *Kassel Documenta* (2002). Ackerman's recent films remain innovative and diverse: both *The Captive* (2000) and *Tomorrow We Move* (2003) star young actress Sylvie Testud. The former film is a mystery based on Proust and inspired by Hitchcock; the latter is a comedy exploring such themes as the interrelation between literary and café life. Her documentary *From The Other Side* (2002) chronicles the tragic disappearance of a Mexican immigrant in California and the plight, more broadly, of undocumented aliens in the context of a globalized economy. Ackerman is considered by many critics to be the greatest woman director in the history of cinema.[7]

Catherine Breillat (1948–) is another filmmaker from the women's liberation movement. Over the course of the last four decades she has explored the relationship between women, pornography, and the nature of the female identity. Most of her films are restricted to adult audiences. Her films include *From A True Young Woman* (1976), *Night Disturbance* (1979), *36 Filette* (1988), *Dirty as a Angel* (1991), *Romance* (1999), *Sex Is Comedy* (2002), and *Anatomy of Hell* (2004). Breillat based *Sex Is Comedy* on the gender relations of actors she had observed while shooting a previous film. She has retained a gritty integrity inspired by Italian neorealism; she constantly explores the unstable boundaries between exhibitionism and reflection. Beyond making films, Breillat has worked with Bernard Bertolucci, appearing in his *Last Tango in Paris* (1972), and has written screen plays for Maurice Pialat—for example, *Police* (1985), Frederico Fellini's *And the Ship Sails On* (1983), and Liliana Cavani's *The Skin* (1981).[8]

One of the ironies of the 1970s is that, as many French directors moved to the far left, the audience increasingly moved right, in front of the television. As the government created more television stations and allowed them to produce more shows and movies with broader entertainment value, the French increasingly stopped going to the movies and stayed home. As a result of the shrinking movie audience—ticket sales declined from the high of 400 million annually in the late 1950s to around 130 million during the 1970s and early 1980s—movie theater owners divided their theatres into more halls and cut down on the length of time movies were shown. Thus small-budget movies, such as the new wave had produced, became more infrequent. Even some of the established new wave directors such as Resnais and Varda found it hard to get their movies distributed in the more restricted and commercialized market of the 1970s. Some, as in the case of Chabrol, made banal comedies. Nevertheless, Resnais's *Stavisky* (1974) and *My American Uncle* (1980) and Chabrol's *Violette* (1978) and *The Horse of Pride* (1979) did show that both filmmakers still had their touch. Nevertheless, the emergence of television cine clubs on Antenne 2 and Cinéma de Minuit on FR3 and the television broadcasts of the French academy awards (the Césars, which began in 1976) ensured that the new generation coming of age watching television was aware of the French cinematic heritage and of the latest developments.

French cinema adapted creatively to these transformations that paradoxically brought great politicization, liberalization, and commercialization to the cinema. One response was to create a new genre of political thriller that combined radical politics and a critical historical perspective with Hollywood action. Some of the most important films in this genre included Constantin Costa-Gravas's *Z* (1969), the story of the generals' coup in 1960s Greece; *Confession* (1970), about the Stalinist purge trials in 1950s Czechoslovakia; *State of Siege* (1972), about CIA repression in Uruguay in the 1960s (filmed in Chile before the coup that toppled Allende); and *Missing* (1982), about the CIA and Chilean generals' repression during their coup d'état against Allende. France's behavior in World War II was especially covered. After Jean-Pierre Melville's *The Shadow Army* (1969), which emphasized the selfless nature of the Resistance, directors took a much more critical look at the notion that the France had been a nation of heroes in World War II. Max Ophuls's initially banned documentary, *The Sorrow and the Pity* (1972), Louis Malle's *Lacombe Lucien* (1974), and Joseph Losey's *Mr. Klein* (1976), were films that stirred great controversy with their unheroic portrayal of occupied France and the ways in which people stumbled into political actions rather than making rational and principled commitments. Another response to this new environment was the rise of an overt pornographic industry and films that explored gay and lesbian themes. Just Jaeckin's *Emmanuelle* series (starting in 1974) had worldwide popularity, and Edouard Molinaro's satire on gay/straight relations, *Cage aux Folles* (1978), inspired two sequels and an American remake *(The Bird Cage,* 1998).

Traditional detective films continued to be popular, but this was a genre that was losing vitality by the end of the 1970s. Nevertheless, Alain Delon, the most bankable French star of the decade, achieved his fame in this genre. The foundation of his success in this genre was Jean-Pierre Melville's *The Samurai* (1967). Few French movies of the past 40 years have had a greater influence on American cinema, inspiring the work of Martin Scorsese, Quentin Tarantino, and John Woo. Another of Delon's major roles was in Henry Verneuil's *The Sicilian Clan* (1969), in which he teamed with two of France's most enduring stars, the venerable Jean Gabin and Lino Ventura.

Some new wave directors achieved new nuances as they matured, and other members of the generation developed a much more personal style. François Truffaut proved the most enduring of the new wave directors, scoring at least moderately successful films throughout the period: *The Wild Child* (1970), the story of the attempt to civilize a child found in the forests of eighteenth-century Europe, *Day for Night* (1973), an exploration into the making of a contemporary film (the ever-more-common international coproductions), and then an especially well-received movie in America, *The Story of Adele H,* which launched Isabelle Adjani into a major film career (no other French actress has won as many Césars as she, with four through 2005). This film about a woman's unrequited love was followed by the story of a banal but enterprising Don Juan in *The Man Who Loved Women* (1977). Even though the movie has a unique and seemingly feminist twist—the female editor of his autobiography narrates the story—many feminists deemed it sexist. Critics also were not overly impressed by Truffaut's final film in his string of autobiographical films starring Jean-Pierre Léaud (due largely to Truffaut using clips from earlier in the series). The film nevertheless concluded one of the most systematic autobiographical explorations by a French director. As we shall see shortly, more cinematic triumphs awaited him. In 1975 Truffaut also brought out a well-received book, *The Films of My Life.*

Two other members of Truffaut's generation, after languishing during the crest of the new wave, achieved prominence from the late 1960s and into the 1970s and beyond. This was especially true for Eric Rohmer (1920–), Truffaut's colleague at the *Cahiers de Cinéma,* and Claude Sautet. From the late 1960s, Rohmer's romantic and lyrical movies—such as *My Night at Maud's* (1969), *Claire's Knee* (1970), and *Chloé in the Afternoon* (1972) as well as those he continued to make in the 1980s and 1990s—gained not only a solid reputation and a string of awards at major film festivals, but also a devoted audience. A few years younger than Rohmer but a decade older than Truffaut, Claude Sautet (1924–2000) achieved directorial success only in 1969 (with *The Things of Life).* During the 1970s he would hit his stride with a run of impressive movies usually starring his favorite actors, Yves Montand and Romy Schneider. His greatest movie and the one this is often considered the best French film of the decade was *César and Rosalie.* Montand and especially Schneider reworked the romantic triangle in the context of the evolving sensibility of the 1970s. A few years later, in *Vincent, François, Paul and Others,* Sautet explore the poignancy of love among those over 40.

Bertrand Blier and Bernard Tavernier were the two most important new young directors of the 1970s. Rather than establishing a new credo or movement, both directors focused on creating powerful story lines rather than innovative cinematic techniques. Blier focused on surveying the dramatic changes in personal morality, sexual relations, and gender morality that emerged after May 1968. In films such as *Going Places* (1974)—with his two favorite actors, the young sensations Patrick Dewaere and Gérard Depardieu, the most important up-and-coming male actors of the 1970s—Blier traced the amorality and nihilism that personal liberation often brought. Two of Blier's other films, *Get Out Your Handkerchiefs* (1978) and *Cold Cuts,* again featured Depardieu and surveyed the toll that a soulless modern urbanism of concrete and cars had taken upon humanity. Both films proved highly influential, with *Handkerchiefs* winning best foreign film at the Oscars (1978). Tavernier's movies, on the contrary, took a more introspective and historical turn. While in *The Clockmaker of Saint Paul* (1974) Tavernier explored the lives of ordinary provincial artisans after the fashion of Marcel Carné and Jacques Prevert, in *The Judge and the Assassin* (1975) he probed the ravages of bourgeois privilege, the plight of the working class, and the sexism inflicted upon women in late nineteenth-century French society.

What we might call the long 1980s for French cinema essentially began with François Mitterrand's victory in the presidential election of 1981. Indeed, his two seven-year terms (1981–1995) mark a distinct crisis period for French cinema due to the growth of television, the associated new technologies and rising production costs, and the growing power of the American cinema. Ironically, by the time this first Socialist president left office, the policies initiated under his tenure to rejuvenate French cinema began to bear fruit and lay the foundations for a decade of prosperity and renewal. Indeed, even though the Socialists were no longer in power when the 1993 GATT negotiations on trade occurred, Lang's notion of a French exception was vigorously defended by the new conservative minister of culture and his team plus French directors such as Claude Berri. Although a difficult period for French cinema, the fourteen years from 1981–1995 saw much individual creativity and renewal even if no clear school dominated. The case of the director Claude Berri is emblematic, as we shall see. Although leading the chorus for protecting European films from Hollywood domination, Berri was also one of the most successful French directors, equaling Hollywood in the ability to create big-budget international hits.

The deregulation and diversification of television during the Mitterrand years had a profound impact on French cinema. Initially, the growing number of channels and the rise of video home system (VHS) players and recorders seemed to pose a dire threat to the industry. But by the 1990s, French governments and the cinema had found a creative solution to this challenge in a proliferation of television stations and formats. In 1982 the French bought 202 million cinema tickets, a decade later (1992) the number of tickets sold stood at almost half: 116 million. During this decline, indeed right in its middle (1985), the number of movies shown on television surpassed the number shown in theatres. Moreover films increasingly earned most of their revenues on television rather than in the theatres. By 1985, films earned 25 percent of revenue in the theatres; by 1990, it was less than 20 percent in theatres, with 40 percent from television, 8 percent video, and 15 percent from international distribution. The growth of Canal Plus posed an especially big challenge. After its creation in 1984, the number of subscribers climbed slowly. By 1987 there were still only 230,000 subscribers. Subsequently,

Canal Plus added increasing numbers of films. Subscriptions soared to 3 million in 1990—by then, the service was adding one new film per day to its list. Also by this date over thirty percent of French homes had a VHS player.[9]

At the same time the French public became more enamored of big-budget American films. This was another trend that appeared from the middle of the 1980s, with the percentage of gross receipts taken by the Americans shooting from 36 percent in 1983 to 58 percent in 1986 and remaining above 50 percent for the next 14 years. Nevertheless, despite French complaints American productions were much less dominant in France, than, for example, in the United Kingdom or Italy where Hollywood gained a 75 percent market share. Rising production costs were also hurting French film production. Costs soared 17 percent in 1978 and 35 percent in 1988, for example. Across the 1980s, as a result, productions in the fashion of the 1960s new wave or the 1970s political cinema declined due to decreasing demand and rising costs. Directors increasingly took their cue from the market rather than their own creative imaginations. As a result "pastiche" replaced originality. Television- and cable-funded movie production aimed at high ratings with family entertainment rather than critical praise from the cinephiles. From the 1980s young directors increasingly came from backgrounds in television, advertising, music, video, and comic-book production rather than just a grounding in the cinema and its history. As we shall see, this would be true of such figures as J-J Annaud and Luc Besson.

As part of his attempt to promote French culture and combat the American infiltration, As part of his attempt promote French culture and combat the American cultural domination, Mitterrand's minister of culture, Jack Lang (1981–1986 and 1989–1993), developed an extensive three-part program to revive French film production. First, in 1982 he doubled funds devoted to the advances on tickets system. This helped increase the number of first filmmakers; in this period between 15 and 20 new directors debuted annually. Second, in 1985 he created a novel type of public/private company known as SOFICAs (Societes de Financement des Industries Cinematographiques et Audiovisuels). While these were private regional companies specializing in film production, their bylaws permitted any investor to write off their investments as a tax deduction. In this way Lang hoped to create small-scale and local film companies that would not be in the grip of the large international entertainment conglomerates and their mass-market blockbusters. Lang's SOFICA system has helped fund a wide variety of documentary and art films. For example, Claude Lanzmann was able to gain support for the production of his profound meditation on the Holocaust (Shoah, 1984), which might not have been able to be funded otherwise. The new wave directors Agnès Varda and Alain Resnais, who had had a hard time through the 1970s and early 1980s getting films either made or distributed, now brought out new films: Resnais's *Love Is Dead* (1984) and Varda's *Vagabond* (1985). Young directors have also benefited, for example, Luc Besson with *Money* (1983). Third, under his tenure French television steadily increased its underwriting of movies for both the small and the big screen. In early 1980s French TV co-produced about 20 percent of French films, but at the end of the decade more than half. Canal Plus played an especially pivotal role. By 1993, 80 percent of French film benefited from its subsidies, and this percentage has remained around the same since.[10]

Many critics unfairly dismiss the 1980s as a period lacking in a clear cinematic style. Granted, the generation and political revolts of the previous two decades had receded and no new distinct school took the place of the new wave. But the term "pastiche," which some have applied to the era, is harsh given the abundance of quality films during the period. Take the case of François Truffaut. As the decade began he had one of his greatest hits with a tense psychological study of Parisian theater life during the German occupation, *The Last Metro* (1980). This film drew 3.3 million spectators and won a record 10 Césars. The following year he returned to one of his favorite themes, obsessive love, with *The Woman Next Door* (1981). This film was also commercially successful and critically acclaimed. Tragically, a brain tumor and hemorrhage would claim Truffaut at the age of 52 in 1984. Clearly the French and international cinema markets would have continued to welcome Truffaut's work, since he had many projects set to go, if he had lived.

Bernard Tavernier and Bertrand Blier consolidated their preeminence with more provocative and distinctive films. Tavernier's best films included *A Sunday in the Country* (1984), an impressionistic and atmospheric study of a pre–World War I artist reflecting on his creative legacy at his country home as he is visited by his conservative middle-class son and the son's family and his protofeminist daughter, and *Round Midnight* (1986), which explored the complex and multilayered life of an American jazz musician in Europe. Tavernier also displayed his literary and critical talents by writing a history of American cinema. But it was Blier in the 1980s who filmed the most provocative mainstream movie about contemporary life: *Father In Law* (1981), a complex social drama starring Patrick Dewaere as a modest composer and night-club singer who tries to take on the role of father for the daughter of his lover after she is killed in an auto accident. Although a superb and well-received film, it was overshadowed by his next film *Household (Ménage,* 1986), which stirred much controversy. Starring the renowned and infamous hard-living singer-celebrity Starring the ubiquitous Gérard Depardieu, Michel Blanc, and Miou Miou, this movie returned once again to a subject dear to the heart of French cinema, the love triangle. But in this groundbreaking film, homosexual dynamics complicated the traditional heterosexual story and as a result a probing exploration of gender dynamics in relation to questions of love, hate, submission, and domination emerged. In 1989 Blier's film *Too Beautiful for You* was the toast of the Cannes film festival. This time Gerard Depardieu coped simultaneously with a midlife crisis and love at first sight.

During the 1980s, Maurice Pialat continued the tradition of late-blooming directors, with the most important films of his long career (dating back to the 1960s). In *Loulou* (1980) he explored the continuing power of social class in French society as Isabelle Huppert falls in love with a working-class lowlife (Gérard Depardieu). His *Under the Sun of Satan* (1987) won the Palme d'Or at Cannes, the first French film to do so since *A Man and A Woman* (1966). In Bressonian fashion Pialat traced the trials, temptations, and sense of failure of a young country priest (another adaptation of a Georges Bernanos novel).

The one new current, but not really a school, was the *cinéma du look*. The young directors grouped under this term took much of their inspiration not from Marxism but from the mercantile world of advertising and fashion. Jean-Jacque Beineix's *Diva* (1981) a neopolar (in essence a contemporary detective drama), enjoyed much success not only in France (winning four Césars) but also in the United States. His next film, *Betty Blue* (1986), combined rich and sensuous cinematography (crane shots and sliding camera) of the ocean juxtaposed with a doomed human relationship. Another director, Luc Besson, also demonstrated the appropriateness of the term, with ostentatious visuals in his film *Subway* (1984), shot mostly in the Paris metro and portraying a world of punk-rock music that is both violent and mercenary. At this point we are a long way from Carné's poetic realism; aesthetics is now driven by technology, not artistry. After the commercial success of *Subway*, Besson's next film, *Big Blue* (1988), became one of the most important cult movies of the decade. Indeed, in its interplay between the dynamics of human love and the mystical depths of the ocean, it became a manifesto about contemporary youth. Two years later Besson's story of a young female assassin, *Nikita* (1990), would be another hit and would be remade by Hollywood shortly thereafter.

Indeed, Besson would be one of many French directors who would prove able to make the crossover to Hollywood productions. His lush visuals translated well with the gritty crime drama *The Professional* (1994), the ostentatious science fiction fantasy *The Fifth Element* (1997), and a visually striking retelling of the life of Joan of Arc, *The Messenger* (1999), all done in English. Another French director, Jean-Jacques Annaud, though not usually classed with the cinema du look, brought much of this same sensibility to the screen with his characteristically contemporary background as a graduate of the National Film Scholl (IDHEC) and a director of television ads. His *Quest for Fire* (1981) explored how humanity may have gained power over this element. In *The Name of the Rose* (1987) a Franco-Hollywood production with Sean Connery, he translated the international best-selling crime thriller set in a medieval monastery by Umberto Eco. Annaud's next big hit was done in French, an adaptation of Duras's acclaimed *The Lover* (1991), about French colonialism in Indochina during the 1930s. In the late 1990s and early 2000s Annaud continued, however, to make films in the United States: *Seven Years in Tibet* (1997), with Brad Pitt, and *Enemy at the Gates* (2001), about the Nazi siege of Stalingrad, with Ed Harris and Jude Law.

Another emergent film director of the 1980s, Claude Berri, proved that French film could make blockbusters on its own terms. Indeed, he was able to combine the broad appeal of the blockbuster with artistic integrity. His first major hit, *Techao Pantin!* (1983) is an especially good case in point. It stars France's most famous comedian, Coluche—a stand-up comedian who came out of the café theater tradition, "ran" for president in 1981, and later opened a series of "restaurants from the heart" to feed the urban poor—in a vast panorama of the Parisian suburban underworld. Berri next turned two Maurice Pagnol novels, *Jean de Florette* (1986) and *Manon of the Springs* (1987), into not merely French but also international hits. An all-star French cast including Yves Montand, Daniel Auteuil, and Emmanuel Béart reaped many French Césars. In the same year as the GATT negotiations (1993), Berri released a new version of Emile Zola's epic novel *Germinal*. The film, starring Depardieu and the Parisian singer of working-class life, Renaud, not only recreated the oppressive atmosphere of the French Industrial Revolution of the late nineteenth century, but also cast an ironic and implicit gaze—with its premiere in the northern formerly industrial heartland city of Lille—on the virtual elimination of the industry by the time it was made.

Berri's successes helped spawn a number of historical epics during the early and mid-1990s. Many dealt with French colonial experience, for example, Pierre Schoendoerffer's *Dien Bien Phu* (1992) and Regis Wargnier's *Indochine* (1992). Both received several Césars but were criticized for insufficient critical rigor in dealing with the imperial exploitation. *Indochine* provided yet another triumph for Catherine Deneuve, a true film and French cultural icon since the early 1960s (indeed her face has been used as the model for the French symbol of the Republic, Marianne). Patrice Chereau's *Queen Margot* (1994) combined the luxurious and the lurid in a film adaptation of Alexander Dumas's novel of French royalty during the French religious wars (1570s). Jean-Paul Rappeneau's *Cyrano de Bergerac* (1990) was the most acclaimed of the historical epics. Equaling Truffaut's 10 Césars for *The Last Metro*, Rappeneau directed Gerard Depardieu in the Rostand play in such as masterful fashion that the stage nature of the lines blended seamlessly with location shots.

Although big-budget French films and expatriate directors in Hollywood showed that the French film industry was far from dead, what really launched the mid-1990s revival of French cinema was a string of masterful and highly successful comedies. One of the first comedies in this trend was Coline Serreau's *Three Men and A Cradle* (1985). This movie drew over 10.25 million viewers, which ranked it as the fifth most attended movie in French history. This French hit was almost immediately remade by Hollywood as *Three Men and a Baby*. (Another big comedy in the 1990s and in the top 20 of attendance, Herve Palud's *An Indian in the City* [1994] would also be remade by Hollywood.) Claude Zidi's comedy *My New Partner* (1985) became one of the few comedies ever to receive a César. But it would be the comedies of Jean-Marie Poire that would really mark a turning point. Already famous for a satire on Santa Claus, *Le Pere Noel est une ordure* (1982), and one of most famous comedies of the last 20 years, Poire built upon his critical reputation with tremendous popular acclaim with *Operation Corned Beef* (1991). Then his 1993 sensation, *The Visitors,* a Monty Pythonesque tale about twelfth-century knights suddenly transported to the present, leaped to second on the all-time list of most attended French films (almost 14 million tickets sold).[11] This came on the heels of the abysmal turnout of 1992, when French film attendance reached an all-time low of 116 million. Helped by the success of *The Visitors,* French film attendance jumped to almost 133 million the following year.[12]

Since *The Visitors,* French comedies have continued to shine at the box office. The 1998 sequel to *The Visitors* had the biggest opening day ever and went on to land among the top 20 grossing French films of all time, with over 8 million attendees. But it was not the biggest comedic film of that year. Instead François Veber's *The Dinner Game* (1998) topped it by a million tickets. This comedy about a successful and wealthy sadistic practical joker being outwitted by his "simple guest" was also a critical success. Between 1999 and 2002 the biggest comedic box office hits would be film adaptations of the Asterix comics. The first, by Claude Zidi, *Asterix and Obélix against César,* took in over 9 1/4 million tickets, and the second, by Alain Chabat, *Astérix et Obélix: Mission Cléopatra* (2002), became the second-largest film in French history, with 14,220,000 watching in theatres.

The decade spanning the end of the 1990s and the start of the new millennium has produced a dramatic renaissance in French film. Remarkably, 9 of the top 20 French films in terms of attendance have been made in the last 15 years. This is astonishing when one considers that film audiences, even with a sizeable upturn since the mid-1990s, are half of what they were in the

1950s. From 2001 French films recaptured enough of the market to push American films below the 50 percent mark in market share. What have been the causes of this turnaround?

By the mid-1990s the film-production system Lang had reconfigured began to bear fruit. The advances on profits and SOFICA system of capitalization have been vital tools for generating investment in film. Television, moreover, which had decimated film in the 1980s, was now able to rehabilitate the medium. Canal Plus now produces half of all French film and dominates European production and, in conjunction with Pathé, distribution. Moreover, with almost five thousand screens, France is among the European leaders and tops Europe in terms of film production. Indeed, with an average of 150 films per year, France ranks behind India (800) and the United States (500) in annual movie production. Although a distant second to the United States, with only 3–4 percent of the market, France is still second in film exports. Profits on film exports have become more and more vital to French cinema, and by the early twenty-first century 85 percent of its revenue come from abroad (40 percent from Western Europe, 26 percent from the United States, 16 percent from Germany and Japanese, and 10 percent from Italy). In 2001 France achieved one of its biggest pan-European hits with *Brotherhood of the Wolf*. While this haunting atmospheric tale out of eighteenth-century life was the fourth most seen film in France (with 5,580,000 tickets sold), it netted a $44 million profit in the rest of Europe.[13]

Along with comedies, almost all genres of French film have been renewed over the past decade (1995–2005). Cinematic realism has had its most important refashioning, with films about the French suburbs and urban street life. As we shall see more fully in the last chapter, French urban life is in some ways the reverse of the American pattern. Rather than the poor being trapped in inner cities as in the United States, they have faced spatial marginalization by being forced to live in outlying suburbs while the wealthy, for the most part, have continued to live in the central cities. The films of Mathieu Kassovitz epitomize what has been called the young cinema, which often deals with suburban marginalization. In *Hate (La haine*, 1995), *Métisse* (1993), *Assassin(s)* (1997), and *The Crimson Rivers* (2000), Kassovitz brings humanity to the unemployed youth. In his most famous movie, *Hate*, for example, a diverse collection of youths (of Jewish, North African, and Sub-Saharan African descent) confront the crisis of a broken family, the drug culture, and police brutality. Kassovitz's innovative use of handheld cameras and a sound track featuring the leading French rap artists (MC Solar, Iam, FFF) reveals the desperation of the underside of French society and resulted in his winning a Cesar in his directing debut. Since 2000 a young Algerian filmmaker, Nadir Mokneche, has been pioneering a French-Algerian hybrid cinema. One of the most compelling French-Algerian coproductions is *Viva Laldjerie* (2002) about the slums of Algiers and France and the economic migrants that connect the two nations together.

In 2000, 105 years after the Lumière brothers, French film again was at the forefront of cinematic innovation. Jean-Christophe Comar, with his thriller about 1830s Paris and one of the first modern detectives, known as Vidocq, made the first all-digital film. Although *Vidocq* has not been hailed as a major film, the implications of digital cinema that it heralds are momentous. The lighter cameras and more efficient filming (one can immediately see the results rather than having to wait for the rushes) result in a more nuanced and upgraded notion of the camera as pen *(camera stylo)*. Only time will tell whether digital filming will provide France with yet another "new wave." Already, however, the most innovative of young French directors are rejuvenating French cinematic traditions.

In both her life and her films, Claire Denis (1948-) has experienced the transformation of France from a colonial power to a multicultural society and a global presence. Raised in Cameron by her parents (who worked in the French foreign civil service) until the age of 14, she had a long and distinguished apprenticeship in the films of Wim Wenders, Jim Jarmusch, and Constantin Costa-Gravas before she started making her own films. *Chocolate* (1988) is a visually rich and evocative exploration of the experience of a young French woman growing up in decolonizing French West Africa during the 1950s. *I Can't Sleep* (1994) explores the multi-ethnic and familial tensions of a Parisian neighborhood based on the true story of the so-called grammy killer who terrorized Paris during the 1990s. The 1999 film *Good Work* reframes Herman Melville's *Billy Budd* to the French Foreign legion in contemporary East Africa. Most recently, her film *The Intruder* (2005) explores the lives of individuals who have literally lived around the world and examines the interactions among space, culture, family, and personal identity. According to some critics she ranks among the elite of French directors.[14]

Over the past decade (1995–2005), poetic realism and lyricism, the French cinematic traditions most in need of revival, have been transformed in unexpected ways. Renewal of this uniquely French lyrical tradition has been done by using high technology. One might call the synthesis digital lyricism. At the center of this French film renaissance are Jean-Pierre Jeunet, who started in advertising, and Marc Caro, who got his start in comics. Both started work in music videos and cartoons in the 1980s. *Delicatessen* (1991) was their first joint project. The famous comic-book author Gilles Adrien did the screen play, Jeunet directed, and Caro did the visuals in a gothic comic-strip screen style. The movie used the language of 1950s American science fiction movies to explore a world after a war using atomic bombs (that is, World War III) in which cannibalism has become predominant and a band of vegetarian troglodytes fights to restore human values. This unique and innovative blend of dark humor and special effects was given a new twist in their second film: *The City of Lost Children* (1994). Amidst a rich cinematic decor that references Méliès, Gustave Doré, Jules Verne, and Marcel Carné, a mad scientist (with the appropriate name of Krank) who has lost the ability to dream survives by stealing the dreams of children. Ultimately he is vanquished when one of the stolen dreams turns into a nightmare. This was one of most original films of the decade and brilliantly confronted humanity's eternal imaginative quest with the potential tyrannies of technological control. Before retuning to the lyrical vein, Jeunet directed the American megaproduction, *Alien: Resurrection* (1997).

Jeunet's greatest success so far has been *Amélie*, which starred actress Audrey Tautou (2001). This contemporary fairy tale of traditional Parisian character types helped spur dramatic increase in attendance—24 percent over the previous year (from 165.5 million in 2000 to 187.1 in 2001)—and helped French films regain half of the market share in the hexagon. Done on a small budget (only one-tenth of *Alien: Resurrection)*, Amelie tells the story of an imaginative but overprotected child who flees from her comfortable suburban cocoon to find adventure in the simple pleasures of Parisian life and in helping the lonely, alienated, and persecuted. The social and imaginative lives of this latter-day Lady Bountiful are seamlessly blended through deft use of special effects with a loving gaze on the contemporary Parisian cityscape, which recalls the classic photographers of Paris, especially Robert Doisneau. In 2004 Jeunet and Tautou joined forces again for a haunting film of loss and anxiety during World War I, based on a Sebastien Japrisot novel, *A Very Long Engagement.* Done in a starker palette, this movie did well but did not match the success of *Amélie*.[15]

Even more than Jeunet, Erick Zonca is seen as the young French filmmaker with the greatest potential. Like many of his generation, he has spent extensive time outside of France, living, for example, in New York City for many years. His *Dream Life of Angels* (1998) captured many Césars, including best film, best actress, and most promising young actress in a year that seemed to be filled with a number of young actresses. This film is a poignant tale of contemporary homelessness and street life in the bleak northern city of Lille. Scored by Yann Tiersen, the same composer who did the popular music for *Amelie*, the film explores the interface of the psychological and the picturesque through an exploration of the character's imaginations. Zonca achieved great success too with the release of *The Little Thief* (1999) and *The Secret* (2000).

In 2003, French film innovated in the genre of the adult animated feature with *The Triplets of Belleville.* Inspired by the comic books of his youth, trained first as a comic-book artist in London, and now living in Canada, Sylvain Chomet blends genres as seamlessly as cultural styles. With stunning decors done by the Russian émigré Evgeni Tomov, Chomet blends the story of a working-class Portuguese immigrant grandmother trying to ensure the success of her grandson in his quest to win the Tour de France. The joy of French wine and the classic music hall songs of the 1920 through the 1950s mix with the danger of the grandchild being kidnapped by a French criminal gang. In this extraordinary cultural synthesis, the references to French traditions of mime jostle with cinematic images drawn from the films of Jacques Tati.

By 2005 the most acclaimed young French film makers included Jacques Audiard, for such films as *The Beat My Heart Skipped* (8 Césars in 2006), Michael Haneke (director of *Hidden* [Caché]), and Philippe Garrel with *Regular Lovers*. Other promising film makers were Arnauld Desplechin and Agnès Jaoui. Desplechin (1960–) has been seen as a successor to Truffaut and with good reason: Desplechin's film, *The Sentinel* (1992) is considered by some to be the foremost film depicting the end of the Cold War. In 1996, he explored male/female relations in *My Sex Life or How I got into an Argument*; in 2000 his film in English, *Esther Kahn* (2000) centered on the dynamics of theatre life and creativity; and in *Kings and Queen* (2004) he focused on the nature of psychoanalysis amidst a larger probing of interpersonal relations in contemporary society and references to classical mythology.

In writing his screen plays, which invariably provide multiple dimensions, Desplechin says he follows Truffaut's maxim: Never write a scene of four minutes to explore one idea, but fit four ideas into each one-minute scene! Just as Truffaut had his favorite actors so does Desplechin, favoring Amalric in particular. One of the most striking lines in *Kings and Queen* occurs when the troubled musician Ishmael provocatively defines the soul in contemporary life "A soul is the manner of negotiating the question of being amidst daily life." At another point, this anguished musician stridently proclaims that "women have no souls!" but the film reveals that only through his encounters with women therapists is he able to achieve any sort of resolution to his neuroses. In this interweaving of gender with popular and classical culture the film offers a complex view of life in a new millennium.[16]

Agnès Jaoui (1964–) is considered one of the most multitalented artists in the French film industry today. Already an award-winning actress, screenwriter, and director (César for best screen play in 1997 and supporting actress in 1998, she also won another César for best film in her directing debut, *The Taste of Others* in 2001. Her films have probed the nature of sexual relations, especially why opposites so often attract and just as often have unexpected results. Her newest film, *Look at Me,* is considered one of best of 2005, according to the *New York Times*. The setting is the Parisian literary world, and the dynamic revolves around issues of cultural distinction and power, à la Bourdieu. Her films illuminate the fascinating ways in which even ordinary individuals—such as voice teachers and house painters—recognize and appreciate novelists, in part due to watching literary talk shows on television, but also how such familiarity with culture often results in more subtle forms of power relations.[17]

In few other areas of culture today is France better placed for continued creativity and influence on the world stage. The percentage of the French population going to the movies in on an upswing: from 55.4 in 1994 to a peak of 62.2 in 1998. Recently, the percentage has diminished somewhat to 59.9 in 2002, but is still virtually five percentage points higher than a decade earlier. This increase is largely due to a spurt in attendance by older age groups. Counter to the American experience, over the last ten years the percentage of movie attendees between 50 and 59 has increased from 5.2 to 11.8 percent of ticket sales, and the rise is even bigger among those in their 60s: from 6.8 to 12.1 percent in the same period. While a mature audience may help fill the seats of theatres showing more sophisticated films, the fact is that aside from children aged 6 to 10 (whose percentage of tickets bought increased during this period from 5.7 to 6.6 percent), the percentages for other age groups has declined: for 11–14-year-olds, ticket sales dropped from 7.9 to 7.2 percent; for the 15–19 age group, a troubling drop from 14.8 to 11.5 percent; and for those in the 20–24 bracket, an even steeper drop from 20.6 to 14.6 percent. Older age groups have also seen a diminished percentage, but not by as much: 25–34-year-old ticket sales have fallen from 18.9 to 14.5, and the 35–49 group actually experienced a slight increase, from 20.1 to 20.7 percent. On a more positive note, the explosive rise of the DVD player does not appear to be putting a dent in these attendance figures.[18]

At a time when the American box office is increasingly dominated by young male audiences primarily in search of distraction and thrills, the mature and sophisticated films of France remain a continuing source of inspiration for Hollywood. As the leading cinematic nation in Europe since 2001, France has been producing over 200 movies per year and has more than 5,000 movie screens. Innovative in its technology and open to the dynamics of an increasingly multi-cultural society, France's second century of the seventh art should be even more creative than its first.

Notes

1. On the reaction of the first cinema audience see Rae Beth Gordon, "Laughing Hysterically: Gesture, Movement and Spectatorship in Early French Cinema," in *Moving Forward, Holding Fast: The Dynamics of Nineteenth-Century French Culture*, eds. Barbara T, Cooper and Mary Donaldson-Evans (Atlanta, GA: Rodopi, 1997), 217–37.

2. Rémi Fournier Lanzoni, *French Cinema: From the Beginnings to the Present* (New York: Continuum, 2004). Also, Susan Hayward, *French National Cinema*, (London and New York: Rutledge, 1993), 25.

3. Lanzoni, *French Cinema.*

4. David Lewis, "Able Gance" in *All Movie Guide,* www.allmovie.com.

5. Kerry Segrave, *American Films Abroad: Hollywood's Domination of the World's Movie Screens from the 1890s to the Present* (Jefferson, NC: McFarland & Co., Inc., 1997), 167 and 269.

6. Jean Douchet and Cedric Anger, *French New Wave,* Trans. Robert Bonnono (Paris: Editions Hazan, Cinematheque francaise) 1998.

7. For assessment see www.frif.com/new2004/chant.html. For book length study see Gwendolyn A. Foster, *Identity and Memory: The Films of Chantal Ackerman* (1998; Carbondale: Southern Illinois University Press, 2003).

8. See www.sensesofcinema.com/ contents/directors/02/breillat.html.

9. Lanzoni, 308–312. Also, Gérard Mermet, *Francoscopie: Pour comprendre les français 2005* (Paris: Larousse, 2004), 419.

10. Lanzoni, *French Cinema,* 313.

11. See Lanzoni, *French Cinema,* on list of most-attended films, 432.

12. Janine Cardona and Chantal Lacroix, *Statistiques de la culture: Chiffres clés* (Paris: Documentation Française, 2005) for cinema attendance in the years between 1991 and 2005.

13. Rémi Fournier Lanzoni, *French Cinema: From the Beginnings to the Present* (New York: Continuum, 2004), 313, and 354–57; Jannine Cardona and Chantal Lacroix, *Chiffres clés 2006: Statistiques de la culture* (Paris: La Documentation Française, 2006), 129.

14. Judith Layne, *Claire Denis* (Champagne: University of Illinois Press, 2005), and Martine Beugnet, *Claire Denis* (Manchester: Manchester University Press, 2004).

15. Rémi Fournier Lanzoni, *French Cinema: From the Beginnings to the Present* (New York: Continuum, 2004), 372. Also, Jannine Cardona and Chantal Lacroix, *Chiffres clés 2006: Statistiques de la culture* (Paris: La Documentation Française, 2006), 131.

16. See Retrospective: Arnaud Desplechin presented at the Wexner Center, www.wexarts.org/fv/pdfs/DesplechinBooklet.pdf. Also, for quote see Arnaud Desplechin, Roger Bohbot, *Rois & Reine* (Paris: Denoël, 2005), 48. For comparison with Truffaut see Sura Wood, "Vive la France The newest of the New Wave speak and screen at Stanford French film festival," www.metroactive.com/papers/metro/02.16.05/france-0507.html.

17. See *A Family Affair,* trans. Agnes Jaoui and Jean-Pierre Barcri (London: Oberon Books, 2001). Also, A. O. Scott, "Lively Bonbons with a Bitter Taste," Review of *Look at Me, New York Times,* April 1, 2005. Finally, see Brandon Judell, "Hailing a New 'World-Class' Director NYFF Toasts Jaoui, Alongside Modern Masters Almodovar and Godard," *Indiewire: On the Scene.* www.indiewire.com/onthescene/onthescene_041001nyff.html.

18. My compilation from *Chiffres Clés* (1994–2006), statistics on demographics of French film audience. See the cinema section. All published by La Documentation française.

9

Performing Arts

THE PERFORMING ARTS of theatre, dance, and music exist and flourish through a creative mixture of state subsidies and imaginative and popular creativity. Theatre and dance in France have had very different historical evolutions than that of music. Since the age of Louis XIV (1643–1715) drama and dance have been well-subsidized elite activities; until recently music did not receive the same amount of governmental attention. Since the 1960s, however, an explosion of new musical styles, and increased government support, has increased France's visibility on the world's musical stage. Thus music has now joined French drama and dance in having an important influence around the world.

THEATRE

In an age saturated with media, it is easy to forget how central theatre was to societies before the age of movies, radio, television, computers, and DVDs—it was the main public entertainment for society. For this reason, as we shall see at various points below, controversies surrounding plays often had large resonances on all parts of social life in the same way that movies, television, and the Internet have today.

French theatre, though born in the Church, also took its inspiration from the street and the marketplace. Passion plays in Latin for the sacred and vulgar farces in evolving French based on ordinary life were two sides of the Middle Ages, centuries in which the sacred and the profane were dramatically juxtaposed, especially on the stage. The French royal court intervened early in the history of French theatre. Thus Charles VI licensed the Confraternity, a troupe of lay nonprofessionals, as the sole legal theatre company in Paris (1402), and they staged religious dramas.

Buildings specifically designed as theatres emerged only during the Italian Renaissance and then spread across Europe. The first theatre in France was, not surprisingly, in Paris, the Hotel de Bourgogne (1548), constructed for a lay religious organization (Confraternity of the Passion) on the second floor of the duke of Burgundy's house. The founder of the French Academy, Cardinal Richelieu, was also a patron of the theatre, having the first freestanding theatre (the Palais Cardinal, 1641) built in Paris (also the first containing a proscenium stage). Moliere later took over Richelieu's Palais Cardinal, by this time known as the *Palais Royal.* Seven years after Moliere's death, Louis XIV amalgamated Moliere's troupe with two other acting companies to establish the Comédie Française (1680). Under royal patronage this troupe set the norm for state sponsorship of theatre across Europe, and by 1689 they had their own theatre. In general, French theatres followed the Italian model of having boxes on both sides and allowing those members of the upper classes who sat in them to see as well as to be seen. The lower classes in theatres were relegated to the pit *(parterre* in French) in front of the stage or the highest and farthest of the seats in the upper rows (these seats came to be known in the nineteenth century as "the paradise"—from which the title of Carné's film comes).

The French monarchy also dictated the nature of French drama. The event that trigged the Academie Française was the staging of Corneille's *Le Cid* (1636). The dramatic controversy that swirled around this work resulted in the august body virtually legislating five rules on what would become French classical drama (or neoclassicism) in the Judgment of the Academy on Le Cid: (1) All events occurring in a play also have to be able to occur off the stage (must conform to "reality"); (2) all plays must teach a moral lesson—good must triumph over bad; (3) genres cannot be blended; plays must either be comedies or tragedies; (4) any stage representation must have a unity of time, place, and action; and (5) a play must have five acts. The rules would essentially be observed until the romantic age.

What made these five rules so formidable was not merely the power of the French monarchy but also the genius of the French dramatists. Down to the present France reveres the tragedians Pierre Corneille (1606–1684) and Jean Racine (1639–1699) and the comedian Moliere (1622–1673) as the greatest playwrights in their history. Indeed, during the seventeenth and eighteenth century many critics put Racine above Shakespeare. Voltaire, for example, called Racine's Phaedra, the "masterpiece of the human mind." Most of Europe's aristocracy and upper middle classes, along with its writers, saw French classicism under Louis XIV as the epitome of civilization and as an antidote to the anarchy and fanaticisms that had wracked Europe during its age of religious strife in the previous generation (from the 1570s through the 1640s). In their masterpieces, these dramatists seemed to have distilled the greatest insights from Greek and Roman dramatists and philosophers.

After the death of the great dramatists and their patron, Louis XIV (1715), eighteenth-century French dramatists, while continuing to follow the rules of neoclassical drama, also developed new dramatic formulas. Bourgeois tragedy (tragedie bourgeoise), dealt with ordinary people in their daily lives and usually had happy endings; sentimental comedy (comédie larmoyante) followed the same formula but emphasized humor; and small comedies (comedietta) were small comedic sketches that would remain popular in the nineteenth century. The most famous dramatist across the eighteenth century was Voltaire. With the success of *Oedipe* (1718), he soared to the top of the theatrical firmament. During the next 50 years he would write 20 tragedies and 12 comedies. Although at some points expressing admiration for Shakespeare, this paragon of French classical drama concluded that he was "a savage with some imagination." Though Voltaire would return to Paris in 1778 after decades of exile, to be feted by an adoring city, his work is now seldom performed. Voltaire has been largely eclipsed by Pierre Carlet de Chamberlain de Marivaux (1688–1763). Many of Marivaux's 30 plays are still staged regularly, and his subtle, nuanced, and delicate emotional language has been immortalized with its own term: *marivaudage.* In his emphasis of emotions, especially love, rather than actions, Marivaux anticipated the emergence of romantic and middle-class drama.

After 1750, Enlightenment ideas began to penetrate French drama. One of the leading members of this movement advocating a more empirical, secular, and democratic society, Denis Diderot, called for a new type of theatre, one that explored the lives of ordinary people in modern society rather than glorifying classical heroes or the aristocracy. Even though his plays, such as *Le fils naturel* and *Le père de famille,* were not very successful then and are not part of the current repertoire, his theories on what one might call middle-class drama (drame borgeois), had a major impact. This influence is epitomized in the plays of the great French playwright of the last 20 years of the monarchy, Pierre-Augustin Beaumarchais (1732–1799). With a life almost as intriguing as his plays—as a clock maker to Louis XV and a music teacher to the king's daughters—and his marriage to a wealthy widow and patronage of the American Revolution, Beaumarchais brought a new sophistication to the theme of aristocrat/commoner interaction. Although his tragedy about the life of the lower orders, *Eugénie* (1767), left audiences unmoved,

The Barber of Seville (1775)—about a witty and clever servant—caught the public's imagination. The age-old tale of servant insubordination resonated with a population growing dissatisfied with what they felt was an aristocratic autocracy in France. Beaumarchais returned to the same servant character (Figaro) in *The Marriage of Figaro*. Banned for several years before its premiere (1784) because it was judged seditious, the premiere produced a near riot. Even though the play stigmatized them as essentially pompous fools, aristocrats often staged their own versions in their palaces and town houses in the years leading up to the French Revolution. These two plays would also dazzle the upper classes of Europe subsequently as operas, in Rossini's *The Barber of Seville* and Mozart's *The Marriage of Figaro*.

Due to upheavals and periodic repression, the revolutionary and Napoleonic eras were not fruitful for the theatre. One can argue that with so much drama in real life it was hard for the stage to compete. Actors dominated this turbulent age. The most famous was François-Joseph Talma (1763–1826). Talma brought an enhanced realism to the stage by wearing a toga, rather than contemporary dress, for the part (as was the custom at the time) and fully embraced the most radical phase of the Revolution, playing a model sansculotte on stage. His close friendships with one of the heroes of the first years of the Revolution, Danton, the great painter of the age, Jacques Louis David, and the great political and military figure, Napoleon, enhanced his celebrity. (With the growing dissemination of newspapers this term starts to be relevant in this age.) Political conflict at the Comédie Française during the opening years of the Revolution led Talma to create a new theatre, one of the dozens in Paris (indeed 78 theatres at one point) and the hundreds across France that emerged with the end of monarchial restrictions on the theatre during the early stages of the Revolution. After 1793, successive revolutionary governments, Napoleon, and then the Restoration (1814–1830) imposed new and varying restrictions on the number and content of theatres, keeping the number at around 11. As part of Napoleon's consolidation of French culture and society, the Comédie Française again assumed its central role. Its power on the Parisian Right Bank was balanced by the other national theatre, the Odeon, on the Left Bank.

French drama again blossomed as the romantic movement made its delayed entry into France during the late 1820s. Again, as during the controversy over *Le Cid*, drama was the cynosure of new literary and artistic controversies. The leader of French romanticism was the young 25-year-old dramatist Victor Hugo. Hugo's opening shot in the war against classicism was the preface to his play *Cromwell* (1827), which ironically would never be performed, in which he called for the overthrow of the unities of time, place, and action and called for the freedom to deal with subjects and characters that might be viewed by the larger society as bizarre or unbelievable. Classical literature and drama, he argued, was similar to Louis XIV's royal palace at Versailles: "well leveled, well pruned, well raked, well sanded," whereas the "Poet should have only one model, nature; only one guide, truth" and argued for "the freedom of art against the despotism of systems of rules and codes."[1] This powerful statement quickly became the manifesto for French romantic literature as a whole.

The premiere of Hugo's play *Hernani* (1830) produced a near riot and is often known as the battle of Hernani. In this and in his other plays, Hugo developed a lyrical style that was new to the French stage. Indeed, so volatile were the conflicts that for almost two months, tensions between romantics and classicists simmered beneath the stage. As can be imagined from Hugo's programmatic statement above, Shakespeare was now a hero. This is also more evident with Stendhal's play *Racine et Shakespeare* (1823) and Alfred de Vigny's version of *Othello* (1829). Alexandre Dumas, both father and son, would also produce romantic plays, the most famous of which is *Camille* (1852). This tale of love doomed due to tuberculosis later became an opera (Giuseppe Verdi's *La Traviata)* and the basis for numerous movies in France and Hollywood.

By the 1830s Paris theatre had evolved into a well-known set of theatres catering to the various tastes and classes of society. While the Comédie Française and the Odeon staged the classics, what became known as boulevard theatre emerged for the growing middle class on the increasingly affluent western side of Paris. The greatest figure of the boulevard theatres was Sarah Bernhardt, with a career that would span 50 years and every continent. On the generally poorer eastern side of the city, the *"boulevard du crime"* held a series of theatres that appealed to lower-middle and working-class tastes. These eastern theatres are the subject of Carné's movie *The Children of Paradise.* The most famous theatre catering to the proletarians was the Funambules. Here a famous mime, Jean-Gaspard Deburau, himself risen from the street, dazzled an audience that eventually included much of high society by the 1850s. These theatres would be demolished as part of Prefect of the Seine, Baron Haussmann's urban renewal of Paris in the early 1860s. After this point workers often went to theatres in the new peripheral districts of Paris or to new café concerts, and later in the century, to theatres in the suburbs. Over the course of the nineteenth century, Parisian dramatists would produce around 32,000 plays (with production steadily rising across the century). By the 1880s about a quarter (500,000) of the Parisian population went to the theatre once a week, and half (1,000,000 to 1,200,000) went at least once a month. The French provincial urban population, moreover, contained theatregoers as assiduous as the Parisians.[2]

After Napoleon III restored freedom of commerce to the theatre industry in 1864, the Parisian theatre enjoyed a golden age. The number of theatres more than doubled (from 11 in 1828 to 23 in 1882), and total revenue from the theatre shot up almost 500 percent between the 1820s and the early 1880s (4,789,000 to 20,168,000), a period of negligible inflation. Most theatres saw their revenues at least double over this period. After 1883, however, theatre attendance declined for the following decade (through 1893), before leveling off between 1893 and 1903. First the café concert and then the cinema would end theatre's role as the great universal entertainment. We have discussed the role of the cinema already in chapter eight and will discuss the role of the café concert below.[3]

The best example of late romantic drama is the work of Edmond Rostand (1868–1918). Although famous for a variety of plays in his time, one of the most famous being *The Eaglet* starring Sarah Bernhardt (about the life of Napoleon's short-lived son—he would die at 20—in exile in Austria), he is now best know for *Cyrano de Bergerac* (1897), the story of a swashbuckling noble solder with a big nose in unrequited love with his cousin Roxanne. Cyrano had the longest run of any French play (December 28, 1897, to May 3, 1913) of the long nineteenth century (1789–1914) and has been adapted as a movie in France and Hollywood numerous times.

The most characteristic of playwrights for the boulevard theatres were Eugène Scribe (1791–1861), Victorien Sardou (1831–1908), and especially Georges Feydeau (1862–1921). No boulevard playwright was more a master at giving his upper-middle-class audience what they wanted: smart, witty, and complex farces with unexpected twists and turns about the lives of wealthy men and shady women. Such complicated plots lead critics to call these types of plays well made. Feydeau wrote 60 plays, the most important being *L'Hôtel du libre échange* (translated as *Hotel Paradiso,* 1894), *Le Dindon* (*Sauce for the Goose,* 1896), *Une puce à l'oreille* (*A Flea In Her Ear,* 1907), *La Dame de Chez Maxim* (*The Girl from Maxim's,* 1899), and *Hortense a dit: "J'm'en fous!"* (*Hortense says, "I don't give a damn!"* 1916). Feydeau's life was as colorful as his characters. After marrying a rich widow and with the profits from his plays, he could be a true man about town and boulevardier (man of the boulevards), with a reserved table at Maxim's restaurant and a chair at every gambling club. Divorce, World War I, and a venereal disease would however mar the end of his life. Once dismissed as superficial by the twentieth-century avant-garde, critics now detect elements of surrealism in his plays, which continue to be widely performed.

The international prestige of French theatre during the nineteenth century is best illustrated by the triumphant world tours of Sarah Bernhardt. Between the late 1870s and the early 1910s, Madame Sarah, as she was known, toured the world to sold-out houses. Always doing her plays in French, she dazzled English factory workers, American cowboys, Argentinean dockworkers, and Japanese businessmen. The foundation of her success was the network of French-speaking theatre companies that could be found around the world at this time. The range of Bernhardt's acting is extraordinary: Not only did she play women of all different classes and historical eras, she continued to play the role of either male or female children well into her sixties (for example, Napoleon's son). By 1895 she was a living monument and would be able not only to maintain her presence in the theatre but also to make her presence felt in the new art of the movies before she died in 1923.

By the 1880s a French theatrical avant-garde started to emerge to overturn what seemed to them a romanticism that had become tepid and conventional. French theatre first experienced a big dose of unconventionality with the emergence of cabaret in the cafés of Montmartre in the 1880s that had combined poetry, music, song, and even early forms of animation in offbeat shows. But much more central to the emerging theatrical avant-garde was Andre Antoine. He was convinced that French theatre must take account of the innovative new naturalistic drama emerging in Scandinavia, especially from Henrik Ibsen and August Strindberg. He was also convinced that the realistic style of novelists such as France's Emile Zola and Russia's Leo Tolstoy must be brought to the stage. He would stage plays or adaptations of novels at this Theatre Libre from 1887. This venue attracted a more artistic and intellectual clientele than the regular theatregoers and stressed the theatre as a place to focus on the message of the play rather than to see and socialize with others in the audience. Antoine's impact, but not his audience, would be tremendous not only on future generations of directors and actors in France but also in inspiring an independent theatre movement in the major cities of the world.

Within a decade of Antoine's experiments in theatre management, experimental theatre erupted in France. The best examples of this new vision of the theatre was Alfred Jarry, whose 1896 play, *King Ubu,* sparked a riot when its eponymous character walked out onto the middle of the stage and said "S**t." At the end of World War I the avant-garde poet and art critic Guillaume Apollinaire's *The Breast of Tiresias* (1917) blended themes from Greek mythology with an exploration of the human unconscious and the indeterminacy of language. This play would be a good example of a word he would coin but of a movement he could not join (due to his death from influenza on the day of the armistice ending World War I in November 1918): surrealism.

The disillusionment and disgust with conventional culture that dadist and surrealists felt after World War I quickly translated to the theatre. Both Tristan Tzara (with *The Gas Heart*, 1920) and Andre Breton (*If You Please*, 1920, with Soupault) wrote for the theatre and further developed the disorienting techniques and themes of Jarry and Apollinaire. But more influential than either of them would be a director rather than a playwright. Jacques Copeau (1879–1949), steeped in the origins of theatre in the Greek chorus, the medieval mystery plays, and the street performance of the multitalented Italian Renaissance Comedia dell'arte, set out to cleanse French theatre and to restore the basic human energies animating theatre. From 1913 to 1924 he directed a theatre on the Left Bank of Paris, the Vieux-Colombier. He had the theatre's rococo interior completely renovated, tearing out its loges, its chandeliers, and its gold ornamentation. In the renovated theatre all attention focused on a stage that connected rather than separated the audience from the actors and that was bathed in subtle indirect lighting. Despairing of the decadent, cloistered, and nonchalant nature of Parisian life, in 1924 Copeau went to the French provinces in the hopes of reenergizing national life at its popular foundations and thus planting the seeds for a true theatrical renaissance. He left behind him, however, two students who in turn would be central to French theatre in the twentieth century: Charles Dullin and Louis Jouvet.

Although French theatre thrived in the interwar period, the French government after the horrible bloodletting became concerned about the state of French theatre. Boulevard theatre found a new leading playwright after 1918, the son of the distinguished actor Lucien Guitry, Sacha Guitry. Through the 1950s, this updated version of the Parisian boulevardier would delight upperclass theatre audiences with the jaunty and saucy repartee of the character in his productions such as *Nono* (1905), *Dream Making* (*Faisons un reve*, 1916), *My Father Was Right* (1919), *Quadrille* (1937). and *Don't Listen Ladies* (1942). While an exhausted population found diversion and excitement in such fare, the French state feared that the nation's moral fiber needed to be restored through more edifying material. Thus in 1920 the government provided funds for a National Popular Theatre in Paris under the direction of an actor with working-class origins who had already tried to create such an institution on his own, Firmin Gémier. Gémier's vision entailed making classic theatre, such as Racine and Shakespeare, rather than boulevard or avantgarde, accessible to the masses. Thus he located his theatre on the edge of Paris and charged low ticket prices. In 1927 Gémier would go on to found, with the assistance of the League of Nations, the Societe Universel du Theatre. This organization achieved little but became the precursor of the present International Theatre Institute run by UNESCO. Much more consequential was Gémier's success in bringing the Russian director Meyerhold, a specialist in a popular theatre after the Russian Revolution, to Paris.

Another director, Russian émigré Georges Pitoëff, also played a vital role in opening up French theatre. A member of the famous "cartel of directors" (Jouvet, Dullin, and Gaston Baty), Pitoëff was nevertheless resented by Antoine, who feared that the French stage was becoming too foreign during the interwar period. Perhaps Pitoëff's greatest accomplishment in a distinguished career was to stage the first French production of Pirandello's *Six Characters in Search of an Author* (1924), a play at the very center of modern theatre and a vital inspiration for the later theatre of the absurd.

Antonin Artaud (1896–1949), playwright, actor, director, poet, and dramatic theorist, distilled the most powerful statement of theatrical transformation in the interwar years, calling for a "theatre of cruelty." After having been part of Breton's surrealist movement in the mid-1920s, he broke away and founded the Theatre Alfred Jarry. There he would stage some of his works and those of other surrealists, such as Roger Vitrac. Like many surrealists, he was entranced by non-Western cultures and was especially impressed by a Balinese play at the 1931 French Colonial Exposition. But his own tortured life and unstable psychological state pushed Artaud beyond the boundaries of even the interwar avant-garde. Artaud desired to create a radical, confessional, and purgative theatre in which the audience would face their own subconscious and unconscious demons. "The spectator who comes to us knows that he has agreed to undergo a true operation, where not only his mind, but his senses and his flesh are going to come into play." His writings on the theatre would be collected in *The Theatre and Its Double* (1938). Although respected but largely unappreciated in the 1930s and 1940s, he would become a major inspiration for French theatre's greatest era of accomplishment: the theatre of the absurd during the 1950s and 1960s.

The most successful French dramatists between the two world wars, who combined both critical and commercial success and have remained popular into the twenty-first century, created what has been called a genre of mythic theatre. For example, one of these playwrights, Jean Giraudoux, is generally considered the greatest French playwright of this era. His plays often explore the attempts to reconcile the great dichotomies of life: man and God in *Amphitryon 38* (1929), paganism and the Hebrew testament in *Judith* (1931), man and woman in *Sodom et Gomorrah,* and war and peace in *The Trojan War Will Not Take Place* (1935). This latter play was banned due to its antiwar message when it was first produced (by Jouvet). Ironically Giraudoux would later be head of French propaganda services in the prewar government. His last play, *La folle de Chaillot* (1945; *The Madwoman of Chaillot,* 1947), explored the dynamics of human needs versus monetary profit, a theme of great resonance during the Nazi occupation of Paris. The younger Jean Anouilh was at one point Jouvet's secretary and was influenced by Giraudoux. This prolific playwright, who would produce works into the late 1970s, groups his plays into thematic series (for example, rosy and black or sparkling and grating). Anouilh's greatest work, *Antigone* (1942), used Greek myth to explore the dynamics of political occupation and resistance.

As would be the case with many other French dramatists, Greek myths provided a safe distance from the harsh realities of the 1930s and 1940s. Jean Cocteau, although often working with the avant-garde of the theatre (we will discuss his multigenre *Parade* in the section on dance), was always haunted by the myth of Orpheus. Pitoëff would stage Cocteau's play on this theme in 1926, and Cocteau himself would later direct two films on the story. Paul Claudel combined a unique blend of profound Christian piety, a passionate appreciation for avant-garde poets such as Rimbaud, and an innovative conception of the relationship between voice, movement, and music in drama. This latter interest stemmed from Emile Jacques-Dalcroze's book *Rhythm, Music, and Education* (1922). In his play *Break of Noon* (originally written in 1905; produced 1948) Claudel explores the dynamic interaction of the flesh and the spirit not only through the story line but also in exquisite detail as far as body language and dialogue. The tensions between secular and profane visions of life very much color this play, generally considered one of the greatest of the twentieth-century French repertoire. Each of these dramatists drew upon Greek and Christian myths to illuminate and deepen their theatre. Their use of myth had a psychological and anthropological edge not found in the seventeenth-century classical dramatists. This probing of the human psychic interior had been stimulated by Freud and other psychologists and honed by the displacements of modern technological society and the devastations of modern war.

The second world war within a generation, as we see above, spurred many of these dramatists to deepen their explorations in myth and created a new younger school of playwrights inspired by the new philosophic theory of existentialism. Not far from the Vieux-Colombier theatre lie the cafés of the Saint German des Pres neighborhood that would become the center of this sober but liberating philosophy that was molded by the wartime deprivation and dissent. Jean-Paul Sartre, Albert Camus, and Simone de Beauvoir would also write plays along with their other prolific literary and philosophic output. Some of the most famous of their plays are Sartre's *The Flies* (1943), *No Exit* (1944), *Death Without a Burial* (1946), *The Respectful Prostitute* (1948), and *Dirty Hands* (1948); Camus's *The Misunderstanding* (1944), *Caligula* (1945), *The State of Siege* (1948), and *The Just Assassins* (1949); and Simone de Beauvoir's *Useless Mouths* (1944). All these plays dealt with the questions of freedom and constraint under the impact of war or racism. The staging and timing of *No Exit* was especially historically charged. Premiering 10 days before the Allied landing of D-Day (June 9, 1944), this play opened in Copeau's Vieux-Colombier and was a fitting example of the renewal of French theatre. Sartre would later remark upon how the oppressive claustrophobia of the Nazi occupation not only heightened his sense of freedom, in particular the necessity to choose your own actions, but also heightened his sense of the power of the three unities of French classical drama.

The continuities that Sartre could find between his dramas and the classics were something that cannot be said of the most important creative playwrights writing in France during the twentieth century, those of the theatre of the absurd. The term absurd comes from Camus's 1943 essay *The Myth of Sisyphus,* which denied that the universe contained any meaning except that which humanity made for itself through its actions. For Camus such a world need not necessarily produce despair. This was not the opinion of most of these dramatists however. During the 1950s, Samuel Beckett, Arthur Adamov, Eugene Ionesco, Jean Genet, Fernando Arabel, and others, however, would shock the international theatre with a series of plays that called into question, if not overturned, every theatrical convention. Ionesco would term his plays "antiplays." Indeed, the very idea that humanity, even if God did not exist, might be able to construct meaning in any coherent or satisfying fashion was questioned.

Although Ionesco's *The Bald Soprano* (1950)—a thorough deconstruction of the plot and dialogue of boulevard theatre—was the first great statement of the new school, its success was not as immediate or intense as Beckett's *Waiting for Godot* (1953). In this short play with four characters, the plight of humanity—waiting senselessly and witlessly for a character by the name of Godot (God?) who never shows up—is revealed to be nonsensical absurdity. In the plays of Jean Genet, such as *The Balcony* (1956) and *The Blacks* (1958), notions of love and intimacy are subjected to the same savage gaze, and the result is an exploration of the infinite complexities of dominance, submission, power, and pleasure, along with race and gender. Perhaps the play that best represents the culmination of this school of theatre is Beckett's 1970 play *Breath,* in which no actors or speech is seen or heard, just a 30-second clip of human breathing.

This collection of dramatists, especially conspicuous for their international origins—Beckett from Ireland, Ionesco from Rumania, Adamov from Russia, and Arable from Spain—showed that Paris remained at the center of world culture and still produced dramatic innovations. Perhaps the secret to the success of the theatre of the absurd is the same as that of Paris itself: the ability to synthesize a broad range of artistic styles. Certainly in the case of the absurdists we see them drawing upon Ibsen, Pirandello, dadism, surrealism, Artaud's theories of the theatre of cruelty, the mythic playwrights, and the existentialists. The theatre of the absurd would have a broad influence across diverse cultures and subsequent generations into the twenty-first century. Despite its worldwide renown, the theatre of the absurd did not find a mass audience. It was staged in the small avant-garde theatres of the Left Bank and similar venues around the world.

Following the end of World War II, the alternate trend we have been following, attempts to broaden theatre's appeal, also received new impetus. Copeau's vision of decentralizing the theatre was carried on and brought unexpected successes (judging from past failures). Jean Vilar, inspired by Dullin aesthetics and Gémier's sense that theatre could be a means of national regeneration and unification, had toured the provinces during the war. In 1945 the success of his staging of T. S. Eliot's *Murder in the Cathedral* in the southern city of Avignon led to his creating an annual summer theatre festival in the city starting in 1947. Through the next 20 years Vilar would use the dramatic settings of the palaces of the late medieval papacy to create stunningly original theatre settings. Indeed, he explored the possibilities of virtually turning a city into one big stage. The festival, ever creative and expanding, has become one of the major theatrical moments every year. Since its inception in the late 1940s tens of millions of spectators have gained a new appreciation of every type of theatre. His success in Avignon led to his appointment as head of the National Popular Theatre (Théâtre Nationale Populaire, TNP) at the Chaillot Palace in Paris. (Here he enlisted the aid of the CGT labor union to fill his shows.) In his desire to reach the masses he would draw especially from the theory and practice of the Marxist Bertolt Brecht's Epic Theatre. Indeed, it was through Vilar that Brecht's Berliner Ensemble came to France in the early 1950s and would have a dramatic impact on the theatre and politics, especially in the late 1960s.

Vilar's dramatic success at Avignon inspired successive French governments through the Fourth and Fifth Republics to decentralize theatre. The creation of National Dramatic Centers (CDN) began in 1947, and by 2003 an extraordinary network of theatres, drama companies, and festivals covered France: 30 National Dramatic Centers (CDN), 9 Regional Centers (CDR), and 4 National Centers for Children and Adolescents (CDNEJ). Moreover, there are 5,000 amateur acting associations, with 1,250 of them belonging to a national federation. Financing for these regional centers is often split into the following percentages: 44 percent national government, 20 percent local government, and 36 percent by the theatre's own fundraising and ticket sales. An important step in the creation of this network was Andre Malraux's creation in the 1960s of *maisons de culture* (literally houses of culture, best translated as cultural centers) in regional cities such as Bourges, Amiens, Grenoble, Reims, Nevers, Firminy, and the Paris suburb of Créteil. The first of the CDNs at Strasboug later became the National Theatre at Strasbourg and is the only national theatre outside of Paris (in Paris we find the Comédie Française, the Odeon, the Theatre National de Colline in an eastern suburb of Paris, and the Theatre National de Chaillot—Vilar's former theatre). The decentralization of theatres increased a trend we have seen across the twentieth century: the growing power of the director. Provincial directors had more freedom to experiment according to their own inclinations rather than follow the trends of Paris.

The mid-1960s also brought a renewal of France's cabaret tradition with the café-theatre. In venues that were fully working cafés, rather than theatres, young acting talent could get its start through intimate interaction with the audience. Anouilh admired this form of theatre, and one of the absurdist playwrights, Arable, would write for it. The first one was Café Royal, created in February 1966 by Bernard da Costa. Its success led to others in Paris such as Café Edgar, La Vieielle Grille, Les Blancs Manteaux, and Café de la Gare, and to some in provincial cities, the most famous of which was Bordeaux's L'Oenyx. By the late 1960s its success became so assured that café theatre had become a rubric in Parisian entertainment guides. In 1968 Vilar welcomed café theatre to Avignon. The list of French actors who started in the café-theatre over the past 40 years is impressive: Coluche, Depardieu, Victory Haïm, and Michel May.

The events of May 1968 brought yet another radical rethinking of the theatre. The director of the venerable Odeon theatre on the Left Bank near the center of the near-revolution, Jean-Louis Barrault, himself a student of Charles Dullin, and the actor who played Debaru in Carné's *The Children of Paradise,* disobeyed the government order to close the theatre as the rioting erupted. Instead Barrault allowed the students to turn the theatre into an open forum in which a free-ranging debate on every possible topic raged for weeks in May and early June. Sadly Barrault was caught in the middle: The government removed him as director and the students barred him from the theatre because they saw no more need for a director. This attempt to fuse theatre and revolution also occurred even after the end of the May–June 1968 near-revolution when the Avignon Festival was disrupted by militants wanting to rethink the assumptions of bringing high culture to the masses.

What appeared like anarchy to many conservatives really made more sense than might first appear. In the late 1960s, notions of "living theatre" came from the English-speaking world and fused with the concept of collective creation that had already been developing in France before May–June 1968. Barrault had been moving in this direction, advocating less emphasis on the text and more creative input from the theatre ensemble and the audience, but now he saw his more tentative formulations being superseded by those that were more radical.

The origins of collective creation date from the early part of the 1960s. Ariane Mnouchkine and other Sorbonne students formed a theatrical society in 1961 and then in 1964 opened Theatre du Soleil in an abandoned cartridge factory in the suburb of Vincennes. Here she and her circle synthesized Artaud's theatre of cruelty with older participatory traditions of the theatre, from the Greek and Roman farces to the French medieval mystery plays to the Italian Renaissance Comedia dell'arte. Especially crucial was Artaud's statement that "the director becomes author—that is to say, creator." The director's role was to create a theatrical environment in which the spontaneity of the actors rather than the text of an author would animate the stage. Indeed, the wide open space of the former factory proved an ideal setting to reconfigure the world of the theatre. Even more than in Left Bank experimental theatres, the distinction between the stage and the actors and the seating and the audience dissolved. The audience was seated without distinction based on their ticket prices. Moreover, all members of the acting troupe, including the set designers and the technical crew, were paid the same salary and given freedom to express their talents. For collective creation to flourish it was necessary to establish a feeling of friendliness and openness in the theatre. Hence the notion of collective creation seemed to be realized in this onetime factory. Not at all disillusioned by the failure to create a revolution in May 1968, Mnouchkine created the most dramatic, popular, and famous plays based on notions of collective creation. She staged a series of plays that dramatized the French Revolution during the early to mid-1970s. The first part of this cycle, focusing on 1789, was the most successful, as it literally mobilized the audience as the extras that take the Bastille.

As befits a time of popular ferment, Mnouchkine and her group were not alone in these ideas and Paris was not the only site of radical experimentation. By 1970 another group dedicated to collective creation, the Theatre de l'Aquarium, also used the Vincennes venue. In the provinces similar experiments took place, the most notable being the Theatre Populaire de Lorraine in this eastern region. The most important animator of collective creations after Mnouchkine was Jérôme Savary. In 1965, along with the absurdist playwright Arabel, he had created Le Grand Theatre Panique. Then he developed the Grand Magic Circus, which combined the cabaret's social satire with a sense of procession found in the circus. The two most famous collective creations of the Grand Magic Circus were *Zartan, The Unloved Friend of Tarzan* (1970) and *Cinderella and the Class Struggle* (1973). The TNP was also radicalized during 1968. The successor to Jean Vilar, Georges Wilson, was fired, and Roger Planchon, a director committed to radical politics after the fashion of Brecht, took over. Feeling that he could have more impact in the provinces, Planchon moved the TNP to Lyon in 1970s and fused his productions with Marxist analysis.

The emphasis on the director over the text waxed through the mid-1970s but waned by the early 1980s. The decline in the use of written plays, especially new ones, led to some theatre publishing firms going out of business. But by the early 1980s Mnouchkine and Savary returned to a closer reading of the texts. Both produced the classics from Greek, French, and English theatre: Aeschylus, Sophocles, Euripides, Moliere, and Shakespeare. In the mid-1990s, Mnouchkine staged several plays of the leading feminist Helene Cixous. Such a return to the text did not imply any loss of creativity. Mnouchkine has remained at the Theatre de Soleil in Vincennes and explored staging Western plays in Japanese Kabuki style. The 1994 staging of Cixous's *La Ville Parjure* explored how the traditions of a third world society, were based on gift giving rather than monetary exchange; returing to this gift giving tradition might provide a means of reconciliation between Western and non-Western societies. Since 1986, however, Savary has been the director of the National Theatre of Chaillot and has done cycles of classics.

The Socialists arrived in power (1981–1993) at a paradoxical period. On the one hand, French society voted them in due to dissatisfaction with a conservative and often imperious Gaullist government. On the other hand, the radical energies of May 1968 had largely dissipated. Nevertheless, the culture minister, Jack Lang, who himself had been a theatre director, had a strong commitment to funding the theatre (indeed he more than doubled its budget) and his tenure was one in which theatrical production flourished. Collective creation was no longer a dominant trend, but its influence was still felt in the continuing openness to innovation and in a greater freedom that actors, set designers, and the technical crews felt in the theatre. Moreover, Lang was assiduous in expanding the number of national dramatic centers and creating a network of theatrical festivals across France (as we shall see below).

The French stage between 1980 and the early twenty-first century has not seen the continual emergence of new dominant theatrical styles or schools as in the previous periods. Although still powerful, directors have ceded some of the power gained in the 1960s and 1970s back to the playwrights. The new generation of playwrights since the 1980s has been extraordinarily prolific in terms of the number of authors, the quantity of plays, and the range of subjects and styles. Nevertheless, despite this diversity the term often used to sum up this period is the theatre of daily life. The most distinctive members of this school include Bernard-Marie Koltès (1948–1989), who published only six plays during his short life. Koltès's plays include *Black Battles with Dogs* and *Return to the Desert* and explore the social margins of French society today, the way in which everyone is trying to make a "deal," and the questions of drugs, gender, and the influence of such historical processes as French colonialism and the Algerian War. Koltès, who died of AIDS in 1989, has found his greatest success posthumously in the play *Roberto Zucco* (1990). This is the contemporary French play most performed internationally today, and its status is also confirmed in a recent anthology on French drama between 1950 and 2000 entitled *De Godot a Zucco*. Inspired by a well-publicized murder, the play probes the unsettling relationship between murder, language, and identity. Michel Vinaver (1927–), whose plays include *Overboard, The Neighbors, Portrait of a Woman*, and *The Television Program*, brings a distinctive perspective to the theatre, since he has been both the CEO of the Gillette company in France and a novelist. His wide-ranging work moves between family dynamics, the impact of unemployment, and the power of television in contemporary French society. Feminist theorist Helen Cixous (1937–) has also written brilliantly for the theatre: *Sihounouk* (1985), *L'Indiade* (1987), and *La Ville Parjure ou les Erinyes* (1994).

Playwrights who have emerged since 1980 have often been very productive. This is especially the case with Philippe Minyana (1946–), who has written more than 30 plays since 1980. Minyana has brought a lyrical rhythmic quality to his exploration of daily life and the crisis of self-identity that he finds in contemporary society. In *Brief Dramas* (1995 and 1997), for example, he explores without pathos the way in which daughters react to the death of their mother. Michel Deutsch (1948–) has written over 25 plays since 1980, many of them, especially *Histories of France* (1997), focusing on the ways in which contemporary politics and literature feel as if they are being manipulated by a grimacing puppeteer. Yasmina Reza (1959–) has not published many plays, but the ones she has have already been translated into 33 languages, won a Tony award, and been collected in a mass-market paperback edition (*Theatre,* 1999). Her plays expose the dynamics of intense moments, as in *After a Burial*

(1986), or, in *Art* (1994), the complexity of feelings among three friends. Noelle Renaude (1949) is one of the most ambitious of contemporary playwrights, having written not only 20 plays but also a theatre-novel, *My Solange, How You Write My Disaster, Alex Roux* (1996), involving over a thousand characters and combining all theatrical styles and genres. As one might expect this has not yet been staged. Her work explores the emptiness of contemporary life with a surprising wit and humor (see *Touristic Diversions*, 1989). Finally, the powerful work of Jean-Paul Wenzel (1947–) perhaps best sums up the feelings of playwrights since the theatre of the absurd in their attitudes about daily life in the contemporary world. In *Far from Hagondange* (1975), he explores the subtle brutality of factory work through the lives of some retired workers. In *The Uncertain* (1979) we see one character utter an especially poignant line: "emptiness makes me sick to my stomach."[4]

By the early twenty-first century experimental and heritage theatres were found throughout France and complemented the continuing vitality of Parisian boulevard theatre. Across France there are 27 national dramatic centers, 10 dramatic centers, and 6 national dramatic centers for youth. In general about 18 percent of the adult population goes to the theatre each year, with about two-thirds of the theatregoing public still located in Paris. A high percentage of them, however, are from the upper and educated classes, thus defeating the dreams of theatre innovators over the past century, who had hoped that increasing numbers of workers would attend. Even so, the theatre still attracts a more diverse audience than dance or musical performances. The numerous Parisian theatre and entertainment guides, *L'officiel des spectacles* and *Pariscope* being two of the most prominent, usually list more than 180 theatrical events daily.[5]

Paris and France remain in the early twenty-first century at the center of world theatre. Whereas playwrights and writers came to Paris mainly due to its cultural opportunities before World War II, they increasingly now have the opportunity to get training or funding or to showcase their work at festivals. Jacques Lecoq created the International School of Theatre in Paris in the late 1950s, and it has become preeminent in attracting students from around the world. Andre Malraux's Theatre des Nations (1961) brought a series of directors and playwrights such as Peter Brook and his International Center of Theatrical Creations and Augusto Boal and his theatre of the oppressed. A number of festivals have been created devoted to the theatres of the various nations of the world. For example, a future culture minister under Giscard D'Estaing, Michel Guy, created the Festival d'Automne in 1972 to showcase new plays from around the world. When Lang was culture minister in the 1980s, he established the Nancy International Theatre Festival and the Limoges

Francophone Theatre Festival. Moreover, Lang transformed the mission of the Odeon theatre, making it a venue for theatre from across Europe.

Thus French theatre's long and proud history continues vibrantly into the twenty-first century, infused now with a creative mix of state intervention, popular participation, and creative aspiration that spans the diverse populations not only of France and the French-speaking world, but also the international theatrical world.

DANCE

This performing art of dance has had a complex history over the course of the last 50 years. France's distinguished dance heritage has been renewed in recent decades and has gained unprecedented popularity. Today, after soccer (known by the French as football), dancing is the second most popular physical activity, and dance productions draw 12 percent of the French population above the age of 15 (as opposed to the 25 percent who attend concerts).[6]

Throughout most of its history, dance has played a dual role in France, as in virtually all other stratified societies. On the one hand, dance has been a means by which local communities display their unity and solidarity. Dances involved the entire community rather than just one age group and were an expression of local customs and traditions. On the other hand, the different social classes have used dance as a means of distinguishing themselves from the others. From medieval times to the eighteenth century the aristocracy set itself apart by its expertise in dance. Although famed for his dancing, Louis XIV was not unusual in having devoted time each day to honing his skills with his dance instructor. The rest of the French aristocracy followed suit, naturally. As the middle classes gained in wealth and power, one of their cultural goals, in order to legitimate their rise in society, was to learn how to become adept at dancing. Moliere, writing *The Bourgeois Gentleman* in the reign of the Sun King, pokes great fun at such seeming impertinence. The assumption of the age was that aristocrats had a "natural" flair for dancing that their plebian counterparts could never match. The dances of the bourgeoisie or the peasantry were viewed as almost genetic expressions of their inferior and vulgar station in society.

Although dance had long been prized, the Italian Renaissance codified notions of aristocratic dancing for the rest of Europe. Catherine de Medici brought not only Italian cuisine but also dancing with her to France in the sixteenth century and helped initiate a golden age of court ballet. (The Italian word *balletti* had originally referred to dancing in royal and aristocratic ballrooms.) The movement of ballet out of the court and palace and onto the public stage began under Louis XIV. Nevertheless, while aristocrats might go to the opera to see ballet, they almost always dance in their own town houses or at the royal court.

In 1661, with the creation of the Royal Academy of Dance and the Paris Opera Ballet, Louis XIV not only consecrated the role of ballet in French culture but also established a model that was followed by most other ballet companies around the world. Louis XIV's favorite court composer, Jean-Baptiste Lully, composed opera with extensive dance sequences that laid the foundations for modern ballet compositions. During the 1690s the first public dances, requiring just a ticket, started in Paris.

By the eighteenth century, Paris had become the leading city for dance in Europe, and Pierre Rameau's book *The Dancing Master* became an authoritative guide. By this time the quadrille (a square dance probably of Italian origin for four couples) had become the basic dance in aristocratic and upper-middle-class society (as the French bourgeoisie wealth grew, so did their demand for dancing instruction). Variants on the durable quadrille would only fully die out after World War I. By the mid-1700s the Paris opera staged a public ball at the time of Carnival (in February) open to anyone who could pay the entrance fee.[7]

The French Revolution did not have a major impact on dance styles but did dramatize and accentuate class differences. There was a big difference between the aristocratic minuet, pavane, and courante, all various on the quadrille and danced in aristocratic salons, and the popular carmagnole, which consisted of people in the street or in public squares forming a circle and periodically stamping the ground and speeding up in tune to the music and song. Here was dramatic evidence of class differences, with the upper classes declaring their distinctiveness and refinement and the people their solidarity and power through their dances. The French Revolution opened up the possibilities of commercial dancing by lifting restrictions on theatres, public drinking establishments, and other commercial recreation venues (that is, by abolishing the royal monopoly granted to the Opera and the Comedie Italienne). Even during the Terror (1793–1794) Paris had 1,800 dancing halls and 23 theatres. Most of these theatres had ballet performances as part of their entertainment, and this would remain the case across the nineteenth century. Nevertheless, the gruesome and paranoid period did take its toll on Parisian dance instructors, many of whom fled to the provinces and took their expertise with them.

Only with Napoleon's rise to power did ballet companies regain their former coherence, and private dance for the elite also resumed. Across the nineteenth century urban ballet became more fully engrained in the national heritage.

Filippo Taglioni was one of the most important directors of the Parisian Opera ballet during the first half of the nineteenth century. He would stage some of the century's most famous ballets—*La Sylphide* and *Giselle*—using the leading ballerinas of the day (who were mainly of Italian or Spanish origin).

During the early nineteenth century, as the middle classes gained power and society in general, but not in equal measure, became wealthier, dancing became both more pervasive and more stratified. At the top of the dancing pyramid-were aristocratic dances, still almost always held in aristocratic town houses. These balls took many forms: costumed or masked, as well as official governmental and charity balls. Middle-class dances, often held in halls rented for the purpose, were usually based on occupational, associational, or regional affiliation. University students had their own balls, the most distinctive being the ones organized by Beau Arts students at the end of the nineteenth century. The nineteenth century also witnessed a proliferation of commercial dancing halls such as the Bal Mabille and Bal Bullier, on the Left Bank of Paris, and the Bal Moulin Rouge and the Bal du Moulin de la Galette, both on the north side of the city. These latter two balls have become world famous due to their depiction in the paintings of Jean Renoir and Paul Henri de Toulouse-Lautrec. For the most part the clientele of these two balls ranged from middle to lower middle class. But dance halls in cafés and taverns on the outskirts of Paris, frequented primarily by the working class, acquired a criminal reputation. By the 1850s the large immigration from the mountainous south central region of France, the Auvergne, produced a distinctive type of dance hall, known as *bal musette* (after an early version of the accordion).

Nineteenth-century Parisians were constantly exposed to new dances. The great age of the traditional quadrilles lasted from 1820 to 1844, with the cancan, a dance with popular origins, emerging in the 1840s and being danced at opera by young German Fanny Elssler (the main rival to Taglioni) and then becoming a craze at Parisian lower-class dance halls (it was considered vulgar in the salons of the upper classes). Subsequently the polka and the mazurka arrived from Poland by the mid-1840s, and a dance from Scotland (known in France as the *schottische)* by the late 1840s. The 1848 Revolution brought a temporary lull in dancing, but by the 1850s and 1860s the French accepted dances from new immigrant groups from the Austrian empire. One such new dance was the waltz, which had caused a scandal when it first hit Paris in the 1820s (due to the close proximity of the couple and the lack of exchange as found in square dances). It become more respectable when Johann Strauss Senior came to Paris in 1837–1838 along with Philippe Musard, king of the quadrille, and it became the most popular dance of the second half of the century. At the end of the century American variants of the waltz arrived—*la mattchiche* from Brazil and Boston from the United States (a variation on an English waltz). Then in the last decade and a half before the war African American and Argentinean dances arrived: the cake walk and then the tango.

Late nineteenth-century Paris became especially well known for its dance reviews, especially at the Moulin Rouge and the Casino de Paris, where the dances of the Parisian working and criminal classes, such as the cancan and, after 1880, the apache dance, moved from the floor to the stage. These dances became the staple of a stable of talented dances with working-class origins and names made famous by painters such as Henri de Toulouse-Lautrec: *la goulue* (the glutton), *grille d'egout* (manhole grating), *nini-patte-en-l'air* (nine foot-in-air), and *la mome fromage* (the cheese urchin), a dance from Spain. Carolina Otéro also became famous in these dance halls. Before World War I a young music hall singer, Mistinguett, and Max Dearly became especially famous for their rendition of the apache dance. These dances and traditions continue to this day at the Moulin Rouge, the Crazy Horse, and the Lido, but now are museum pieces. Nevertheless, contemporary choreographers Léonide Massine and Maurice Béjart have incorporated elements of the cancan into their productions.

As the pace of innovation in popular dance increased, rural and provincial France looked ever more stagnant and dull. Traditional rural and local dances remained strong, especially early in the century. Only after mid-century, as a national railroad network connected the country more closely together and as provincial towns increased the number of theatres, operas, and café concerts, did dances become more standardized around France, and the quadrille, polka, and waltz replaced such traditional rural and local dances as the branle, the rigadoon, and the gavotte. A few regions, however, kept their traditional dances, for example, the bourrée in Auvers, the Sardane in the Basque country and the farandole in Provence.

While popular dancing in Paris flourished in the late nineteenth century, ballet stagnated. During the Second Empire (1851–1870), the upper-class audiences preferred operettas (such as those of Jacques Offenbach), and the lower-middle to working classes the café concert, rather than the ballet. Although composer Léo Delibes wrote music for ballet, few stagings had much distinction or innovation. The Paris opera ballet would remain a bastion of conservatism and tradition until almost 1910.

By the 1890s Paris had became a site more of consumption than creation of ballet and the emerging modern dance movement. From the early 1890s, a series of women dancers created sensations through their innovative solos. In 1892 the American Loïe Fuller was one of the first to captivate not only with her movement but also with brilliant staging using electric lights that made it seem as if she was on fire. The Russian Anna Pavlova and the Argentinean La Argentina followed and also had great success. But Fuller and an American successor, Isadora Duncan, perhaps had the biggest impact because both captured the imaginations of artists and became immortalized in paintings and posters by Henri de Toulouse-Lautrec (Fuller) and in stone by Auguste Rodin and Antoine Bourdelle (Duncan). These dancers came to Europe due to its reputation as the capital of Western culture, to be able to work with great writers and artists, and because its audiences were discerning and appreciated their innovations in dance.

The foreign dancers who had the biggest impact, however, were not individuals but companies. Serge Diaghilev's Ballets Russes (1909–1929) helped make Paris again the center of dance, with brilliant and provocative lead dancer Vaslav Nijinsky and the pioneering music of Igor Stravinsky. Their ballet *The Rite of Spring* literally caused a riot in Paris when it first premiered in 1913. The collaboration between dance, music, art, and literature that the Ballet Russes helped inspire became even stronger when the Swedish Ballet (Ballets Sudeois) arrived after World War I in the early 1920s. Writers such as Paul Claudel and Jean Cocteau, artists such as Pablo Picasso and Georges Braque, and composers such as Darius Milhaud and François Poulenc were just some of the artists contributing to the artistic synergy of this company and others.

After World War I, Paris went mad for American jazz music and dancing and the entire spectrum of dances that made the 1920s roar in the United States. The result would be a so-called desacralization, as European notions of good form and restraint were thrown to the winds in the aftermath of a war that had shown the limitations of the European notions of will power and rational self-control. These dances included the Charleston, the shimmy, the fox trot, and the *paso doble*. The African American expatriate Josephine Baker would personify this new freedom of dance on French music hall stages and movie screens through the interwar era. The only dance to emerge from France during these decades was the java, a product of the Ball Musettes.

Amidst the cataclysmic events of the period from 1914 to 1930, French ballet began a renaissance, and modern dance started to develop. The Paris Opéra Ballet again became innovative under Jacques Roché, who had worked with Natalia Trouhanova and her innovative blend of modern dance and music (including the music of Paul Dukas, Vincent d'Indy, and Maurice Ravel) at the Chatelet Theatre. Modern dance gained one of its first French patrons in Count Etienne de Beaumont, who started a ballet sea*son (les soirees de Paris)*. Two important events occurred in 1931. First, a former choreographer of the Ballets Russes, Bronislava Nijinska, formed a chamber ballet and worked with Ida Rubinstein to create ballet for Ravel's Bolero; second, Rolf de Maré founded the Archives International de la Danse (AID) and hosted some of the first modern dance competitions. The following year the Ballet Russes reconstituted themselves as the Ballets Russes de Monte Carlo and brought in the Russian expatriate who would later be at the center of American ballet, George Balanchine.[8]

The Paris Opera Ballet continued to innovate after 1929 under the Russian-born Serge Lifar, who had danced with Diaghilev. Lifar would create more than 50 ballets, including one, *Icarus* (1935), which was especially innovative since it was danced without any musical accompaniment. In addition, as we shall see below, some of his students would be decisive on the evolution of French dance during the 1950s. Unlike theatre, dance during World War II did not flourish. Only with the return of peace and the start of the postwar boom would dance regain its élan.

One of the few innovative manifestations of dance during the Nazi oc-cupation of Paris and France was the embrace of American swing music. Brought to France in the late 1930s, it was danced by groups of middle-class youths (known as the *zazous)* who continued to dance the jitterbug, the lindy hop, and other dances during the war and then helped implant bebop, the mambo, and the cha-cha-cha after the war.

In the late 1950s and through the 1970s American rock 'n' roll had a major impact on popular dancing. The arrival of the new era of dance was dramati-cally announced by the French baby boomers themselves in June 1963 (on what has become known at "the night of the nation") when a concert that was expected to draw 20,000, according to the popular radio show on Europe 1, *Salut les copains,* instead brought 100,000 to see the new teen idols Johnny Hallyday, Sylvie Vartan, and Richard Anthony. On vivid display that night were the new dances of rock 'n' roll such as the twist. Later in the decade came the jerk, the mashed potato, the hully gully, and a French rock 'n' roll dance called le Madison.

While a new generation was being captivated by popular dance, French ballet was also being renewed. In the immediate postwar years, two of Lifar's students, Roland Petit and Janine Charrat, put a distinctive French stamp on modern ballet. The style that they helped formulate has been called "theatri-cal, daring, chic, and sexy" by one of the leading scholars of the field. To be free of the constraints of the Paris Opera Ballet, Petit founded the Ballet des Champs Elysées with Diaghilev's former secretary and the help of Jean Coc-teau. Here Janine Charrat staged an innovative and influential version of Igor Stravinsky's *Jeu des Cartes* (1945) danced by one of the greatest of the new generation of French dancers, Jean Babilée. Petit also collaborated with Cocteau on a stunning *Le Jeune Homme et la Mort* (1946), which juxtaposed the serene music of Bach with a story of sadism and death. Babilée also directed himself, along with his wife Nathalie Philippart, in *L'Amour et Son Amour* (1948), a retelling of the Greek myth of Eros and Psyche. These dancers/chorographers then expanded their influence by founding their own companies.

The mid- to late 1950s brought the emergence of more new talent, new dance competitions, and new teachers. In the early 1950s Maurice Béjart, one of the great names in French modern ballet, started his stellar career. In 1954 Béjart created the Ballet de L'Etoile in Paris, but this company later was amalgamated with others, and he wound up in Brussels as the director of the Ballet of the Twentieth Century (1960–1987). Françoise and Dominique Dupuy formed Les Ballets Moderns de Paris and won first prize at the inaugural International Festival of Modern Dance in Paris (1958). By the end of the decade three foreign-born dancers—Jerome Andrews (United States), Jacqueline Robinson (UK), and Karin Waehner (Germany)—had settled in France and would introduce France, via their own dance companies, to the latest developments from their native lands. Jerome Andrews would be the most influential.[9]

After 1960 modern ballet spread to the provinces. Roland Petit went to Marseille and directed an eclectic and exciting mixture ranging from rock 'n' roll ballet based on the music of Pink Floyd (1972) to such classics such as *The Nutcracker* and the waltzes of Ravel. Joseph Lazzini was especially assiduous in promoting provincial ballet, moving from Marseille to Amiens to Anger. Other troupes emerged in Nancy, Lille, Roubaix, and Strasboug. The ambition of the Nancy Ballet-Theatre, under Jean-Albert Cartier and Hélène Trailine, was especially immense: They performed a cycle of all the major twentieth-century dance works before moved on to Nice.

By the late 1960s French ballet and modern dance had clearly been rejuvenated, but over the next 20 years they would gain unprecedented popularity and exposure across France. The renaissance of French dancing really began in earnest after May 1968 when an interest in almost every form of dance accelerated. Inspired by the American counterculture, the growing popularity of modern dance, and interest in the religions and martial arts of Asia, student radicals in particular and French youth culture in general put a new emphasis on the body and freedom of movement. Moreover, as part of an attempt to spread culture through the provinces, dance companies were set up in provincial cities. At the same time, in 1969, the first Choreographic Festival at Bagnolet (a suburb of Paris) occurred. Since this date winning its annual prize has become a major honor in the world of dance.

After the Socialist Party won power in 1981, French dance received greater attention and funding. By 1987 it had achieved greater autonomy within the Ministry of Culture, and the following year was proclaimed "the year of dance in France." This merely confirmed the modern dance boom that erupted across France in the 1980s and continues strong into the twenty-first century. One hundred new dance companies emerged during these years. By 2005 there are over 140 dance festivals in France each year spanning the spectrum of dance from classical ballet to folkloric, including salsa, swing, rock 'n' roll, hip-hop, disco house, and techno.

Modern dance companies have achieved extraordinary reach across all of France, and are thus a true dream come true for those wishing to see culture decentralized, if not democratized. For example, Jean-Claude Gallotta in Grenoble had created a range of modern dance styles: from the highly theoretical and geometrical four steps to a more emotional exuberance in Yves P to humor in Ulysses 84. Maguy Marin, who achieved an international sensation with May B—a chilling translation of Becket's theatre of the absurd into dance (1981)—headed the National Drama Center in the Parisian suburb of Creteil for many years (1989–1998). In 1985 she scored another success in *Cinderella* for the Lyon Opera Ballet and then headed the National Drama Center in Rilleux-la-Pape, a suburb of Lyon. Regine Chopinot, whose career was launched after winning the Bagnolet competition in 1981 and whose productions such as *Delices* (1983) have incorporated costumes by Jean-Pierre Gaultier, headed the National Drama Center of Poitou-Charentes at La Rochelle. Finally, Daniel Larrieu, working out of the National Drama Center at Tours, has creatively inserted absurdity amidst the banality of daily life in *One Lump or Two (of Sugar)* (1983) and in *Skin and Bones* (1984).

Modern dance choreographers have also been brilliant at utilizing a wide diversity of influence from contemporary popular music to Asian theories of body movement. Marie-Christine Gheorghiu incorporated rock music in *Pole to Pole* (1983) and Josette Baiz's punk rock in *Blue Beard*. Hideyuki Yano's exploration of new ways to interconnect dance and the body, especially the effects of falling, has been incorporated by Karine Saporta's Hypnotic Circus.

The fact that some recent choreographers have also incorporated techno music into their programs shows the ever-growing contact between different levels of French dance. The popularity of raves—in essence large free-form music and dance parties often with techno or hip-hop music, has been growing since the late 1980s. As with so many earlier forms of popular culture, raves began in the United States (in the mid-1980s in Detroit). The dances of these large formless parties, usually held in large warehouses and former factories in the suburbs, have taken the trends of spontaneity and informality about as far as they can go. The couple has been dissolved into a free-floating mass of humanity. Members of the May-1968 generation may not like the music, but they can certainly understand these sentiments of festivity and fraternity expressed so fully.

MIME

Modern European mime is a creation of nineteenth-century France, growing out of royal (before 1789) and Napoleonic (after 1807) decrees that prevented any speaking on the Parisian stage by companies other than the Comédie Française and the Paris Opera. This constraint on silence produced, starting in 1819, the career of Jean-Gaspard Deburau (1792–1846) at the Funambules Theatre. Deburau would create the character of Pierrot, with white face and long, loose white smock and pants, which was immortalized in Carné's *The Children of Paradise*. Mime declined after his death and the abolition of the restriction on speaking on the Parisian stage. Only with the advent of Jacques Copeau and his school at the Theatre du Vieux-Colombier did mime become renewed. The renaissance stemmed from Copeau's emphasis on the actor's body as much as the text as the conveyor of meaning and his call for actors to have a rigorous training in gymnastics and mime (all part of the traditions of the ancient Greeks, Commedia dell'arte, and Japanese stages that Copeau believed could renew French theatre). One of Copeau's students, Etienne Decroux (1898–1991), would develop what Decroux termed a corporal mime (as opposed to the nineteenth-century pantomime that concentrated on face and hands). Decroux developed this style not only as a teacher but also as author in his book *Words on Mime* (1985). Decroux's first student was Jean-Louis Barrault (1910–1994), who would star as Deburau in Carné's *The Children of Paradise* and was also a part of Dullin's Atelier Theatre. Another of Decroux's students is the most famous mime of the past half century, Marcel Marceau (1923–), who has transgressed his master's theory by incorporating mime and pantomime. Moreover, mime is a vital part of Jacques Lecoq's (1912–) school. Since the 1980s a series of French and international mime festivals have inspired a new school of postmodern mime.

MUSIC

In contrast to drama and dance, music never received consecrated status. Indeed, from Jean-Jacques Rousseau in the eighteenth century to Andre Malraux in the twentieth, many have asserted that the French are not a

musical people. Nevertheless, France has produced composers of conse-
quence, especially Guillaume de Machaut in the Middle Ages and Guillaume
Dufay in the Renaissance. Composers since the seventeenth century include Louis Couperin (1626?–1651), Jean-Philippe Rameau (1683–1764),
Hector Berlioz (1803–1869), and Claude Debussy (1862–1918). In the
interwar and immediate postwar periods, France produced jazz musicians
such as Django Reinhardt and Stephen Grappelli and popular singers such
as Maurice Chevalier, Edith Piaf, and Yves Montand, who gained and have
retained an international reputation. Although George Brassens, Leo Ferre,
and Jacques Brel never attained such an international reputation, they did
achieve an unprecedented statue in literary circles and high culture for their
lyrics. Since the 1990s, French techno, known as French Touch, rap, rai (a
fusion of North African and French music), and African (these latter often
lumped under the term World Music) have gained prominence.

Although both classical music and jazz count a large percentage of the
intelligentsia as fans, the overall audience for these musical genres in France
today is small. Classical music accounts for only 5 percent of recorded music
sales; classical, jazz, and blues make up only 2 percent of the music played on the
radio. Among concert goers, however, classical music holds its own, with jazz distinctly trailing. French music heads the list of most popular concerts, attracting
43 percent of the live music audience, followed by nonopera classical music at
26 percent, just slightly ahead of world or regional music (25 percent), international pop (24 percent), then rock (19 percent), and jazz (14 percent). Operas
are only attended by 4 percent of the concert going public. The last categories
include musical styles simply listed as "other" followed by techno (6 percent),
and rap (4 percent).[10]

Classical Music

Classical music developed out of polyphonic choral church music especially
centered around Paris during the tenth century (the Notre Dame School). By
the twelfth century, polyphonic music (based on several singers with different
melodies) had developed into a more structured form known as the *motet.*
The leading composer in the ars nova school of French composers was Guillaume de Machaut (ca. 1300–1377). The succeeding generation of French
composers became known as the *ars subtilior* for their more complex and
intricate compositions. In southern France during the twelfth and thirteenth
centuries the troubadours created various genres of poetic love songs either
for aristocratic court ladies or, in some cases, shepherdesses. Sadly little of
the notation for this highly influential form has been preserved. Aristocrats
were the primary composers of this music, such as Guillaume IX of Aquitaine
(1071–1127). During the Renaissance, Burgundy became a vital musical

center, producing a Burgundian school whose most important composer was Guillaume Dufay (ca. 1397–1474). Dufay is also considered the most illustrious and influential composer in Europe around 1450 and helped create the Netherlands School, which exerted a profound influence across Europe through 1600. Nevertheless, his masses, though technically brilliant, are not considered to be highly innovative, and for this reason his work is usually not classed with the great Italian, German, and Viennese masters.

The next age (the baroque, roughly from 1600 to 1750) brought the emergence of French opera and ballet. Although the first French opera debuted in the 1640s, it was only a generation later, with Louis XIV's favorite composer Giovanni Battista Lulli (1632–1687), also famous for his ballets done in collaboration with Moliere, that French tragic opera emerged (roughly at the same time as the great French dramatists). During this same period François Couperin (1668–1773) wrote masterpieces for the organ and especially the harpsichord and brilliantly synthesized the warring French and Italian musical styles of the era. The most famous and influential composer of the era, however, was Jean-Philippe Rameau (1683–1764). He made a significant and lasting contribution to musical theory with his treatises, especially the one on harmony, and his light and deft opera-ballets.

The most important development during the French Revolution was the creation of the Paris Conservatory, which would make Paris a center of music training over the coming centuries and bring such composers as Frederic Chopin (1810–1839) and Jacques Offenbach (1819–1880) to the city of light. Despite the long shadow cast by the great German romantics (such as Beethoven and Schubert) Hector Berlioz produced some of the most creative and individual music of the era. In similar fashion French comic opera composers such as Offenbach, Georges Bizet (1838–1875), and Jules Massenet (1842–1912) produced immortal operas such as *Orpheus in the under World, Carmen,* and *Manon* despite the hegemony of Wagner and Verdi. In the late nineteenth century, French classical music took an especially innovative turn with the impressionism of Claude Debussy and the more classically restrained but later jazz-inflected work of Maurice Ravel. Debussy's wide range of music production, from operas to concert tone poems, piano, song, and chamber music, broke not only with late romanticism after the fashion of Wagner but also opened Western music to Asian influences from Japan and Indonesia. Along with Igor Stravinsky, another expatriate composer who made his home in Paris before World War I, and Arnold Schoenberg, Debussy is one of the great innovators of modern music with its break from traditional notions of harmony, chordal progression, and melody. As World War I commenced, however, France lost one of its most innovative composers, Edgar Varèse

(1883–1965), to the United States. In New York Varèse would become a pioneer in the use of percussion and electronics in modern music.

After World War I a new school of young composers emerged, known as les six (the six, a term coined by critic Henri Collet). Reacting against all forms of lush romanticism, including Debussy and Ravel, and inspired by the mocking minimalism of Erik Satie (1866–1925), who was their mentor, and the refined classicism of Jean Cocteau, who was their literary spokesperson, the six included Arthur Honegger (1892–1955), Darius Milhaud (1892–1974), François Poulenc (1899–1963), and the most important members of the group, Georges Auric (1899–1983), Louis Durey (1888–1979), and Germaine Tailleferre (1892–1983). Like most avant-garde groups of the era they did not remain a cohesive group for long but, as their ages suggest, remained influential across the twentieth century. During their lifetimes they incorporated a wide variety of musical genres and styles into French music: from Stravinsky's rhythms and Schoenberg's serialism to American jazz and Brazilian bosa nova. Perhaps the greatest accomplishment of these composers were Poulenc's three post–World War II operas: *Les Mamelles de Tiresias* (1947; *The Breasts of Tiresias),* inspired by Apollinaire, *Les Dialogues des Carmélites* (1957; *The Dialogues of the Carmelites),* inspired by a novel about antireligious violence during the French Revolution, and a one-act tragedy by Jean Cocteau, *La Voix Humaine* (1959, *The Human Voice).*

Following World War II France witnessed an even fuller flowing of classical composers. Henri Dutilleux (1916–) fused the late romantic traditions of Debussy and Ravel with more complete assimilation of Schoenberg's serialism in compositions, such as his two symphonies (1951 and 1959), *Métaboles* (1964–64), and *Timbres, espace, mouvement* (1977–78), which are examples of his abiding quest to explore the relationship between sonority and spatialization. The two most important composers were Olivier Messiaen (1908–1992) and Pierre Boulez. Both have been more than just composers, Messiaen an influential teacher and Boulez an especially articulate music theorist. Messiaen began in the jeune France group of composers in the 1930s and began his prolific career as a composer and professor at the Paris Conservatory, where his students included a stellar list of modern composers: Pierre Boulez (1925–), Jean Barrqué (1928–1973), the Greek Iannis Xenakis (1922–2001), and Tristan Murail (1947–). Messiaen combined a broad eclecticism—for example, the inspiration for his *Turangalîla Symphony* (1946–48) was the Balinese gamelan, or his *Seven Haiku, Japanese Sketches* (1962), inspired by the Japanese poetic form, and many works inspired by birdsongs from the 1940s through the 1980s—but especially in an intense Catholicism seen in such pieces as his Pentecost Mass for organ

(1950), the orchestral work *The Transformation of Our Lord Jesus Christ, Nine Meditations on the Mystery of the Holy Trinity* (1965–69), for organ, and the opera *Saint Francis Assisi* (1975–1983). His deep piety, however, did not preclude his frequent use of serialism. Boulez not only is the most significant combination of composer, conductor, and theorist of the century but also in such works as *Structures for Two Pianos* (1951–61) and *Le marteau sans maître* (1954) took serialism to as complete a form and as logical a conclusion as so far had been seen. From 1974 to 1991 he directed the new Parisian institution devoted to contemporary electronic and acoustic music (IRCAM), which has also been instrumental in showcasing younger generations of composers and has since had some affiliation with another new Parisian institution, La Cité de la Musique. He has continued his composing with such recent work as *Anthèmes 2* (1997) for violin and electronic device *(dispositif électronique)* and *Dérive 2* for 11 instruments (1988–2002).

In the late 1970s a new movement emerged that has become known as the spectral music movement, though as always the composers within it generally do not wish to be affiliated with any rigid category. In general composers that have come of age since the 1960s and are associated with this style have striven to develop a new range of harmonies (thus breaking with the serialist disregard for this musical component). The concept was first developed by Hughes Dufour (1943–) in a 1979 article, and the movements of other chief composers include Gerard Grisey (1946–1998) and Tristan Murail. While Murail's piano has been especially well received, such as in *The Work and the Days*, along with his orchestral compositions such as *The Aura of the Dunes (L'Esprit des Dunes)*, Grisey has been most famous for his works for percussion, such as *Tempus ex machina* for the orchestral piece *Drifts (Dérives)*, which begins as soon as the musicians begin to tune their instruments, and *Day, Counter Day (Jour, contre-jour)*, which starts and concludes with soft notes that blend into audience applause. Other young composers inspired by this group include Philippe Hurel, Philippe Leroux, Marc-André Dalbavie, Jean-Luc Hervé, Fabien Lévy, and Thierry Blondeau.

Jazz

Almost from the moment of its creation in the United States, the new musical form jazz was incorporated into compositions by French musicians. A turn of the century African American dance, the cakewalk, inspired Debussy, and this trend has continued ever since. During and after World War I African American soldiers or entertainers, either fighting in France or entertaining the troops, introduced a music that the French quickly took to their hearts. The arrival of Josephine Baker (1906–1975) in France in 1925 and the sensation she caused cemented this link, and Baker would eventually become a French citizen and icon (participating in the Resistance during World War II and remaining a star until her death). In general American jazz greats, such as Louis Armstrong and Duke Ellington, came to France often and in great numbers at time when racism remained virulent in the United States and Paris seemed to be at the center of world culture. Inspired by such examples, Jacques Hélian and Ray Ventura created jazz orchestras, and instrumentalists such as guitarist Django Reinhardt (1910–1953) and violinist Stephane Grappelli (1908–1997), with their *Quartet du Hot Club de France* made original and lasting contributions to the genre. French music critics also made vital contributions. Hugues Panaissé was the first great non-American jazz critic; beginning her career at the age of 18, becoming president of the Hot club de Jazz de France, editing the magazine *Jazz Hot* from 1936 to 1947, and writing the book *(Le Jazz Hot)*. The other founder of *Le Jazz Hot,* Charles Delaunay, the child of the famous painters, continued to edit the magazine until 1980, and it continues to be published to this day.

After World War II, trumpeter Boris Vian and American expatriates such as clarinetist and saxophonist Sidney Bechet helped make the Saint-Germain des Prés district of Paris the new center of jazz (displacing Montmartre). Vian also doubled as a jazz critic (see his *Chroniques de Jazz).* But by the mid-1950s Paris could no longer compete with New York as a center of jazz, and figures such as Miles Davis were not as attracted to long stays in France as were the older generations. Nevertheless, Paris in particular and France in general have one of the densest concentrations of jazz clubs and festivals in the world. Since the 1960s such French jazz artists and composers as Bernard Peiffer (1922–1976), Jean-Claude Fohrenbach and François Jeanneau (saxophone), André Hodeir (1921–), Dominique Pifarély (1957–), Jean-Luc Ponty (1942–), Pierre Blanchard (1956–) (violin), and Henri Texier (1945) (bass) have been especially prominent. In 1992 Lang's Ministry of Culture created a National Jazz Orchestra (ONT) and a jazz department in the National Conservatory of Music and Dance in Paris. Today, approximately 3,000 jazz musicians live in France, half in Paris and half in the provinces.

POPULAR MUSIC (CHANSON) ACROSS THE CENTURIES

Before the emergence of modern popular music in the mid-nineteenth century, most of the French population was primarily acquainted with the music of their communities and regions, known as folk music and chanson. This latter term is another unique feature of French culture in that it carries a greater prestige and history than the term popular song would in English. Often seen as having origins in the poetry of François Villion and the troubadours, this tradition has been continued over the last century and a half by such singers as Theresa, Aristide Bruant, Edith Piaf, and George Brassens. Even before the modern age of recordings, Chanson often transcended local areas. French folk music, on the contrary, has usually started and often remained rooted in a specific locality. French folk music is as diverse as all other cultural forms we have studied; each French region having its own unique traditions of song and music. Yet, the amount of variation was limited. For example, almost all regions had variations on bagpipe (indeed more than in any other European nation) and the hurdy gurdy (known in France as the *vielle-à-roue*, the hurdy gurdy is a cross between a violin and a piano accordion). The most peripheral areas of France had the most distinctive instruments, thus Corsican musical instruments include the bagpipe *(caramusa),* 16-stringed lute *(cetera),* mandolin, fife *(pifana),* and the diatonic accordion *(urganettu).*

The most successful and distinctive folk music, based on its persistence and popularity, is that of Brittany. As early as the 1830s a pioneering musicologist, Hersart de la Villemarqué, published a treatise on the region's music, *Barzaz-Breizh* (1839), which helped to keep Breton traditions alive. After the folk revival of the late 1960s exploded, Breton music was again in the forefront. Indeed, one native Breton son, Alan Stivell, is perhaps the most influential folk-rock performer of continental Europe. After his 1971 album *Renaissance of the Celtic Harp,* Breton and other Celtic traditional music achieved mainstream success internationally. With Dan Ar Bras, he then released *Chemins de Terre* (1974), which launched Breton folk-rock. This set the stage for stars like Malicorne in the ensuing decades. Uniquely Celtic in character, Breton folk music has had perhaps the most successful revival of its traditions of any regional folk music, partially due to the success of Lorient, France's most popular music festival.

Even before the age of recordings, folk music, especially in the nineteenth century, had a vital impact on Paris. For example, the mighty stream of Auvergnat immigrants to Paris across the nineteenth and early twentieth century brought the region's tradition of the *bal musette,* based on the hurdy gurdy and later fused with the accordion from Italy, to produce a distinctive type of dance hall still found in some neighborhoods in Paris. Breton music and other regional music did not have as much of an impact on Parisian life due to the fact that no other region's immigrants became so dominant in the café trade where much music often took place.

In the first half of the nineteenth century, most singing was still an amateur activity. Middle-class men usually met in what were known as *caveaus* (vaults), singing societies in fashionable restaurants and clubs in Paris and in the provinces. The working classes had similar though less elegant venues, in inexpensive cafés and taverns known as *goguettes.* Even in the late eighteenth century, however, some street singers and some formal concert halls, usually attached to cafés, emerged. The rise of the professional singer and songwriter began in earnest with the creation in 1851 of SACEM (Society of Writers, Composer, and Editors of Music; société des auteurs, compositeurs et éditeurs musicaux) which introduced the concept of copyright into songs and music. France pioneered this new type of intellectual property. The result would be the emergence of popular music as a true profession. One of the first results, and one that would continue to be part of French street and café culture into the 1940s, was the sale, in shops and on the street, by composers (often doubling as singers) of their music.

Modern popular music, with its star system, first emerged during the Second Empire (1851–1870). On the one hand, the self-proclaimed Napoleon III effectively outlawed caveaus and goguettes in 1852 when, as part of his coup d'etat, all meetings now required police authorization and surveillance. At the same time the sale of sheet music and song, and singing in cafés and restaurants, had been increasingly repressed (as part of the growing fear of radicalism following the 1848 revolution). By the late 1850s, however, the imperial government started to lift restrictions on singing in cafés and restaurants. As a result spacious new concert stages attached to restaurants emerged, especially in Paris (l'Alcazar, l'Eldorado, La Scala, l'Horloge, and Les Ambassadeurs). In 1864 and 1867 Napoleon III lifted the monopoly that theatres had hitherto enjoyed as far as wearing costumes and performing in character. The result would be the emergence of the café concert. Often called the "Opera house of the people,"[11] these hybrid institutions (in part a synthesis of caveau and goguette) become much more diverse in their musical repertoire and would eventually produce such music, dance, and sex spectacles as those at the Moulin Rouge. The first great popular music star of France was Emma Valadon, nicknamed Theresa (1837–1913). She helped launch the tradition of nationwide tours that brought the new popular music of the capital to the budding café concert scene across the nation. Considered "the diva of the gutter," Theresa would become the prototype of the realist singers such as Aristide Bruant in the late nineteenth century and Renaud in the early twenty-first. She reigned as the queen of the Parisian café concert during the 1860s and 1870s. The measure of Valadon's success and the prestige of chanson in the late nineteenth century is that she also sang the songs of Jacques Offenbach (1819–1880), that popular composer who constantly mixed high and popular culture in his operas and brought the cancan to the opera stage with *Orpheus in the Underworld*.

Around 1900, Aristide Bruant (1851–1925) and Yvette Guilbert (1867–1944), both immortalized in the painting and posters of Toulouse-Lautrec, entertained and challenged Parisians and tourists in their nightclubs and café concerts. By 1894 Paris had as many café concerts as theatres, and in 1900 the most successful of them, the Olympia, earned two million francs; this gross was higher than that of the Comédie Française. Indeed, between the 1890s and World War I café concerts enjoyed their golden age, in between the dominance of the theatre and that of the movies. These places, at their height numbering around 360 in Paris alone, were cheap and informal and allowed Parisians to eat, smoke, drink, and watch a show all at the same time.[12]

After World War I, the usually small-scale and homespun café concert gave way to the bigger and more sophisticated music hall (the English institution helped inspire the change, and the English word became naturalized in French). Performers such as Mistinguette and Frehel and especially Maurice Chevalier consolidated their prewar popularity and became major stars. Indeed, Chevalier would become an international celebrity with hit recordings and films not only in France but also in Hollywood. By the middle of the decade a young singer from the south of France, Charles Trenet, had fused American swing music with his own inimitable style. (For example, his song *La Mer* would become a major hit in the United States as *Beyond the Sea* by Bobby Darin in the 1950s and has been recorded in 4,000 different versions around the world.)[13]

At the end of the 1930s, Edith Piaf, a disadvantaged child and street singer, emerged to become a major star. Until her death in 1963, her singing, songs, and life would incarnate the ordinary people of Paris, their passions (loves, heartbreaks, hatreds, and joys) and their spaces (the street and its entertainers and merchants, the cafés, dance halls, churches, rivers, and the metro). Few singers have led a more tragic but also a more productive life. Her legendary concerts at Parisian music halls helped stave off their bankruptcy. She died in 1963 one year before the Beatles began their climb to dominance of the world's popular youth culture.

After World War II, Piaf continued to be a power and helped young singers, most prominently Yves Montand, but also Charles Aznavour, to achieve stardom. At the same time, in the Saint Germain des Pres neighborhood of Paris, Juliette Greco developed her own distinctive style of song tied to the urban realism of such poets as Jacques Prevert and the philosopher Jean-Paul Sartre (who wrote a song for her). Charles Trenet remained a force through the 1950s and helped to inspire the post–World War II generation of singer-songwriters, including Léo Ferré (1916–1993), Georges Brassens (1921–1981), and Jacques Brel (1929–1978). Each of these three singer-songwriters has become a popular classic, as famous for his lyrics as for his music. Indeed, even though about 50 percent of his output was banned as obscene in the 1950, Brassens's lyrics in 1967 won the poetry prize of the Academie Française. Son of pious mother and an atheist father, Brassens, like so many provincials, fell in love with Paris and its street culture and café life. His earthy reflections on love and friendship are in a tradition stretching back to Villon but especially focused on Verlaine (many of whose poems he recorded). Jacques Brel, a native of Belgium, initially in the 1950s brought a youthful romanticism and lyricism to songs about love and woman, but by the end of the decade and into the 1960s attacked middle-class life as stodgy and unreflective. By the late 1960s and 1970s his songs has become more resigned, and he starred in a version of Don Quixote that captured well the mood of the era. Léo Ferré also came from the provinces, out of a particularly repressive Catholic family. After being demobilized following World War II, he turned to fusing cabaret with a more intense poetic and political strain than had been hitherto common. Constantly challenging his audience on political matters and demanding the freedom to be creative, he also expressed tender and profound emotions for the sea and for the animal world. Each of these so-called canonical chansonniers—confirmed when each of them had their lyrics and poetry become part of the prestigious Seghers poetry series—saw it as their task, as had generations of bohemians before them, to unsettle the smug life of the French middle classes.

One of the most original singer-songwriters in the 1950s was Serge Gainsbourg (1928–1991). In the late 1950s he worked with Boris Vian and won an award, the Grand Prix de l'Académie Charles Cros, in 1959, with his first album, which included a song "Le poinçonneur des Lilas" that immediately entered the repertoire of French chanson. But Gainsbourg's omnivorous musical genius would lead him into virtually every musical style that emerged over the 30 years, from rock 'n' roll, to the early French variant *yéyé,* to hard rock, folk-rock, reggae, and funk. Along the way Gainsbourg would work with such famous female singers as France Gall, Jane Birkin, and Vanessa Paradis. He never lost the touch to provoke, as when he set the French National anthem, "La Marseillaise" to a reggae beat. Gainsbourg would be one of the initiators of musical mixing (known as *metissage,* the hallmark of French music, especially since 1968).

In 1962 Andre Malraux, the great champion of spreading high culture among the masses, called for a revision of musical education that, ironically, helped launch new generations of French chansonniers. In 1966 the inaugural minister of culture charged Marcel Landowski, both a composer and administrator of music at the Comédie Française and at the Ministry of Culture, with mapping out a 10-year plan of music education (Plan Landowski). Only after the events of May 1968 did Landowski have a chance to implement his plan, but since he remained at his post until 1975, he accomplished much of what he desired. By the late 1970s the national budget for music had increased twelve-fold over the previous decade, and after 1973 studies showed a steady increase in the musical training of French youth. In 1977, Daniel Colling, one of the directors of Malraux's *maisons de la culture* based in Orleans, created one of the most successful of the music festivals that have now become so common across France.

The Bourges Spring Festival has become the main venue to preserve and promote French song. In a small town south of Orleans, Charles Trenet was able to connect with a new generation and keep his name current in popular French music. The audience for these live concerts has grown from 12,000 in its first year (1977) to 45,000 by 1980, with an average annual attendance over the past two decades of 100,000. At these concerts established stars such as Trenet or Georges Moustaki have been able to meet and hear new generations of singers. Other music festivals—such as the International Music Festival in Aix-en-Provence, the Nice jazz festival, and the Rennes rock festival— have also been popular and show a shift in French music listening away from a daily or weekly patronizing of music halls or cabarets and toward big concerts in Paris or summer music festivals.

The Bourges Festival also helped confirm the reputation of a new generation of French chansonniers who emerged in the 1970s. This was especially the case with Renaud (1952–) and Alain Souchon (1945–), initially compared to Léo Ferré, and Jacques Higelin (1940–), compared to Trenet. But these two artists were part of a much larger movement that included Maxime Le Forestier (1945–), who was hailed as a new George Brassens and was among the best-selling artists between 1973 and 1977, Francis Cabrel (1953–), Bernard Lavilliers (1946–), Yves Simon (1945–), and Jean-Jacques Goldman (1951–). Increasingly in the 1980s these artists infused the French chanson tradition with musical style from around the world, especially Africa. For example, in the bicentennial year of the French Revolution (1989) Maxime Le Forestier made a comeback with a song entitled "Né quelque part" ("Born Somewhere") expressing solidarity with the universalist aspirations of the French revolutionary tradition and against the rise of the National Front. During the 1980s and 1990s, another generation of chansonniers, including Patricia Kaas, Patrick Bruel, and Zazie, has sustained the genre even while continuing to experiment with fusing the chanson tradition with a wide variety of musical styles. In 2002 and 2004, for example, *variété française* held between 59 and 64 percent of the music sales in France (*variété française* is a broad category that, in this context, includes essentially all French music); as we shall see below, government intervention is also partly responsible for these strong percentages. In recent years, Anglo-American-inspired shows searching for new musical talent have been immensely popular *(Popstars,* on the M6 channel, and *Star Academy,* on the TF1 channel) and will perhaps be another source to maintain the tradition.[14]

FRENCH ROCK: FROM *YÉYÉ* TO POP TO ALTERNATIVE

The emergence of American and then British rock 'n' roll transformed the French music scene during the 1960s. In the early 1960s a group of young singers imitating Elvis and the early Beatles became known as the *yéyés* (the French translation of yea-yea). One of them in particular, Johnny Hallyday, has become a national institution. Over the last 40 years (1963–2003), he has sold 80 million records (18 of which have gone platinum) and sung to 15 million people (eventually, Hallyday would be an extra in an Elvis Presley motion picture filmed in Paris, *Loving You.*)[15] Virtually none of this first generation of French rockers continued the tradition of the singer-songwriter (aside from Françoise Hardy), and although their records continued to sell their status was soon diminished in France with the arrival of the Beatles. By the end of the 1960s, in the wake of the escalation of the Vietnam War and the events of May 1968, French youths switched to a steady diet of the Beatles, the Rolling Stones, Jimi Hendrix, the Grateful Dead, and Bob Dylan.

By the end of the 1970s, with the emergence of punk and then alternative styles of rock music, French rock 'n' roll developed a more authentic voice. The virtuoso Jacques Higelin was one of the first to create a distinctive French punk sound, and he was followed by bands such as Métal Urbain, Starshooter, Indochine, and the relatively long-lasting Telephone (1981–1990). Nevertheless, it was groups in the second half of the 1980s that proved most distinctive and successful, such as Les Negresses Vertes, Têtes raides, Mano Negra, and especially the duo of Les Rita Mitsouko. This last duo, Catherine Ringer and Fred Chichin, produced in 1985 a single entitled "Marcia Baïla," which supposedly has received more play on French radio than any other song.[16] One of the members of Mano Negra, Manu Chao, went on in the 1990s to become a solo act and in the late 1990s and early 2000s sold over4 million copies of *Clandestino* (1998), making it one of the best-selling albums in France and in the rest of the world ever for a French artist.[17]

THE RISE OF MUSICAL MULTICULTURALISM: RAI, AFRICA, WORLD

The 1980s brought a musical revolution to France. First, Socialist victory in the presidential and parliamentary elections brought Jack Lang to the Ministry of Culture, and he and his party at once transformed the musical scene. While Lang increased musical subsidies at both the national and regional levels, the parliament freed the airwaves of regulation to allow for a spate of new FM stations. Lang also created the Fete de la Musique, one of the most successful festivals in France and now celebrated in dozens of countries each June 21. In addition, under his administration expansive and flexible new concert halls were built in Paris and the provinces (Le Zenith, 1982 and La Cite de la Musique, 1985–96). Just as France was becoming a more diverse society, its musical outlets, from concerts to radio stations, also became more diverse. Thus in 1981 Radio Beur in Paris and Radio Galèere in Marseilles began broadcasting the rai music that had been a staple of Algerian culture since 1900 but was largely absent from a monotone French radio before this date.

The deregulation of radio has had an especially pronounced effect on French society. In 1970 radio was still used primarily for news, but by the 1990s and 2000s, music and talk had become predominant. Even in the early 1970s under 10 percent of French households had hi-fi equipment; by 1997 this figure had jumped to 74 percent; and in 2002 was still moving higher at 81.4 percent. This overall figure hides significant disparities by age; in 1997 for example, 41 percent of those over age 65 and 23 percent above age 55 lacked hi-fi equipment.[18]

Rai radio stations and those catering to other music promoted the development of distinctive hybrid sounds across France's increasingly diverse urban landscape. In 1984 Karim Kacel's song "Banlieues Bleues," expressed the new sensibility of the Parisian and Lyonaise suburbs that had become ethnic and religious melting post since the 1950s. The first rai festival occurred in the northern Parisian suburb of Bobigny in 1986 and propelled Cheb Khaled, later known simply as Khaled, into stardom. In the same year another rai group, Carte de Sejour (the French word for visa) released a version of Charles Trenet's "Sweet France" at a time when the conservatives who controlled the French parliament passed a more restrictive set of laws on French nationality. The song displayed the complexities of multicultural identity in a postcolonial world. Carte de Sejour broke up shortly thereafter, but its main singer, Rachid Taha, along with Khaled, Cheb Mami, and Faudel are the leading synthesizers of North African music with contemporary popular music. Many of the themes of their music, such as Faudel's song "Maintes-La-Jolie," express the love of neighborhood that has been a traditional part of French popular song.

During the 1980s, also in part due to Lang's inspiration, Paris became a center of what has become known as world music. Spanning folk and popular music from around the world, this genre of music is incredibly diverse, ranging from the Celtic harp of Alain Stivell, from Brittany, to the Africans Salif Keita of Mali and Youssou N'Dour Al Farka Touré and Xalam of Senegal to the zouk genre developed by Kassav and other artists from Guadeloupe and Martinique. Indeed, in the 1980s Paris became the capital of African music.

FRENCH RAP, HIP-HOP, AND DANCE MUSIC (FRENCH TOUCH)

One of the most innovative and unique products of the new musical ferment has been French rap and hip-hop. First aired on French TV and radio, these creations of marginalized African Americans quickly resonated in the impoverished suburbs of France. Between 1990 and 1992, two compilations of French rap appeared, including *Rapattitude,* which was the spring board for most of the major artists of the last fifteen years. Today France is the second-largest market for rap and hip-hop in the world, with rappers such as MC Solar and groups such as IAM, both of whom have gold albums. Hardcore rap is represented by such groups as Suprême NTM, the last letters standing for a French translation of a well-known epithet. French rap and hip-hop have also produced the biggest sensation in the English-speaking world for French music in decades: Les Nubians. Known as an "Afropean hip-hop/R&B duo," these multiracial sisters come from the southwestern port of Bordeaux. With a French father who is an accountant and a mother from the African nation of Cameron, they have lived both in Bordeaux and amidst the civil war of Chad (where they went when their father donated his expertise for the Red Cross). In 1999 Americans bought almost 400,000 copies of their first album *Princesses Nubiennes,* and worldwide they sold just about one million. Indeed, their overseas success made their reputation in France.[19]

As French rap has developed and evolved, it has been synthesized with a wide variety of regional musics. Thus in southwestern France an Occitan rap has emerged, with such artists or groups as Claude Sicre, Ange B, from Toulouse, the Massilia Sound System, from Marseilles, and the Beur rap group Alliance Ethnik from the suburbs north of Paris. Finally, another Toulousian group, Zebda, has combined rap, rai, and reggae.

In the mid-1990s French musicians made a major mark in techno (a new wave of electronic music with roots in disco). French techno achieved so much success, especially in England, that this style has become known by the title bestowed by English music critics: French touch. While some musicians in this movement originate from the poorer suburbs around Paris, such as Bagnolet, most come from affluent suburbs such as Versailles. Groups and individuals, such as Saint-Germain, Daft Punk, DJ Cam, Cassius, Air, Mr. Oizo, Bob Sinclair, and Modjo are all children of the 1980s and its musical styles: disco, funk, new wave, and rock. These French touch artists are also tied to new forms of entertainment, sociability, and youth culture that emerged in the early 1990s at raves and free parties, which usually occurred in clubs on the outskirts of Paris and other major cities. The big breakthrough came on January 18, 1992, at a rave at La Defense hosted by the Fnac (the nation-wide French department store specializing in music, books, and electronic media)Dance Division, which 4,000 attended. The biggest hit single by these French techno groups was by Stardust: "Music Sounds Better with You," which is one of the biggest hits in techno history, selling over two million copies. Then in 1998 the group Air produced *Moon Safari,* an album that sold 1.6 million copies, and the following year the first album by Cassius topped the English charts. French touch is the major reason French music exports have jumped so dramatically (see below). Thus it is quite logical that in February 2005 the Minister of Culture Renaud Donnedieu de Vabres decorated the group Air, Philippe Zdar (half of Cassius), and Dimitri from Paris for their contributions to the diffusion of French culture.[20]

Government Intervention Since 1981

Surveying the extraordinary musical energy coming from immigrant groups, Lang was at the forefront in establishing the Francophone Council of Song (1985) and the Bureau of French Music (1993). This latter organization directs marketing of French music worldwide and has had phenomenal success, with exports growing from 1.5 million in 1992 to 39 million in 2000. The success of the French program has led the Germans to create a similar system. In 1996, fearing the effects of growing globalization, the French Parliament passed what has become known as the Pelchat amendment mandating that 40 percent of all music broadcast during the day and evening (from 6:30 A.M. to 10:30 P.M.) be French, and at last 20 percent be recent releases.[21]

Today France ranks as the fifth-largest music market in the world and the third biggest in Europe. Despite the recent general decline in worldwide music sales, due especially to new Internet sites and means of distribution, France earns more money on the export of its music than its films (but both sales figures are below those of books). The French music industry, as in every other developed country, is dominated by a few multinationals (BMG, EMI, Sony Music, Universal Music, Virgin Music France, and Warner Music). "Hypermarkets" and large specialty stores, such as FNAC, which specializes in books, music and entertainment, and computer technology, now sell over 75 percent of all music (compared to 54 percent as recently as 1993). Despite this concentration in both the production and the distribution of music, the growing diversity of French society and the sustained commitment of its government to promote creativity should ensure that France remains a worldwide leader in music.[22]

This rapid survey has shown that France is home both of a great heritage and of much contemporary ferment in the performing arts.

NOTES

1. For "Preface to Cromwell," see www.bartleby.com/39/40.html.

2. See F.W.J. Hemmings, *The Theatre Industry in Nineteenth-Century France* (Cambridge: Cambridge University Press, 1993), 2.

3. See Hemmings and Sally Debra Charnow, *Theatre, Politics, and Markets in Fin-de-Siecle Paris: Staging Modernity* (New York and London: Palgrave Macmillan, 2005).

4. Michel Azama, ed., *De Godot à Zucco: Anthologie des auteurs dramatiques de langue française (1950–2000),* Vol 3 (Paris: Éditions Théâtrales, 2005), 200.

5. Jannine Cardona and Chantal Lacroix, *Chiffres clés 2006: Statistiques de la culture* (Paris: La Documentation Française, 2006), 124 for theatre statistics. Please check the website of *L'officiel des spectacles* at www.corsini.org/lofficieldesspectacles.htm and for *Pariscope*, www.pariscope.com.

6. Jannine Cardona and Chantal Lacroix, *Chiffres clés 2006: Statistiques de la culture* (Paris: La Documentation Française, 2006), 114.

7. David Looseley, "In from the Margins: Chanson, Pop and Cultural Legitimacy," in Hugh Dauncey and Steve Cannon, eds., *Popular Music in France from Chanson to Techno: Culture, Identity and Society* (Aldershot UK: Ashgrate, 2003), 29.

8. Vicki Woolf, *Dancing in the Vortex: The Story of Ida Rubinstein* (Choreography and Dance Studies Series) (Amsterdam: Harwood Academic Pub, 2001).

9. See Jacqueline Robinson, "Modern Dance Education," in *International Encyclopedia of Dance*, vol. III (New York and Oxford: Oxford University Press, 1998), 83–84.

10. Jannine Cardona and Chantal Lacroix, *Chiffres clés 2006: Statistiques de la culture* (Paris: La Documentation Française, 2006), 95, 100, and 114.

11. David Looseley, "In From the Margins: *Chanson*, Pop and Cultural Legitimacy," in Hugh Dauncey and Steve Cannon, eds., *Popular Music in France from Chanson to Techno: Culture, Identity and Society* (Burlington Vt.: Ashgrate, 2003), 29.

12. F.W.J. Hemmings, *Theatre and State in France, 1760–1905* (Cambridge: Cambridge University Press, 1994), 195. For the number of café concerts, see Ludovic Tournès, "Reproduire l'oeuvre: la nouvelle économie lusicale," Jean-Pierre Riouw and Jean-François Sirinelli, *La culture de lasse en France: de la Belle Époqe à aujoud'hui* (Paris: Fayard, 2002), 223.

13. Bertrand Bonnieux, et al., *Souvenirs, souvenirs . . . Cent ans de chanson française* (Paris: Editions Gallimard, 2004), 126.

14. Jannine Cardona and Chantal Lacroix, *Chiffres clés . . . : Statistiques de la culture.* Series (2001–2006). Sec. "disques." Also, the graph "Répartititon par repertoire," shows how French music sales compare with the other types of music: classical, jazz and international (that is contemporary music that is not French). Specifically in the 2006 edition, Jannine Cardona and Chantal Lacroix, *Chiffres clés 2006: Statistiques de la culture* (Paris: La Documentation Française, 2006), 95. (The 2004 edition had the same graph on the same page.)

15. www.experts.about.com/e/j/jo/Johnny_Hallyday.htm.

16. David L. Loosely, *Popular Music in Contemporary France: Authenticity, Politics, Debate* (Oxford, New York: Berg, 2003), 49.

17. See biography of Manu Chao at www.rfimusique.com/siteEn/biographie/ biographie_6191.asp. (The best way to access Manu Chao's biography and any other at RFI Musique is to go to their site www.rfimusique.com, click on the English version and then search for the biography of the artist desired.) For statistic of the 4 million copies of Chao's album Clandestino sold, see Delfin Vigil, "Addicted to Manu," in *San Francisco Chronicle, Datebook*, Sunday July 23, 2006, 46.

18. Olivier Donnat, *Les pratiques culturelles des français, enquête 1997* (Paris: La Documentation française, 1998), 99; and Gérard Mermet, *Francoscopie: Pour comprendre les français 2005* (Paris: Larousse, 2004), 438.

19. Chris Tinker, "Music," in Hugh Dauncy, ed., *French Popular Culture: An Introduction* (London: Arnold, 2003), 94 and Marianna Childress, "Les Nubians— One Step Forward," Globo Beat. *Global Music.* Satuday, July 12, 2003. Accessed at www.theglobalist.com/DBWeb/StoryId.aspx?StoryId=.

20. Stéphane Jourdain, *French Touch: Des raves aux supermarchés, l'histoire d'une epopee electro* (Bordeau: Castor Music, 2005), 10, 92, 124, 135, and 165.

21. For terms of Pelchat Amendment in English see *USENGLISH Foundation Official Language Research—France: Legislation.* Available online: www.us-english. org/foundation/research/olp/viewResearch.asp?CID=59&TID=1.

22. Ben Cardew, "CD Sales Decline as Discounts Lose Lustre," *Music Week*, October 15, 2005, 5. Stéphane Jourdain, 144; Jannine Cardona and Chantal Lacroix, *Chiffres clés 2006: Statistiques de la culture* (Paris: La Documentation Française, 2006), 208, 214, and 299.

10

Art, Architecture, and Housing

THE DEMOCRATIZATION OF CULTURE has been one of the underlying themes of this book. This process is seen most dramatically when we look at the evolution of art, architecture, and housing across the last hundred years. In essence the once most sacrosanct bastions of aristocratic culture—art and architecture— under the influence of the French and Industrial Revolutions and the artistic avant-garde have steadily became more oriented to the well-being of ordinary people rather than to celebrating aristocratic, much less middle-class, glory and taste. In art we can see this especially since the French Revolution, which created the world's first modern museums, through the romantic period in literature and art, which emphasized the virtues of the people, to the modernist school, with such figures as Marcel Duchamp and Pablo Picasso, who radically expanded the notion of art to include everyday objects. French photographers across the last century have been especially skilled at portraying the drama and sentiment of French daily life, and their work has thus complemented that of these painters. After World War I, France produced one of the greatest modern architects, Le Corbusier, who reoriented architecture away from grandeur and luxury and toward the concept of "machines" for living. After the twentieth century's second horrible war, postwar governments spent unprecedented amounts of capital not only to solve France's centuries-long housing crisis but also to inject new forms of cultural animation into urban life. At the same time, recent trends in art have increasingly focused on environments and thus have helped spur the intersection of culture and everyday life. Whereas French culture in the Old Regime focused on elite patronage, and in the long century of republican consolidation (1789–1981) on the artistic creation, we may be moving into an era in which consumer enjoyment takes center stage in French culture.

FRENCH ART

Almost everyone associates France with great art. Only Italy can compare with the length and complexity of the French artistic heritage. The greatest ages of French art both predate and postdate the Italian Renaissance. Between roughly the life of Nicholas Poussin (1594–1665) and the late 1960s French art achieved its greatest expression. Whether the French can regain their former primacy in art and again have Paris as the capital of art is hard to know, but certainly, as we shall see, the nation is making a concerted effort to do so.

France's artistic heritage goes back well before recorded history, to cave art. The paintings of Lascaux in the Dordogne valley of southwestern France were accidentally discovered at the start of World War II (1940). These remarkably sophisticated paintings, dating from about 15,000 B.C.E., were thought to be the oldest in France until in 1994 and 1999 serendipity again struck with the discovery of remarkably realistic paintings in limestone caves at Grotte Chauvet in southeastern France dating from about 14,000 years earlier (ca. 30,000 B.C.E.). Depicting the animals these people hunted and worshiped, often in ritual fashion, this art expressed the collective dreams and realities of an entire people, since hunter-gatherer societies had little if any social hierarchies.

The next major traces of art in France come from the Celtic peoples and are stone megaliths similar to Stonehenge in England found especially in contemporary Brittany (in the northwest near the Atlantic coast). Dating from 2000 B.C.E. from what is known as the Beaker culture, after their pottery and ceramics, these monuments are believed to have functioned as ritual spaces to plot the movement of the stars and thus to determine the pattern of their daily lives. While a class of priests, the Druids, had clearly emerged, art was still integral to the functioning of the entire society. We possess little idea of what other types of painting or sculpture may have been part of pre-Roman Gaul due perhaps to the Roman's own destruction of such evidence after Caesar's conquest (58–56 B.C.E) or such evidence perishing with the collapse of Roman power by 400 C.E.

The centuries-long disintegration of the Roman Empire and its classical culture saw the slow erosion of Greco-Roman painting and the urban environment that sustained it. The culture of the Germanic barbarian tribes that became the new rulers of France was antithetical to painting because it was centered on the horse rather than the house, raiding and plunder more than settlement and administration. As a result, once the various German tribes had conquered and occupied Roman Gaul, they would set up fortified camps rather than take over the Roman cities. Thus their art centered on objects that could be carried rather than permanently displayed, such as small pieces of jewelry and metalwork. This point is vital to understanding why the Greco-Roman tradition of art was so completely shattered by 500 C.E and why French painting emerged much later into glory than French architecture or sculpture and why Paris did not emerge as a center of art until very late (in the early nineteenth century).

Until the seventeenth century, as we shall see, France's greatest contributions to Western civilization would be in the fields of architecture and sculpture rather than in painting. Indeed, it may come as a shock to realize how relatively late French painting emerged; certainly for centuries it lagged behind not only Italian but also Flemish. In the Romanesque era (ca. 1100) for example, the most famous "paintings" in France are the Bayeux Tapestry rather than the murals of the Saint Savin-sur-Gartempe church near Poitiers. The next great pictorial developments were stained glass, especially in the Chartres cathedral (particularly 1194–1220), and miniature painting, especially in books. This first instance of Parisian art is found in the books of hours (essentially spiritual and secular guide books for living the good life) that became popular for the aristocratic elite in the fifteenth century. (See for example the *Psalter of Saint Louis* [1253–1270], the *Tres Riches Heures de Duc de Berry* [ca. 1413–1416], and the *Rohan Book of Hours* [ca. 1418–1425].) These early French artistic achievement were largely inspired by Italian and Flemish models. Only in the mid-1400s did the first great French painter emerge: Jean Fouquet. Born in Tours and working there, in Paris, and in Italy, Fouquet produced both panel portraits in churches and manuscript illuminations (see especially the *Book of Hours of Etienne Chevalier* [ca. 1455]).

Only with the advent of the Italian Renaissance and French involvement in Italian politics did French painting start to become a major current in Western Civilization. In 1494 Charles VIII (ruled 1483–1498) invaded Italy and inaugurated a long conflict not only on the Italian peninsula but also with Spain. Out of this struggle numerous Italian painters, sculptures, and architects would come to France and transform its culture (we have already see the example of Marie de Medicis in cuisine and will see her again with architecture). Francis I (ruled 1515–1547) aspired to outdo Italian princes as a patron of the arts, and towards this end he brought Leonardo da Vinci to France (where he lived his remaining few years at the Ambois chateau in the Loire Valley and died in 1519). He brought other artists as well to add artistic glory to his reign and to transform one of his hunting lodges, Fontainebleau, into a pinnacle of Renaissance architecture and art (with murals, painting and stucco work, for example).

Out of Francis I's patronage emerged the first French school of painting, the school of Fontainebleau. Leonardo's tenure in France was too brief to have much of an impact, but this was not the case with the Italian artists that worked at Fontainebleau during the 1530s through the 1560s, Rosso Fiorentino, Francesco Primaticcio, and Niccolò dell'Abate. These artists worked in the mannerist style, which came after the High Renaissance. The school also included Jean Cousin and Antoine Caron. All of these artists worked in painting, murals, and stucco and made Fontainebleau into one of the wonders of the age.

French painting was disrupted by turmoil surrounding the French wars of religion (the 1560s through the 1590s) and their aftermath. The most arresting record of this era's violence came from Antoine Caron, who transposed the instability to the time of the Roman Empire (*Massacres under the Triumvirate,* 1566). After he had secured stability and restored prosperity, Henry IV (ruled 1598–1610) continued work on the Fontainebleau palace. The second Fontainebleau school, however, is not as highly regarded as the first as it reveals the exhaustion of the mannerist style. One must turn to the provinces to find artists of greater talent at this time. One of the most interesting is the etcher Jacques Callot of Nancy (then in the independent duchy of Lorraine). Following his work in Florence for its grand duke (1611–1621)—almost obligatory at this time for French artists—Callot returned to Nancy and continued to do scenes of daily life and festivals and then recorded the ravages of war in *The Miseries and Horrors of War* (1633), as Lorraine was forcibly brought into France by Cardinal Richelieu during the Thirty Years War (1618–1648).

By the mid-sixteenth century, Paris started to become a magnet for artists. The extensive building program of Henri VI attracted many, and the growing centralization of the monarchy under Cardinal Richelieu had the same effect. Philippe de Champaigne, with his masterly rendering of Louis XIII, was the foremost portrait painter of the era. Although rooted in his native Lorraine, as were so many other French artists of this era, Georges de la Tour came to Paris after Louis XIII expressed interest in his paintings and gave him a royal appointment. Largely forgotten after his life, this artist deftly used the contrast of light and darkness, after the manner of the Italian Caravaggio, to evoke both strong and subtle if not mystical emotions out of biblical and genre scenes. Also influenced by Caravaggio, the Le Nain brothers, Antoine, Louis, and Mathieu, moved from the Champaign region to Paris in 1630 and there composed their almost ethnographic ensemble paintings of peasants (for example, *The Peasant's Meal,* 1642).

Simon Vouet (1590–1649) renewed French art by bringing the new baroque style back from Italy and by training many influential painters, especially Charles Lebrun, who consolidated the French style. Vouet's studio in Paris became the center of French art, and like his predecessors he worked in many media: paintings, murals, and decorative artwork on walls and ceilings. His most important student, Charles Lebrun, was not only a major painter (see his *Chancellor Séguier*), but also a central figure in the creation of the French academic system of painting. Lebrun played a major role in the creation of the Royal Academy of Painting and Sculpture, becoming its secretary in 1661 and director in 1683. In 1662 he became the official painter for Louis XIV and then head of the Gobelins factory that made tapestry and other exquisite pieces of furniture and interior decoration. Lebrun also worked on Louis XIV's palaces, especially Versailles, and helped craft the flamboyant and grandiose style, composed of order, clarity, and rigor, that made this not only the largest but also the most envied royal residence in Europe. In short, Lebrun was the classic example of the court painter at the center of power. He was also a pioneer in producing heroic portraits of Louis XIV for what we would call propaganda purposes.

Ironically, the two greatest French painters of the age worked almost exclusively in Italy. The life and work of Nicholas Poussin (1594–1665) and Claude Lorrain (1600–1682) complemented and contrasted with each other. Steeped in classical learning, Poussin moved to Italy at the age of 30, developed close ties to the papacy at Rome, and was highly regarded by the Spanish who then dominated the Italian peninsula. He reluctantly returned to France on the orders of Richelieu to work for Louis XIII. But disputes with Vouet and the royal court led to his returning to Italy for the rest of his life. He is generally regarded as the greatest European painter of his age and the epitome of classical order and harmony, with his paintings that concerned dramatic and decisive moments in classical and biblical history (*Moses Saved from the Waters, Rape of the Sabine Women, Shepherds of Arcadia, The Inspiration of the Poet,* and his series on such subjects at the seven holy sacraments). Indeed, this outsider would become the ideal stylist for French art until the mid-twentieth century. One of the first great debates in art theory in France concerned whether Poussin's emphasis on line and composition made him a better painter than the Flemish Peter Paul Rubens, with his focus on color and texture. A good friend of Poussin, Claude Lorrain, on the contrary, was of peasant origin and devoted his life to painting the Roman countryside. Although often having mythological or biblical references, his landscapes reveal a direct and intimate acquaintance with nature rather than an accumulation of references to past masters. His close observation of real life made his art highly innovative, and he was considered the standard by which all landscape painting was judged well into the nineteenth century.

After the heroic age of Louis XIV, French painting through most of the eighteenth century became lighter and more playful. This style has become known as the rococo. The greatest practitioner of the rococo, coming from the only recently incorporated territory of what would become French Flanders, was Antoine Watteau (1684–1721). What lends Watteau's paintings of seemingly superficial aristocratic garden parties (*fête galantes*) and dances their power is the sense that all of this joy is fleeting. Watteau had a deeply personal sense of the shortness of life, since he contracted tuberculosis shortly after having arrived in Paris. The restrained Rubenesque characteristics of Watteau's work gave way to a luxuriant celebration of female bodies in the mid-century work of François Boucher (1703–1770) (especially in his *Nude Girl,* 1751). Art historians believe the painting depicts one of Louis XV's mistresses. Jean-Honoré Fragonard (1732–1806) continued his master's style with such famous paintings as *The Swing* (1767). The paintings in his series entitled *The Progress of Love* (around 1770–1773) were so sensual that his patron, one of Louis XV's last mistresses, Madame du Barry, declined them due in part to the growing sense of modesty in the last years of this debauched Bourbon's reign.

By the 1770s a more sober style returned to French painting: neoclassicism. The beginnings of this trend can be seen in Jean-Siméon Chardin (1699–1779) who brought discerning realism to genre scenes, such as *Girl Scraping Vegetables* (1738) that was inspired by the Dutch school that so closely and minutely recorded daily life. The shift from rococo to neoclassicism registered in the work of one of greatest of women painters in the early modern European world. Marie Louis Elisabeth Vigée-Lebrun, working with her father and encouraged by one of the masters of the rococo, Greuze, became the friend of Marie Antoinette and painted the queen surrounded by her children. She was also influenced by the classicism and incipient republicanism of Diderot and Rousseau and painted herself and her daughter after a fashion to epitomize the ideal of motherly love and daughterly respect. She would flee France during the Revolution, returning only after it was over.

The complexities of neoclassicism are fully on display in its greatest artist, Jacques Louis David (1748–1825). On the one hand, in paintings such as the *Oath of the Horatii* (1784–1785), David celebrated Roman republican patriotism. With its implicit criticism of aristocratic decadence, this painting helped create the mindset that would overturn the monarchy and try to recreate ancient virtue in modern France. Indeed, after the assassination of the radical revolutionary Jean-Paul Marat, David painted one of his greatest paintings of the dead leader in his bath (1793) (where Marat had been murdered). On the other hand, the explicit sexism of the picture (the men on one side ready to die for their republic, the women on the other fainting in fear of losing their sons, brothers, and husbands) and its celebration of power reveal how David could later become the court painter of the Emperor Napoleon (creating, for example, the heroic image of Napoleon crossing the Alps). Looking at this picture we get a good sense of why Vigée-Lebrun would leave France as the Revolution became more extreme. Neoclassicism, however, had great staying power. Reaching its height under Napoleon with such other painters as Antoine-Jean Gros and Anne-Louis Girodet, it would continue to have a profound influence into the mid-century due to the genius of David's most accomplished student, August Dominique Ingres (1780–1867). The versatile Ingres excelled at painting a wide range of subject and styles: from heroic and mythological panoramas *(Oedipus and the Sphinx,* 1808) to intimate portraits *(Madame Devauçay,* 1807) to the early-nineteenth-century vogue for exotic Middle Eastern and Asian societies *(The Turkish Bath,* 1863). Although anticipating romanticism in his *The Dreams of Ossian* (1813) (based on the story of a supposed northern European equivalent of Homer), Ingres rejected all the various artistic movements that would sprout after 1820 and became prominent defender of academic art.

As we have noted in the first chapter, romanticism was more than just a philosophy or a theory but an expansive and expressive urge to transform all facets of Western art and personal expression. The utopian socialist Charles Henri Duke Saint Simon (1760–1825) anticipated the direction this sentimental revolution would take in terms of art when he applied the military term avant-garde to the artist rather than the soldier. Regardless of the field, the artist was charged with leading humanity forward with new insights and artistic revelations rather than simply upholding the traditional notions of taste and style that had been prevalent in previous ages. One of the most visionary and intensely focused of French romantic artists was Théodore Géricault (1791–1824). In his brief life, itself an emblem of romantic tragedy, he explored emotions and situations few French artists have ever touched. His *The Raft of the Medusa* (1819), based on an actual shipwreck, used brilliant colors and an innovative composition to depict the psychological and physical horror of being shipwrecked and then of being saved. The most important French romantic painter was Eugène Delacroix (1798–1863), who started painting dramatic scenes from literature, Dante, and Virgil in hell, then created exotic scenes of life in North African harems and horsemen, and finally ended up doing murals on government buildings. A lively debate flourished across his career, reminiscent with the one between the partisans of Poussin and Rubens, over the relative merits of line versus color.

While many painters were drawn to Paris as it became ever more a hothouse for artistic theories and an incubator, though its studios, museums, and cafés, of new styles, some painters focused on the French countryside. Camille Corot (1796–1875) would be the first of a long line of nineteenth-century French painters to view nature as the best teacher. Reviving, renewing, and elaborating on Lorrain's attempts to paint from nature, Corot went into the fields and thus painted on location. His brisk and bold brush strokes had a fundamental influence on the Barbizon school, which followed him into nature, in their case into the forest near Fontainebleau. The Barbizon school was a group of painters who rejected traditional depictions of the countryside found in academic art and went directly out into nature—in their case, around the French town south of Paris from which derives their name—especially during and after the 1848 Revolution through the 1860s. This informal grouping of painters included Jean-François Millet (1814–1875), Theodore Rousseau (1812–1867), Narcissus Díaz de la Peña (1807–1876), Charles-François Daubigny (1817–1876), and Constant Troyon (1810–1865). Their sympathies for rough nature and simple peasants made some critics suspect they were political radicals, but this was not the case. Their paintings would influence the impressionists more than political radicals.

The first painter to incarnate Saint Simon's ideal of an avant-garde artist was Gustave Courbet (1819–1877). He combined radicalism in both style and subject matter. At the half century (1850) his *Burial at Ornans* astonished art critics by depicting the funeral of a peasant villager on a huge canvas traditionally reserved for mythological gods or historical rulers. Courbet painted in a spare "realist" style that attempted to evoke both the banality and the dignity of ordinary people. His radicalism would eventually take him into the government of the Paris Commune during the Franco Prussian War (1870–71). (His activities there will be covered under architecture.) Following his participation in the commune, Courbet would flee to Switzerland. His "realism," the name given to his style, though highly influential, did not produce a school of painting.

Although not a political radical in the fashion of Courbet, Edouard Manet's elaboration on Courbet's experiments in mixing genres and refiguring painterly technique would produce the real revolution in art and lead to the rise of the first school of modern art, the impressionists. Courbet's influence is clearly seen in Manet's 1863 paintings *Le Déjeuner sur l'Herbe* and *Olympia*. What made these paintings about women so shocking is not that they were nude, as this had long been acceptable in a mythological setting, but that they were depicted in contemporary Parisian society with expressions not of serenity but of either enjoyment or defiance. Thus a nude woman on the grass of a Parisian park caused a scandal at the famous Salon des Refusés (1863). For critics whose criteria derived from academic painting, this canvas reeked of immorality and depravity, though Manet saw himself as merely creating a new art for a new, modern world. (In many ways fulfilling the agenda that Baudelaire, as we have noted in chapter one, called for.)

By the mid-1860s, Manet attracted a circle of novice painters around him who would become known as the impressionists. This was another grouping based more on affinity than any clear ideology and included Edgar Degas (1834–1917), Claude Monet (1840–1926), Camille Pissarro (1830–1903), August Renoir (1841–1919), Alfred Sisley (1839–1899), Gustave Caillebotte (1848–1873), Armand Guillaumin (1841–1927), and Berthe Morisot

(1841–1895). What first brought them together was the initial impression- ist exhibition in 1874. A hostile journalist, Louis Leroy, coined the term "impressionist" for Monet's painting *Impression, Sunrise* (1872) which he felt was more an approximation than a fully completed painting. While Monet best personified the *plein-air* ethic, Edgar Degas most fully explored the spaces of modern life: from race tracks to cafés, ballet schools, offices, and laundries. By 1886, the date of their last collective exhibition, the impressionists had es- sentially won the war with the academics. In essence they had radically and de- cisively severed painting from its traditional reliance on "reality" and "elevated" subject matter. By exploring the nature of light and sensation on the human eye, they opened up painting to explore the human mind and to paint not what is seen but what is felt and experienced. All the various schools of modern art would be inconceivable without this crucial shift in focus. Impressionism created not only a new language in colors and subject matter but also led to a proliferation of new schools of painting. This is well attested to in a recent book on the history of artistic movements, which lists only 8 artistic movements between the Renaissance and the nineteenth century, but 22 during the nine- teenth century, 22 from just 1900 to 1945, and 41 since 1945.

In general the next period is known as postimpressionism (roughly 1880 to 1905). The most important painters in this era were Paul Cézanne, Paul Gaugin, Vincent van Gogh, and Georges Seurat. Although he had been part of two impressionist exhibits, Cezanne had been left unsatisfied. Wishing "to make of impressionism something solid and enduring, like the art of the museums," he explored the geometry and line behind the colors and sensa- tions without regard to traditional notions of perspective. His landscapes, such as *Mont Sainte-Victoire* (ca. 1886), his still lifes, and his depictions of card players hint at the revolution that Picasso and Braque would unfold with cubism a few decades later. Georges Seurat (1859–1891) had similar rationalizing ambitions to Cezanne but took them in the direction of color, not line. Through a painting technique involving thousands of colored dots that would provide through opposition and contrast the lines of the painting (a style that would become known as pointillism), Seurat wished to achieve a sort of science of perception and painting. (See for example his *Afternoon on the Island of La Grande Jatte,* 1884–1886.) While Cezanne systematically ex- plored line and perspective and Seurat color and line, Gaugin and van Gogh used colors to express not outward appearances but inner emotions (thus they were precursors to the various schools of expressionism that emerged after 1900). Despite their artistic affinities, Gauguin and van Gogh expressed very different attitudes toward France. While van Gogh was one of the first foreign artists to make France his home, Gaugin wished to abandon a civili- zation that he felt had become corrupt and inauthentic and to rediscover the basic elements of life among the premodern societies, first in Brittany and then in the French colony of Tahiti. Henri Toulouse-Lautrec took the opposite approach, plunging into the bohemian and proletarian underworld/demi monde of Paris's Montmartre district and making its dancers and singers famous across the following centuries.

Symbolist painting also emerged in the postimpressionist era. Symbolist art, however, was neither as influential nor as successful as it was in literature. Nevertheless, it includes artists such as Gustave Moreau, Pierre Puvis de Chavannes, and Odilon Redon, although their works are not now as highly regarded as the schools noted above and below and did have considerable influence on the symbolist painters that emerged in other nations. Their obsessive quest to encode their paintings with symbols that would tap into the unconscious helped inspire the Norwegian Edward Munch and the Austrian Gustave Klimt for example.

While the symbolists tried to create paintings with intellectual and metaphysical depth, yet another nineteenth-century school explored the painting surface, the canvas. Named the Nabis, the Hebrew word for prophet, by poet Henri Cazalis, this group formed around him and the aesthetician, artist, and friend of Gaugin, Paul Sérusier. Most of the other members of the group had also studied at one of the Paris art academies (Julien) and included Edouard Vuillard, Felix Vallotton, Louis Valtat, Paul Ranson, and Pierre Bonnard. This school showed the growing link between literature and art. For example, another writer connected with the group, Maurice Denis wrote (in 1890) "a tableaux is essentially a surface plane covered by colors in a certain assembled order." In short, the nabis continued the impressionist quest to rethink the nature of painting by exploring the nature of assembling images on a canvas.

The beginning of the twentieth century saw no diminution in the attempt to probe the nature of painting. Still feeling the constraints of academicism, a new generation strove to expand the range of art through a more intense expression of emotions via the use of dramatic coloring. They were dubbed wild beasts (fauves in French) by the critic Louis Vauxcelles at the 1905 Autumn Salon. Again a critic's harsh judgment quickly became a term of description not denigration for the work of a group of artists who would travel in many different directions over the course of their very productive lives: André Derain (1880–1954), Albert Marquet (1875–1957), Georges Rouault (1871–1958), Maurice Vlaminck (1876–1958), Raoul Dufy (1877–1953), Henri Matisse (1869–1954), and Georges Braque (1883–1963). By 1907 this group had disintegrated and the artists developed their own unique styles, but all of them would remain at the center of the French art world past 1950, especially Braque and Matisse, who would rank among the greatest of the twentieth century.

By 1900, with a century of incessant artistic and political innovation already accomplished, Paris stood at the pinnacle of world art. Artists from around the world, following in the footsteps of van Gogh, were pulled by this artistic magnet to the streets, cafés, parks, and countryside of this world capital of art. Across the twentieth century "French" art or the school of Paris would welcome a wide variety of foreigners. In a world about to descend into a paroxysm of nationalism (with two world wars) Paris was an oasis of cosmopolitanism. At the center of the expatriate art community was a young Spaniard, Pablo Picasso (1882–1973), whose art would best epitomize the fervent quest for innovation across the twentieth century.

Although his artistic genius was apparent from his early teens and would transform any genre or medium in which he worked throughout his life, Picasso's first and greatest innovation was cubism. The line and geometric exploration of Cezanne were raised to a new level of sophistication with his *Les Demoiselles d'Avignon* (1906–1907) and fused with Picasso's research into African art. Thus this painting encompasses much of the most vital energy of early-twentieth-century art: the search for new techniques and sources of inspiration outside of the Western world. Braque was so impressed by this painting that he joined Picasso in developing cubism. The first years of cubism brought what scholar call an "analytical" phase, in which objects were reexamined in the light of geometric shapes and then, in a second phase— "synthetic cubism"—placed into larger ensemble painting (with a variety of objects displayed in geometric fashion). Other artists also using this new style were Albert Gleizes (1881–1953) and Jean Metzinger (1883–1937). In essence, cubism deconstructed space and perspective and allowed the artist to explore multiple lines, dimensions, and perspectives simultaneously. Cubism questioned the basic notion of a painterly "object" and would this lay the foundation for abstract art. Although abstract art would especially flourish in Germany, some of the first explorations of this style occurred in Paris. Francis Picabia's (1879–1953) painting *Caoutchouc* (1909) was the first clear artistic expression of abstractionism that would be further developed by Robert (1885–1941) and Sonia Delaunay (1885–1979), Czech expatriate Frank Kupka (1871–1957), and the former cubists Jean Hélion (1904–1987) and August Herbin (1882–1960).[1]

The foundational idea of art—that it is something somehow beautiful and distinct from ordinary utilitarian objects—was interrogated by another titan of twentieth-century French art, Marcel Duchamp (1887–1968). With his *Nude Descending a Staircase* (1912), he fused the scientific study of movement with art. Even before the rise of dada during World War I, Duchamp had developed the notion of the "ready-made" by turning a urinal and other ordinary manufactured objects into art (see his *Fountain,* 1916) based upon his authority as an artist. Duchamp's iconoclasm would help inspire conceptual art at the end of the century and erode such distinctions between painting and sculpture and art and life.

Thus the antiwar avant-garde art movements—dada during World War I and surrealism afterwards—became part of a broader reexamination of traditional notions of representation in the Western world. What these movements brought to art—from the dadaist Francis Picabia to the surrealists Salvador Dali (1904–1989), Andre Masson (1896–1987), and Yves Tanguy (1900–1955)—was an exploration of the subconscious mind through either a free flow of images or thought processes personified in elaborate detail. (For example, to portray the experience of time passing Dali created images of clocks that had melted onto surfaces.)

During the late 1920s and 1930s, as totalitarian states emerged in Stalinist Russia and Nazi Germany, Parisian artistic cosmopolitanism became ever more pronounced. One result was that scores of modern artists, such as the pioneering Russian abstractionist Wassily Kandinsky, moved to Paris, and the city became the center of abstract art as Russian and German artists fled the totalitarian regimes of Hitler and Stalin. At the same time the art world, like the rest of society, became polarized politically to an unprecedented degree. By 1930 abstract artists in Paris had formed an association (Concrete Art: Art Concrete) which expanded to over 400 members the following year and become known as abstraction-creation. As a result of these organizations, Paris would see the first art shows devoted entirely to abstract art. In 1941 yet another new school emerged, nonfigurative art, which synthesized elements of fauvism, cubism, and abstraction with a return to paintings depicting daily life. Some of its members would have long careers, for example Jean Bazaine (1904–2002), Alfred Manessier (1911–1993), Charles Lapicque (1898–1988), and Russian-born Paris resident Serge Poliakoff (1900–1969). Conservative artists, those still wishing to follow the traditions of Poussin, formed their own group, *forces nouvelels* (new forces), in 1934 and staged their own shows through 1943. Ironically this group declined rather than thrived under Vichy.

Defeat and German occupation devastated the Parisian art world. Many of the best artistic minds, such as the founder of surrealism, André Breton, moved to New York, but Pablo Picasso stayed in Paris as an act of resistance and then after World War II joined the Communist Party. It is from this point that New York started its rise as a world art center and would eventually displace Paris by the late 1960s. Rather than a time of innovation as in the theatre, art during and immediately after World War II coped with the unimaginable devastations of total war and genocide. Free of any immediate connection to the horrors going on across the Atlantic, New York artists had the luxury of government assistance during the New Deal and its aftermath with the GI Bill, of developing new schools (such as abstract expressionism), and getting training both in the United States and in Europe after the war. Increasingly from the 1950s, reversing the first half of the century, trends would start in the New York and then move to Paris.

Confronting the horrors of modern war and the Holocaust has been one of the most distinctive aspects of French art after 1945. The German social critic Theodor Adorno's meditation on whether poetry was possible after Auschwitz found resonance in French art, perhaps most fully in the raw art *(art brut)* of Jean Dubuffet (1901–1985), who tried to explore the boundaries of human creativity—from children's drawing to the art of hunter-gatherer societies, the artistic efforts of the mentally ill, and the unconscious and banal traces of art found in graffiti. Jean Fautrier (1898–1964), who had taken refuge in an asylum during the war and witnessed Nazi atrocities, evoked the horror of torture and dismemberment in the *Hostages* series (1945). Bernard Buffet (1928–1999) captured the sense of isolation and futility of an inhumane world (see his self-portrait, 1956)

Paris remained an international art center and a cauldron for new artistic currents. By 1948 André Breton had returned and continued to host surrealist meetings in cafés and joined with Dubuffet in creating the Society for Raw Art. As the Cold War descended on Europe, artisan and political activist Andre Fougeron (1912–1998) penned a manifesto, *The Painter on His Battlements,* calling on artists not to surrender to U.S. imperialism, also the subject of one of his famous pictures, *Atlantic Civilization* (1953), which has at its center a Cadillac. Nearby a greedy capitalist takes off his top hat and bows as a Nazi German soldier comes out of the top of the luxury sedan with an aimed rifle. Around him are the oppressed workers of the developed and Third Worlds. In 1948, at the Café Notre Dame in Paris, a group of artists from Copenhagen, Brussels, and Amsterdam formed a new group called COBRA (from the first letters of the names of these cities). Including the Danish painter Asger Jorn, who would also play an important role in the situationist international, along with other painters such as Pierre Alechinsky, Karel Appel, Carl-Henning Pederson, and the French Jean-Michel Atlan, this group synthesized Marxism, surrealism, and Norse mythology into a critique of the Cold War culture then emerging. By the mid-1950s a group of young Latin Americans (Venezuelan Jesus-Raphel Soto and Argentinians Julio Le Parc and Horacio Garcia Rossi) made Paris their home in the hopes of avoiding the constraints of U.S. imperialism in their homelands.

As American art styles became more influential with the great success of the New York abstract expressionist school in the 1950s, French artists turned to irony and what would later be called deconstruction to assimilate and accommodate to their own work. For example, American abstract expressionism became abstract lyricism for the German-expatriate Parisian painter Georges Mathieu (1921–). Moreover, Jackson Pollack's action painting was reconfigured through the phenomenological philosophy of Maurice Merleau-Ponty's notion of the inseparability of mind and body. As a result, Mathieu's and other French abstractionist paintings by Pierre Soulages (1919–) or the early work of Simon Hantai (1922–) tend to be more decorative and less harsh than their American counterparts, in short with more patterns.

The next American style (the pop art of the last 1950s and 1960s) was assimilated into a new realist *(nouveau réalisme)* trend in France (founded in 1960). In general, French artists in this school had a more satirical and mystical edge than did Jasper Johns or Robert Rauschenberg. This school of art continued the questioning, first begun by Duchamp, of the compartmentalization of art into painting and sculpture that will become increasingly common in the following decades. An offshoot of this movement was GRAV (Group des recherches d'art visual), in which artists such as Julio Le Parc (1928–) wished to abolish the distinction between artists and the public and who took their art into the street to make their point.

The work of Yves Klein (1928–1962) and Jean Tinguely (1925–1991) gained widespread notoriety in a fashion that had not been seen since the turn of the century and helped inspire numerous subsequent trends. Klein's *The Void* (1958), which was simply a studio devoid of any paintings, for example helped inspire minimalism. Tinguely's *Metamecaniques* (1954–55) were the first of the many machines he built which literally smashed themselves apart and thus provoked a reexamination of art in an industrial world. Such exhibitions anticipated the kinetic art movement that Tinguely would also join during the mid-1950s. Klein had a deeply mystical streak that was especially apparent in the reverence for the color blue; indeed, he would develop and patent a special shade of the color that has become known as International Klein Blue (IKB). He explored its symbolism not only in exhibitions of differently priced but identical monochromes, but also by having a woman bathe herself in his blue and then become a "woman paintbrush," using her body became the means of applying the blue paint to canvas, per Klein's instructions.. For Klein, "Color itself was painting."[2] This latter exhibition would anticipate the "happenings" of the 1960s and the performance art that emerged in the 1980s and beyond.

Niki de Saint-Phalle (1930–) brought a protofeminist aesthetic to nouveau réalisme. She first made an impression on the public with a satire on informal abstract art techniques. With her so-called rifle shot reliefs, the spectator could shoot at bottles containing paint, which would then run onto canvasses. Then in conjunction with Jean Tinguely she created a huge and hollow 20-foot seated woman, which one entered by the vagina and inside encountered outrageously painted women on the theme of brides and whores (*Brides et Nanas*).

The artist Christo, originally from Bulgaria, developed his art in the context of neorealism. His "wrappings" have taken the notion of found objects to new heights and have been among the most public ways in which the separation between art and reality has been rethought. His wrapping objects and making them into gifts for the spectator also calls into question the nature of the museum experience. Indeed, his works have often been seen as example of another artistic school: land art.

France in the 1960s also participated in the development of artistic happenings that first sprouted in the fluxus group in New York. Jean-Louis Lebel, author of first French anthology of beat poetry (1965), brought happenings to Europe in the spirit of Marcel Duchamp and fluxus (as in flow) and organized "art laboratories of the future" with multimedia capabilities in which the artist blends into their materials and the ego is transcended.[3] The fluxus movement in France had as its main proponents Robert Filliou (1926–1987) who believed "Art is a function of life more than a fiction. Art is what makes life more interesting than art" and Ben (Benjamin Vautier, 1935–) for whom "art is everything."[4]

By the mid-1960s, a new generation of French artists had moved closer to American pop art's embrace of contemporary popular culture and ironic glances at art history. This emerged most fully in two movements, narrative figuration *(figuration narrative)* and photographic art *(photographie d'art)*. The name of the first group comes from one of the expositions that formed the style: Myths of Daily Life (1964) and Narrative Figuration (1965). Artists such Gilles Aillaud (1928–), Henri Cueco (1928–), Bernard Rancillac (1931–), Jacques Monory (1934–), Valerio Adami (1935–), Peter Klasen (1935–), Hervé Télemaque (1937–), Eduardo Arroyo (1937–), Gérard Fromanger (1939–), and AlainJacquet (1939–) wished to expose, after the fashion of Roland Barthes, the ideological rationalizations and obfuscations of daily life and break with what they saw as a cozy and symbiotic relationship between artists and museums.

The photographic art movement often used irony and pathos as major tools. Alain Jacquet's ironic photographic reformulation of Manet's *Lunch on the Grass* (1964) is one of the best examples. Martial Raysse's *Simple and Quiet Painting* (1965), mixes photography and painting. Among more recent works are those of Gérard Garouste (1946–), whose parodies of classic Western art from Tintoretto to Picasso have fused pop art with postmodernism. Christian Boltanski (1944–) as a self-taught painter has extended and updated Dubuffet's *art bruit* into experimental art borrowing from Japanese motifs and with references to the Holocaust.

Between late 1966 and 1967 four young artists, Daniel Buren (1938–), the Swiss expatriate, Olivier Mosset (1938–2000), Michel Parmentier (1938–2000), and Niele Toroni (1937–) joined under the aegis of art critic Marcelin Pleynet to form a new movement, B.M.P.T. (after the initials of their last names). In their various "manifestations" (sequentially numbered) they tried "to make paintings without being painters" and to break with the banalities of aesthetic and romantic idealism of the notion of the creative artist.[5]

In May 1968 came an outpouring of posters and the occupation of the Ecole des Beaux Arts. Pierre Buraglio helped found and direct a people's workshop that established links with factory workers and tried to inspire the workers to create art on the job. Moreover, the Salon of Young Painters was more traditionally militant in protesting the Vietnam War and supporting strikes and promoting a realist style of painting similar to Soviet "socialist realism." The May events also led to the establishment of artistic cooperatives and communes, the most important of which was the Malassis cooperative in the Parisian suburb of Bagnolet. Gérard Tisserand (1934–) and the artists that surrounded him—(Henri Cueco (1929–), Lucien Fleury (1928–2004), Jean-Claude Latil (1932–), Michel Parré (1938–), and Christian Zeimart (1934–)—tried to take the gravity out of art and turn it into a joyous act of collective creation, using the large format style popular with poster and graffiti artists during the May 1968 events.

By 1970 virtually all critics and historians believe that New York had surpassed Paris to become the world's art capital. Nevertheless, the birthplace of modern art has continued to attract and develop a diverse set of new artists and movements. The most important movement of the 1970s was supports/surfaces, a French response and variation on American minimalism. Although it only existed as a coherent avant-garde movement during the early 1970s, its deconstructive aesthetic—painting is not dead but it must take as its subject the nature of painting itself—remained important throughout the decade. Associated with the avant-garde review *Tel Quel,* and especially with its art critic Marcelin Pleynet, this movement tried to inject a Marxist and deconstructionist perspective on art, exposing the material foundations of this supposedly "spiritual" activity though a constant interrogation and comparison between the material used and the meanings generated by art. As a result, a wide variety of material from traditional paints to floor carpet was enlisted to jar viewers out of their complacency regarding art. See for example Louis Cane's (1943–) *Toiles decoupes,* composed of large felt squares, or his rubber stamps bearing his name, or Claude Viallat's (1936–) use of rope in *Multiple Disappearances,* or Daniel Dezeuze's (1942–) use of a ladder in *Brown and Green Wooden Ladder.*

In the middle of the 1970s another movement called *nouvelle subjectivité* emerged with the encouragement of the conservateur and art critic Jean Clair in Paris and inspired by foreign artists such as David Hockney and the German artists of the 1920s. Their 1976 exposition at the Paris Museum of Modern Art launched the careers of Alberto Gironella (1929–, born in Mexico), Olivier O. Olivier (1931–) Michel Parré (1938–1998), formerly of the Malassis cooperative, Sam Szafran (1934–), and Christian Zeimart. In essence these painters returned to oils and canvasses and to portraits and landscapes.

By the end of the 1970s critics began to wonder if the avant-garde had dissolved or died. The debate started in 1977 when critic Philippe Solliers in *Tel Quel* and critic Dominique Jameux in *Musique en jeu* raised the issue and then debated it with art critic and historian Catherine Millet at the Centre Pompidou. The biennial of Venice in 1980 reflected this new perception, with its focus on the trans-avant-garde. Lyotard's notion of a "postmodern condition" and Gilles Lipovetsky's concept of the "era of the void" also fit into this mood. Thus the end of grand narratives in history and politics; also seemed to affect the art world. Moreover the Socialist cultural subsidy policies regarding art, especially the FRAC (regional funding of contemporary art), gave artists a cushion against the caprices of the marketplace, which had so often enraged artists since the romantic era.

The first new movement to emerge in the 1980s was first known as the new figurations *(nouvelles figurations)*. Ben (Benjamin Vautier 1935–), along with the critic Bernard Lamarche-Vadel, brought coherence to this disparate group of young painters. Ben dubbed this new tendency free figuration *(figuration libre),* but the group more permanently has been divided into two tendencies: 1) popular figuration—including artists Robert Combas, (1957–), Hervé Di Rosa (1959–), Richard Di Rosa, (1963–), and Rémy Blanchard (1958–1993)—so called for their references to popular and urban culture; and 2) figuration *savante,* which has utilized high culture and includes Jean-Michel Alberola (1953–), Jean-Charles Blais (1956–), and Gérard Garouste (1946–). Whether inspired by popular or elite images, both groups have explored art beyond the question of beauty (indeed this was the theme of their first exposition). Two characteristic ways in which these artists revised figuration are illustrated by Robert Combas's painting, *R.F.*, of a brilliantly blue-skinned, sexually explicit Marianne with a red Phrygian bonnet, waving the French flag; also, Jean-Charles Blais's Paris metro station for the National Assembly with posters of the head of politicians (controversial because there were no female heads).

Although there may no longer be a true avant-garde in France and though the number of formal or even coherent schools or movements has declined, contemporary art still holds great power to shock, provoke, and stimulate. An excellent case is the work of Daniel Buren, which has grown increasingly conceptual over the decades. When he won the commission to install an art exhibit in the courtyard of that bastion of French architectural and political power, the Palais Royal (right next to the Council of State and the Ministry of Culture), his sculpture of white and black columns of various sizes quickly brought howls of outrage from critics who saw it as flippant and cheap, among other epithets. The multimedia feminist Orlan (1947–) is most famous for her "carnal art" that has reversed Christian metaphysics by turning the flesh into word via operations on her body that she directs while she is awake (thus also embodying Artaud's concept of the theatre of cruelty). She has also worked with computers and photography (one especially memorable one portrays her as a half machine that dispenses kisses). Orlan's art has provoked a heated debate as to whether her art undermines or strengthens male power over women. On the contrary, the seemingly "classical" representational artist Balthus (1908–2001) angered many for his preoccupation with painting prepubescent women. The graffiti art movement that emerged with the introduction of African American rap and hip-hop into France in the late 1980s and early 1990s also became controversial, especially when Lang and other culture ministers funded various graffiti artist groups.

The last decade and a half (1990–2005) has witnessed a continued acceleration in the pace of change in the French art world. As noted below, a new network of museums now covers France and complements the growing government intervention in art noted above. Moreover, a number of private foundations have emerged. For example, in 1994 Gilles Fuchs founds the ADIAF, Association de défense internationale de l'art française (www.adiaf.com), which now annually awards a Marcel Duchamp prize to the person judged the best French artist. Artists have also become more empowered, with an explosion in the middle of the 1990s of art galleries directed by artists themselves (autogérés). Over the past fifteen years the main aesthetic theories have explored the relationship between art, artist, and consumer in an increasing media- and image-saturated society. Across the 1990s French critics were extraordinarily preoccupied by the status of contemporary painting, with philosophers such as Jean Baudrillard and the former director of the Ecole des Beaux Arts, Yves Michaud, weighing in against an art that seemed to have become, in their eyes, sterile, obscure, and devoid of meaningful criteria of judgment. Defenders of contemporary art, such as Catherine Millet and Rainer Rochlitz, defended contemporary art essentially as a whole. The sociologist of art Nathalie Heinich and the critic Nicolas Bourriaud developed the most novel, interesting, and consequential responses. Heinich explored what she termed the "permissive paradox," in which contemporary artists must follow what has now become a traditional and ironic injunction: Be transgressive! Bourriaud's notion of relational aesthetics revisioned the artist as a social worker. For Richard Leydier, notions of a relational aesthetic have been at the foundation of art over the last decade. As we see below, this is a useful prism on this era. Finally, another polemic erupted when the sociologist Alain Quemin submitted the report on French art in international context that the Minister of Foreign Affairs had requested in June 2001. In essence, this report found that contemporary French art had little resonance around the world with only a few exceptions (such as Christian Boltanski, Daniel Buren, Pierre Huyghe, and Sophie Calle).

Despite this bleak assessment, French art remains provocative. For example, as far as notions of relationality, Pierre Huyghe has put a television at the disposal of the viewers of some of his exhibits, and Philippe Parreno invites museumgoers to do their preferred pastimes. The expatriate Thai, Rirkrit Tiravanija has prepared Thai soup and put pinball machines at the disposition of the viewers. The artist duo of Sylvian Grout and Stéphane Mazéas took this invitational turn one step further when they invited the museumgoers to destroy furniture in the gallery Georges Verney-Caron.[6] Alberto Sorbelli has been one of the recent artists making video as vital a part of art as it had been in the 1970s and 1980s. One of his pieces features a film of a woman playing a prostitute and trying to pick up customers in the Louvre by Da Vinci's Mona Lisa.

Other artists have begun an active engagement with deprived urban spaces or marginal people. Olivier Blanckart has filmed reactions to his playing a homeless person who appears to be making his home in an art gallery during a *vernissage*. Melik Ohanian (1969–) has extensively photographed and audio-recorded France's *banlieues* (especially prescient in light of the recent riots) and filmed the Liverpool docks in such a fashion that the various layers of experience, from its time as a bustling port to the era of strikes and now in its eclipse as the site of ocean traffic due to globalization, shine through. Pierre Huyghe (1962–) has explored urban space in a wide variety of fashions: from developing rituals for a community in the Hudson valley of upstate New York to creating a puppet opera on the life and work of Le Corbusier to operating a television station for artists. Thomas Hirschhorn (1957–) has constructed a wide range of artworks out of "ramshackle materials" and placed monuments, one for example in honor of George Bataille, in an impoverished suburb where immigrants are in the majority. Expatriate Anri Sala (1974–) has explored the drab Stalinist urbanism of his native Albania through photography and film. Dominique Gonzalez-Foerster (1965–), in her explorations of space, has one installation piece entitled: *Park—A Place for Escape*. Bruno Peinado has subverted and reconfigured a staple of modern advertising, the Michelin Man (Bibendum), into Afro-Michelin Man, with his fist raised in a Black Power salute. The work's title: *One Big World* presents a fascinating reconceptualization of globalization.

Philippe Parreno (1964–) perhaps best encapsulates the trend on relational aesthetics when he notes that through his widespread artistic collaborations with other artists and their use of a Japanese animated character in some of their exhibitions, the notion of the museum and exposition space is constantly in flux: "An exhibition space is not only a display of objects but also a space of negotiation, a place where a series of games can be played."[7]

SCULPTURE

Sculpture emerged as a complement to Romanesque architecture. Indeed, the first French artist we know by name was Gislebertus, who carved his name under his extraordinary rendering of the *Last Judgment* (c. 1140) above the west entrance to the Autun Cathedral in Burgundy. We know little about the sculptors who created masterpieces on other cathedrals. The next great age of French sculpture emerged during the Renaissance, the first great age of artistic individualism. Jean Goujon (1510–1566) and Germain Pilon (1537–1590) translated the styles of such Italian masters as Donatello and Michelangelo into a French idiom. Goujon's work is ubiquitous across the landscape of Paris even to this day, on the facades of the Louvre, the bas-reliefs of the Saint Germain l'Auxerrois church and the Carnavalet Museum (formerly the Hotel de Ligneris), and the six nymphs of the Fountain of the Innocents. Goujon's architectural work reveals the persistence of the architect-artisan tradition into the French Renaissance. The favorite sculptor of Catherine de Medici, Pilon did some of his greatest work on her tombs (and that of Henry II) at Saint Denis and also contributed sculptures at the Louvre, Fontainebleau, and Saint Jean François church in Paris. Pilon was deft at combining and anticipating numerous styles: realism from the French style, idealism from the Italian Renaissance, and an emotionalism that anticipated the baroque. In the age of Mansart, Jacques Sarazin (1588–1660) meshed his style with the architectural master at Maisons-Laffitte and contributed work to the Louvre and to the funerary sculptures for ecclesiastical dignitaries.

The construction of Versailles provided great opportunities for a new generation of sculptors. The two favorite sculptors of the age of Louis XIV are Antoine Coysevox (1640–1720) and François Girardon (1628–1715). This is not surprising, since along with accomplished technical mastery they were superb at depicting the glories of Louis XIV's reign. Perhaps the most creative of seventeenth-century French sculptors was Pierre Puget (1628–1715). His life shows the importance of the power of patronage in the age of aristocracy. Puget lost royal and aristocratic favor when one of his first patrons, the famous Fouquet, fell from the favor of Louis XIV. Puget then worked for French towns and the Catholic Church. While his depiction of Atlantes over the doorway of the Toulouse city hall ranks as one of his first great works, his Saint Sebastian is considered the most powerful work of baroque sculpture outside of Bernini. Puget would eventually do work for Louis at Versailles, but his inability to win favor at court prevented him from being one of the chief sculptures at the palace. Only with the romantic movement in the early nineteenth century did this baroque master receive his due recognition as the greatest French sculptor of his age (in part of course because he fit the romantic paradigm of the artistic genius unappreciated in his own time).

The eighteenth century was an eclectic age for sculpture. The rococo style is found especially in his extensive production of female nudes, but Étienne Maurice Falconet (1716–1791) had many talents. The Enlightenment thinker Denis Diderot believed his *Pygmalion and Galatee* to be a masterpiece, but his generally acknowledged masterpiece is the equestrian statue of Peter the Great in Saint Petersburg (considered the best statue of its genre from the eighteenth century). Adept at court politics, he became a favorite of Louis XV's mistress Madame de Pompadour. Jean-Antoine Houdon (1741–1828) steeped himself in Greco-Roman sculpture and put his love for antique republicanism to good use with statues of some of the greatest figures of both the Enlightenment and the American Revolution. See *Voltaire, Rousseau, Benjamin Franklin,* and *George Washington.* Finally Jean-Baptiste Pigalle (1714–1785) also gained the favor of Madame de Pompadour and excelled at intimate rococo scenes such as *Love and Friendship,* a baroque battle, and crowd scenes (see his tomb for Marshall Saxe). But he too did penetrating busts of Voltaire and Diderot, showing how much the Enlightenment won the heart and minds of the art world at the end of the century. Along with Houdon we see signs of the classical revival in the work of Edme Bouchardon (1698–1762) from his *Neptune* in the gardens of Versailles to the now destroyed (during the French Revolution, 1792) equestrian statue of Louis XV in the Place de la Concorde.

The crisis in political identity that the French Revolution unleashed has led some historians to talk of a nineteenth-century "statue-mania" as the successive regimes of the century tried to secure their power in stone. Across the century republicans eventually agree that a female figure, which would become known as Marianne, would stand for the French Republic. Haltingly after the 1848 revolution, but with much greater confidence after 1880, statues of Marianne became a feature of virtually every French town and city by World War I.

Although admiring Puget, the romantic age did not produce many sculptors of enduring merit. One of the few is François Rude, whose most famous work is *The Departure of the Volunteers* (usually called *La Marseillaise)* on the Arc de Triomphe. In his relatively short life (1784–1855), Rude's sculpture shifted from academic classicism (as in his statue of the painter David, 1826) to romantic, (as in *Joan of Arc Listening to her Voices,* 1852). In the work of Aime-Jules Dalou (1838–1902), we see the emergence of naturalism in sculpture. This left-wing militant depicted the plight of the working class, joined the Paris Commune in 1871, and crowned his life with the famous *Triumph of the Republic* statue in the Place de la Republique in eastern Paris (1889). In essence "Marianne" is depicted as leading the eastern working-class districts, which are at her back, forward into the Republic.

This assertion of a republican identity and the attempt to implant republican values during the 1880s, when the French Third Republic still felt threatened, explains the gift of the Statue of Liberty to the United States. At the time France and the United States were the only two republics in the world. Frédéric-Auguste Bartholdi (1834–1904) was the sculpture of the statue, whose official title is *Liberty Lighting the World.* Bartholdi also sculpted the *Lion of Belfort* out of the side of a mountain in Belfort and did a copy of the Lion, which is now in the middle of the Place Denfert-Rochereau in Paris.

Auguste Rodin (1840–1917) towers over rest of late nineteenth- and early twentieth-century French sculptors. In essence he did for sculpting what the impressionists did for painting—he freed it from the weight of the academic tradition. As a youth he failed his entrance examination at Ecole des Beaux Arts and had his pieces rejected by the Salon. He thus experienced similar rejection as did the impressionist painters. The unfinished look of much of his work, however, was inspired not by the impressionists, but from seeing Michelangelo's unfinished work in Italy. Rodin's greatest work, such as his series on Balzac and the *Bourgeois of Calais,* endowed these middle-class figures with a heroic energy appropriate for a democratic age. *The Kiss* and *The Thinker* have become true icons of the modern world. His studio by the Invalides on the Left Bank has now become a museum where one can see *Gates of Hell* (1880–1917), a massive but uncompleted work.

One of Rodin's assistants, Antoine Bourdelle (1861–1929) became not only an important sculptor in his own right, largely in the style of Rodin, but also an influential teacher, as we shall see below.

One of the trends started by the impressionist was for painters also to do sculpting. Indeed, some of the best late nineteenth- and twentieth-century sculptors in France were also painters. For example, both Degas and Renoir did impressive work in three dimensions. (Degas is especially famous for his young female ballet dancers.) During the twentieth century Picasso was also a leading sculpture, with works such as *Glass of Absinthe* (1914), *Head of Bull* (1943), and *Goat* (1950).

Twentieth-century sculpture has seen many of the same styles and debates as in painting. But the controversies have not been as intense and there has not been the same tendency to cluster into schools. Even more than in painting, many of the most important sculptors came from outside of France and absorbed the various artistic and intellectual trends of Paris. As far as official sculptures in public places, after an initial boom in sculptures commemorating the casualties of the Great War, public sculpture went into eclipse during the crises of the 1930s through the 1960s.

Constantin Brancusi (1876–1957) was of Rumanian origin, the son of poor peasant, and was largely self-taught. He came to Paris in 1904 and was greatly influenced by Rodin, African sculpture, cubism, and the poet and art critic who coined the term surrealism, Guillaume Apollinaire. Brancusi stripped his work of everything he considered excessive to his message and tried to uncover the basic energy of primitive sculpture. His *Sleeping Muse* (1910) and *Sorcerer* (1916) tried to unlock the power of magic, and in his series on Madame Pogany (1912–1933), he tried to remove all outside reference and concentrate on the inner being. He also did some monumental work, such as *Column without End* (1937–1938).

Alberto Giacometti (1901–1966) was born in Switzerland and came to Paris just before World War I (1912) and was influenced by Bourdelle, Brancusi, African art, and surrealism. World War II also deeply influenced him, and he moved sculpture even farther from its mimetic moorings in the outside world after 1945 than did Brancusi, with a wide-ranging exploration of forms in space. Often his statues of humans seem literally to grow out of the statue's base or as if their bodies had been burned by an atomic explosion. (See his *Nude Standing Woman* in bronze.)

Working in a similar mode to Giacometti was Germaine Richier (1904–1959) a student of Bourdelle. Her sculpture was especially influenced by the horrors of World War II. Many of her most powerful works are "hybrids" of humans, animals, and plants, such as *Praying Mantis* (1946), *The Storm* (1948), and *The Ogre* (1951), which showcase the bestial side of modern humanity, the implication being also, that evolution has not been as progressive as nineteenth-century optimists had hoped.

The 1960s brought the new realist school to sculpture as well as to painting. César (César Baldaccini, 1921–1998) covered an extraordinary range of styles. He moved through an expressive and emotional figuration (*The Man from Draguignon,* 1958) to a tranquil repose in such works as *Venus de Villetaneuse* (1962) then on to *Compressions* (1960), which involved literally compressing parts of automobiles into sculptures and displaying the resulting aleatory effects. In the late 1960s he used plastics to create a similar art of the serendipitous. When the French film industry created its own "Oscars," they named their statue César. Arman (Armand Fernandez, 1928–) is another prominent member of this loose artistic grouping (as we have seen this looseness is true of all "artistic 'schools" since the impressionists). Arman has elaborated on Duchamp's tradition of the ready-made, working with cars in his series *Multiples* and *Long Term Parking* and with forks in the Place Jean-Troisgros in the eastern provincial city of Roanne.

During the 1980s and 1990s President Mitterrand and Culture Minister Jack Lang revived state support and subsidies for public statues. The allegorical figures of the past gave way to abstraction, new realism, and new tendencies such as installation art. If the fluid bronze statue of a Jean-Paul Sartre striding forth on the Paris streets in a courtyard of the Old National Library on the Rue de Richelieu is a good example of contemporary naturalism, then Spitzer's 1994 memorial to the Jewish victims of the 1942 round-up at the Paris bicycle stadium (Velodorome d'hiver)—which is just a suitcase and a doll—testifies to the power of contemporary minimalism to evoke the horrors of the Holocaust. Daniel Buren's installation art, a series of different sized and black-and- white striped columns at the Palais Royal in central Paris, develops the themes that have guided his career. In the playful and critical spirit of situationism, Buren's previous covering of buildings (Samaritaine department stores and the Louvre museum) with banners of alternating colors interrogates the nature of art in the public sphere in contemporary society. Doing so in the very center of classic Paris, next to the Comédie-Française at the Palais Royal is but one of his most enduring explorations in this genre. When Christo (1938–) installed the banners in Central Park in 2005 he provided an instance of the continued vitality of this installation art.

The 1990s to the middle of the first decade of the twenty-first century has brought new experimentation. Jean-Pierre Ray has built his own house in which the arrangement of rooms and home appliances is slightly out of usual order. By doing so he visualizes and problematizes Le Corbusier's notion that space educates and highlights the artistic nature of much of daily life. Anne Poirier (1941–) and Patrick Poirier (1942–) have explored the aesthetics of memory. Their early 1990s creation *Mnémosyne* explores the nature of human memory via an innovative integration of castings and books. Richard Baquié (1952–1996), a Marseilles-based sculptor, used all sorts of material found in the region, for example, old machines and autos, for what were called "large-scale haikus of sheet metal" made of cut-up cars and machines.[8]

MUSEUMS

While France during its 1789 Revolution pioneered in the creation of the modern museum, over the past 30 years the nation has set about radically rethinking the function and purpose of the museum in the contemporary world. The result has been some of the most innovative museum buildings in the world. This evolution in the conception of the museum reveals important insights into the evolution of thought on both art and architecture and thus serves to connect the preceding and succeeding parts of this chapter.

From the 1789 Revolution to the present France has pioneered in the creation of the modern museum. In 1793 the revolutionary government, which had just a year earlier guillotined the king, opened the royal palace in Paris, the Louvre, to the public, thus creating a public place for education and edification out of what had been a private space of prestige and power. Provincial cities gained when an 1801 law allowed surplus paintings to be transferred to their own collections, which also often resided in former aristocratic palaces. Nineteenth-century museums, for all their democratization of previously aristocratic space, remained intimidating spaces for the lower classes. (Emile Zola in his novel concerning working-class café life and alcoholism, *L'Assomoir,* provides a penetrating exposition of this cultural gap.)

The opening of a National Museum of Modern Art (1947) did not lead to much change in the closed and reserved nature of the museum space, which usually took over without much thought the processional and hierarchical distribution of rooms in royal palaces and aristocratic town houses. Openness, informality, and unconventionality—avant-garde attributes par excellence— were not found at this site dedicated to the movement.

Attitudes about museums started to change in the late 1960s as Christo wrapped the Berne Art Museum (Kunsthalle), thus turning it into a "gift" in 1968, the same year students and workers across France demanded a growing openness to culture and provided an example of this by filling the streets with posters. Subsequently the 1970s brought a revolution in museum curating through an attempt to desanctify and democratize.

Ironically, a politician who had incurred special wrath in 1968 as a master mining the dismantling of the student and worker near-revolution conceived a new type of museum for modern art while serving as president between 1969 and 1974. Pompidou would die in office before his dream was realized at Beaubourg in central Paris in 1977. The international architectural team of Richard Rogers and Renzo Piano (United Kingdom and Italy) created a multifunctional and flexible museum space that allowed curators, artists, and the public to create novel spatial relationships. Their creation concretized the desires of the new school of museumology. Despite much controversy among the critics, the success of the museum, measured in attendance figures and the animation generated around the institution by a rich street and café life, made the museum a potential model.

When Mitterrand won election as president four years later, the Beaubourg was indeed the model that he and Culture Minister Jack Lang wished to emulate with their "*grands projets.*" American I. M. Pei's proposed pyramid at the

Louvre achieved much the same results for the oldest and largest museum both in France and the world. With the opening up of the entire courtyard to an underground reception center that had abundant light, thanks to the pyramid, Pei united tradition and modernity, elitism and democratization. A similar honesty and transparency has marked most of the other new museums and entertainment centers in Paris. (The glaring exception being the Musée d'Orsay, where the various genres and periods of nineteenth-century French art and sculpture have been isolated with little real organic connection in this renovated late nineteenth-century train station not far from the Eiffel Tower on the Left Bank.)

After Mitterrand, museums have continued to be built at a rapid pace. By 2005 in Paris the Jeu-de-pomme has been incorporated into the National Center of Photography, and two new museums have opened: the Plateau, along the Buttes de Chaumont, and the Palais de Tokyo, on the Avenue President Wilson, not far from the Champs Elysées. In addition, the network of regional galleries, often tied to the regional art organizations (FRAC—*Fonds régional d'art contemporain*) have also been increased with dramatic new buildings, such as one by Renzo Piano in Lyon, the Pompidou Center in Metz, another Modern and Contemporary Art Museum in Strasbourg, and the transformation of Toulouse's old slaughterhouses into another museum. In addition a new museum devoted to French regional, European, and Mediterranean cultures is scheduled to open in Marseilles. Another for the art of Africa, Asia, and the Pacific, on the quai Branley not far from the Eiffel Tower, has opened in the summer of 2006 to mixed reviews. Not surprisingly these proposals and openings have generated great controversy but show France's commitment to multiculturalism.

Today in France there are over 1,000 museums. Over 72 percent of them are municipal and devoted to a variety of objects. Virtually every department and region is now well served by museums (another success of postwar decentralization). The most famous museums belong to the national government and are directed by the minister of culture through an association of national museums. Attendance at French museums has fluctuated between 12 million in the years following the terrorist attacks of September 11, 2001, and over 16 million in the year after the bicentennial of the French Revolution (1990). Over 60 percent of these visitors tend to be foreigners, and the biggest percentage is in the age between high school and college (18 to 25, at almost one-quarter of the attendance). The percentage then drops for those between 25 and 34 (around 18 percent) and then rises to about 22 percent for those between 35 and 49 years of age. Those above 50 years of age slightly outnumber those under 18 (a little over 18 percent as compared to a little under this figure).

Despite the more open and inviting nature of museums in the early twenty-first century, the educated urbanized middle and upper classes, still dominate museum attendance. As one moves up the educational scale, the likelihood of going to a museum increases dramatically. For example of those who have not graduated from the French equivalent of high school, only 11 percent go to museums in any given year. This percentage steadily rises—to between 22 and 29 percent—for those who have gained professional training by the end of high school, and to 35 percent for those who have passed their college entrance exams (the *baccalauréat*). The attendance numbers then jump to 48 percent for those who have completed two years of college, and rise again to 64 percent for those who have had at least two years of graduate school. There is also a sharp urban/rural differentiation, with only 21 percent of those living in rural regions going to museums each year, as opposed to the highest percentage, 57 percent, which are Parisians. As far as gender, there is virtually no difference (31 percent for women and 28 percent for men) in overall museum attendence. However, in terms of the Louvre women heavily predominate (57 to 43 percent) as do foreign tourists (67 percent) as compared to French visits (33 percent). Despite the more open and inviting nature of museums in the early twenty-first century, the educated middle and upper classes, especially students, still dominate museum attendance. The high percentage—almost 38 percent—of students provides hope that habits learned early in life will carry over into their adult life regardless of their occupation. What is most unexpected is the low percentage of retirees, slightly below 6 percent, less than half the percentage of white- and blue-collar workers (12 1/2 percent). Certainly the figure for retirees will change once the large French baby-boom generation starts to retire.[9]

ARCHITECTURE

Unlike painting, French genius quickly manifested itself in the built-environment. One of the ironies of French cultural history is that over the last few centuries, as painting has flourished, architecture has not been as influential as in past centuries. Nevertheless, since the 1970s the architectural renaissance that has occurred in France is in the process of transforming the French urban landscape for the twenty-first century.

Within 500 years of the collapse of the Roman Empire, while much of culture remained mired in chaos, French architects and builders will remain forever obscure. We know few details of the construction of most buildings from this era due to the lack of documentation, chiefly because of the illiteracy of the era. Almost certainly teams of artisans rather than architects in the modern sense constructed most buildings. It is only in the fourteenth century that we see the emergence of architectural attribution.

The first architectural style to emerge after the fall of the Roman Empire, the Romanesque, was largely concentrated in what would become France. The main manifestations of this powerful but unsophisticated architecture— with large walls and small windows due to a lack of technical ability—were churches. The main patron of their construction was the Cluniac monasteries founded in 910, which had their origin at Cluny in France but spread in a dense network with over 1,000 sites across Europe and into the Holy Lands of the Middle East (brought due to the Crusades). A monk by the name of Raoul Glaber, writing shortly after the year 1000 c.e., records the excitement of that building spree: "It was as if the world renewed itself, spreading a glittering robe of churches over everything."[10]

By the time the original monastic complex in Cluny was completed in 1085, it was the biggest church in the West and epitomized Romanesque style. Largely destroyed during the French Revolution, French Romanesque architecture today is best epitomized by the cathedral of Saint-Sernin in the southern city of Toulouse (ca. 1080–1120) and the abbey of Saint-Etienne in the northern city of Caen. The diffusion of the Romanesque style across what was becoming France demonstrates the important role architecture would play in the emergence of a French cultural identity. French Romanesque architecture helped fashion a national identity because this style was not uniform and varied across Europe.

France was at the very center of the next revolution in European architecture, the Gothic style. Indeed, after the renovation of the abbey church of Saint-Denis under the direction of Abbot Suger, essentially the prime minister of the king between 1140 and 1144, this much more soaring, light, and airy architecture (due to the flying buttresses that supported the vaulting) spread across Europe. Suger renovated the church at Saint-Denis not just for religious but also for political reasons. This church would become the great burial grounds for French kings until the French Revolution, when it was looted. Sadly much of the church was then renovated during the nineteenth century and lost some of its original character.

During the next century Gothic cathedrals sprouted across the French landscape (most of them near the capital of Paris) and influenced all building styles. These cathedrals, including Notre Dame in Paris (1163–1250), Bourges (ca. 1190–1275), Chartres (especially 1194–1220), Reims (1211), and Amiens (1220–1270) personified what would become known as High Gothic. Chartres is commonly considered the crown jewel of this architectural style. The Gothic style would remain a powerful force in France and northern Europe into the sixteenth century, evolving into *rayonnant* (ca. 1240–1350) and flamboyant (to about 1550) variations (referring to the styles—radiating or flaming—of stained glass windows found in the cathedrals). The church of Saint-Maclou in Rouen (finished 1531) is one of the last examples of the Gothic style. This same attention to soaring grandeur and minute detail can also be found in the few surviving houses and city walls of the era.

The Italian Renaissance architectural style came to France, much as with painting, due to the French invasion of the peninsula in 1494 and the succeeding period of warfare. By transforming a hunting lodge into a royal palace at Fontainebleau, and by renovating the Louvre (then the king's palace in Paris), Francis I (ruled 1515–1547) became the primary initiator of the Renaissance style in France. One of the Italian architects that Francis imported to work on Fontainebleau, Sebastiano Serlio, would also be highly influential in diffusing the Renaissance style in his multivolume and profusely illustrated *L'Architettura* (1537–1547). One of the French architects used for the Louvre, Pierre Lescot (1515–1578) created its famous facades. Another, Philibert Delorme, also became one of the leading advocates for the Renaissance style in France and the greatest French architect of his age. With his own studies of architecture, first in Italy and then in two books, *New Inventions To Build Better at Less Cost* and *Architecture,* Delorme asserted, in good Renaissance fashion, not only his own individuality but also the nobility of the profession of architect as master thinker and designer, not simply a master craftsman, as architects had been though in the Middle Ages. (Indeed, his father had been a stone mason.) Jacques Androuet de Cerceau (1510–1585) consolidated the rising stature of the architect particularly with his two-volume *The Most Excellent Buildings of France* (1576–1579), which provided a summa on the French Renaissance style, and by founding a dynasty of architects ending with his grandson Jean (1585–1649).

After terminating the age of religious warfare in 1598, Henry IV revived work on Fontainebleau and brought Renaissance urban planning to Paris. This was most evident with the construction after 1605 of the Place Royale on the eastern side of Paris (today known as the Place des Vosges). This square was right below the Marais (literally meaning the swamp), a neighborhood in which aristocrats were building sumptuous townhouses (hotels), one of the most famous being the Hotel de Sully (1624–1629) by Jean de Cerceau. A decade earlier than Cerceau's efforts were those of the leading architect of the era, Salomon de Brosse, on the Luxembourg Palace on the Left Bank. The Florentine references included in this palace were at the behest of the building's patron Marie de Medicis (wife of Henri IV).

The transition from the Italian Renaissance to the French classical style is epitomized in the work of one of France's greatest architects, François Mansart (1598–1666). Most famous for his distinctive roofs that covered not only the top of buildings but extended down over the last story (which had really first been used by Lescot and his teacher Solomon de Brosse), Mansart did not complete many projects because he demanded complete control in building and was seldom satisfied (sometimes tearing down what had just been completed). He is best known for his work on private town houses for the rich and powerful (his masterpiece was what is now known as Maisons-Laffitte outside Paris) and for churches and chapels. Without abandoning Renaissance principles of order, Mansart added a more abundant proportion and refined symmetry that pointed towards the age of Louis XIV.

Following in the footstep of Francis I, the Sun King rebuilt the hunting lodge of his father at Versailles into the largest building in Europe and the model for subsequent royal and aristocratic architecture across Europe through the eighteenth century. From the broad and stately boulevard leading up to the massive facade of the palace, to the miles of gardens and the artificial lake, the viewer is both dazzled and awed by both monumentality and regularity. Seldom has architecture been so successfully melded with political power. As befits a king who claimed absolute power over his kingdom, Louis XIV employed the most talented architects and artisans. Over the 46 years that Louis worked on his dream palace (from 1669 until his death in 1715), he employed Louis Le Vau (1612–1670) through the first decade and then Jules Hardouin-Mansart (1646–1708) (great-nephew of Francis) as his principal architects for the buildings and Andre Le Nôtre for the gardens. Le Vau and Le Nôtre had earlier worked as a team (along with the painter and muralist Charles Le Brun) on a chateau for an official by the name of Fouquet, Vaux-le Vicomte (1657–1661, Seine-et-Marne), that was so magnificent that it elicited Louis XIV's envy and confirmed their talent. Thus he used the same team for Versailles.

Between the death of the Sun King (1715) and the French Revolution (1789) French architecture first caught its breath and returned to the ancients, and then theorized a new world. The rococo style had an architectural analogue in the works of Ange-Jacques Gabriel (1698–1782), in particular the graceful and delicate Petit Trianon (1761–1768), on the grounds of Versailles, and in innumerable hotels in the Paris region. A more robust neoclassical style is found in the buildings around what is now the Place de la Concorde. The epitome of French neoclassicism, combining a deep knowledge of antique style with a lightness and elegance that is especially French, is found in the work of Jacques-Germain Soufflot (1713–1780). The culmination of his work is the Saint Genèvieve church (1757–1790) which after the Revolution became the Pantheon, dedicated to the memory of the greatest talents of the nation. Claude-Nicholas Ledoux also worked in the neoclassical vein, first with private town houses (hotels) in Paris and then on a series of toll-gates for the collection of municipal taxes on goods entering Paris. His most innovative structure was a theatre in the southern city of Besançon, which eliminated the loges and relegated the parterre to the rear of the theatre and seated the audience in chairs. During the Revolution Ledoux spent time in prison and there composed a treatise on architecture in relation to its political and social context and envisioned utopian projects. His visionary tendencies, however, seem tame next to those of Étienne-Louis Boullée (1728–1799). Bred from an intense study of ancient architecture and immense travel in the Near East, and inspired by the grandiose architectural imagination of the Italian Piranese, Boullée envisioned gargantuan monuments to the scientist Sir Isaac Newton (1784) and a stadium that could hold 300,000 spectators. Naturally the French Revolution had neither the time nor the money to build these colossal ventures, but his ideas of a new public architecture do prefigure the Russian avant-gardists following the Russian Revolution (1917–1922). Seldom has an age careened so violently between the miniature and the megalomaniacal in its architectural theory and practice.

By contrast the nineteenth century seems rather conservative. Reversing the trend of the Middle Ages, France in the nineteenth and early twentieth centuries was at the forefront of painting, but not of architecture. This statement must be qualified to the degree that nineteenth-century architecture around the world did not experience one of its most innovative periods. For example, the building program of Baron Georges Haussmann during the Second Empire (1852–1870) was much more innovative in its theory of provisioning Paris with better transportation, water, sewage, and recreation facilities than in its architecture, which followed a mixture of classical and neoclassical styles, or in its creation of broad boulevards with scenic vistas onto monuments (already pioneered in Rome during the Renaissance). The greatest architect of the Haussmann era was Charles Garnier (1825–1898). His Paris Opéra (1861–1874), along with the casino at Monte Carlo and the Marigny theatre in Paris, typified the eclectic tending toward baroque mix of styles.

Only at the end of the century did the new industrial architecture, utilizing iron and then steel, become a palpable presence in France. The first use of these materials as well as glass had been with train stations. For the most part, however, these buildings did not attract a lot of attention (but the impressionists did love to paint them due not only to their modernity but to the way in which all the steam in these places allowed the painter to experiment with subtle shadings). The building that really announced a new age of architecture in France was the Eiffel Tower. Although luminaries such as Charles Garnier petitioned against the new structure, its popularity (over two million visitors) during the 1889 centennial exposition of the French Revolution (1889) quickly made it into an icon of French identity in particular and modernity in general. By 1900 the architect Hector Guimard (1867–1942) was using iron in his *art nouveau* inspired metro stations. But most of Guimard's other buildings did not use this industrial material.

Architecture received a thoroughgoing reappraisal only in the aftermath of World War I. Charles-Edward Jeanneret, known as Le Corbusier (1887–1965), stands in the middle of the new theorizing of architecture from the 1920s until his death. After studying art and architecture in his native Switzerland, he built his first house in 1905 and then traveled extensively between 1907 and 1911 studying different styles (from peasant buildings to the first skyscrapers) and discussing them with most of the innovative architects of the period. Returning to Paris, he would publish *After Cubism* (1918), *Towards a New Architecture* (1923), and *The Decorative Art of Today* and *Urbanism* (1925). Indeed, Le Corbusier did advocate what can be seen as a "cubist" architecture based on solid shapes and masses and discarding ornamentation. Seeking sponsors, Le Corbusier traveled to the Soviet Union in the 1930s and to Brazil in the 1930 and 1940s. He was at the forefront of the international style—eschewing traditional decorative motifs on buildings and the pedestrian sidewalks of the nineteenth-century city—that was formulated during the interwar period and became dominant afterwards. After World War II, with his theories of modular construction, he helped pioneer the construction of massive apartment complexes.

The period between 1945 and the late 1970s was an age of poorly assimilated international style architecture in France. Often known in French as "hard France," the style lacked much reference to any French traditions. Le Corbusier became the emblematic figure of this transformation even though he did not have much actual impact on construction, just building a few individual apartment blocks in Marseille, along with some commissions, especially churches. (See his especially famous church, Notre Dame du Haut Ronchamp, 1955.) Le Corbusier's influence, even if diffuse, was pervasive, inspiring the notorious *grands ensembles* (large concrete housing projects) across France. The massive use of prefabricated concrete sections for housing estates, however, was inspired more by the work of architect Marcel Lods between the 1930s and the 1960s than Le Corbusier. Massive uniform concrete buildings, either for business or housing, became known as "hard French" (these English words were used in the French expression).

In the late 1970s another ironic turn occurred. The man who many critics saw as wanting simplemindedly to "marry Paris to the twentieth century" by running highways across much of the traditional Paris territory after the fashion of a bureaucratic Le Corbusier, and who had seemed to many of the May 1968 generation to embody insensitive state repression, Georges Pompidou, envisioned creating a museum to his great artistic passion: modern art. He would not live to see the realization of his dream in the late 1970s, and he might be surprised at the results.[11]

Rather than sparking a renaissance in French art, the Centre Pompidou, also known as Beaubourg (completed in 1977), has sparked a renewal in French architecture. By 2005, France can point to some of the most innovative architectural accomplishments of the previous quarter-century in the world. Many of these building, starting with the Centre Pompidou, have not been built by French architects, but by architects chosen via competitive biddings open to architects from around the world. For example, the Centre Pompidou competition was won by an Anglo-Italian combination of Renzo Piano and Richard Rogers. The same competitive process was used by François Mitterrand in his *grands projets* between 1981 and 1995.

After François Mitterrand became the first Socialist president in 1981, he set in motion an ambitious building program. Over the course of his 14 years as president he would, among other projects, place a glass pyramid in the center of the courtyard of the Louvre (designed by I. M. Pei), build a Grand Arche (designed by Johann Otto von Spreckelsen) on the axis of the Arc de Triomphe, the Champs Elysées, and the Louvre, and construct an Institute for the Arab World (designed by Jean Nouvel), a City of Music (designed by Christian de Portzamparc), and a new French National Library (designed by Dominique Perrault). As the names of the architects indicate, Mitterrand used both foreign and French architects. In general these projects conformed to the postmodern aesthetic by blending with the surrounding architectural forms. Moreover, the use of glass and steel rather than concrete also indicated a shift from the international style of the Montparnasse Tower (completed under Pompidou in 1973).

PHOTOGRAPHY

Along with film, photography is one of the modern technological innovations whose cultural implications were especially well elaborated in France. But the nation's scientists were also decisive in the creation of the technology itself. Nevertheless, the development of modern painting, especially impressionism, is hard to imagine without the impetus of photography. As impressionism set out to chronicle the nature of human perception, French photography first turned to what once had been the function of painting, documentation of great people, events, and daily life. By the 1920s avant-garde movements turned to photography as yet another avenue to transform art and society. Then by the 1930s the birth of modern photojournalism brought photography even more intimately into the center of modern mass culture than it had been. Since World War II, photography has been one of the most pervasive cultural practices, spanning the social and cultural spectrum from amateurs to the contemporary avant-garde. Despite this extraordinary cultural resonance, intellectuals from Baudelaire to Bourdieu have denigrated photography as an inferior art. Nevertheless, the work of Roland Barthes in the early 1980s has been on the forefront of an influential new vision of photography that informs current artistic and intellectual debate.

The forerunner of modern photography was the *camera obscura* (Latin for dark room), a technique dating from the ancient world via Muslim civilization that allowed an image to be projected on a wall or piece of paper. Leonardo da Vinci is the first artist to have recorded his use of this technique. Other famous artists also used the technique, but the first real advance into what we consider to be modern photography occurred when in the summer of 1826 Joseph Nicéphore Niépce (1768–1833) produced the first photography using a polished pewter plate coated with bitumen of Judea, a substance highly sensitive to light. Following upon these experiments, Louis Jacques Mandé Daguerre (1787–1851), both a collaborator and rival of Niépce, drew an important lesson from an accident. After unintentionally putting an exposed copper plate in his closet in 1835 he discovered that an image had appeared. Daguerre concluded that mercury fumes from a broken thermometer had caused the reaction. Thus by chance was modern photography born. Daguerre went on to perfect a process that allowed pictures to be developed in half a minute or so, a great convenience. His name became so intimately associated with the first photographs that they became known as daguerreotypes. By the 1850s, however, the English inventor William Henry Fox Talbot's negative/positive photographic process, which, unlike Daguerre's system, allowed the production of multiple copies, had become standard.

By the 1850s the first professional photographers emerged. Again France was in the forefront with Gaspard Félix Tournachon, known by his nickname, Nadar. In 1854 he opened what would become one of the first great photographic studios and captured the distinctive personality of France's contemporary luminaries and celebrities: Victor Hugo the writer, Sarah Bernhardt the actress, Deburau the mime, Baudelaire the poet, and Alexandre Dumas, père, the novelist. Later in his career, in 1887, Nadar pioneered the modern photo interview with the centenarian chemist Eugene Chevreul. During the 1860s the racy and fashionable world of Second Empire high society was captured by Pierre-Louis Pierson. Some of his most famous pictures were of the Countess de Castiglione, a mistress of Napoleon III and fashion plate of the new Parisian haute couture. The first generation of photographers also took photographs for personalized visiting cards for the Parisian elite and provided some solace to grieving parents. Photographs of dead children were popular at this time of high infant mortality rates as a means by which parents could cope with their unbearable loss. In France, with the Paris Commune in 1871, as in the United States during the Civil War, armed conflict assumed center stage, and the bodies of the dead soldiers were especially prominent. The late nineteenth century brought the moralistic and sentimental genres to the forefront at the height of the Victorian age.

During the 1880s, new innovations coming from England and the United States democratized photography. The glass plates coated with a gelatin emulsion that Richard Maddox developed across the English Channel and the box camera that George Eastman created across the Atlantic resulted in photography requiring less time and expertise and increased the ability of photographers to take pictures spontaneously rather than having their subjects pose for the camera. During the 1880s the modern amateur photographer emerged and founded a variety of photographic societies; by 1907 there were 120 amateur associations. Increasingly, scientists turned to photography to record their fields more minutely and fully. Thus criminologist Alphonse Bertillon (1832–1898) photographed thousands of criminals not only for identification but also in the hopes of the delineation of the "criminal type." Albert Londe, under the direction of Jean-Martin Charcot, attempted the same sort of classification of mental illness, especially for women "hysterics," at the Salpêtrière Hospital in Paris. While astronomers shifted to photographs to record the movements of the stars, a young physiologist and so-called chronophotographer, Etienne-Jules Marey (1830–1904), minutely photographed the movements of humans and animals running and walking. His innovative photography helped inspire not only cinema but also avant-garde art, especially Marcel Duchamp's *Nude Descending a Staircase*.

After 1900, photographers increasingly asserted the artistic nature of their profession and, as in the case with Duchamp, the avant-garde annexed photography into their cause. During the 1840s and 1850s, while most painters and art critics, such as Baudelaire, initially had seen photography as mere documentation, they had also been intrigued by the freedom photography could give the artist to explore worlds other than what had been considered objective reality. French photographers and the impressionists often collaborated; for example, Nadar let the impressionists use his studio for the 1874 Exhibition. Many impressionists and postimpressionists also used photography as an aid for their own painting. Around the turn of the century, photographers around the world began a systematic campaign to make photography into a fine art. This movement became known as the photo secession and featured figures such as Alfred Stieglitz in New York. In France Leon Robert Demachy (1859–1937) and Constant Puyo (1857–1933) were founding members of the Photo Club of Paris, which had broken away from the more staid French

Society of Photography. They and other secessionist photographers published in such photographic journals as *L'Art photographique* (1899–1900) and *La Revue de photographie* (1903–1908). For Demachy "A straight print may be beautiful, and it may prove . . . that its author is an artist; but it cannot be a work of art . . . A work of art must be a transcription, not a copy, of nature . . . If a man slavishly copies nature, no matter if it is with hand and pencil or through a photographic lens, he may be a supreme artist all the while, but that particular work of his cannot be called a work of art . . . "[12]

The two most distinguished practitioners of the photographic art, Eugene Atget (1856–1927) and Jacques-Henri Lartigue (1894–1986), however, were productive much more than polemical. Atget spent his life documenting Paris, its monuments, shops, and streets, when no one was on the street. Bereft of people, his photographs of the Parisian built-environment take on simultaneously both a great solidity and a profound mystery. At his death he left 1,797 glass plates and about 10,000 prints that were preserved in large part due to the American photographer Bernice Abbott, who became his champion. While Atget chronicled the commercial and monumental side of Paris, Lartigue during his long career documented first Parisian high society after the fashion of Proust, then the great sports and artistic personalities of the interwar years, and then achieved triumphs with a show in the Museum of Modern Art in New York (1963) and the publication of his *Diary of a Century* (1966). He became world famous and was appointed official photographer by the new president of France Valery Giscard d'Estaing during his term in the Elysée. At the end of his life he photographed the painter Marc Chagall and then donated his entire work to the French state. For both Atget and Lartigue there was no necessary contradiction between objectivity and artistry.

During the interwar years Paris attracted some of the greatest photographers in the world. Many of them were influenced by the avant-garde theories of dadaism and surrealism. This was especially true with the American expatriate Man Ray (1890–1976), whose highly individual and innovative photographs (which he called *Rayographs* or *Rayograms*) involved putting objects on photographic paper and exposing them to light to create unexpected images or, for example, fusing the motifs of a violin onto a photograph of a nude's backside (this was found in a portrait of the Montparnasse artistic model, his lover, Kiki, in his *The Violin of Ingres*). Breaking less radically from representation were the Hungarian expatriates André Kertész (1984–1985) and Gyula Halász, who would become known in France as Brassaï (1899–1984). Their great innovation was to use the much more portable new Leica cameras that appeared after 1924. These cameras fit into a coat pocket and could be used immediately, allowing these photographers to capture moods quickly. While Kertész focused on more ordinary street scenes, Brassaï lingered over the faces and bodies of artists, writers, toughs, and prostitutes of Pigalle and other artistic and entertainment haunts of 1930s, especially at night. It is thus no wonder that the American writer Henry Miller noted of Brassaï, "When you meet the man you see at once that he is equipped with no ordinary eyes." By the end of the 1930s the Leica camera has inspired a young generation of French photographers such as Henri Cartier-Bresson and Robert Doisneau and helped spawn modern photojournalism, especially with the American publication *Life,* but also with such French publications as *Regards* and *Vu.*

The world-rending and transforming events of the 1930s and the 1940s gave rise to the contemporary self-conscious photojournalist. The first modern press agency was created in Paris by another Hungarian émigré, Charles Rado, in 1933. Brassaï and some young French photographers, Robert Doisneau and Willy Ronis, soon joined the agency. Rado closed the agency during the war and moved it to New York City. At the end of World War II, Raymond Grosset reopened the Paris branch and became its director. Doisneau, Ronis, and others returned, and the agency gained international fame and influence. Doisneau's photographs of the daily life of the middle and working classes of the Paris region from the 1930s through the 1960s have become true icons (endlessly reproduced in calendars, organizers, and books) for the French who often view these decades through a nostalgic lens at the poetry and poverty and street and café life that they have lost. Since the 1990s a young generation of photographers such as Daniel Colagrossi has continued to explore some of these subjects, especially café life.

In 1947 another photographic agency opened up in Paris, Magnum, founded by the American veteran photographer Robert Capa (who had filmed extensively and famously in the Spanish Civil War and in Paris during its liberation in August 1944), Henri Cartier-Bresson, and another American, David Seymour. Both these agencies exist into the early twenty-first century and remain at the center of photojournalism. They have been witnesses to the most important and typical events of the past 60 years, the French and then the American wars in Vietnam and Indochina for example, and have embodied a photographic humanism, especially in the postwar French photojournalist magazine *Paris Match* (from 1949). The exhibitions in Paris and New York in 1955–1956 and the book *The Family of Man* represented the high point of these agencies' influence and their style of capturing, in Cartier-Bresson's famous phrase, "the decisive moment" on film.

From the 1960s through the 1980s, French photography became more reflective and self-critical. Roland Barthes in his *Mythologies* attacked what he saw as a sentimental and smug humanism in these photojournalists, which dulled the sensitivities of the public rather than sharpening their critical faculties. Pierre Bourdieu in his *On Photography* persuaded many that photography was both a highly structured and rather banal leisure activity that sustained rather than undermined the social structure. At the same time, a new generation of photographers and photojournalists emerged, epitomized by Raymond Depardon (1942–), who started his professional life at the age of 14 and founded the photojournalism agency Gamma (1967) with Gilles Caron, Hubert Henrotte, and Hugues Vassal, but then gave it up in the later 1960s after one of his colleagues (Gilles Caron) died while working. Subsequently, in 1971, he returned to photography, joining the Magnum agency and doing a wide range of subjects from a *Playboy* issue to covering sporting events, the revolution and repression in Chile (1970–1973), and the Civil War in Chad during the late 1970s. He has published numerous photo essays containing both photographs and commentary and directed over 17 films. Critics note his ability to turn the banal into magic and his reticence to intellectualize his subjects or to try to interpret them. Instead he reflects more upon his own condition as he takes pictures (the highly autobiographical nature of his numerous photographic essays; see for example *Errance, Seuil*, 2000).

After May 1968 French photography incorporated more democratic impulses and new theoretical influences. When the French National Library renovated its photographic archives the public gained much easier street access to its holdings. When the French National Library renovated its photographic archives, the public gained much easier street access to its holdings. In 1969 Lucien Clergue—a photographer, a friend of Picasso, and an author of books on artists and on subjects as diverse as gypsies, nudes, and his native province—launched the Recontres Internationales de la Photographie in his hometown of Arles. It has become Europe's premier annual photography meeting. In 1976 the city of Paris hosted the first biannual Photo Month (Mois de Photo), which is another showcase for aspiring photographers. Then in 1982 the new Socialist government created a National School of Photography (ENP) at Arles and established an annual prize for photos and for booklength photographic essays.

In 1980, one year before he was to die in an auto accident, social theorist Roland Barthes published what has become one of the leading mediations on the meaning of photography, *Camera Lucida* (working off of the original term *camera obscura*). After the death of his mother, Barthes confronted the relationships between images, time, and death. His theory that time is both confirmed and dispersed in what he termed the "photographic ecstasy" has helped reorient the study of photography towards the consciousness of the viewer and the visual language that both the photographer draw upon.

One of the most important photographers since the 1970s is Sophie Calle. As with so many other artists since May 1968, her work defies easy categorization, spanning the boundaries between photojournalism and feminism and between conceptual and installation art. Born in 1953 in Paris, Calle's work has drawn upon the notion of creativity of constraints found in the literary movement Oulipo or critiquing the objectification of women that is at the heart of feminism. She also brilliantly anticipated the rise of reality television. For example, in *Suite Venitienne* (1979) she stalked a man she had met at a party in Paris across Europe to Venice and there donned disguises to photograph him in the fabled city. As with other contemporary photographers, this work includes both photographs and textual commentary. In *Address Book* (1983), she published a series of articles that had first appeared in the newspaper *Liberation* on the consequences of her contacting every person she found in an address book she had found on the street (then photocopied and returned to the owner, documentary filmmaker Pierre Baudry). This work explores again in a novel fashion the boundaries between public and private life (almost the legal nature of these distinctions, since the owner of the address book threatened a lawsuit). In *True Stories* (1994) she combined pictures and personal memoirs of women to explore the nature of women's experience in contemporary society. Then in 2003, the same year she staged *The Sleepers* at the top of the Eiffel Tower, which involved 28 people reading her bedtime stories as she lay in a bed she had brought up, she also had her first show at the Pompidou Center.

French photography in the first decade of the twenty-first century remains among the best in the world. A major reason for this success is the superb training provided at the ENSP in Arles and at the Gobelins in Paris, the continuing draw of Paris as a site and object of photography, and the power of the theory and history in photographic training. In general, young photographers at the turn of the twenty-first century receive much more grounding in the theory and history of photography than did past generations. Moreover, raised in an age of ubiquitous television they virtually never resort to the black-and-white photographs common through the generation of Depardon. They also no longer follow the credo of trying to capture the "objective truth." Instead they search out the subjects neglected by the media and explore the underlying structures of society rather than dramatic moments. Finally, the growing use of digital photography and computers to alter and shape images has challenged traditional notions of the photographic universe. and this generation is exploring the limits and implications of these new technologies.

Among France's new generation a number of photographers stand out. Raphael Dallaporta (1980–) explores a dramatic range of underrepresented subjects, from landmines to the interior of churches. Gérald Garbez (1973–) combines in unique ways a focus on interior and exterior spaces often seen as empty or unimportant (closets, hallways, vacant lots) with portraits of people in these spaces. The viewer is invited in and compelled to draw their own conclusions (based on the writings of Japanese authors Haruki Murakami). Although born in Belgium, Aimée Hoving (1978–) does much of her photography in Paris, capturing debutants and their mothers as well as white-collar workers and their offices. Through such seemingly ordinary slices of life seismic shifts in attitudes and behavior are revealed. Rémy Lidereau (1979–) combines in creative and unexpected ways urban landscapes with his own computer work, challenging the viewer to explore the relationship between photographic reality and computer-generated art. Last in enumeration but not in importance is Valérie Rouyer (1972–) whose photographs of the human body on the operating table explore the nature of corporeality, of the interior and exterior of the physical body and its organs, in a fashion that complements the explorations in the boundaries between the public and the private done by Calle and others.

In short, French photography remains vital, inspired, and not encumbered by its rich history.

Housing

As we have noted above, architecture for most of French history, as has been the case for other nations, has focused on the elites. Only in the mid-nineteenth century did writers from across the political spectrum begin seriously to consider how to house the masses. By the end of the nineteenth century, public officials in a variety of sectors—urban administration, medicine, public health, and law enforcement—began to systematize a body of knowledge that has since World War I become known as urbanism.

After World War I, ambitious programs of urban renewal foundered on fears of political and financial instability. Compared to Great Britain and Germany, France built much less public housing. Only on the outskirts of Paris did extensive and inexpensive housing appear for the lower classes. Even in affluent neighborhoods, the stone of prewar building was replaced with brick. Thousands of Parisian-area workers wound up constructing their own homes in farmland, often without sewage or sidewalks, rather than living in planned garden cities advocated by the Socialist mayor of the suburban Suresnes, Henri Sellier. A national program of low-cost housing emerged after the passage of the Loucheur Law in 1928 which created inexpensive government housing (known at the time, in French, as HBM—*(habitations à Bon Marché)*. Fiscal restraints and government timidity during the interwar period limited construction of this type of housing to about one million apartments (200,000 or so in the Paris region).

In the middle years of the 1950s, with industrial production and transportation not only up and running after the war years but now positively booming, the French state turned its attention to transforming its cities. Laws passed in 1955 and subsequent years provided the central government with broad powers to plan new cities and towns (especially the ability to control the price of land to prevent speculation). Two important tools were the creations of two types of urban creation and renewal: the ZUP (zones of priority urbanization) and the ZAD (in essence zones of redevelopment). With these measures the new towns were built on the periphery of old cities, and the designated slums of urban and suburban were torn down or renovated.

With industrial techniques of prefabrication and construction, the housing problem that had plagued France from the early nineteenth century seemed to be solved. After having built only 1.7 million housing units between 1915 and 1948, and about 2 million units between 1949 and 1969, the number jumped to 4,338,1000 units between 1970 and 1978. Although the pace of construction fell after this latter date, it remained historically high. In 1970, over 66 percent of French housing still predated 1946; by 1978 that figure had fallen to a little over 51 percent, in 1984 to 43 percent, and in 2002 it stood at 33.2 percent.[13]

Even more impressive was the addition of household amenities. At the start of the 1960s only 30 percent of French housing had a shower or bathtub and 60 percent lacked an interior toilet; today under 3 percent of the housing stock lacks these items. At the same time the number of residences having a refrigerator or washing machine climbed from 7.5 and 8.4 percent to 92.9 and 75 percent respectively. As far as cars and televisions, these percentages also soared dramatically in a short period of time: from 30 percent in 1960 to 50 percent by 1966 for autos, and from 26 percent in 1962 to 50 percent in 1966 in the case of TVs. With subsequent innovations in home entertainment, VCRs, cable television, and later the Internet, similar rates of diffusion would be seen. In short, by the 1980s the home had become the primary site of leisure activities.

While French housing was renewed and modern consumer durables for the home amassed, a generalized discontent grew about living in large and seemingly impersonal housing complexes. By the mid-1970s, intellectuals, urbanists, a growing percentage of the population, and even architects turned against Le Corbusier and the rejection of human scale and the street. Valery Giscard d'Estaing, after being elected president in 1974, rescinded many of the plans of his predecessor, Georges Pompidou, to add more high-rises and highways to Paris. The growing disenchantment with modern architecture would produce a French variant on the postmodern school of architecture by the 1980s. This school stressed a return to smaller-scale architecture, a shift back to brick, stone, and glass, and a rejection of concrete as the primary building material.

During the 1970s, not only the traditional urban neighborhood but also the rural home became an object of nostalgia. One measure of the attachment the French still had for rural and country life was the explosion in second homes. Today almost 10 percent of the French population owns a second home. With a total population in 2004 standing at over 61 million this is an impressive increase on an already substantial number of the population owning second homes during the mid-1970s (1.7 million, but only 330,000 in 1954).[14]

As the public face of Paris was being renewed, underlying shifts in the housing market were producing new tensions. Between 1970 and 2000 new patterns at the top and bottom of the housing market coincided with a growing influx of immigrants from non-European countries, usually former French colonies. On the one hand, the number of private, owner-occupied homes grew dramatically. From 35 percent of the French population in 1954, the figure now stands at over 56 percent. On the other hand, subsidized government-built housing also climbed dramatically, from 300,000 units in 1950 to 3.8 million in 2002. At this latter date almost 10 million people lived in HLMs (the postwar term that replaced HBM, and stands for housing at moderate pricing), or one French person in six. Increasingly, immigrant families and their children reside in government housing or in the now deteriorating *grands ensembles*. Families from the traditional working class or second- or third-generation rural migrants increasingly moved out of the large urban and suburban housing complexes and into private homes.

As a result, a fear developed after the 1980s of growing social and economic polarization. Although residential segregation in France has not and does not reach the level found in the United States, concern has risen that an underclass of people trapped in poverty is growing. The great irony is that while the United States worries about the "inner city," in France the concern focuses on the *banlieues* (the French word for suburb). This is an effect of Haussmann's renovation in Paris in the 1850s and 1860s and similar transformation across urban France in the nineteenth century that made the center of the city the site of middle-class life. First workers, then rural migrants, and now foreign migrants locate in the outer districts of Paris and in the outlying suburbs. In general, however, the poorest suburbs are on the eastern side of Paris, while in the west affluent suburbs have emerged, especially around Versailles.

In order to halt and reverse urban deterioration and promote a more open society, French lawmakers in 1999 passed three laws aimed at dealing with urban and suburban problems within a metropolitan context. The Voynet Act furnishes a plan to direct urban development, the Chevènement Act paves the way for closer and more direct coordination between cities and suburbs within metropolitan areas, and the Solidarity and Urban Renewal Law aims to provide well-designed housing based on the needs and participation of the local residents (thus overcoming, it is hoped, the alienation of the grands ensembles).

These measures quickly seemed ineffective when weeks of rioting erupted in October and November 2005. Even though French impoverished neighborhoods and suburbs do not contain the level or long history of neglect or segregation found in the United States, the riots nevertheless highlighted the fact that France contains 700 neighborhoods, almost all on the periphery of its cities, that contain almost five million people (8 percent of the population) who have unemployment rates often running at 40 percent for youths under 30. Aimless life, even when cushioned by an extensive welfare state, has clearly proven to be explosive. The goal of many reformers to tear down the large apartment blocs has gained further momentum after these riots. But many question whether low-rise and more human-scale buildings will end the alienation and frustration unless jobs are created. Part of the despair in these communities derives from the fact that the French who are white gained the chance to move out of these housing estates in the 1980s, but that immigrants have not had the same opportunities since. In short, what seemed to badly housed urban workers or rural peasants a dream in the early 1960s now looks like a nightmare.

Whether these new laws will have their intended effects is difficult to say. All that is certain is that the French state is deeply committed to furnishing the tools to allow its citizens to improve their lives through better housing and urban life.

NOTES

1. *Robert Delaunay: 1906–1914, de L'Impressionnisme A L'Abstraction: Exposition Presentee Au Centre Georges Pompidou* (Paris: Centre Georges Pompidou, 1999). Also, Stanley Baron and Jacques Damase, *Sonia Delaunay: The Life of an Artist* (London: Thames & Hudson, 1995).

2. Patricia Fride-Carrassat and Isabelle Marcadé, *Les Mouvements dans la peinture* (Paris: Larousse, 2005), 175. Also, Jean-Louis Pradel, *L'art contemporain* (Paris: Larousse, 2004), 60.

3. Marc Jimenez, *La querelle de l'art contemporain* (Paris: Gallimard, 2005), 90–91).

4. Patricia Fride-Carrassat and Isabelle Marcadé, *Les Mouvements dans la peinture* (Paris: Larousse, 2005), 181–182.

5. Marc Jimenez, *La querelle de l'art contemporain* (Paris: Gallimard, 2005), 85–87.

6. Richard Leydier, "Le triomphe de l'art contemporain?" in Millet, *L'Art Contemporain*, 335.

7. Uta Grosenick, ed., *Art Now,* Vol. 2 (Kölin: Tashen, 2005), 386.

8. Phrase from Anne Rochette and Wade Sanders from *Art in America,* October 1998. Accessed online: www.artinamericamagazine.com.

9. Jannine Cardona and Chantal Lacroix, *Chiffres clés 2006: Statistiques de la culture* (Paris: La Documentation Française, 2006), 43.

10. www.uk.encarta.msn.com/encyclopedia_781533637/French_Art_and_Architecture.html.

11. These sentiments much more closely follow the feelings of Prefect of the Seine during the 1960s, Paul Delouvrier, see Norma Evenson, *Paris a Century of Change, 1878–1978* (New Haven, CT: Yale University Press, 1979), 58. On Pompidou's actual and more complex attitude regards the car and the capital see, Matthieu Flonneau, *Paris et l'authomobile* (Paris: Hachette, 2005), 193–196.

12. Stephen Bann, *Parallel Lines: Printmakers, Painters, and Photographers in Nineteenth-Century France* (New Haven, CT: Yale University Press, 2001).

13. *L'État de la France 2004* (Paris La Découverte, 2004).

14. See chapter three on gender and family for more details.

Bibliography

CHAPTER 1

Clark [Furguson], Priscille Parkhurt. *Literary France: The Making of a Culture* (Berkeley: University of California Press, 1987).

DeJean, Joan. *The Essence of Style: How the French Invented High Fashion, Fine Food, Chic Cafés, Style, Sophistication, and Glamour* (New York: The Free Press, 2005).

Feldblum, Miriam. *Reconstructing Citizenship: The Politics of Nationality* (Albany: State University of New York Press, 1999).

Gordon, Bertram M. "The Decline of a Cultural Icon: France in American Perspective," *French Historical Studies* 22 (1999): 625–651.

Kuisel, Richard. *Seducing the French: The Dilemma of Americanization* (Berkeley: University of California Press, 1997).

Lebovics, Herman. *Bringing the Empire Back Home: France in the Global Age* (Durham, NC: Duke University Press, 2004).

———. *Mona Lisa's Escort: Andre Malraux and the Reinvention of French Culture* (Ithaca: Cornell University Press, 1999), 99.

———. *True France: The Wars over Cultural Identity, 1900–1945* (Ithaca: Cornell University Press, 1994).

Looseley, David L. "Back to the Future: Rethinking French Cultural Policy, 1997–2002," *International Journal of Cultural Policy* 9.2 (July 2003): 227–234.

———. *The Politics of Fun: Cultural Policy and Debate in Contemporary France* (Oxford: Berg Publishers, 1997).

Noiriel, Gerard. *The French Melting Pot: Immigration, Citizenship, and National Identity*, Translated by Geoffroy De Laforcade (Minneapolis: University of Minnesota Press, 1996).

Ross, Kristen. *May '68 and Its Afterlives* (Chicago: University of Chicago Press, 2002).

Stovall, Tyler, and George Van Den Abbeele, eds. *French Civilization and its Discontents: Nationalism, Colonialism, Race* (Lanham, MD: Lexington Books, 2003).

CHAPTER 2

Bourg, Julian. *After the Deluge: New Perspectives on Postwar French Intellectual and Cultural History* (Lanham MD: Lexington Books, 2004).
Byrnes, Joseph F. *Catholic and French Forever: Religious and National Identity in Modern France* (University Park: Pennsylvania State University Press, 2005).
Drake, David. *French Intellectuals and Politics from the Dreyfus Affair to the Occupation* (New York: Palgrave Macmillan, 2005).
————. *Intellectuals and Politics in Post-War France* (Basingstoke, UK: Palgrave Macmillan, 2002).
Fetzer, Joel S., and J. Christopher Soper, eds. *Muslims and the State in Britain, France, and Germany* (New York: Cambridge University Press, 2004).
Hollier, Dennis, and Jeffrey Mehlman, eds. *Literary Debate: Texts and Contexts: Postwar French Thought,* Vol. II, Translated by Ramona Naddaff and Arthur Goldhammer (New York: New Press, 2001).
Judt, Tony. *Past Imperfect: French Intellectuals, 1944–1956* (Berkeley: University of California Press, 1992).
Kritzman, Lawrence D., ed. *The Columbia History of Twentieth-Century French Thought,* translated by Malcolm DeBevoise (New York: Columbia University Press, 2005).
Laurence, Jonathan, and Justin Vaisse. *Integrating Islam: Political and Religious Challenges in Contemporary France* (Washington, DC: Brookings Institution Press, 2006).
Tippett-Spirtou, Sandy. *French Catholicism: Church, State and Society in a Changing Era* (New York: St. Martin's Press, 2000).
Zayzafoon, Lamia Ben Youssef. *The Production of the Muslim Woman: Negotiating Text, History, and Ideology* (Lanham, MD: Lexington Books, 2005).

CHAPTER 3

Caron, David. *AIDS in French Culture: Social Ills, Literary Cures* (Madison: The University of Wisconsin Press, 2001).
Celestin, Roger, Elaine DalMolin, and Isabelle de Courtivron, eds. *Beyond French Feminisms: Debates on Women, Politics, and Culture in France, 1981–2001* (London: Palgrave Macmillan; 2003).
Duchen, Claire, ed. *French Connections: Voices from the Women's Movement in France* (Amherst: University of Massachusetts, 1987).
Foley, Susan K. *Women in France since 1789: The Meaning of Difference* (New York: Palgrave Macmillan, 2004).
Ford, Caroline. *Divided Houses: Religion and Gender in Modern France* (Ithaca: Cornell University Press, 2005).

Gregory, Abigail, and Ursula Tidd, eds. *Women in Contemporary France* (New York: Berg Publishers, 2000).

Killian, Caitlin. *North African Women in France: Gender, Culture, and Identity* (Stanford: Stanford University Press, 2006).

Martel, Frederic. *The Pink and the Black: Homosexuals in France since 1968,* Translated by Jane Marie Todd (Stanford: Stanford University Press, 1999).

Oliver, Kelly. *French Feminism Reader* (New York Rowman & Littlefield Publishers, Inc., 2000).

Smith, Timothy B. *France in Crisis: Welfare, Inequality and Globalization since 1980.* (Cambridge: Cambridge University Press, 2004).

CHAPTER 4

Corbin, Alain. *The Lure of the Sea: The Discovery of the Seaside in the Western World 1750–1840,* translated by Jocelyn Phelps (Berkeley: University of California Press, 1994).

Cross, Gary. *A Quest for Time: The Reduction of Work in Britain and France, 1840–1940* (Berkeley: University of California Press, 1989).

Dauncy, Hugh, and Geoff Hare, eds. *France and the 1998 World Cup: The National Impact of a World Sporting Event* (London: Frank Cass, 1999).

Engelman, Larry. *The Goddess and the American Girl: The Story of Suzanne Lenglen and Helen Wills* (Oxford: Oxford University Press, 1988).

Furlough, Ellen. "Packaging Pleasure: Club Mediterranee and French Consumer Culture, 1950–1968." In Richard Golden, *The Social Dimension of Western Civilization,* 5th ed. Vol. 2 (Boston: Bedford/St. Martin's, 2003).

Haine, W. Scott. *The World of the Paris Café: Sociability among the French Working Class, 1789–1914* (Baltimore: Johns Hopkins University Press, 1996).

Hare, Geoff. *Football in France; A Cultural History* (Oxford: Berg, 2003).

Harp, Stephen L. *Marketing Michelin: Advertising and Cultural Identity in Twentieth-Century France.* (Baltimore: Johns Hopkins University Press, 2001).

Harris, Sue. *Festivals and Fetes Populaires.* In William Kidd and Siân Reynolds, *Contemporary French Cultural Studies* (London: Arnold, 2000).

Holt, Richard *Sport and Society in Modern France* (Oxford: Oxford University Press, 1981).

Mendras, Henri, and Laurence Duboys Fresney. *Francais comme vous avez change: Historie des Français depuis 1945* (Paris: Tallandier, 2004).

Muchembled, Robert. *Popular Culture and Elite Culture in France, 1400–1750,* Translated by Lydia Cochrane (Baton Rouge: Louisiana State University Press, 1985).

Ozouf, Mona. *Festivals and the French Revolution,* translated by Alan Sheridan (Cambridge: Harvard University Press, 1988).

Ring, Jim. *The Riviera: The Rise and Rise of the Cote D'Azur* (London: John Murray Publishers Ltd., 2004).

Thompson, Richad, Philip Dennis Cate, and Mary Weaver-Chapin. *Toulouse-Lautrec and Montmartre* (Princeton: Princeton University Press, 2005).

CHAPTER 5

Andre, Jean-Louis, and Jean-Daniel Sudres. *Dishes of France: An Insider's Tour of the Regions and Recipes* (New York: Rizzoli, 2002).

Blum, Dilys E. *Shocking! The Art and Fashion of Elsa Schiaparelli* (New Haven, CT: Yale University Press, 2003).

Bocuse, Paul. *Paul Bocuse's French Cooking* (New York: Pantheon, 1977).

Bocuse, Paul, and Dietmar Frege. *Bocuse's Regional French Cooking* (New York: Flammarion, 1992).

Charles-Roux, Edmonde. *Chanel and Her World* (New York: Vendome Press, 2005).

Charpentier, Marolyn. *La France Gourmande: A Food Lover's Guide to French Festivals* (London: Pavilion Books, 2003).

Chenoune, Farid. *Jean Paul Gaultier* (New York: Assouline, 2005).

de Rethy, Esmeralda, and Jean-Louis Perreau. *Christian Dior: The Glory Years 1947–1957,* translator unknown (New York: Vendome Press, 2002).

Djerlal, Sophie, ed. *Alaia,* "Preface" by Michel Tournier (Göttingen: Steidl, 1998).

Ducasse, Alain, Linda Dannenberg, and Pierre Houssenot. *Flavors of France* (New York: Artisan, 1998).

Guiliano, Mireille. *French Women Don't Get Fat: The Secret of Eating for Pleasure* (New York: Knopf, 2004).

Jouve, Marie-Andree. *Balenciaga* (Paris: Assouline, 2004).

Kawamura, Yuniya. *The Japanese Revolution in Paris Fashion* (Oxford: Berg Publishers, 2004).

Koda, Harold, Andrew Bolton, et al. *Chanel* (New York: Metropolitan Museum of Art, 2005).

Langle, Elisabeth. *Pierre Cardin* (London: Vendome Press, 2005)

La Varenne, Francois Pierre. *The French Cook,* "Introduction" by Philip and Mary Hyman (Lewes, UK: Southover Press, 2001).

Luneau, Gilles. *The World Is Not for Sale: Farmers against Junk Food* (London: Verso, 2002).

Mauries, Patrick, ed. *Pieces of a Pattern: Lacroix by Lacroix* (London: Thames and Hudson, 1997).

Mauries, Patrick. *Sonia Rykiel* (New York: Universe, 1998).

McCoy, Elin. *The Emperor of Wine: The Rise of Robert M. Parker, Jr. and the Reign of American Taste* (New York: HarperCollins/Ecco, 2005).

Mennell, Stephen. *All Manners of Food: Eating and Taste in England and France from the Middle Ages to the Present,* 2nd ed. (Urbana: University of Illinois Press, 1995) .

Moreau, Roger. *Les Secrets de la Mère Brazier,* Rev. ed., "Preface" by Paul Bocuse (Paris: Éditions Solar, 2001).

Pochna, Marie-France. *Dior* (Paris: Assouline, 2005).

Safina, Rosario, and Judith Sutton. *Truffles: Ultimate Luxury, Everyday Pleasure* (New York: Wiley, 2002).

Spang, Rebecca L. *The Invention of the Restaurant: Paris and Modern Gastronomic Culture* (Cambridge MA: Harvard University Press, 2000).

Steele, Valerie. *Paris Fashion: A Cultural History,* 2nd rev. ed. (New York: Berg Publishers, 1998)

Teboul, David. *Yves Saint Laurent 5, avenue Marceau, 75116 Paris, France* (New York: Harry N. Abrams, 2002).

Troisgros, Jean. *The Nouvelle Cuisine of Jean & Pierre Troisgros* (New York: Quill, 1985).

CHAPTER 6

Bair, Deirdre. *Simone de Beauvoir: A Biography* (New York: Touchstone, 1991).

Bellos, David. *Georges Perec: A Life in Words: A Biography,* 1st ed. (New York: David R. Godine, 1993).

Cohen-Solal, Annie. *Sartre: A Life,* edited by Norman McAfee, translated by Anna Cancogni (New York: Pantheon Books, 1987).

Davis, Colin, and Elizabeth Fallaize. *French Fiction in the Mitterrand Years: Memory, Narrative, Desire* (Oxford: Oxford University Press, 2000).

Hewitt, Nicholas. *The Life of Celine: A Critical Biography* (New York: Blackwell Publishers, 1999).

Ibnlfassi, Laila, Nicki Hitchcott, Sam Haigh, Rosemary Chapman, Malcolm Offord, and M. H. Offord, eds. *Francophone Literatures: A Literary and Linguistic Companion* (London: Routledge, 2001).

Kay, Sarah, Terence Cave, and Malcolm Bowie. *A Short History of French Literature* (Oxford: Oxford University Press, 2006).

Kesteloot, Lilyan. *Black Writers in French: A Literary History of Negritude,* translated by Ellen Conroy Kennedy (Washington, DC: Howard University Press, 1991).

Le Sage, Laurent. *The French New Novel: An Introduction and a Sampler* (University Park: Pennsylvania State University Press, 1962).

Lofficier, Jean-Marc. *Shadowmen: Heroes and Villains of French Pulp Fiction,* 2 vols. translated by Randy Lofficier (Encino, CA: Black Coat Press, 2003).

Lottman, Herbert. *Albert Camus: A Biography* (Garden City, NY: Doubleday, 1979).

Macey, David. *Frantz Fanon: A Biography* (London: Picador, 2002).

Oppenheim, Lois. *Three Decades of the French New Novel* (Champagne: University of Illinois Press, 1987).

Powrie, Phil, and Margaret Attack, eds. *Contemporary French Fiction by Women: Feminist Perspectives* (Manchester: Manchester University Press, 1991).

Thompson, William, ed. *The Contemporary Novel in France* (Gainesville, University Press of Florida, 1995).

Tilby, Michael, ed. *Beyond the Nouveau Roman: Essays on the Contemporary French Novel* (New York: Berg, 1990).

Todd, Olivier. *Albert Camus: A Life,* translated by Benjamin Ivry (New York: Alfred A. Knopf, 1997).
———. *Malraux: A Life,* Translated by Joseph West (New York: Alfred A. Knopf, 2005).

CHAPTER 7

Kuhn, Raymond. *The Media in France* (London: Routledge, 1995).

Orange, Martine, and Jo Johnson. *The Man Who Tried to Buy the World: Jean-Marie Messier and Vivendi Universal* (New York: Portfolio, 2003).

Popkin, Jeremy D. *Revolutionary News: The Press in France, 1789–1799* (Durham, NC: Duke University Press, 1990).

Scriven, Michael, and Monia Lecomte, eds. *Television Broadcasting in Contemporary France and Britain* (New York: Berghahn Books, 1999).

Walz, Robin. Review of *L'Encre et le sang: recits de crimes et sociéte à la Belle Epoque,* by Dominique Kalifa, *H-France* (July 1996), Society for French Historical Studies. Available: www.h-france.net/.

CHAPTER 8

Atack, Margaret. *May '68 in French Fiction and Film: Rethinking Society, Rethinking Representation* (Oxford, UK: Oxford University Press, 1999).

Beauchamp, Cari, and Henri Hehar. *Hollywood on the Riviera: The Inside Story of the Cannes Film Festival,* 1st ed. (New York: William Morrow and Co., 1992).

Brody, Richard. *Everything Is Cinema: The Working Life of Jean-Luc Godard* (New York: Henry Holt and Co., 2006).

de Baecque, Antoine, and Serge Toubiana. *Truffaut: A Biography.* Translated by Catherine Temerson (Berkeley: University of California Press, 1999).

Douchet, Jean. *Nouvelle vague* in collaboration de Cedric Anger, translated by Robert Bonnono (New York: Distributed Art Pulishers, Inc., in association with Editions Hazan/Cinémathèque Française, 1999).

Durham, Carolyn A. *Double Takes: Culture and Gender in French Films and Their American Remakes* (Hanover, NH: Dartmouth: University Press of New England, 1998).

Flitterman-Lewis, Sandy. *To Desire Differently: Feminism and the French Cinema.* (New York: Columbia University Press, 1996).

Forbes, Jill. *The Cinema in France after the New Wave* (Bloomington: Indiana University Press, 1994).

Foster, Gwendolyn A. *Identity and Memory: The Films of Chantal Ackerman* (Carbondale: Southern Illinois University Press, 2003).

Harris, Sue. *Bertrand Blier* (Manchester, UK: Manchester University Press, 2001).

Hayward, Susan. *Luc Besson* (Manchester: Manchester University Press, 1998).

Heathcote, Owen, Alex Hughes and James S. Williams, eds. *Gay Signatures: Gay and Lesbian Theory, Fiction and Film in France, 1945–1995* (New York: Berg, 1998).

Layne, Judith. *Claire Denis* (Champagne: University of Illinois Press, 2005).

Neupert, Richard John. *A History of the French New Wave Cinema.* (Madison: University of Wisconsin Press, 2002).

Powrie, Phil, ed. *French Cinema in the 1990s: Continuity and Difference: Essays* (New York: Oxford University Press, 1999).

———. *Jean-Jacques Beineix.* (Manchester: Manchester University Press, 2001).

Sherzer, Dina, ed. *Cinema, Colonialism, Postcolonialism: Perspectives from the French and Francophone World,* 1st ed. (Austin: University of Texas Press, 1996).

Slavin, David Henry. *Colonial Cinema and Imperial France, 1919–1939: White Blind Spots, Male Fantasies, Settler Myths* (Baltimore: Johns Hopkins University Press, 2001).

Smith, Alison. *Agnès Varda* (Manchester: Manchester University Press, 1999).

Tarr, Carrie. *Reframing Difference: Beur and Banlieue Filmmaking in France* (Manchester: Manchester University Press, 2005).

Tarr, Carrie, and Brigitte Rollet. *Cinema and the Second Sex: Women's Filmmaking in France in the 1980s and 1990s* (New York: Continuum, 2001).

Wilson, Emma. *Alain Resnais* (Manchester: Manchester University Press, 2006).

CHAPTER 9

Barber, Stephen. *Artaud: The Screaming Body: Films, Drawings and Recordings* (London: Creation Books, 2005).

Behr, Edward. *Thank Heaven for Little Girls: The True Story of Maurice Chevalier's Life and Times* (New York: Villard Books, 1993).

Blake, Jody. *Le Tumulte Noir: Modernist Art and Popular Entertainment in Jazz-Age Paris, 1900–1930* (University Park: Pennsylvania State University Press, 2003).

Bradby, David. *Mise En Scene: French Theatre Now* (London: Methuen, 1997).

———. *Modern French Drama 1940–1990* (Cambridge: Cambridge University Press, 1991).

———. *Theatre of Roger Planchon* (Cambridge, UK: Chadwyck-Healey, 1984).

Bradby, David and Maria Delgado, eds. *The Paris Jigsaw: Internationalism and the City's Stages* (Manchester, UK: Manchester University Press, 2002).

Conway, Kelley. *Chanteuse in the City: The Realist Singer in French Film* (Berkeley: University of California Press, 2004).

Daoust, Yvette. *Roger Planchon: Director and Playwright* (Cambridge: Cambridge University Press, 1981).

Dauncey, Hugh and Steve Cannon, eds. *Popular Music in France from Chanson to Techno: Culture, Identity and Society* (Aldershot, UK: Ashgrate, 2003), 139–170.

Durand, Alain-Philippe, ed. *Black, Blanc, Beur: Rap Music and Hip-Hop Culture in the Francophone World* (Lanham, MD: The Scarecrow Press, 2002).

Elstob, Kevin. *The Plays of Michel Vinaver: Political Theatre in France* (New York: Peter Lang Publishing, 1992).

Esslin, Marrin. *The Theatre of the Absurd* (New York: Vintage, 2004).

Felner, Mira. *Apostles of Silence: The Modern French Mimes* (Rutherford, NJ: Fairleigh Dickinson University Press, 1985).

Freeman, E., and Ted Freeman, *Theatres of War: French Committed Theatre from the Second World War to the Cold War* (Exeter, UK: University of Exeter Press, 1998).

Fulcher, Jane F., ed. *Debussy and His World* (Princeton, NJ: Princeton University Press, 2001).

Gaensbauer, Deborah B. *Eugene Ionesco Revisited* (New York: Twayne Publishers, 1996).

Garafola, Lynn. *Diaghilev's Ballets Russes* (New York: Da Capo Press, 1998).

Hopkins, Patricia M., and Wendell M. Aycock, eds. *Myths and Realities of Contemporary French Theater: Comparative Views* (Lubbock: Texas Tech University Press, 1985).

Jameux, Dominiqu. *Pierre Boulez,* translated by Susan Bradshaw (Cambridge, MA: Harvard University Press, 1991).

Jean-Aubry, Georges. *French Music of Today and Musicians of Today,* translated by Edwin Evans (Freeport, NY: Books for Libraries Press, 1976).

Kiernander, Adrian, and Christopher Innes, eds. *Ariane Mnouchine and Théâtre du Soleil* (Cambridge: Cambridge University Press, 1993).

Loosely, David. *Popular Music in Contemporary France: Authenticity, Politics, Debate* (Oxford, UK: Berg, 2003).

McMillan, Dougald, and Martha Fehsenfeld. *Beckett in the Theatre: The Author as Practical Playwright and Director: From Waiting for Godot to Krapp's Last Tape* (London: Calder Publications, 1988).

McMullan, Anna. *Theatre on Trial: Samuel Beckett's Later Drama* (New York: Routledge, 1993).

Mellers, Wilfrid. *Francis Poulenc* (New York: Oxford University Press, 1995).

Tinker, Chris. *Georges Brassens and Jacques Brel: Personal and Social Narratives in Post-War Chanson* (Liverpool, UK: Liverpool University Press, 2006).

Winders, James A. *Paris Africain: Rythyms of the African Diaspora* (New York, NY: Palgrave Macmillan, 2006).

Chapter 10

Arbaizar, Philippe, Jean Clair, Claude Cookman, and Robert Delpire. *Henri Cartier-Bresson: The Man, the Image and the World: A Retrospective* (London: Thames and Hudson, 2003).

Bach, Friedrich Teja, Margit Rowell, and Ann Temkin. *Constantin Brancusi, 1876–1957* (Philadelphia: Philadelphia Museum of Art, 1995).

Berggrun, Olivier, Max Hollein, and Ingrid Pfeiffer, eds. *Yves Klein* (Kassel, Germany: Hatje Cantz Publishers, 2004).

Boltanski, Christian. *Christian Boltanski* (London: Phaidon Press, 1997).

Buffet, Anabelle, and Jean-Claude Lamy eds. *Bernard Buffet: The Secret Studio*, photographs by Luc Fournol and Benjamin Auger, translated by Deke Dusinberre (Paris: Flammarion, 2004).

Christo and Jeanne-Claude. *The Gates: Central Park, New York City, 1979–2005*. Photographs by Wolfgang Volz. Picture notes by Jonathen Henry (Köln: Taschen, 2005).

Cuito, Aurora, and Cristina Montes. *Jean Nouvel* (London: Te Neues Publishing Company, 2003).

Danchin, Laurent. *Jean Dubuffet* (New York: International, 2001).

Depardon, Raymond. *Depardon Voyages*, English-French ed. (Paris: Editions Hazan, 1998).

Ewing, William A., Natalie Herschdorfer, and Jean-Christophe Blaser. *Regeneration: 50 Photographers of Tomorrow* (New York: Aperture, 2006).

Fierro, Annette. *The Glass State: The Technology of the Spectacle, Paris 1981–1998* (Boston: MIT Press, 2002).

Franck, Dan. *Bohemian Paris: Picasso, Modigliani, Matisse, and the Birth of Modern Art*, translated by Cynthia Liebow (New York: Grove Press, 2001).

Guilbaut, Serge. *How New York Stole the Idea of Modern Art*, translated by Arthur Goldhammer (Chicago: University of Chicago Press, 1985).

Hamilton, Peter. *Robert Doisneau: A Photographer's Life* (New York: Abbeville Press, 1995).

Harris, Steven. *Surrealist Art and Thought in the 1930s: Art, Politics, and the Psyche* (Cambridge: Cambridge University Press, 2004).

Jaquand-Goddefroy, Corinne. *Young French Architects*, translated by Claus Käppliner and S. Parsons (London: Birkhauser, 1999).

Jencks, Charles. *Le Corbusier and the Continual Revolution in Architecture* (New York: Monacelli, 2000).

Karmel, Pepe. *Picasso and the Invention of Cubism* (New Haven, CT: Yale University Press, 2003).

Lelong, Guy. *Daniel Buren* (New York: Flammarion, 2002).

Loew, Sebastien. *Modern Architecture in Historic Cities: Policy, Planning and Building in Contemporary France* (London: Routledge, 1998).

Macel, Christine, Ive-Alan Bois, Yve-Alain Bois, and Olivier Rolin. *Sophie Calle: Did You See Me?* (New York: Prestel, 2004).

Masboungi, Ariella. *Projects Urbains en France/French Urban Strategies* (Paris: Éditions du Moniteur, 2002).

Mathieu, Georges. *The Art of Lyrical Abstraction*. Exhibition (New York: Wally Findlay Galleries, 1985).

McClellan, Andrew. *Inventing the Louvre: Art, Politics, and the Origins of the Modern Museum in Eighteenth-Century Paris* (Berkeley: University of California Press, 1999).

Miller, Russell. *Magnum: Fifty Years at the Front Line of History: The Story of the Legendary Photo Agency* (New York: Grove Press, 1999).

O'Brien, C. Jill. *Carnal Art: Orlan's Refacing* (Minneapolis: University of Minnesota Press, 2005).

Parente, Janice, Pierre Restany, Yoko Masuda, and Michel de Grece. *Niki De Saint Phalle: Monograph* (Bern: Benteli Verlag, 2005).

Peiry, Lucienne. *Art Brut: The Origins of Outsider Art* (Paris: Flammarion, 2001).

Ronte, Dieter. "Christo and Jeanne-Claude: The Würth Collection." Essay. Translated by Michael Foster. Curated by Sonja Klee (London: Philip Wilson Publishers, 2004).

Schneider, Angela. *Alberto Giacometti: Sculptures, Paintings, Drawings* (New York: Prestel Publishing, 1994).

Sherman, Daniel J. *The Construction of Memory in Interwar France* (Chicago: University of Chicago Press, 2001).

Sherman, Daniel J. *Worthy Monuments: Art Museums and the Politics of Culture in Nineteenth-Century France* (Cambridge, MA: Harvard University Press, 1989).

Tomkins, Calvin. *Duchamp: A Biography* (New York: Owl Books, 1998).

Walker, Ian. *City Gorged with Dreams: Surrealism and Documentary Photography in Interwar Paris* (Manchester, UK: Manchester University Press, 2002).

Warehimel, Maria. *Brassai: Images of Culture and the Surrealist Observer* (Baton Rouge: Louisiana State University Press, 1996).

Index

About the Author

W. SCOTT HAINE is Lecturer in European History at Holy Names University, Oakland, California.